JESUS

Also by Marcus J. Borg

Jesus: A New Vision

Meeting Jesus Again for the First Time

The God We Never Knew

The Meaning of Jesus
(with N. T. Wright)

Reading the Bible Again for the First Time

The Heart of Christianity

The Last Week
(with John Dominic Crossan)

The First Christmas
(with John Dominic Crossan)

JESUS

UNCOVERING

THE LIFE,

TEACHINGS,

AND RELEVANCE OF

A RELIGIOUS REVOLUTIONARY

MARCUS J. BORG

HarperOne
An Imprint of HarperCollins*Publishers*

HarperOne

JESUS: *Uncovering the Life, Teachings, and Relevance of a Religious Revolutionary.* Copyright © 2006 by Marcus J. Borg. All rights reserved. Printed in the United States of America. No part of this book may be used or reproduced in any manner whatsoever without written permission except in the case of brief quotations embodied in critical articles and reviews. For information address HarperCollins Publishers, 10 East 53rd Street, New York, NY 10022.

HarperCollins books may be purchased for educational, business, or sales promotional use. For information please write: Special Markets Department, HarperCollins Publishers, 10 East 53rd Street, New York, NY 10022.

HarperCollins Web site: http://www.harpercollins.com
HarperCollins®, 📖®, and HarperOne™ are
trademarks of HarperCollins Publishers

FIRST HARPERCOLLINS PAPERBACK EDITION PUBLISHED IN 2008

Designed by Joseph Rutt

Library of Congress Cataloging-in-Publication Data is available.

ISBN: 978–0–06–143434–1

08 09 10 11 12 RRD (H) 10 9 8 7 6 5 4 3 2

For Dom and Sarah Crossan,
dear friends, teachers,
and companions on the way

Contents

Preface   1

ONE Jesus Today
     Telling His Story   3

TWO The Gospels
     Memory and Testimony   27

THREE The Gospels
       Memory, Metaphor, and Method   51

FOUR The Shaping of Jesus
      Jewish Tradition in an Imperial World   77

FIVE The Shaping of Jesus
      His Experience of God   109

SIX The Big Picture
     The Synoptic Profile of Jesus   137

SEVEN God
       God's Character and Passion   165

EIGHT Wisdom
       The Broad Way and the Narrow Way   191

Contents

NINE Resistance
The Kingdom and the Domination System   225

TEN Executed by Rome, Vindicated by God   261

Epilogue
Jesus and American Christianity Today   293

Notes   313

Author Index   337

Scripture Index   339

Preface

This may be the last comprehensive book about Jesus that I write. I do not imagine that it is my last book on topics related to Jesus, the Bible, and Christianity. But it may be my last attempt to treat the "whole" of the story of Jesus as a figure of history who became Christianity's Lord.

I say this not because of intimations of imminent mortality. But I am in the first half of my sixties, and I do not imagine writing another book like this for at least twenty years. By then, I may not be here, or I may be more interested in simply living life and resting in God.

This book has a history. Twenty years ago, I wrote *Jesus: A New Vision,* my first somewhat comprehensive treatment of Jesus for a general audience. This book began three or four years ago as a "revised edition" of that book. It was to be a modest revision: an updating of bibliography and footnotes, an integration of important historical Jesus research from the last twenty years, and a modification of some content. A year or so later, it became a more thorough revision, so much so that I learned that it constituted a "new edition." The difference, I have been told, is that a revised edition has less than 25 percent new content, and a new edition more than that. Now, two years later, it has become a replacement book—which is to say, a new book. Only a few paragraphs here and there are more or less the same as what I wrote twenty years ago.

I still affirm most of what I wrote in *Jesus: A New Vision,* the basic sketch of Jesus that I drew as well as the historical method that I used. But my understanding of Jesus and my pedagogy—my way of teaching about Jesus—have developed over the past twenty years. The result is that I see Jesus somewhat differently now and speak about him somewhat differently. I would say I see Jesus more fully now—but that is for others to judge.

This book has two cultural contexts, the first century and the twenty-first century. It suggests a way of seeing Jesus shaped by historical scholarship even as it is also addressed to Christians (and interested inquirers) in our cultural context. It thus moves back and forth between the first century and our time. How does what we can discern about Jesus *then* matter for *now*? I imagine that three audiences might be interested in it: Christians seeking to understand more fully what being Christian is about; undergraduates in religious studies courses and seminarians in divinity schools; and those curious about a way of seeing Jesus that breaks out of conventional ways of perceiving his life and activity.

The older I get, the more difficult it is to name all the people to whom I am indebted for what I have come to glimpse of Jesus. They include the professors who taught me; my students in college, university, and seminary courses; lay and clergy audiences in my life "on the road"; and my predecessors and contemporaries in the academy. I acknowledge especially my indebtedness to John Dominic Crossan. Our friendship and working relationship go back many years, and I have learned more from him than from any contemporary. To Dom and his wife, Sarah, I dedicate this book.

I want to acknowledge the assistance and above all the patience of several people on the staff of Harper San Francisco as they waited for this manuscript and then expedited turning it into a book—especially my publisher, Mark Tauber, my editor, Mickey Maudlin, my copy editor, Ann Moru, and the editorial production team of Lisa Zuniga and Terri Leonard. I would also like to thank my very able assistant and colleague at Oregon State, Dr. Judy Ringle.

Finally, I want to thank the families of Al Hundere and Ike Kampmann, both of San Antonio, Texas. The financial support provided by Al and Ike to support my work at Oregon State University has made much of my writing possible.

ONE

Jesus Today

Telling His Story

We live in a "Christ-haunted" and "Christ-forgetting" culture. So wrote Walker Percy over thirty years ago at the beginning of his novel *Love in the Ruins:*

> Now in these dread latter days of the old violent beloved U.S.A. and of the *Christ-forgetting* and *Christ-haunted* death-dealing Western world I came to myself in a grove of young pines [italics added].

The passage strikes a more ominous tone than I intend, but its description of our culture rings true. Even as we forget Jesus in many ways, we remain fascinated by him.

The last few years have witnessed several epiphanies of our fascination. In 2004, Mel Gibson's movie *The Passion of the Christ* was a major cultural event. Its graphic portrayal of the torture and execution of Jesus generated front-page stories in hundreds of newspapers across the nation, cover features by the three major weekly news magazines, and prime-time specials on several television networks.

That year's best-selling novel, *The Da Vinci Code* (still on the *New York Times* best-seller list) also has Jesus at its center. Its attention-getting hook is the possible discovery of evidence that Jesus and Mary Magdalene were lovers and had a child together. The novel spawned magazine stories and television shows about what we can know or guess about Mary of Magdala, the most important of Jesus's women followers. It also created strong interest in early Christian writings that did not make it into the New Testament.

The sales record of a very different genre of fiction, the Left Behind novels, provides another illustration of an abiding fascination with Jesus. Set in the near future and claiming to be based on biblical prophecy, these novels tell the story of events leading up to the second coming of Jesus. All twelve have been on the *New York Times* best-selling list (fiction). By 2004, the series had sold over sixty-five million copies.[1]

A year earlier, in 2003, two books about Jesus in the history of the United States were published, *Jesus in America* and *American Jesus*. Each chronicles the remarkable resilience of Jesus in American culture as well as the diverse ways in which he has been seen, from the beginning of European settlement to the present.[2]

All of this should strike us as extraordinary: almost two thousand years after his death, Jesus continues to be front-page news in the United States. It is not so in other countries of the historically Christian world. Colleagues in Britain and Europe are amazed by our preoccupation with Jesus. We are indeed "Christ-haunted."

The primary reason, of course, is the high percentage of Americans who affirm Christianity, higher than in any other country. According to a recent poll, over 80 percent of Americans identify themselves as Christian, well over two hundred million people. According to another poll, 84 percent agree with the statement "Jesus is the Son of God."[3]

These numbers are remarkable. They also seem too high, for they are significantly greater than the number of people who participate in the life of a church. Only about half as many do, but even this lower figure amounts to over a hundred million. Jesus matters to a whole lot of people.

Yet Christians in the United States today are deeply divided about what it means to follow him:

- Many followers of Jesus oppose evolution and defend the literal-factual truth of the Bible's stories of creation. Yet followers of Jesus were the first to reconcile evolution with the

Bible by understanding the Genesis stories symbolically and not literally.

- Followers of Jesus are among the strongest supporters of our nation's invasion and continuing occupation of Iraq. Followers of Jesus are among its strongest critics.

- Followers of Jesus are among the strongest opponents of gay marriage. Followers of Jesus are among its strongest advocates.

- Followers of Jesus are among the strongest supporters of an economic and tax policy that benefits especially the wealthy and powerful. Followers of Jesus are among its most vocal critics on the biblical grounds that such a policy betrays God's passion for economic justice for the poor.

Examples could be multiplied, but these illustrate sharp disagreement among American Christians about what it means to take Jesus seriously. Our culture wars are to a considerable extent Jesus wars.

TELLING THE STORY OF JESUS

I have a memory from childhood of singing hymns about telling the story of Jesus:

> Tell me the story of Jesus,
> Write on my heart every word;
> Tell me the story most precious,
> Sweetest that ever was heard.

Another one is even more familiar:

> I love to tell the story
> Of unseen things above;
> Of Jesus and his glory,
> Of Jesus and his love.

What I sang, I believed. For me as a child, the story of Jesus was the most important story in the world. The conviction has remained with me. But as I have grown older, I have realized there is an equally important issue: *how* we tell the story of Jesus. There are many ways of telling his story, and how we tell it matters crucially.

To say the obvious, this is because of Jesus's extraordinary significance for Christians. In the testimony of his early followers in the New Testament, he is spoken of in the most exalted terms imaginable: as the Son of God, Messiah, and Lord; as the Word Made Flesh, the Light of the World, the Lamb of God, the Bread of Life, the Living Water, the Way and the Truth and the Life, the Great High Priest and Sacrifice; the Son of Man who will come again to gather the elect and judge the world. The fourth-century Nicene Creed, the most universal of the Christian creeds, affirms:

> One Lord Jesus Christ, the only-begotten Son of God, begotten of his Father before all worlds, God of God, Light of Light, very God of very God, begotten, not made, being of one substance with the Father, by whom all things were made.

In fourth- and fifth-century Christian trinitarian language, he is the second person of the Trinity and one with God.

Thus, for Christians, Jesus is utterly central. In a concise sentence, *Jesus is for Christians the decisive revelation of God.* Slightly more fully, Jesus reveals, discloses, what can be seen of God in a human life and what a life filled with God looks like. This affirmation defines what it means to be Christian. Christians find the decisive revelation of God and life with God in Jesus, just as Jews find the decisive revelation of God in the Torah and Muslims find the decisive revelation of God in the Qur'an.

For Christians, the decisive revelation of God is *a person*. As Son of God, he reveals God; as the Word become flesh, he embodies what can be seen of God in a human life; as the Light of the World, he enlightens us about the nature and will of God and about the way to life.

Of course, Christians also speak of the Bible as the revelation of God, indeed as the "Word of God." Yet orthodox Christian theology from ancient times has affirmed that *the* decisive revelation of God is

Jesus. The Bible is "the Word" become *words*, God's revelation in human words; Jesus is "the Word" become *flesh*, God's revelation in a human life. Thus Jesus is more decisive than the Bible.

Importantly, Jesus is not the revelation of "all" of God, but of what can be seen of God in a human life. Some of God's traditional attributes or qualities cannot be seen in a human life. The omnipresence of God cannot be seen in a human life—a human being cannot be present everywhere. The infinity of God cannot be seen in a human life—a human being by definition is finite. So also omnipotence: a human being cannot be all-powerful and still be human. So also omniscience: what could it mean to say that a human is "omniscient" and that Jesus in particular was? That he would "know everything"— including, for example, the theory of relativity and the capital of Oregon?

So there is much of God that cannot be seen in a human life. But—and this is what matters—what can be seen is the character and passion of God. By the "character of God," I mean simply "what God is like." By the "passion of God," I mean simply "what God is passionate about," what God most cares about, what concerns God most. The first is often called the nature of God, the second the will of God. This is what Jesus reveals: the character and passion, the nature and will, of God.

Thus how Christians tell the story of Jesus deeply affects how we see God and the Christian life. There are several ways of telling his story in the United States today. Each version produces a different vision of God's character and passion and thus what it means to take Christianity seriously. These visions often clash with each other, religiously and politically.

The Dying Savior: Jesus Died for Our Sins

One way of telling Jesus's story emphasizes his death on a cross. Gibson's *The Passion of the Christ* is a vivid and violent example. The movie focuses on the last eighteen hours of Jesus's life, from his arrest on Thursday evening through his crucifixion on Good Friday. It opens with a verse from the prophet Isaiah in the Jewish Bible:

> He was wounded for our transgressions, crushed for our
> iniquities; by His wounds we are healed (Isa. 53.5).

The verse frames the movie as a whole, and its effect is clear: the primary purpose of Jesus's life was to die for the sins of the world.

This way of telling the story is very familiar. The majority of Christians—Catholics, evangelical and mainline Protestants, Pentecostals—grew up with it. For many people, Christians and non-Christians, "Jesus died for your sins" is the one-sentence summary of Jesus's significance.

Like all ways of telling the story, this version shapes a vision of God and the Christian life. Because it highlights Jesus as the sacrifice who makes forgiveness possible, it leads to an image of God as primarily a lawgiver and judge whose commandments we have violated. We are all sinners. Nevertheless, God loves us. But God will not or cannot forgive us unless adequate atonement is made. Hence the necessity of Jesus's death. As the one sinless human being, without spot or blemish, he is the sacrifice who atones for the sins of the world and makes forgiveness possible.

This emphasis upon Jesus as substitutionary sacrifice leads to a vision of the Christian life as centered in sin, guilt, and forgiveness. Though this way of telling the story most often also emphasizes trying to follow the teachings of Jesus and the Bible, it highlights our repeated failure to do so. Thus our central need is forgiveness; only so can we be right with God. This vision is widespread; the worship services of most denominations consistently include a confession of sin followed by a proclamation of forgiveness. So also the celebration of the Eucharist (also called the Mass, the Lord's Supper, and Holy Communion) most commonly emphasizes sin, sacrifice, and forgiveness.

Jesus as the Divine Human: God in Human Form

Another way of telling the story of Jesus sees him as God in human form. This way is frequently combined with the first one, even as it has a distinctive emphasis. It emphasizes that Jesus was divine, unlike the rest of us—that even during his earthly life he had divine power and divine knowledge. Though he looked like us and seemed to be one of us, he was really God in human form (and thus not really one of us). So familiar is this way of thinking that many people take it for granted that it is orthodox Christian theology. Many of us have been asked by Christians who are quite sure they are orthodox, "Do you believe Jesus was God?"

But this view is actually one of the earliest Christian heresies, known as docetism (pronounced doh´-sit-izm), from a Greek word meaning "to seem" or "to appear." Jesus seemed, appeared, to be human, but really wasn't—rather, he was really God. Most Christians would deny being docetic, if they've heard the term. But Christians have commonly seen Jesus as having divine knowledge—that's why he could speak with God's authority and know the future—and as having divine power—that's why he could walk on water, heal the sick, change water into wine, raise the dead, and so forth.

This image of the earthly Jesus as a divine and therefore superhuman figure is described whimsically (and, I trust, not offensively) by Robert Capon, a contemporary Christian writer. "The true paradigm of the ordinary American view of Jesus is Superman," Capon writes. Then he quotes the well-known words that opened each episode of the *Superman* series on both radio and television:

> Faster than a speeding bullet, more powerful than a locomotive, able to leap tall buildings in a single bound. It's Superman! Strange visitor from another planet, who came to earth with powers and abilities far beyond those of mortal men, and who, disguised as Clark Kent, mild-mannered reporter for a great metropolitan newspaper, fights a never-ending battle for truth, justice, and the American way.

Capon continues:

> If that isn't popular christology, I'll eat my hat. Jesus—gentle, meek and mild, but with secret, souped-up, more-than-human insides—bumbles around for thirty-three years, nearly gets

himself done in for good by the Kryptonite Kross, but at the
last minute struggles into the phone booth of the Empty Tomb,
changes into his Easter suit and with a single bound, leaps back
up to the planet Heaven. It's got it all—including, just so you
shouldn't miss the lesson, kiddies: He never once touches Lois
Lane.[4]

But a figure who has superhuman powers is ultimately not one of us.
Jesus's humanity disappears.

This way of telling the story leads to a vision of the Christian life
that stresses *believing*—believing that Jesus as the Son of God was
divine and thus capable of divine feats. God was his father; he was
conceived by God's Spirit in the virgin Mary. He had miraculous
powers and did things that no mere human can do: he healed the sick,
gave sight to the blind, forgave sins, changed water into wine, stilled a
storm, walked on water, fed multitudes with a few loaves and fishes,
raised Lazarus from the dead, and so forth. It also stresses that Jesus is
the *unique* revelation of God—only in Jesus has God become human.

In addition to being docetic, this way of telling Jesus's story has an
additional problem. Namely, if Jesus had superhuman power and
knowledge, he cannot be a model for human behavior. Yet the New
Testament often speaks of him as such. The gospels speak of following Jesus, and Paul speaks of imitating Christ and being transformed
into the likeness of Christ. But if Jesus was really God (and thus not
really human), it makes no sense to speak of imitating him and becoming like him.

The Apocalyptic Jesus: The End Is Near

The apocalyptic way of telling the story of Jesus commonly includes
the first two ways, but it emphasizes the future end of the story: the
Christian apocalypse—the second coming of Jesus and the last judgment—will happen soon. This is the Jesus of the Left Behind novels,
though the notion is older. Several books in the New Testament
affirm that Jesus will come again. The affirmation is enshrined in the
Christian creeds. And from time to time, again and again, Christians

have claimed that "the time is near." They did so as the year 1000 approached, during the Reformation of the sixteenth century, and among some Christian groups since; they do so as well today.

In the 1970s, this expectation was popularized in books by Hal Lindsey, such as *The Late Great Planet Earth*, which sold over thirty million copies. Lindsey emphasized that the "rapture" and the final seven years of world history were at hand. When the "rapture" happens, true Christians will be taken up to heaven in order to be spared the seven years of "tribulation," a period of suffering that will precede the second coming of Jesus. Those not taken up to heaven in the "rapture" are the "left behind." Though they will need to live through the suffering and conflict of the time of tribulation, they will have the opportunity to repent.

The Left Behind novels build on this understanding. They begin with the "rapture" and then narrate the tumultuous events of the final seven years of world history, marked by tribulation, war, and the final judgment. The series culminates with the battle of Armageddon, the second coming, and the last judgment, in which the vast majority of humankind is annihilated and condemned to eternal torment.

It is an odd way of telling the story of Jesus. Though its advocates say they're taking the book of Revelation literally, their interpretation is far from literal. They see the image-laden first-century language of Revelation as referring to events of our time and imminent future. Giant locusts with stingers in their tails whose wings make a noise like many chariots become helicopters. Stars falling to the earth as the sky vanishes like a scroll being rolled up refers to a thermonuclear exchange. A force of cavalry numbering two hundred million (lit., "twice times ten thousand times ten thousand") riding on horses with heads like lions refers to a future army (perhaps Chinese). Moreover, the notion that there will be a "rapture" is not ancient Christian teaching, but is less than two centuries old. Most who take the "rapture" seriously do not know this.[5]

It is also a pernicious way of telling the story of Jesus. Violence abounds. The central Christian characters are members of a "tribulation force" who fight with modern weapons against the armies of evil. It is Christian holy war, and God and Jesus fight on their side.

The scenes of judgment and annihilation are described in graphic language:

> Men and women, soldiers and horses, seemed to explode where they stood. It was as if the very words of the Lord had super-heated their blood, causing it to burst through their veins and skin.... Their innards and entrails gushed to the desert floor, and as those around them turned to run, they too were slain, their blood pooling and rising in the unforgiving brightness of the glory of Christ.[6]

This is a horrific vision of Jesus and of God. This is the "killer God" and the "killer Jesus." God and Jesus are going to "get us" unless we believe the right things, try to live the right way, and seek forgiveness for our shortcomings. Though today's apocalyptic Christians also affirm the gospels and the rest of the New Testament, their way of telling Jesus's story does not emphasize the compassionate Jesus who was a friend of sinners, but the warrior Jesus of Revelation riding a white horse and leading the armies of heaven against "the beast and the kings of the earth with their armies" (Rev. 19.11–21).

Like all ways of telling the story of Jesus, it shapes a vision of the Christian life. Being Christian means *being ready, being prepared,* for the "rapture," the second coming, and the final judgment. Only by belonging to the category of "true believers" will one be saved when the end time arrives. It stresses intensity of belief and purity of behavior—the world is divided even now between righteous and wicked, pure and impure, believers and unbelievers. And this view normally leads to a relative disregard for taking care of this world. How much does the environment matter if everything is going to end soon? How much does working for justice matter if all political systems will soon be irrelevant? Why work for peace when the Bible teaches that the future will be filled with war? Indeed, violence seems to be God's way. What *does* matter is believing and doing what is necessary in order to be in the in-group, the saved, when the "rapture" occurs or, failing that, when Jesus returns. This is the most important decision we face, for we risk annihilation in this world and condemnation in the next.

How many of the millions of readers of the Left Behind series affirm its theology is difficult to know. Some may simply find the books entertaining, good for reading on the beach. But according to a recent poll, over 20 percent of American Christians are "certain" that Jesus will return in the next fifty years, and another 20 percent think he "probably" will. In their minds, the second coming of Jesus, the end of the world, and the final judgment are near.[7]

Jesus as Teacher: Guidance for the Moral Life

All Christians agree that Jesus was a teacher. Some, however, focus on his teaching role as a comprehensive way of telling his story. This view is most often held by people who aren't sure what to make of theological claims about Jesus. Was he really the divinely begotten and only Son of God? Is he the only way of salvation? Are the miracles attributed to him really possible? Skepticism about these matters leads some to affirm that the importance of Jesus lies in his moral teaching.

Thomas Jefferson's way of seeing Jesus provides a striking example. While president, he spent some evenings with the gospels and a pair of scissors cutting out the parts that in his judgment did not go back to Jesus. (One wonders what would happen if a president were to do this today.) What remained was the moral teaching of Jesus, purified of the miraculous, provincial, and time-bound elements, including much of the theology. The result was *The Jefferson Bible,* a collection of the moral wisdom of Jesus.[8]

Few advocates of this way of seeing Jesus actually use a scissors. But seeing him primarily as a teacher is quite common. For some, his teaching included social and political imperatives. But most see his teaching more individualistically: he taught us how to behave toward one another.

Within this framework, Jesus's teaching is often reduced to very general moral precepts that could be put on a greeting card: "Love one another," "Do unto others as you would have them do unto you,"

"Love your neighbor as yourself." No doubt the world would be a better place if we lived according to these principles. But Jesus's teaching was edgier than this. After all, it got him killed. Authorities do not commonly execute somebody whose message abounds with benign banalities: be kind, be nice, be good. A persuasive image of Jesus must make sense of why he was crucified by the powers that ruled his world.

This way of telling the story of Jesus leads to a moralistic vision of following him. It minimizes or sets aside the explicitly religious dimension of his life and message. When his message is separated from its grounding in God, it easily becomes "good advice." But it doesn't address the issue of how we become more loving people through a deep centering in God that transforms lives. The problem with "Jesus as teacher" is not that it's wrong, but that it's shallow.

A LARGER DIVISION:
TWO PARADIGMS FOR SEEING JESUS

In addition to these different ways of telling the story of Jesus, there is an even broader division among American Christians today. Two very different *paradigms* for seeing Jesus conflict sharply with each other, producing very different understandings of Jesus. To define this important term with three short synonymous phrases, a paradigm is *a way of seeing a whole;* it is *a comprehensive way of seeing;* it is *a large framework within which we see.* As a way of seeing a whole, it affects how the particulars, the specifics, are seen.

To illustrate from the history of astronomy, the Ptolemaic and Copernican ways of seeing the earth in relationship to the universe were paradigms, comprehensive ways of seeing. Each affected how the movements of the heavenly bodies were understood. The Ptolemaic paradigm placed the earth at the center of the universe and understood the particulars, the data—the observable movements of the sun, moon, planets, and stars—in relationship to a stationary earth at the center. It worked pretty well and even made accurate predictions of eclipses possible.

For about fifteen hundred years, until Copernicus and Galileo in the 1500s and 1600s, it was the accepted scientific view, indeed taken for granted. But then it was replaced by the Copernican paradigm, which removed the earth from the center and placed the sun at the center of what now became a solar system (indeed, to speak of a solar system prior to the 1500s and 1600s is an anachronism). And the change in paradigms affected how the data—the movements of the heavenly bodies—were seen.[9]

This illustration not only explains what paradigms are and how they affect our seeing, but also helps us to understand a major conflict—perhaps *the* major conflict—in American Christianity today. We are experiencing conflict between two very different paradigms for seeing the "data" of Christianity: the Bible (including the gospels), Jesus, postbiblical teachings and doctrines (including the creeds), the nature of Christian language, and ultimately the nature of the Christian life. Both are Christian paradigms—millions of Christians affirm each. So it is not that one of them is Christian and the other not. And it is not that one of them is "traditional" Christianity and the other an abandonment of much of the Christian tradition. Rather, both are ways of seeing the Christian tradition and what it says about the Bible, God, Jesus, and what it means to follow him.

There is as yet no commonly agreed-upon terminology for naming these two paradigms. To use a chronological way of naming them, the first is an earlier paradigm, the second an emerging paradigm. To use more substantive ways of naming them, the first is *belief-centered;* it emphasizes the importance of holding Christian beliefs about Jesus, God, and the Bible. The second is *way-centered;* it emphasizes that Christianity is about following Jesus on a path, a path of transformation. The first emphasizes the *literal* meaning of Christian language, including the Bible; the second emphasizes the *more-than-literal* meaning of Christian language, what I will soon call the metaphorical meaning of Christian language. The differences between these two paradigms and their effects on telling the story of Jesus will become clear as we continue.

Jesus Within an Earlier Christian Paradigm

We are very familiar with seeing Jesus within an earlier Christian paradigm because, with the exception of "Jesus as teacher," all of the ways of telling the story of Jesus mentioned so far fall into this category. Most of us over fifty grew up with it, as have many under fifty, and it continues to be the most common way of seeing Jesus in America today. Because it dominates Christian radio and television, it is also the most publicly visible. But though very familiar, and though I call it an earlier paradigm, its distinctive features are not ancient or traditional. Rather, as I explain at the end of this section, they are the product of the last three to four centuries. I now summarize the earlier paradigm by describing its four central characteristics.

1. *The earlier paradigm sees Jesus through a Christian doctrinal lens.* It sees Jesus through a lens shaped by later Christian doctrine, especially the creeds of the fourth and fifth centuries. According to these, he is a divine figure: "God's only Son, our Lord," very God of very God, and of one substance with God; he is the second person of the Trinity and coeternal with God. Of course, he was also human; he is "true man" as well as "true God," two natures in one person. The creeds also highlight his death as the central purpose of his life: "For us and for our salvation he came down from heaven.... For our sake he was crucified under Pontius Pilate."

Throughout the centuries, most Christians have brought these doctrinal understandings to their hearing and reading of the gospels. Thus the first-century Jesus is seen as already "all of this." Even those Protestant groups who reject "doctrine" and affirm the Bible alone are affected by the doctrinal lens, for they accept its central claims about Jesus and see the gospels within its framework.

Not surprisingly, a doctrinal lens produces a doctrinal understanding of Jesus. Its central elements become the framework for seeing Jesus: he was (is) the only Son of God, both human and divine; he died for the sins of the world; and he is now one with God, indeed coequal with God. And the lens operates even (and especially) when we're not conscious of it. It shapes not only how many Christians see

Jesus, but also how most non-Christians do. If they've heard anything at all about Jesus, this is most likely what they've heard.

But when we see Jesus and the gospels primarily through a later doctrinal lens, we impose its understandings on the texts and often miss their first-century meaning. Even as a doctrinal lens highlights much of importance, it also casts much into shadow. Even as it illumines, it obscures.

My claim is not that later Christian doctrines are wrong and should be discarded. Not at all. I belong to a church that recites the creeds in its worship services, and I have no difficulty doing so. But this is because I understand the creeds as later Christian testimony to the significance of Jesus. In *their* language (language that had developed over a few centuries) these Christians expressed their deepest convictions about Jesus—about who he was (and is) and why he matters. These convictions flowed out of their continuing experience of the presence of Jesus, their worship and devotion, and their thought. But I do not see them as expressing beliefs or understandings that were already there in the first century, already there in the mind of Jesus and his earliest followers.

2. *The earlier paradigm sees the gospels and Jesus within the framework of biblical literalism.* "Biblical literalism" is shorthand for a way of seeing the Bible that became common over the last three or four centuries. It continues to be affirmed by at least a slight majority of American Christians. It has two primary features: it emphasizes that the Bible is a divine product and that it is to be read literally.

First, the Bible comes from God and therefore has a divine guarantee. Because God inspired the Bible as God has inspired no other document, it is God's truth. This is why it has authority. This view exists in harder and softer forms. The hard form speaks of biblical inerrancy and in American Christianity is affirmed by fundamentalists and most conservative evangelicals, but not commonly by Catholics and mainline Protestants. A softer form is also quite common. It does not insist on biblical inerrancy, but affirms that God inspired the Bible in such a way that it contains no serious errors. The softer form thus does not need to argue that the Bible is scientifically inerrant; it can happily say that science is not the Bible's subject, even as it continues to ground the important truths of the Bible in its divine origin.

Second, the earlier paradigm emphasizes a literal-factual interpretation of the Bible. It not only sees the Bible as true because of its divine origin, but identifies "truth" with "factuality." This also happens in harder and softer forms. The hard form reads the Genesis stories of creation as factually true and thus rejects evolution. The softer form accepts that parts of the Bible may be symbolic or metaphorical (the Genesis stories of creation, the story of Jonah and the big fish, the sun standing still, and so forth), but nevertheless affirms that a core factuality matters. This core of factuality commonly includes what are seen as the really important events: that the sea really did divide in two in the time of the exodus to allow the fleeing Israelites to escape from an Egyptian army; that Jesus really was born of a virgin, really did walk on water, multiply loaves, rise from the dead, and so forth. Thus, though the softer form does not need to fight against modern science, the general factuality of the Bible's central stories continues to be affirmed.

When the gospels are read through the lens of biblical literalism, whether in harder or softer form, the literal factuality of their language is either taken for granted or emphasized. The gospel stories of Jesus's miraculous birth and his spectacular deeds are understood as reporting events that really happened. When John's gospel reports that Jesus said about himself, "I am the light of the world," "I am the way, and the truth, and the life," "The Father and I are one," "Whoever has seen me has seen the Father," and "No one comes to the Father except through me," it means that Jesus really said these things. Thus the stories of Jesus's mighty deeds and his grand self-affirmations are all read as historically factual reports: he did and said these things.

This way of seeing the gospels is the basis for C. S. Lewis's oft-quoted statement from one of his early books:

A man who was merely a man and said the sort of things Jesus said would not be a great moral teacher. He would either be a lunatic—on a level with the man who says he is a poached egg—or else he would be the Devil of Hell. Either this man was, and is, the Son of God; or else a madman or something worse.[10]

The persuasiveness of the statement depends upon a literal-factual reading of the gospels. Its logic works only within this framework.

The first two features of the earlier paradigm—a lens shaped by doctrine and a literal-factual way of reading the gospel—commonly go together and reinforce each other. They produce a way of seeing Jesus that combines the "dying Savior" Jesus with the "divine-human" Jesus. Advocates of the "apocalyptic" Jesus also accept the above, even as they place their emphasis in a different place, namely, on Jesus's imminent return to judge the world.

3. *The earlier paradigm sees Jesus as intrinsically linked to the afterlife.* The afterlife—the promise of heaven and the threat of hell—has been at the center of popular Christianity for centuries. In the minds of many, this is what Christianity is all about. It tells us what we must do to be saved, that is, what we must do in order to go to heaven (and avoid hell). Indeed, for many Christians, this is what the words "saved" and "salvation" mean; they refer to a postdeath state, to the next world and not this world.

Within this framework, Jesus's message is primarily about heaven and how to get there. Two very familiar phrases in the gospels are understood this way: the "kingdom of heaven" and "eternal (or everlasting) life." The first comes from Matthew's gospel, in which the "kingdom of heaven" is central to Jesus's message. The second occurs frequently in John's gospel. But neither phrase means what we commonly understand as "heaven" or "eternal life." For Matthew, the "kingdom of heaven" does not mean an afterlife, but is his substitute for the "kingdom of God," which, as Matthew makes clear, is for the earth, and even in some sense is already here. For John, the Greek phrase translated "eternal life" cannot simply be equated with an afterlife. Rather, it means "the life of the age to come," and John affirms that this is already a present reality.

Nevertheless, when these phrases are seen within a paradigm that emphasizes an afterlife, they are naturally understood to refer to a postdeath state. The effects on how Jesus is seen are obvious. Not only was his message about an afterlife, but so was his death. As the sacrifice for sin, it makes our forgiveness possible, which is the prerequisite for entering heaven. Though being forgiven also makes a difference in our lives now, its primary importance concerns the next world. Thus Jesus—his message and his death—are about the way to heaven. And within this paradigm, he is most commonly seen as the *only* way of salvation. In a sentence, "Believe in Jesus now for the sake of heaven later."

4. *The earlier paradigm emphasizes believing.* In one sense, there is nothing new about this emphasis. Christians from the beginning have affirmed the importance of believing in Jesus. The language goes back to the New Testament. But in the last four hundred years or so, the word "believe" has undergone a radical change of meaning, so that its modern meaning is very different from its premodern Christian meanings. For most modern Christians, believing means believing a set of claims, a set of statements: believing that God exists, that the Bible is the Word of God, that Jesus is the Son of God, that he was born of a virgin, that he died for our sins, that he rose from the dead, that he is the only way of salvation, that he will come again, and so forth. This is believing as affirming a set of beliefs to be true.

But prior to about the year 1600, the verb "believe" had a very different meaning within Christianity as well as in popular usage. It did not mean believing statements to be true; the object of the verb "believe" was always a person, not a statement. This is the difference between *believing that* and *believing in*. To believe *in* a person is quite different from believing *that* a series of statements about the person are true. In premodern English, believing meant *believing in* and thus a relationship of trust, loyalty, and love. Most simply, to believe meant to belove.[11]

Thus, until about four centuries ago, believing in God and Jesus did not mean "I believe *that* the following statements about God and Jesus are true." Rather, to believe in God and Jesus had two primary meanings. It meant to *trust* in God and Jesus. Not to trust in *statements* about God and Jesus (for this would be "believing *that*"), but to trust in God as known in Jesus. This is believing as *fiducia*, to use the

Latin term for faith as "trust." In addition, to "believe" meant to commit one's allegiance, loyalty, and love to God and Jesus. This is believing (and faith) as *fidelitas,* as faithfulness (loyalty, allegiance, commitment) to God as known in Jesus (and not primarily to *statements* about God and Jesus, which, once again, would mean "believing *that*"). *Believing that* and *believing in* are very different. The first leads to an emphasis on correct belief, on believing the right things. The second leads to a transformed life.

Why did this change in the meaning of "believe" happen? Why did "faith" become "believing *that*"? It happened because of the encounter between Christianity and the Enlightenment, the great watershed event in Western cultural history that created the modern world, separating it from all that went before. It began in the seventeenth century with the birth of modern science, which involved both a new way of knowing and a body of knowledge generated by the new way of knowing. Authority and tradition (whether based on revelation or reason) as the basis of knowledge were replaced by experimentation and verification. The new way of knowing led to a new view of the universe as well. Increasingly, it was understood as a self-contained system governed by natural laws operating within the space-time world of matter and energy. The Enlightenment's way of thinking soon spread beyond science to the study of the human world of history, culture, institutions, and religions.

The collision between the Enlightenment and Christianity began with the controversy about whether the earth was at the center of the universe. Though an earth-centered universe was not official Christian doctrine, it had been part of the taken-for-granted Christian worldview for centuries. But in the early 1600s, Galileo's astronomical observations with the newly invented telescope persuaded him that the hypothesis suggested by Copernicus in 1543 was correct: the earth moved around the sun. He became an advocate of a sun-centered solar system. Church authorities arrested, tried, and convicted him of heresy. Compelled to recant, Galileo was confined to his house for the rest of his life.[12]

For modern Christians, the claim that the earth is *not* the center of the universe is not controversial. I don't know any Christians who would argue that it is. But other challenges by Enlightenment science to commonly accepted Christian notions continue to be rejected by some Christians. In the eighteenth and nineteenth centuries, the study of geology generated a picture of the earth as very much older than the Bible implies and of geological features as the product of uniform processes occurring over an immense period of time. In the nineteenth century, Darwin's theory of evolution provided an explanation of the development of species that did not depend upon supernatural creation.

Beyond these specific conflicts, the Enlightenment worldview— its understanding of what is real and what is possible—collided with many Christian convictions. Do divine interventions in the world really happen? Is the Bible the unique revelation of God? Indeed, does direct divine revelation happen? Do supernatural events like the spectacular events reported in the Bible and the gospels really happen? Do virgin births ever happen? Does it ever happen that somebody can walk on water? Is Jesus really the only way of salvation and is there therefore only one true religion, namely, Christianity? Is there really an afterlife, or is it pretty clear that our existence is dependent upon our bodies? Indeed, given the modern understanding of reality as that which can be known by science, is God real?

And so the meaning of "believing" changed from trust and loyalty to *believing that*—believing *that* a set of statements about God, Jesus, and the Bible are true, in spite of reasons to question them. The Enlightenment made Christianity questionable to millions of people in Western culture, especially in the last hundred years. In the twentieth century, Europe became full of nonbelievers, even as the United States remains a country of believers. But most believers and nonbelievers alike agree that being Christian is about believing.

The earlier paradigm's understanding of believing as affirming Christian teachings to be true in spite of reasons for skepticism indicates that it is not ancient, but a product of the collision with the Enlightenment. So are two of its other major features, biblical inerrancy and literalism. The claim that the Bible is "inerrant" in all of its details first appears in a book of theology written in the second half of the seventeenth century, a response to scientific results that seemed to call some of the Bible's teachings into question. So also an emphasis on literal-factual interpretation; because modernity challenged the factuality of the Bible, the response of many Christians was to insist on its factuality. But prior to modernity, the *more-than-literal*, the *more-than-factual* meaning of biblical texts, their *metaphorical* meaning, mattered most. Thus the most distinctive features of the earlier paradigm are not traditional, but a defensive rejection of the Enlightenment whenever it is perceived to threaten the central claims of Christianity.

Jesus Within an Emerging Christian Paradigm

Though naming the second paradigm "emerging" may suggest that it is very recent, it originated in the same period of time as the earlier paradigm. It is also a product of Christianity's encounter with the Enlightenment. It began to emerge in the 1600s among a few intellectuals and gradually gained momentum in academic and theological circles in the eighteenth and nineteenth centuries. In the twentieth century, it became the dominant understanding in divinity schools and seminaries of mainline churches, so that it has been familiar to mainline clergy for a couple of generations. But only recently has it been embraced at the grass-roots level among millions of Christians, laity as well as clergy, even as it continues to be unfamiliar to many.

Rather than involving a defensive rejection of the Enlightenment, it involves a discerning integration of Enlightenment knowledge. It affirms what we have learned about nature from the natural sciences in the last several centuries. It affirms what we have learned about ourselves from the human sciences—from biology, anthropology, sociology, and psychology. It affirms what we have learned from the study of history and culture, including the historical study of religions and the Bible. It takes seriously our growing awareness of religious pluralism, which makes it difficult to believe that only one religion is the true religion. The integration of modern knowledge needs to be discerning and to be done critically, for the perennial pitfall and peril of modern ways of thinking is reductionism, namely, the reduction of reality to what can be known through scientific ways of knowing.

In particular, the emerging paradigm sees the gospels and the Bible very differently. Indeed, for the study of Jesus, this is the most central difference. Rather than seeing them as a divine product and therefore as inerrant, and rather than interpreting them literally and factually, it sees them as human historical products that are to be read as a combination of historical memory and metaphorical narrative.

The process began in the late 1600s when a few European thinkers began to apply Enlightenment ideas to an understanding of the Bible. The pioneers included Richard Simon (1638–1712), a French Catholic, and Baruch Spinoza (1632–77), a Dutch Jew. They argued that the first five books of the Jewish Bible (the Pentateuch) were not written by Moses, as was commonly supposed, but were written over a period of centuries. From this, it followed that the Pentateuch was not to be understood as God's direct revelation to Moses, but as a human historical product, namely, as the product of ancient Israel. Given this, the historical meaning of these texts requires that we set them in the historical context of the community and time in which they were written.

Soon thereafter, this understanding was applied to the gospels and the New Testament. They began to be understood as the products of early Christian communities testifying to what Jesus had become in their lives in the decades after his historical life. They tell us how early Christians told the story of Jesus. They combine memory and testimony. The result was that the Bible as a whole began to be understood as a human historical product. The Jewish Bible (the Christian Old Testament) is the product of ancient Israel, and the New Testament is the product of early Christianity. Thus the Jewish Bible is not *God's story* of Israel, but *Israel's story* of Israel. The gospels are not *God's story* of Jesus, but *early Christianity's story* of Jesus.

Seeing the Bible and the gospels as human products involves no denial of the reality of God or the presence of the Spirit in the process. The form of the emerging paradigm that I advocate includes a robust affirmation of the reality of God. There are reductionistic forms of Enlightenment thought that view the idea of God as nothing more than a mistaken human projection and construction. They do not interest me. For me, Christianity without a robust affirmation of the sacred has no significant importance. Within this framework, the Bible and the gospels (like the sacred scriptures of other religions) are human *responses* to the sacred. They tell us not what God says, but what our spiritual ancestors said.

This change in how the Bible and the gospels are seen is the paradigm shift that marks the birth of the modern historical study of Jesus. It has often been called a "historical-critical" paradigm for reading the Bible in order to distinguish it from an uncritical and unhistorical way of reading. I prefer to speak of it as a "historical-metaphorical" paradigm. This approach integrates the insights of the historical-critical method with the realization that much of the language of the Bible is metaphorical, that is, more-than-literal, more-than-historical, in its meaning.

Because the rest of this book develops the way the gospels and Jesus are seen within this paradigm, I here provide only a preview of its foundations:

- The gospels are the result of a historical process. Written in the last third of the first century, they tell us what Jesus had become in the lives of the communities in which the traditions reported in them developed.

- As such, the gospels combine memory and testimony. Some of what they report is Jesus remembered; some of what they report is the fuller understanding that had developed in the decades between his death and the writing of the gospels.

- The gospels also combine memory and metaphor, historical memory with metaphorical narrative.

- There is a crucial distinction between the pre-Easter Jesus and the post-Easter Jesus. The former is Jesus before his death; the latter is what Jesus became after his death. There are important differences between the two.

These are the foundations of a historical-metaphorical way of telling the story of Jesus. In the next two chapters, I describe them in greater detail. They lead to a way of telling the story of Jesus quite different from the most familiar ways of telling his story. They result in a sketch of Jesus that is persuasive, compelling, inviting—and challenging.

TWO

The Gospels

Memory and Testimony

In this chapter and the next, we consider the nature of the gospels, our primary sources for knowing about Jesus. The gospels are both simple and complex. For centuries, millions of ordinary Christians with no technical training have heard or read them and been shaped and changed by them. On one level, their meaning is obvious: Jesus is the Light of the World, the Bread of Life, and the Son of God; we are to love one another as he loved us; we are to love the Lord our God with all our heart, soul, strength, and mind.

On the other hand, they are complex documents. They are written in an ancient language that most people today do not understand. They have a complex history. They combine pre-Easter memory with post-Easter testimony. They make allusions to the Jewish Bible and to the first-century world that are not always apparent to us. They combine memory and metaphor. But their complexity is not a deficiency or defect to be lamented. Rather, their complexity contributes to their richness.

THE GOSPELS IN CONTEMPORARY SCHOLARSHIP

At the beginning of the first volume of his study of the historical Jesus, the contemporary Catholic scholar John Meier invites us to imagine an "unpapal conclave" composed of four scholars:

Suppose that a Catholic, a Protestant, a Jew and an agnostic—
all honest historians cognizant of 1st-century religious movements—were locked up in the bowels of the Harvard Divinity
School library, put on a spartan diet and not allowed to emerge
until they had hammered out a consensus document on who
Jesus of Nazareth was and what he intended in his own time
and place.[1]

What would they all agree on?

Obviously, there would be disagreements, some perhaps flowing
out of their differing religious commitments. But they would agree
about much of importance. In particular, they would agree about the
foundation and pillars of the modern study of Jesus and Christian
origins, which I describe in this chapter and the next. They are not
only shared by mainstream Jesus scholarship, but define it.

The foundation is a way of seeing the gospels that has emerged
since the Enlightenment. In a sentence, *the gospels are products of early
Christian communities in the last third of the first century*. This short
sentence carries a freight of meaning.

First, it has a negative corollary: the gospels are not a direct divine
product, as notions of biblical inerrancy suppose. Rather, as documents written within early Christian communities, they are human
products. They tell us how our spiritual ancestors in these communities saw Jesus and his significance.

Second, as documents written in the last third of the first century,
they are the result of a developing tradition. During the decades
between Jesus's historical life and the writing of the gospels, the traditions about Jesus *developed*. This is not a supposition, but demon-
strated from the gospels themselves, as I soon illustrate. Thus the
gospels are not simply historical accounts of Jesus's life. Rather, they
tell us how Jesus's followers told and proclaimed his story several decades after his death.

Third, calling them community products means that the gospels
were written from within and for early Christian communities. Of
course, they were written by individuals, but these individuals were
not "authors" in the modern sense of the term. Modern authors most

commonly write for people they don't know, and they seek to be original and creative. But the individuals who wrote the gospels were crystallizing into writing their community's traditions about Jesus as they had developed in the decades since his death. They proclaimed the significance Jesus had come to have in these communities as the first century wound to its end.

Interpreters of the gospels who see them within the earlier paradigm sometimes argue that this understanding of the gospels and the pillars built on it are *presuppositions* that illegitimately shape the way the gospels are seen. But they are actually *conclusions,* not presuppositions, flowing out of detailed study of the gospels. They are the result of such study, not chosen *a priori.* I turn now to a fuller description of this way of seeing the gospels.

SOME BASICS

Because we live in a time when not everybody can be assumed to know what the Bible and the gospels are, I begin with basics.[2] The Christian Bible—the sacred scripture of Christians—includes the Jewish Bible and the Christian New Testament. The Jewish Bible (sometimes referred to as the Hebrew Bible, reflecting the language in which almost all of it was written) is called by Christians the Old Testament. Jews, of course, do not call it that.

Importantly, "Old" Testament does not mean outdated or superceded, despite a continuing Christian predilection to understand it that way. The Jewish Bible was the Bible of Jesus and his followers. In the middle of the second century after Jesus, a Christian named Marcion tried to get rid of the Jewish Bible as sacred scripture for Christians, arguing that it was the revelation of an inferior God. He was unsuccessful, and the orthodox Christian position ever since has been that the Jewish Bible *and* the New Testament are sacred scripture for Christians.

"The gospels" refers to the four gospels of the New Testament: Matthew, Mark, Luke, and John. There were other early Christian gospels, but these four became part of the New Testament. In addition, there are twenty-three other documents in the New Testament.

Most (twenty-one) are letters, epistles, from early Christians to other early Christians. Thirteen of these are attributed to the apostle Paul, and the others to figures such as Peter, James, Jude, and John. The remaining two documents are a "history" of early Christianity, the book of Acts, and an "apocalypse," the book of Revelation. But the gospels are the documents that narrate the life of Jesus. The rest of the New Testament does not purport to do so.

SOURCES FOR KNOWING ABOUT JESUS

With one exception, the only writings from the first century that mention Jesus were written by Christians. Thus we know about him almost exclusively through the testimony of people devoted to him. The exception is a brief passage from a Jewish historian named Josephus, who was born in the Jewish homeland around 37 CE. As a young man, he became commander of Jewish forces in Galilee in the war of revolt against the Roman Empire in 66 CE. Captured early in the war, he endeared himself to the Roman general Vespasian by telling him that a Jewish prophecy had predicted his triumph and elevation to emperor. Vespasian became his patron, and for the rest of his life Josephus lived in Rome, where he wrote a history of the Jewish revolt and a history of the Jewish people.

In a section of the latter work, written around 90 CE, he narrates events in the Jewish homeland while Pontius Pilate was governor some sixty years earlier:

> At this time there appeared Jesus, a wise man. For he was a doer of startling deeds, a teacher of people who received the truth with pleasure. And he gained a following both among many Jews and among many of Greek [meaning "Gentile," that is, non-Jewish] origin. And when Pilate, because of an accusation made by the leading men among us, condemned him to the cross, those who had loved him previously did not cease to do so. And up until this very day, the tribe of Christians (named after him) has not died out.[3]

As the only non-Christian reference to Jesus from the first century, it is interesting and valuable, even though it does not tell us anything we do not know from the gospels. But it discloses how a non-Christian saw Jesus—what he knew about Jesus and how he summarized what he thought most important:

- Jesus was "a wise man"—a teacher of wisdom.

- He did "startling deeds"—minimally, a reference to his reputation as a healer.

- He gained a following among Jews and Gentiles.

- He was crucified by order of the Roman governor after he was accused by "leading men" among the Jews.

- His followers continued to love him after his death.

- His followers became known as Christians and continued to exist when Josephus wrote near the end of the first century.

How did Josephus know about Jesus? There are two possibilities. The first is that he learned his information from followers of Jesus, either while he still lived in the Jewish homeland or later from Christians in Rome. If so, the passage is not an independent non-Christian source, but dependent upon Christians. The other possibility is that he learned about Jesus from non-Christian Jews, probably before moving to Rome in the 60s. Perhaps this is how non-Christian Jews commonly spoke about Jesus. His sketch is not negative, but quite admiring, even if it seems inadequately neutral from a Christian point of view.

In any case, this is the only non-Christian reference to Jesus from the first century. Everything else written about him in the first century comes from his followers. Their lives had been changed by him. They continued to experience him as a divine presence in their midst. For them, as Matthew's gospel puts it, he was "Emmanuel," a Hebrew word that means "God with us." They saw him as the decisive revelation of God—of what can be seen of God in a human life and of what a life filled with God looks like. Our sources for Jesus are testaments of devotion.

The earliest Christian writings are not the gospels, but the genuine letters of Paul, written in the decade of the 50s. But Paul's letters tell us very little about the life and message of Jesus. This does not mean that Jesus's historical life was unimportant to Paul, as some scholars have suggested. Rather, Jesus mattered greatly to Paul. Paul spoke of Jesus as Lord and as God's Son, as did early Christians generally. He wrote about life "in Christ," "Christ crucified," and "imitating Christ." But narrating the story of Jesus was not the purpose of his letters. Rather, as the literary genre of "letters" indicates, Paul was writing to Christian communities about issues that had arisen in their life together.

Thus for our knowledge of Jesus's life, we are almost completely dependent on the four gospels of the New Testament: Matthew, Mark, Luke, and John. Written in the last third of the first century, beginning with Mark around the year 70, they are known as the *canonical* gospels because they are part of the "canon" of the New Testament. There are also Christian *noncanonical* gospels that did not become part of the New Testament. But these are from the second century or later and have little or no importance for glimpsing the life of Jesus.

There is once again an exception: the *Gospel of Thomas,* discovered in Egypt in 1945.[4] Unlike the canonical gospels, *Thomas* has no narratives about Jesus—no stories of his life, miracles, birth, death, or resurrection. Rather, *Thomas* is a collection of teachings attributed to Jesus commonly divided into 114 sayings. Though most likely not written down until 125–40 CE, some of these sayings may be as early as what is in the canonical gospels. Most of this early material has parallels in the canonical gospels and thus does not provide new information. But a few sayings of Jesus found only in *Thomas* may be early as well. They are treated briefly in a later chapter.

A SKETCH OF GOSPEL ORIGINS

The study of the gospels over the past few centuries has resulted in a near consensus among mainstream scholars regarding their origin and relationships to one another. I begin with Matthew, Mark, and Luke, known together as the synoptic gospels.

- Mark is the earliest gospel, written around 70 CE, some four decades after the death of Jesus. It is also the shortest; Matthew and Luke are both about 50 percent longer. Primarily narrative, Mark consists mostly of stories about Jesus, with only a relatively small amount of his teachings. Mark begins with Jesus as an adult. In the first half of the gospel, Mark tells the story of Jesus's public activity; in the second half, he tells the story of Jesus's journey to Jerusalem and death and ends with the empty tomb on Easter morning.

- Matthew and Luke were written a decade or two later. Both used Mark as their primary source for their narrative of Jesus's public activity: 90 percent of Mark also appears in Matthew, and two-thirds appears in Luke. These similarities are the reason Matthew, Mark, and Luke are known as the synoptic gospels. But Matthew and Luke significantly expand Mark by including much more of the teaching of Jesus. In addition, both add to the beginning and end of Mark by prefacing the story of Jesus's public activity with stories of his birth and concluding with Easter stories not found in Mark.

- Before Mark was written, it is likely that there was a written collection of the teachings of Jesus that scholars call "Q." The basis for the hypothesis is that significant portions of Matthew and Luke that do not come from Mark are quite similar to one another, and the most likely explanation is that they come from an additional source used by both Matthew and Luke when they wrote their gospels. This source is Q; it consists of about two hundred verses and may have been put into written form as early as the 50s.

This sketch of the relationships between the synoptic gospels is commonly called the "two-document hypothesis." It says there are two primary written sources for the synoptics, Mark and Q. It is widely accepted by mainstream scholars, even as a small number have misgivings.[5]

John's gospel, also commonly called the Fourth Gospel, is generally thought to be the latest, most likely written in the 90s of the first century. John is very different from the synoptics. Jesus speaks about himself very differently. All of the "I am" sayings are found only in John: "I am the light of the world," "I am the bread of life," "I am the way, and the truth, and the life," and so forth. Only in John does Jesus say, "The Father and I are one" and "Whoever has seen me has seen the Father." The style and content of Jesus's teaching are also very different. Jesus teaches in long and quite abstract discourses rather than in memorable short sayings and parables and much of his teaching is about himself. Finally, John's story of Jesus's public activity is quite different, in both content and sequence. Because of these differences, most scholars see the gospel of John as having a purpose quite different from that of the synoptics. John's language is more symbolic and metaphorical. This awareness is ancient, not modern; it goes back to at least the second century, when Clement of Alexandria commented on John's distinctive quality by calling it the "spiritual gospel."

THE GOSPELS AS A DEVELOPING TRADITION

This sketch of the gospels indicates in a general way the foundational claim of the historical study of Jesus and Christian origins: the gospels are a developing tradition. Matthew and Luke developed Mark; they used and adapted Mark as they wrote their own gospels. They also used and adapted Q. Matthew and Luke also augmented Mark and Q; they each supplemented what they had received from tradition with tradition of their own.

The easiest and most persuasive way to see development within the gospels is by using a "gospel parallels," in which the synoptic gospels are printed in parallel columns.[6] Seeing them laid out side by side discloses their similarities and differences and demonstrates how a later gospel develops an earlier one. I provide three illustrations, the first two quite brief, the third more extensive. I linger over this point because of its importance and to emphasize that this way of seeing the gospels is not a presupposition brought to the texts, but a conclusion flowing out of detailed study of the texts themselves.

The Lord's Prayer

The first illustration is the famous prayer called by Protestants the Lord's Prayer and by Catholics the Our Father. It is found in three different versions in early Christian documents. The first two are in Matthew and Luke. The third is in the *Didache* (a Greek word meaning "teaching" and pronounced dih´-dah-kay), a collection of Christian teachings from around the year 100 but not included in the New Testament.

Matthew 6.9b–13	*Luke 11.2b–4*	*Didache 8.2b–3*
Our Father in heaven,	Father, hallowed be your name.	Our Father in heaven,
hallowed be your name.		hallowed be your name.
Your kingdom come.	Your kingdom come.	Your kingdom come.
Your will be done,		Your will be done,
on earth as it is in heaven.		on earth as it is in heaven.
Give us this day our daily bread.	Give us each day our daily bread.	Give us this day our daily bread.
And forgive us our debts,	And forgive us our sins,	And forgive us our debts,
as we also have forgiven our debtors.	for we ourselves forgive everyone indebted to us.	as we forgive our debtors.
And do not bring us to the time of trial,	And do not bring us to the time of trial.	And do not bring us to the time of trial,
but rescue us from the evil one.		but rescue us from the evil one.
		For the power and the glory are yours forever.

Because Matthew's version is widely used in Christian worship, it is the most familiar. But, at least to Protestants, something is missing from Matthew. It does not have the familiar closing, "For the kingdom and the power and the glory are yours, forever and ever." However, we do find very similar words in the *Didache:* "For the power and the glory are yours forever." The most familiar Protestant form of this prayer thus combines Matthew with the last line from the *Didache,* slightly modified.

Luke's version is shorter and differs in other ways as well. Instead of "Our Father in heaven," Luke has simply "Father." Luke does not have "Your will be done, on earth as it is in heaven." In the lines about bread and forgiveness, the wording is slightly different. Finally, Luke lacks both "Deliver us from the evil one" and "For the kingdom and the power and the glory are yours, forever and ever."

How do we account for these differences? There are two possibilities. The first is that Jesus taught the prayer in all three forms, and all three were memorized and preserved by his followers. Though logically possible, this is improbable. The second explanation is much more likely. Though the core of the prayer probably goes back to Jesus, the prayer was developed in somewhat different ways by early Christian communities and then put into written form by the authors of Matthew, Luke, and the *Didache.* The point is that the three forms of the Lord's Prayer are best explained by seeing them as products of a developing tradition.

Jesus Enters Jerusalem

A second illustration is the story of Jesus entering Jerusalem at the beginning of the final week of his life, the day known to Christians as Palm Sunday. Though the story is found in all four gospels, we focus on the beginning as told in Mark and Matthew:

When they were approaching Jerusalem, at Bethphage and Bethany, near the Mount of Olives, he sent two of his disciples and said to them, "Go into the village ahead of you, and immediately as you enter it, you will find tied there a colt that has never been ridden; untie it and bring it. If anyone says to you, 'Why are you doing this?' just say this, 'The Lord needs it and will send it back here immediately.'" They went away and found a colt tied near a door, outside in the street. As they were untying it, some of the bystanders said to them, "What are you doing, untying the colt?" They told them what Jesus had said; and they allowed them to take it. Then they brought the colt to Jesus and threw their cloaks on it; and he sat on it. (Mark 11.1–7)

When they had come near Jerusalem and had reached Bethphage, at the Mount of Olives, Jesus sent two disciples, saying to them, "Go into the village ahead of you, and immediately you will find a donkey tied, and a colt with her; untie them and bring them to me. If anyone says anything to you, just say this, 'The Lord needs them.' And he will send them immediately." This took place to fulfill what had been spoken through the prophet, saying, "Tell the daughter of Zion, Look, your king is coming to you, humble, and mounted on a donkey, and on a colt, the foal of a donkey." The disciples went and did as Jesus had directed them; they brought the donkey and the colt, and put their cloaks on them, and he sat on them. (Matt. 21.1–7)

The stories are quite similar because the author of Matthew uses Mark as he writes his gospel. But Matthew makes two significant changes as he does so.

First, Matthew adds a quotation from the Jewish Bible. Matthew 21.5 quotes Zechariah 9.9, which refers to a king entering Jerusalem on a colt:

"Tell the daughter of Zion [Jerusalem],
Look, your king is coming to you,

> humble, and mounted on a donkey,
> and on a colt, the foal of a donkey."

According to Zechariah, the "humble" king will be a king of peace. The passage from Zechariah continues: "He will cut off the chariot from Ephraim and the war horse from Jerusalem; and the battle bow shall be cut off, and he shall command peace to the nations" (v. 10). By quoting Zechariah, Matthew makes explicit what is implicit in Mark. Zechariah provides the symbolism (namely, entering the city on a colt) that gives the act of Jesus its meaning.

Second, Matthew adds an animal to the story. Whereas Mark's story has one animal, a colt, Matthew's has two, a donkey and her colt. Seven times Matthew changes Mark's one animal to two animals, including the climactic moment when Jesus mounts up: "They brought the donkey *and* the colt, and put their cloaks on *them*, and he sat on *them*" (Matt. 21.7). According to Matthew, Jesus rides into Jerusalem on two animals. Visualizing this is somewhere between comic and impossible. How does one ride two animals, especially when the animals are presumably of different sizes?

So why does Matthew add a second animal? It flows from Matthew's citation of Zechariah. The author of Matthew understood the text as referring to two animals. Matthew read Zechariah as saying that the humble king would come "mounted on a donkey, *and* on a colt, the foal of a donkey." So he adds an animal.

Ironically, the Zechariah passage in the Hebrew version of the Jewish Bible does not refer to two animals. Rather, it uses a characteristic of Hebrew poetry known as "parallelism," in which the second of two lines repeats or augments the first line. In this case, the second line specifies the meaning of the first line. Thus the Hebrew text of Zechariah says, in effect "on a donkey—*that is,* on a colt, the foal of a donkey." The author of Matthew may have misunderstood the Hebrew text or may have been using a Greek translation of the Jewish Bible that had misunderstood the Hebrew text. In any case, he adds an animal to make the correspondence exact between his reading of Zechariah and the story of Jesus's entry.

This illustration once again shows that the gospels are a developing tradition. Matthew modifies Mark—he develops the tradition he found in Mark. It also shows that the gospel writers felt free to do so. Clearly, Matthew does not see Mark as an "infallible" or "inerrant" account that he must not change. And it raises interesting questions. Did Matthew really think that Jesus rode into Jerusalem on two animals? Did he see himself as writing about the way it *really* happened? Or was making the meaning of the story explicit more important to him than historical exactitude? It seems so.

Christological Development

The third illustration is more extensive. It involves several texts in which we can see *christological* development. "Christology" is a semi-technical theological term whose subject matter is Jesus's identity and status: Jesus as the Messiah, the Son of God, the Light of the World, and so forth. When we carefully compare the gospels, we can see that their christological language develops over time, as three examples demonstrate.

Jesus Stills the Storm. Mark (6.47–52) and Matthew (14.22–33) contain parallel stories of Jesus's walking on the water and stilling a storm on the Sea of Galilee. The disciples are in a boat in a storm at night. They are distressed. Then they see Jesus walking on the sea; he commands the storm to cease, and it does. At the end of the story Mark reports the disciples' reaction: "And they were utterly astounded." Why? According to Mark,

> For they didn't understand about the loaves, but their hearts were hardened. (Mark 6.51–52)

When Matthew copies this story from Mark, he changes the ending. Instead of concluding the story with the disciples' lack of comprehension about the loaves, an ending that may well have puzzled Matthew, Matthew replaces it with an awestruck affirmation, "Those in the boat worshiped him, saying, 'Truly you are the Son of God'"

(Matt. 14.33). The story in Mark has no such exclamation; Matthew adds one.

Jesus's Baptism. The parallel stories of Jesus's baptism by John the Baptizer all include a vision in which Jesus sees the Spirit of God descending upon him accompanied by a voice that names him as God's "beloved Son":

In those days Jesus came from Nazareth of Galilee and was baptized by John in the Jordan. And just as he was coming up out of the water, he saw the heavens torn apart and the Spirit descending like a dove on him. And a voice came from heaven, "You are my Son, the Beloved; with you I am well pleased." (Mark 1.9–11)

Then Jesus came from Galilee to John at the Jordan, to be baptized by him. John would have prevented him, saying, "I need to be baptized by you, and do you come to me?" But Jesus answered him, "Let it be so now; for it is proper for us in this way to fulfill all righteousness." Then he consented. And when Jesus had been baptized, just as he came up from the water, suddenly the heavens were opened to him and he saw the Spirit of God descending like a dove and alighting on him. And a voice from heaven said, "This is my Son, the Beloved, with whom I am well pleased." (Matt. 3.13–17)

Now when all the people were baptized, and when Jesus also had been baptized and was praying, the heaven was opened, and the Holy Spirit descended upon him in bodily form like a dove. And a voice came from heaven, "You are my Son, the Beloved; with you I am well pleased." (Luke 3.21–22)

As Matthew and Luke use Mark, both make some minor stylistic changes. In addition, Luke adds that the vision happened while Jesus "was praying."

Matthew makes two changes that are more substantial. First, he adds to Mark a conversation between Jesus and John not found in the other gospels. When Jesus approaches John to be baptized, John initially refuses: "I need to be baptized by you, and do you come to me?" But Jesus asks John to do so, saying, "Let it be so now; for it is proper for us in this way to fulfill all righteousness." The effects of this addition are twofold. On the one hand, that John baptized Jesus might suggest that John is superior to Jesus. To counter this possibility, Matthew has John recognize Jesus's superiority: "I need to be baptized by you." On the other hand, Matthew counters an impression that could be created by Mark's story. According to Mark 1.4, John was preaching "a baptism of repentance for the forgiveness of sins." From this, it could be inferred that Jesus went to be baptized by John because he thought of himself as a sinner in need of repentance. Matthew's addition makes it clear that Jesus did not *need* to be baptized by John, but did so in order "to fulfill all righteousness."

The second change is more subtle. In Mark (and in Luke), the voice that speaks from heaven during Jesus's vision addresses him in the second person: "*You* are my Son, the Beloved; with *you* I am well pleased." The implication is that this was a private experience of Jesus. Matthew changes the voice to the third person: "*This* is my Son, the Beloved, with *whom* I am well pleased." In Matthew, it becomes a declaration to the crowd, and not a voice addressed to Jesus. Thus, Matthew implies, Jesus's identity as God's Son was made public at his baptism.

Peter's Confession. The famous passage commonly called Peter's confession at Caesarea Philippi is found in Mark 8.27–30, Matthew 16.13–16, and Luke 9.18–20. In Mark it climaxes the first half of the gospel. Jesus's public activity in Galilee is now over with and, right after this story, Mark's narrative begins to move toward Jerusalem and the final week of Jesus's life.

In the setting of this story Jesus asks his disciples, "Who do people say that I am?" And so they report what people are saying.

Some say he is "John the Baptist; and others, Elijah; and still others, one of the prophets." Then Jesus asks, "But who do you say that I am?" The responses:

> Peter answered him, "You are the Messiah." (Mark 8.29)

> Simon Peter answered, "You are the Messiah, the Son of the living God." (Matt. 16.16)

> Peter answered, "The Messiah of God." (Luke 9.20)

As Matthew and Luke take this story over from Mark, they once again make changes. Luke's is very modest. He adds two words to Peter's reply: Jesus is "the Messiah *of God*." This is a change without a difference, for the Messiah is intrinsically "of God," that is, anointed by God. Matthew's change is more substantial. To "You are the Messiah," he adds *the Son of the living God*." Once again, Matthew adds a christological phrase to a text that did not have it.

What we see in these texts reflects a general tendency that can be seen in the gospels. As they develop, they add christological language to their story of Jesus, with John's gospel doing so most overtly and frequently. They are not to be faulted for this, as if they should not have done so. Rather, this language expressed their communities' most central conviction: the Jesus whom they remembered is the decisive revelation of God. He is the Messiah, God's Son, the Light of the World, the Bread of Life, the Living Water, the Word Become Flesh; indeed, he is Lord. In their experience and devotion, he was all of these. This language is their testimony to him. It is gospel.

This understanding of the gospels as a developing tradition is the foundation of modern Jesus scholarship. From it flow a number of implications shared in common by mainstream scholars. Because "foundation" is a construction metaphor, we might think of these implications as "pillars" built upon this foundation. About these pillars, the four scholars in Meier's "unpapal conclave" would also agree.

THE FIRST PILLAR: THE GOSPELS AS MEMORY AND TESTIMONY

We turn now to how seeing the gospels as a developing tradition affects how we read them, interpret them, and understand them. Within this way of seeing them, they look very different from how they look within the earlier paradigm. The latter sees the gospels as based on eyewitness accounts of Jesus and their purpose as providing factually accurate reports of his life and message. The authors are seen as factual-minded writers who depended on their own scrupulous research, the guidance of the Spirit, or both to produce unvarnished history. The gospels are seen primarily as history remembered, as texts whose primary purpose is historical exactitude.

But seeing the gospels as a developing tradition means that they are not primarily concerned with historical reporting. Rather, *the gospels combine memory and testimony*. To express this first pillar in only slightly different language, they combine memory and witness, memory and proclamation, memory and conviction. They contain the communities' memories of the pre-Easter Jesus and their post-Easter proclamation of his significance. They combine Jesus remembered with Jesus proclaimed.

Within this framework, the authors of the gospels are seen as "evangelists," as they have long been called, and not primarily as writers whose primary purpose was historical reporting of the past. The term "evangelist" is based on the Greek word for "gospel," which means "news." As evangelists, the authors of the gospels proclaimed the "news" about Jesus *in* and *for their time and place*. The word "news" suggests updating. They proclaimed Jesus for their "now" by updating the story of Jesus "then." They combined proclamation of Jesus for their now with their memory of Jesus then. In this, they did what any good Christian preacher, teacher, or theologian does—tells us what Jesus *then* means for us *now*. As they did so, they built on memory even as they went beyond memory to include the fuller understandings and convictions that had developed in the decades since Jesus's death.

As a combination of memory and testimony, the gospels contain earlier and later layers of material. The language of "layers" is an archaeological metaphor. To shift to a vocal metaphor, the gospels combine multiple voices: the remembered voice of Jesus and the voices of early Christian communities testifying to what Jesus had become in their lives. The quest for the historical Jesus involves making discerning decisions about what is earlier and what is later, what is the voice of Jesus and what is the voice of the community. The earlier the layer, the earlier the voice, the closer we are to Jesus. The later the layer, the later the voice, the more we are in touch with the testimony of his followers. Importantly, both layers, both voices, matter. The point is not to discard the later layers, but to understand them for what they are—early Christian testimony to what Jesus had become.

THE SECOND PILLAR: THE PRE-EASTER AND POST-EASTER JESUS

The second pillar of Jesus scholarship is a recognition of the difference between the pre-Easter Jesus and the post-Easter Jesus. The former is Jesus *before his death;* and the latter is *what Jesus became after his death.*[7] They are quite different from each other.

One aspect of the difference is obvious: Jesus's followers knew him in a different way after his death from how they had known him before his death. Before his death, they knew him as a finite and mortal human being. He was a flesh-and-blood, corpuscular and protoplasmic Galilean Jew; he weighed around 110 pounds and was a bit over five feet tall; he had to eat and sleep; he was born and he died.[8] *This* Jesus, the pre-Easter Jesus, is a figure of the past, dead and gone, nowhere anymore. This does not deny Easter, but simply recognizes that Easter does not mean that the flesh-and-blood Jesus who weighs 110 pounds is still alive somewhere.

After his death, they knew him in a different way. Paul experienced him on the road to Damascus as a brilliant light and a voice. In one of his letters, Paul says, "Even if we did once know Christ in the flesh, that is not how we know him now" (2 Cor. 5.16, JB). In the gospel stories of Easter, it is clear that Jesus after Easter is different from what he was like before his death. He passes through walls and enters locked rooms. Two of his followers walk with him for several hours and do not recognize him. He appears and then vanishes.

This recognition of a difference between the pre-Easter and post-Easter Jesus is thus ancient, not modern. In Matthew 26.11, Jesus before his death says to his followers, "You will not always have me with you." Two chapters later, after Easter and at the very end of the gospel, Jesus says, "I am with you always, to the end of the age" (28.20). For Matthew, both statements are true. Jesus in the form they had known him before Easter was no longer with them, but Jesus after Easter was with them in a new way—"I am with you always," language that echoes Matthew's theme of Jesus as "Emmanuel," which means "God with us."[9]

Whereas the pre-Easter Jesus was finite and mortal, the post-Easter Jesus is spoken of as a divine reality. In John's gospel, Thomas exclaims as he experiences the risen Jesus, "My Lord and my God!" (20.28). As the Christian tradition develops, the post-Easter Jesus is spoken of as one with God and as having the qualities of God. In the post-Easter language of the Nicene Creed, Jesus is spoken of as "very God of very God" and "of one substance with the Father." So also in Christian devotion and prayer. Consider how Jesus (here named Christ) is spoken of in a well-known prayer from Celtic Christianity:

Christ as a light
Illumine and guide me.
Christ as a shield
O'ershadow me.
Christ under me
Christ over me
Christ beside me
On my left and my right.
This day, be within and
Without me,
Lowly and meek,
Yet all powerful.
Be in the heart
Of each to whom I speak,

In the mouth of each
Who speaks unto me.
This day, be within and
Without me,
Lowly and meek,
Yet all powerful.
Christ as a light
Christ as a shield
Christ beside me
On my left and my right.[10]

How must the Christian who composed this prayer have been thinking of Christ in order for its language to make sense? Christ is like
God, an omnipresent spiritual reality: above me, below me, beside
me, around me, within me. This is the post-Easter Jesus, obviously
different from the flesh-and-blood pre-Easter Jesus.

There is also a not so obvious difference, and this difference is an
important part of the second pillar of modern Jesus scholarship. It
flows directly out of seeing the gospels as a developing tradition.
Namely, *Jesus as spoken of in the gospels is different in important ways
from the pre-Easter Jesus.* The Jesus we meet on the surface level of
the gospels and the New Testament as a whole (the "canonical Jesus,"
as he is sometimes called) is the *post-Easter Jesus of the developing tradition,* the memory of Jesus shaped by the post-Easter convictions of
Christian communities.

This applies especially to christological language. As we have already seen, such language grows as the gospels develop. Seeing this
development raises a broader historical question. Is all christological
language post-Easter? Or does some of it go back to a pre-Easter setting? During his historical life, did Jesus or his followers think of him
and speak of him as the Messiah and the Son of God? Or is christological language the product of the developing tradition after Easter?
Is it part of Jesus's message about himself? Or is it the product—the
testimony—of post-Easter Christian experience and thought?

Importantly, this is a historical question, not a theological question. The issue is not whether Jesus *is* the Son of God, Lord, Light

of the World, and so forth. For Christians, the truth of these affirmations is not dependent upon whether Jesus thought of himself in these terms; rather, this *is* who Jesus is for Christians. Thus the issue is not the truth of christological language, but the historical question of whether it goes back to Jesus. Is such language pre-Easter? Was Jesus's identity part of his message?

We begin with the synoptic gospels. All three affirm that Jesus is the Messiah and the Son of God, but they do not present this as part of his own message. Instead, they report this only in the voice of his followers. In Mark this happens just once, namely, in the story of Peter's affirmation "You are the Messiah." The story ends with Jesus commanding his disciples not to tell anyone what Peter has said (8.30). They obey him; in Mark, this is the only time they speak of Jesus as the Messiah. Thus, according to Mark (and Matthew and Luke), the status of Jesus as the Messiah was not part of the pre-Easter message of Jesus or his disciples. The obvious and direct implication is that Jesus's status as the Messiah and Son of God became part of their proclamation only after Easter.

But in John, as mentioned earlier, Jesus frequently speaks of his christological status. The "I am" sayings and statements like "The Father and I are one" are only in John. How does one reconcile this with the synoptic portrait? There are two logical possibilities. First, Jesus did speak of himself as John reports he did, but Mark (and Matthew and Luke) either did not know this or chose not to report it. Within harder and softer forms of biblical literalism, this is how it is resolved. But this seems unlikely. If Jesus spoke as John says he did, can we imagine that the authors of the synoptics didn't know this? And if they did know this, can we imagine any reason they wouldn't report it? A second possibility seems much more likely: Jesus did not speak of himself as he does in John. Rather, this language is the post-Easter testimony of John and his community.[11]

Why did this happen? How did Jesus, a monotheistic Jew, become spoken of as divine and as "one with God"? There are two major reasons. The first is the impression that he made on his followers during his lifetime. They did not experience him as ordinary, but as extraordinary. There is no other way to explain why they left everything (family, work, village, convention) and risked everything (including death) in order to follow him. They must have experienced a "presence" in and around him, as followers of other major religious figures such as St. Francis and the Buddha and Muhammad did. In the best-known scholarly book about Jesus a half century ago, Günther Bornkamm wrote: "Jesus belongs to this world. Yet in the midst of it, he is of unmistakable otherness."[12] Whatever more needs to be said about Jesus, he was a charismatic Jew in whom his followers sensed the presence of the sacred. I do not think that his pre-Easter followers thought he *was* God. But I can imagine that they exclaimed, "What manner of man is this?"

The second reason is his followers' *experience* of Jesus after his death. They experienced him as a present reality, not simply a figure of the past; and they experienced him as a divine reality, as Lord. This is the central affirmation of early Christianity, of the gospels and the New Testament as a whole. It is also the central affirmation of the Easter stories.

Set aside for now whatever puzzles you about these stories. Do they describe "public events" that anyone could have witnessed? Were the empty tomb and the appearances of Jesus after his death the kinds of events that disinterested observers could have seen, that even Pilate could have seen? Do these stories purport to report the kinds of events that could in principle have been photographed? We will consider the Easter stories in detail later in this book. For now, I emphasize that they are rooted in early Christian *experience* of Jesus after his death, but now known in a radically new way, no longer as a figure of flesh and blood, but as a divine reality having the qualities of God. This is the post-Easter Jesus of Christian experience.

Thus the post-Easter Jesus—what Jesus became after his death— is the Jesus of Christian experience and tradition. This is the Jesus who proclaims his own identity in christological language, and who speaks of the importance of believing in him and his saving significance. But this language almost certainly does not go back to the pre-Easter Jesus.

This claim is alarming to some Christians. In their minds, it calls into question the truth of the gospels and the significance of Jesus. If the gospels say that Jesus said all of these things about himself and he didn't, does this mean that the gospels aren't true? The issue is generated by what might be called "historical fundamentalism" or "fact fundamentalism": if these statements aren't historically factual, then they aren't true; they are exaggeration, fantasy, or even lies. This reasoning is a legacy of the Enlightenment, which led many in Western culture to identify "the true" with "the factual."[13]

Thus I emphasize that there is a difference between testimony and fantasy, witness and exaggeration, conviction and lies. A historical-metaphorical way of reading the gospels does not see them as fantasy or exaggeration or deception, but as the testimony and witness and convictions of Jesus's followers.

To return to the main point, the second pillar of modern Jesus scholarship sees the pre-Easter Jesus as quite different from the post-Easter Jesus. The distinction is important for two primary reasons. First, when the distinction is not made, the divine qualities of the post-Easter Jesus are projected back onto the pre-Easter Jesus. The result is an unreal human being. When the pre-Easter Jesus is thought of as divine, we get Jesus as "Superman," a superhero with powers and knowledge beyond what human beings have. The result is that we underestimate Jesus; we lose track of the utterly remarkable human being that he was. As Albert Nolan, a South African Jesus scholar, wrote about thirty years ago: "Jesus is a much underrated man.... To deprive this man of his humanity is to deprive him of his greatness."[14]

The distinction matters for a second reason. It affects how we see Jesus's message and purpose. A majority of Christians in North America think that his message was primarily about himself—his role in God's plan of salvation, especially his death, and the importance of believing in him. But if, as a historical-metaphorical way of seeing Jesus affirms, the pre-Easter Jesus's message wasn't about himself, what was it about? It was, as I suggest in the rest of this book, about God, "the way," and the kingdom of God.

But before we turn to a sketch of the pre-Easter Jesus, we need to describe the third pillar, the historical-metaphorical way of reading the gospels. Namely, the gospels combine not only memory and testimony, but also memory and metaphor. This is the subject of the next chapter.

THREE

The Gospels

Memory, Metaphor, and Method

The third pillar of modern Jesus scholarship is the recognition that much of the language of the gospels is metaphorical. Whereas the first pillar affirms that the gospels combine *memory and testimony,* the third affirms that they combine *memory and metaphor,* historical memory in metaphorical narrative, *Jesus remembered* with *Jesus metaphorized.* This way of seeing the gospels moves beyond a literal-factual reading and, very importantly, emphasizes their truth as metaphor. Metaphors and metaphorical narratives can be truthful, truth-filled, independently of their literal factuality.

What it means to say that the gospels contain memory is obvious: some of what they report consists of early Christian memories of what Jesus said and did and what happened to him. But the meaning of metaphor and metaphorical narrative needs explanation. I use "metaphor" in a much broader sense than its narrowest meaning, in which it is distinguished from simile. Both are figures of speech, but a simile uses the word "like," and a metaphor does not. Simile: "My love is *like* a red red rose." Metaphor: "My love *is* a red red rose."

In the broader sense in which I am using the term, the metaphorical meaning of language is its *more-than-literal, more-than-factual* meaning. Metaphor refers to the *surplus of meaning* that language can carry. I emphasize *more-than-literal* meaning because of a common tendency in modern Western culture to think that metaphorical language is inferior to factual language. When people first encounter the suggestion that a biblical story is metaphorical, their response

sometimes is, "You mean it's *only* metaphorical?" But metaphor is
about a surplus of meaning, not a deficiency of meaning.

From ancient times, Christian interpreters of the Bible and the
gospels have consistently emphasized their meaning as metaphor.
Only in the last few hundred years have some Christians flattened
biblical language by emphasizing its literal-factual meaning. This insistence upon the literal-factual truth of the gospels often generates
its opposite, skeptical rejection by those who cannot believe them literally. But there is a third way that moves beyond the stark choices of
literalism or its rejection. This third way is provided by seeing the
gospels as a combination of metaphorical narrative and historical
memory.

Because the claim that much of the language of the gospels is
metaphorical is controversial in some Christian circles today, I begin
with examples with which I imagine everybody would agree. As I do
so, my purpose is threefold: to illustrate (1) that much of the language in the gospels is metaphorical; (2) that what matters is the
more-than-literal meaning; and (3) that the more-than-literal meaning does not depend upon the historical factuality of the language.

METAPHORICAL LANGUAGE
IN THE GOSPELS

To start with christological language and at the risk of emphasizing
the obvious, I underline its metaphorical character with examples
from the gospel of John:

- Jesus is the Light of the World. Jesus is not literally a light, a
  candle, or a lamp. But he is metaphorically all of these. He is
  light in the darkness, illumination, revelation, the one who
  enables us to see. As light, he is even flame and fire, as he is in
  the *Gospel of Thomas:* "Whoever is near me is near the fire"
  (82).

- Jesus is the Bread of Life. Of course, Jesus is not literally a
  loaf. But he is metaphorically "bread," the food that satisfies
  our hunger. Likewise, he satisfies our thirst; he is not only

spiritual food but "living water." Indeed, he is "bread" and "wine."

- Jesus is the Gate and the Way. But Jesus is not literally a gate, a door, or a threshold, not literally a way, a path, or a road. But he is metaphorically—he is the gate, the door, the way, the path into a new kind of life.

This language is obviously metaphorical, not literal. What could it mean to take it literally? But for Christians, Jesus really and metaphorically is all of these. The language is not literally true, but metaphorically truthful.

Not only did early Christians use metaphorical language about Jesus, but his own message was full of metaphor. He seems to have had a metaphorical mind. To illustrate with some of his short sayings:

"You strain out a gnat but swallow a camel" (Matt. 23.24). Jesus wasn't talking about eating insects or camels.

"Let the dead bury their own dead" (Matt. 8.2). He wasn't talking about literally dead people, certainly not in the first use of "dead"—and probably not in the second either.

"Figs are not gathered from thorns, nor are grapes picked from a bramble bush" (Luke 6.44). Jesus wasn't talking about where to find figs and grapes.

"Can a blind person guide a blind person? Will not both fall into a pit?" (Luke 6.39). He wasn't talking about literally blind people.

"Why do you see the speck in your neighbor's eye but do not notice the log in your own eye?" (Matt. 7.3). He wasn't talking to people who literally had logs in their eyes.

Taking these sayings literally would miss their meaning. Metaphor is about meaning. Literalism often misses meaning.

In addition, Jesus taught with metaphorical narratives, that is, with parables. Apparently he valued this mode of teaching; more parables are attributed to him than to anybody else in his religious tradition. Importantly, the truth of his parables does not depend upon their being factually true. I know of no Christian who insists that the parable of the good Samaritan "really happened"—that Jesus was telling a story about something that had actually happened on the road from Jerusalem to Jericho. Likewise, I don't know anybody who insists that there really was a prodigal son who was lavishly welcomed home by an overjoyed father and whose older brother objected. To suggest that these stories must be factually true in order to contain truth strikes everybody as foolish. The parables of Jesus are to be read parabolically, that is, as metaphorical narratives. They are about *meaning,* and their truthful and truth-filled meaning does not depend on their factuality.

Thus far, I assume, all Christians would agree. A historical-metaphorical approach to the gospels builds on the above as it also moves beyond. As metaphorical narratives, the gospel stories about Jesus fall into two categories. The first is *memory metaphorized*—stories that contain the memory of something that happened, but that are told in such a way as to give them a more than historical-factual meaning. The second is *purely metaphorical narratives.* These are not based on memory of a particular event and thus are not history remembered, but are stories created for the sake of their metaphorical meaning.

MEMORY METAPHORIZED

I illustrate the first category, memory metaphorized, with two examples: the story of Jesus's journey from Galilee to Jerusalem, and a story of Jesus exorcizing a demon-possessed man. Each has a basis in memory, and each is also given a metaphorical meaning.

Jesus's Journey from Galilee to Jerusalem

Mark's story of Jesus's final journey from Galilee to Jerusalem (8.22–10.52) is at the center of Mark's gospel. This story separates and connects the first and third parts, which treat Jesus's public activity in

Galilee and his climactic final week in Jerusalem. Obviously, the story contains memory: it is as certain as anything can be that Jesus really did make a journey from Galilee to Jerusalem that ended in his execution. This is history remembered.

But the way Mark tells the story of Jesus's journey gives it a more-than-literal, more-than-historical meaning. In Mark, it is a story of *what it means to follow Jesus,* a theme closely linked to two other themes in Mark, "the way" and "discipleship." For Mark (and early Christianity generally), to be *a disciple* is *to follow Jesus* on *the way* that leads to *Jerusalem.*

As Mark (followed by Matthew and Luke) tells the story of this journey, Jesus three times speaks of his impending crucifixion and resurrection: the authorities will kill him, but God will vindicate him (Mark 8.31; 9.31; 10.33–34). According to the third and most detailed anticipation of Jesus's death:

> See, we are going up to Jerusalem, and the Son of Man will be handed over to the chief priests and the scribes, and they will condemn him to death; then they will hand him over to the Gentiles; they will mock him, and spit upon him, and flog him, and kill him; and after three days he will rise again.

After each anticipation, Jesus speaks about what it means to follow him (8.34; 9.35; 10.35–45). The most familiar of these is the first: "If any want to become my followers, let them deny themselves and take up their cross and follow me." To follow Jesus is to follow him to the cross in Jerusalem. Within this story, Jerusalem has a twofold significance. It is the place of death and resurrection, of endings and beginnings, where, to use an old wordplay, the tomb becomes a womb. It is also the place of confrontation with the authorities. To follow Jesus is to join him on this journey of transformation and confrontation. The story of Jesus's final journey is a metaphorical narrative about the meaning of discipleship.[1]

Strikingly, Mark frames this story of following Jesus with two stories of blind men being given their sight. Immediately at the beginning of the section, Jesus restores sight to a blind man in the town of

Bethsaida in Galilee (8.22–26). As the section ends, Jesus restores sight to a blind beggar named Bartimaeus in Jericho, the last stop before Jerusalem (10.46–52). Sitting by the roadside, Bartimaeus calls out for help. Jesus says to him:

> "What do you want me to do for you?" The blind man said to him, "My teacher, let me see again." Jesus said to him, "Go; your faith has made you well." Immediately he regained his sight *and followed Jesus on the way.*" (10.51–52)

That Mark frames the story of Jesus's final journey with these stories gives them a metaphorical meaning. Within Mark's narrative, really seeing, having one's eyes opened, is to see that discipleship means following Jesus on "the way"—the way that leads to Jerusalem, confrontation with the authorities, death, and resurrection.

Do the stories of the blind man of Bethsaida and blind Bartimaeus also contain memory? Possibly. Jesus was a healer, and he may have healed some cases of blindness. But whatever the historical verdict, it is clear that Mark's purpose in these stories is not historical reporting for the sake of historical reporting. Rather, he places these stories where he does because of the way they frame Jesus's final journey. To emphasize their factuality risks missing their meaning as metaphor: they are stories about seeing the way of Jesus.

Jesus Heals a Demoniac

A second example of a text that combines memory and metaphor is the story of Jesus exorcising a host of demons from a possessed man in Mark 5.1–20. It is a dramatic story. The possessed man lives in a graveyard; naked, he howls day and night and bruises himself with stones. With superhuman strength, he breaks the chains with which he is shackled. When Jesus exorcises the unclean spirits, named "Legion," from him, they enter a herd of two thousand pigs, which dash into the sea and drown.

Memory. That Jesus performed exorcisms of people whom he and his contemporaries believed to be possessed by unclean spirits is widely accepted by historical scholars. Even the Jesus Seminar, much maligned for its alleged excessive skepticism, voted by a large majority that Jesus functioned as an exorcist. Whether or not this story reports an actual event, its claim that Jesus exorcised demons is memory.

Metaphor. The central features of this story create a powerful metaphorical narrative. Its details create a vivid picture of impurity. The possessed man lives on the other side of the Sea of Galilee among Gentiles, who are impure. He lives among tombs, which are impure, unclean. Pigs—unclean animals—graze nearby. The demons who possess him are "Legion," a term that points to the Roman (and thus gentile) possessors of the land. Impurity was seen as contagious. But in this story, Jesus is not made impure by the contagion of impurity; rather, the reverse happens. The unclean spirits are exorcised, the unclean animals are destroyed, and the story ends with the man clothed, in his right mind, and restored to community. The point of the story is that the Spirit of God present in Jesus overcomes impurity rather than being overcome by it.

Did it happen as Mark reports it? Or is Mark's telling of the story mostly memory metaphorized? People might decide differently about this. But what is clear is that a reading that emphasizes the factuality of the story without recognizing its more-than-factual meaning misses most of what Mark is saying.

PURELY METAPHORICAL NARRATIVES

Purely metaphorical narratives, the second type, are not based on the memory of particular events, but are symbolic narratives created for their metaphorical meaning. As such, they are not meant as historical reports. Rather, the stories use symbolic language that points beyond a factual meaning. I provide three examples. About all of these, there is widespread agreement among mainstream scholars that their purpose is not to report events that happened.

The Wedding at Cana

The story of Jesus changing over a hundred gallons of water into fine wine at a wedding in the village of Cana (John 2.1–11) is regarded by virtually all mainstream scholars as a purely metaphorical narrative, not as a report of a historical event. As metaphor, what is it saying? What is its parabolic meaning?

We begin with its literary context. It is the opening scene, the inaugural story, of Jesus's public activity in the gospel of John.[2] Inaugural stories are important in the gospels. In each, the opening scene of Jesus's public activity discloses what the story of Jesus, the gospel, is most centrally about. As John's inaugural story, the wedding at Cana functions as his way of saying what the story of Jesus is about, what constitutes the good news.

The first few words of the story are wonderfully evocative: "On the third day ..." Big things happen in the Bible "on the third day," most notably the resurrection of Jesus. Thus at the beginning of his gospel, John anticipates its climax. The next words, "there was a wedding," are equally evocative. Marriage was a rich religious metaphor in Judaism and early Christianity: the marriage of God and Israel, the wedding of heaven and earth, the mystical marriage between an individual and God, the church as the bride of Christ. Moreover, in Jewish peasant life at the time of Jesus, weddings were the most festive of celebrations. Life was hard for peasants, and their diet was basic and meager. It seldom included meat or poultry, which required killing one of their few animals. But a wedding celebration meant momentary release from unremitting labor and enjoying copious amounts of food and wine, accompanied by music and dancing.

These associations help us to understand the power of John's inaugural scene: *the story of Jesus is about a wedding.* And more: it is a wedding at which the wine never runs out. More: it is a wedding at which the best wine is saved for last. All of this flows from a more-than-literal reading, from hearing the story as a metaphorical narrative, from a parabolic reading of it. The other option—a literal reading of the story—emphasizes the factuality of the miracle, and the question then becomes, "Do I believe that this happened?" By shifting the focus to believing or not believing that Jesus could change water into wine, a literal readings risks missing the story's metaphorical meaning.

Peter Walks on the Sea

In the previous chapter as I illustrated how christological language about Jesus develops, I briefly treated how Matthew changed the ending of Mark's story of Jesus walking on the Sea of Galilee and stilling a storm. Now we return to this story to focus on another change Matthew makes, namely, a story of Peter walking on the water (14.28–31).

To review the story, the disciples are in a boat on the Sea of Galilee. It is night, there is a storm, their boat is "battered by the waves," and they are "far from land." They are in peril. In the darkness, Jesus comes toward them, walking on the sea. Terrified, they think he's a ghost, and they cry out in fear. But Jesus says, "Take heart, it is I; *do not be afraid*" (14.27). Then:

> Peter answered Jesus, "Lord, if it is you, command me to come to you on the water." Jesus said, "Come." So Peter got out of the boat, started walking on the water, and came toward Jesus. But when Peter noticed the strong wind, *he became frightened, and beginning to sink, he cried out, "Lord, save me."* Jesus immediately reached out his hand and caught him, saying to him, "You of little faith, why did you doubt?"

It is again illuminating to contrast a literal-factual reading with a metaphorical reading. The first emphasizes that this really happened. Jesus really walked on the sea, and so did Peter, until he became afraid, and then he sank. Read literally, what does this mean? Is it simply a report of a remarkable and unrepeatable incident? Or does it also mean that we can literally walk on water if only we're not afraid and have enough faith in Jesus? Is this the point of the story? That we can walk on water?

Reading it as a metaphorical narrative yields a different emphasis. It is a story about fear and faith. When Peter became afraid, he sank, and his fear is named as "little faith." So it is. With little faith, we sink. But with faith, we stay afloat even in the midst of darkness, storm, and peril. As the nineteenth-century Danish theologian and philosopher Søren Kierkegaard defined faith, faith is like floating in seventy thousand fathoms of water. If we are afraid and struggle, we become exhausted and drown. But faith gives us buoyancy. Denise Levertov's poem "The Avowal" speaks of this meaning of faith:

> As swimmers dare
> to lie face to the sky
> and water bears them,
> as hawks rest upon air
> and air sustains them;
> so would I learn to attain
> free fall and float
> into Creator Spirit's deep embrace,
> knowing no effort earns
> that all-surrounding grace.[3]

This, and more, is meant when this story is heard as a metaphorical narrative.

Hearing the metaphorical meaning of these stories does not require that one deny their factuality. If somebody chooses to believe that Jesus really did change water into wine at Cana, that he really walked on the water, and that Peter also did, it is still important to ask, "What is their more-than-literal meaning?" For these stories were told for their more-than-literal meaning. And so I sometimes say, "Believe whatever you want about whether these stories happened this way—now let's talk about what they mean." Their truth as metaphorical narratives does not depend on their factuality. That is not their purpose. This claim is especially important as we consider a third illustration.

The Stories of Jesus's Birth

The stories of Jesus's birth in Matthew and Luke are among the best-known stories in the gospels. For many Christians, our earliest memories of Jesus, the Bible, and God are associated with these stories. And when we were children, most of us took it for granted that "it happened this way."

But the vast majority of mainstream biblical scholars see these stories as metaphorical narratives rather than as history remembered. Because this claim is surprising to some Christians and controversial to others, I begin with a concise summary of why mainstream scholars see them this way before turning to the more important topic of their rich and provocative meanings as metaphorical narratives. So that what follows will not seem as a debunking of these stories of spectacular events surrounding the birth of Jesus, I emphasize they have great power as truth-filled and truthful stories.[4]

There are a number of reasons why mainstream scholars do not see them as historical reports. First, they are quite late, found only in Matthew and Luke, written in the last two decades of the first century.[5] Neither Mark, the earliest gospel, nor Paul, the earliest writer in the New Testament, speak of Jesus's special birth. Nor does the gospel of John. If stories of Jesus's miraculous birth were important and early in early Christianity, it is difficult to imagine their absence from Mark, Paul, John, and rest of the New Testament.

Second, what happens in the stories—the plot line—is quite different in Matthew and Luke. We often miss this because the stories are typically combined in the celebration of Christmas with wise men and shepherds gathered around the manger.

In Matthew, Joseph learns that Mary is pregnant and is told by an angel in a dream that her pregnancy is "from the Holy Spirit." Then, after Jesus is born, wise men from the East are led to the place of Jesus's birth by a moving star. King Herod learns of the birth and orders the slaughter of all children under the age of two in the area of Bethlehem. In order to escape the slaughter, Mary, Joseph, and Jesus flee to Egypt, where they remain until Herod dies. After his death, they plan to return to their home in Bethlehem, but move to Nazareth in Galilee instead. Strikingly, none of the above is found in Luke.

Moreover, elements familiar from Christmas pageants are missing from Matthew. There is no annunciation to Mary, no journey to Bethlehem, where there is no room in the inn and Jesus is born in a stable, no shepherds, no angels in the night sky singing, "Glory to God in the highest." All of these are found only in Luke, as well as much else.

Forty-five verses are devoted to the story of John the Baptizer's birth to aged and barren parents, which Matthew doesn't mention at all. (Indeed, Matthew uses only thirty-one verses for his whole story of Jesus's birth.) Only Luke has the Magnificat, Benedictus, and Nunc Dimittis, those magnificent hymns that have been part of Christian worship throughout the centuries. Only Luke narrates Jesus's circumcision and the story of Jesus in the temple at age twelve.

The main characters, other than Jesus, are different. In Matthew, Joseph is the central character; Mary is barely mentioned. In Luke, Mary, Zechariah, and Elizabeth are the main characters; Joseph is hardly mentioned. Matthew has the wise men; Luke has the shepherds. Finally, the genealogies, the lists of Jesus's ancestors, are different.[6]

Of course, there are some similarities. These include conception by the Holy Spirit, birth in Bethlehem while Herod the Great was king, the names of Jesus's parents, and Nazareth as the village in which Jesus grew up. But even among these similarities, there are differences. Though both Matthew and Luke report that Jesus was born in Bethlehem, they differ on whether this was the home of Mary and Joseph. In Matthew, they live in Bethlehem. In Luke, they live in Nazareth but journey to Bethlehem because of the census. Though both report that Jesus was conceived by the Holy Spirit, they tell the story quite differently. In Matthew, Joseph learns of it in a dream. In Luke, the angel Gabriel announces it to Mary.

Finally, these stories look like they belong to the literary genre of metaphorical or symbolic narrative. Angels abound. In Matthew, they speak frequently to Joseph in dreams. In Luke, the angel Gabriel speaks to Zechariah, the father of John the Baptizer, and then goes to Nazareth to speak to Mary. Another angel speaks to the shepherds and is then joined by a host of angels singing in the night sky. Characters burst into memorable hymns. A special star moves through the sky leading wise men from the East to the place of Jesus's birth. In both, there is a divine conception. When we find features like these in a story, we commonly conclude that its literary genre is not a literal-factual report, but a metaphorical or symbolic narrative.

These are the primary reasons that mainline scholars do not see the stories of Jesus's birth as historically factual reports, but as metaphorical narratives. Some Christians are uncomfortable with this conclusion. To some, denying the factuality of the virgin birth and the other spectacular happenings in the stories seems like denying the power of God. But that is not the issue. The question is not, "*Can* God do things like this?" Rather, the question is, "What kind of stories are these?" Many of the same Christians think that denying the virgin birth involves denying that Jesus is the "Son of God," as if that status is dependent upon biological conception by God. And so in this context, I repeat what I said earlier: believe whatever you want about whether Jesus's birth happened this way—now let's ask, what do these stories *mean*? To argue about whether the stories narrate what actually happened most often distracts us from the meanings of the stories.

So we turn now to their meanings as metaphorical narratives. As we do so, we will see the importance of a historical *and* metaphorical approach, for their language has rich meanings within the historical context, the historical matrix, of first-century Christianity. Their language resonates with the traditions of Judaism and challenges the world of the Roman Empire.

Light imagery runs through both stories. In Matthew, a special star in the night sky guides the wise men until it stops over Bethlehem (2.10). Luke uses light imagery in his hymns: "The dawn from on high has broken upon us, to give light to those who sit in darkness" (1.78–79); and Jesus is "a light for revelation to the Gentiles" (2.32). Also in Luke, "the glory of the Lord," the radiant luminosity of God, shines upon the shepherds as they keep watch over their flocks by night (2.9). Light is an archetypal religious image, found in all of the world's enduring religions. When the Buddha was born, a great light filled the sky. And "enlightenment" as an image of salvation is central to many religions, including Christianity.

Light as an image of salvation is in the Jewish Bible as well. To illustrate with two passages from Isaiah: "The people who walked in darkness have seen a great light" (9.2); and:

Arise, shine; for your light has come, and the glory of the Lord has risen upon you. For darkness shall cover the earth, and thick darkness the peoples; but the LORD will arise upon you, and God's glory will appear over you. Nations shall come to your light, and kings to the brightness of your dawn. (60.1–3)

The claim made by the use of this light imagery is concisely expressed in John's gospel: Jesus is the light shining in the darkness, the true light that enlightens everyone, indeed the Light of the World (John 1.5, 9; 9.5).

A second theme in the birth stories is that Jesus is the *fulfillment* of ancient Israel's deepest yearnings and hopes. Matthew shows this by quoting five passages from the Jewish Bible that he correlates with events in his story, introducing each with a formulaic phrase saying, in effect, that these events took place to fulfill what had been spoken through the prophet. A close study of the passages, however, reveals that in their contexts in the Jewish Bible, they were not predictions of the future made hundreds of years in advance. Rather, this is Matthew's way of saying that in Jesus the hope of Israel has come to pass.[7]

Luke does this differently. Unlike Matthew, he does not quote passages from the Jewish Bible as if they were predictions. Rather, he includes in his hymns language that echoes the Jewish Bible:

God has brought down the powerful from their thrones, and lifted up the lowly, has filled the hungry with good things, and sent the rich away empty, and has helped God's servant Israel ... according to the promises God made to our ancestors, to Abraham and his descendants forever. (1.52–55)

Blessed be the Lord God of Israel, for God has looked favorably on God's people and redeemed them. God has raised up a mighty savior for us in the house of God's servant David ... that we would be saved from our enemies and from the hand of all who hate us. (1.68–71)

In the words of the aged Simeon:

Master, now you are dismissing your servant in peace, according to your word; for my eyes have seen your salvation, which
you have prepared in the presence of all peoples, a light for revelation to the Gentiles and for glory to your people Israel.
(2.29–32)

The theme of fulfillment is not about the fulfillment of prophetic
predictions, as if the Jewish Bible contains specific predictions of
Jesus. That is an impression created by some passages in the New
Testament (especially in Matthew) and sometimes used in argu-
ments that attempt to prove the supernatural origin of the Bible.
Rather, the theme of fulfillment is an affirmation that in Jesus, to use
the words from the familiar hymn "O Little Town of Bethlehem":
"The hopes and fears of all the years are met in thee tonight." As
metaphorical narratives, the birth stories affirm that Jesus is the fulfillment not only of ancient Israel's yearning, but of the world's great
yearning.

A third theme is a *conception brought about by God* when it is humanly impossible. In the Jewish Bible, this theme is linked to God's
promise to Israel. In Israel's stories of its ancestors, God promises
them that their descendants will be as numerous as the stars of the
sky. And yet Sarah, Rebekah, and Rachel (the wives of Abraham,
Isaac, and Jacob) are all barren. Then, when Sarah is ninety years old,
she conceives and gives birth to Isaac. So also Rebekah and Rachel
are barren until God opens their wombs. Later, Samson and Samuel,
both deliverers of Israel in a time of peril, are born to barren women.
These are not divine conceptions in the sense that no man is involved. But they are seen as conceptions made possible by God when
they were not humanly possible so that God's promise might be fulfilled. So also in the case of Jesus: his conception is an intensification
of this theme.

A fourth theme is Jesus as the *Son of God*. Though this affirmation
is common to all the gospels and the New Testament as a whole,
only Matthew and Luke link this status to Jesus's conception and
birth. Mark and John do not. As already mentioned, neither has a
birth story. In Mark, Jesus's status as God's Son is first disclosed at

his baptism as an adult. Paul speaks of Jesus as "descended from David according to the flesh, and declared to be Son of God with power according to the spirit of holiness by resurrection from the dead" (Rom. 1.3–4). If we hear Paul's words without later Christian teaching affecting how we interpret them, they suggest that Jesus's status as Son of God began at Easter.

But in the birth stories, Jesus as Son of God and divine conception are linked. It is implicit in Matthew and explicit in Luke. In his birth story, Matthew does not refer to Jesus as "Son of God" except indirectly in a quotation from the prophet Hosea: "Out of Egypt have I called my son" (2.15). In Luke, it is explicit. When the angel Gabriel tells Mary that the Holy Spirit will conceive a child in her, Gabriel tells her that he will be the "Son of the Most High," the "Son of God" (1.32, 35). Like the previous theme of conceptions made possible by God when humanly impossible, this theme affirms that what happened in Jesus was "of God," "of the Spirit."

The linkage of divine conception with the status of Son of God leads to a fifth theme: *the birth stories directly challenge a central claim of Roman imperial theology.* Within Rome's imperial theology, the emperor was Son of God because of divine descent. It began with Julius Caesar (the word "Caesar" means "emperor"), who was Son of God as a descendant of the god Venus through her son Aeneas. After he was assassinated in 44 BCE, stories were told of his ascent into heaven to take his permanent place among the gods.

The notion became fully developed in the time of Caesar Augustus, the greatest of Rome's emperors. Born Octavian in 63 BCE, he was the adopted son of Julius Caesar. After the assassination of his father, a great civil war wracked the empire until Octavian defeated Mark Antony and Cleopatra at the battle of Actium off the northwest coast of Greece in 31 BCE. From then until 14 CE, he ruled Rome and its territories as "Caesar Augustus."

A grateful empire gave him extraordinary accolades. He was "Augustus," the divine one. He was the savior who had brought peace on earth by bringing the great civil war to an end. Throughout the empire, coins, inscriptions, and temples—the media of the day—heralded him as "Son of God." His other titles included "god," "god made manifest," "lord," "lord of the whole world," and "savior of the world." In Egypt he was called "god from god."[8]

Given the above, it is not surprising that stories were told about his divine conception. According to the Roman historians Suetonius and Dio Cassius, Augustus was fathered by the god Apollo, who impregnated his mother, Atia, while she slept. The same night, as confirmation of the divine conception, Atia's husband had a dream in which he saw the sun rise from her womb. Portents and premonitions of Augustus's future were revealed to others. Even as an infant and child, his life was marked by remarkable and spectacular deeds.[9]

His birthday marked the beginning of a new era and a new calendar. According to an inscription in Priene on the west coast of present-day Turkey:

> The birthday of the most divine Caesar (Augustus) is … the day which we might justly set on a par with the beginning of everything, in practical terms at least, in that he restored order when everything was disintegrating and falling into chaos and gave a new look to the whole world.… For this reason one might justly take this to be the beginning of life and living.… All the communities should have one and the same New Year's Day, the birthday of the most divine Caesar.

As the inscription continues, it uses the word "gospel," "good tidings," Greek *euaggelia*, to name what Augustus has brought to the world:

> Caesar by his epiphany exceeded the hopes of those who prophesied good tidings (*euaggelia*), not only outdoing benefactors of the past, but also allowing no hope of greater benefactions in the future; and since the birthday of the god first brought to the world the good tidings (*euaggelia*) residing in him …, the Greeks of Asia [Asia Minor] have decided that the New Year in all the cities should begin on 23rd September, the birthday of Augustus.[10]

The new calendar divided history into "Before Caesar Augustus" and "After Caesar Augustus." Thus, "the divine Augustus was not just lord of empire and earth, but also of calendar and time."[11]

The titles of Augustus—god, Son of God, savior, lord, the one who brought peace on earth—continued to be used by the emperors who succeeded him. Within this historical context, we can see the counterimperial message of Luke's birth story. Jesus is "Son of God" by divine conception, and his life will bring down the mighty from their thrones. The challenge is especially clear in the angelic message to the shepherds, which both echoes and counters the language of imperial theology:

> I am bringing you good news (*euaggelion*) of great joy for all the people: to you is born this day in the city of David a Savior, who is the Messiah, the Lord…. Glory to God in the highest heaven, and on earth peace! (Luke 2.10–14)

Jesus, not Augustus and his successors, is the Son of God, Savior, and Lord who brings peace on earth.

Matthew's birth story has an anti-imperial edge as well, even though he does not explicitly echo the language of imperial theology. Rather, Matthew echoes the story of Israel's liberation from the ancient empire of Egypt. He does so with his portrait of Herod the Great as a new Pharaoh. Herod ruled the Jewish homeland on Rome's behalf, and when he learns from the wise men that a child has been born who is to be "king of the Jews," he plots to kill him. Foiled by the wise men's failure to return to report the location of the child, he orders the slaughter of Jewish babies in and around Bethlehem, just as the Pharaoh of Exodus ordered that male babies born to the ancient Hebrews should be killed. Herod as Pharaoh seeks to kill Jesus as the new Moses. He symbolizes the rulers of this world who seek to destroy the true king, whose kingdom, the kingdom of God, stands against the kingdoms of this world. Thus Matthew and Luke, each in his own way, highlight the challenge to empire brought by Jesus and early Christianity.

As metaphorical narratives, the birth stories have multiple and powerful meanings. As post-Easter constructions, they are like overtures to the gospels and the story of Jesus. They sound the central themes of the story: Jesus as light in the darkness, as the wisdom of God that draws the wise men of the Gentiles, as the fulfillment of Israel's hope and God's promise, as the Son of God and Lord and true king, as God's revelation to Israel and the world. Like the gospels as a whole, they affirm that Jesus is all of this.

I conclude this section with a possibly puzzling postscript on the meaning of the word "literal." What is the literal meaning of a parable? Its literal meaning is its parabolic meaning. What is the literal meaning of a poem? Its literal meaning is its poetic meaning. What is the literal meaning of a symbolic or metaphorical narrative? Its literal meaning is its symbolic or metaphorical meaning. But in modern Western culture over the last few centuries, "literal" has most often been confused with "factual," and factuality has been elevated over the metaphorical. Hence when people say they take stories in the Bible and the gospels "literally," they most often mean "factually." Thus the difference is not ultimately a *literal* versus a metaphorical reading, but a *factual* versus a metaphorical reading. And to read a story factually rather than metaphorically often involves a misjudgment about the literary genre of a story. When the metaphorical is understood factually, the result is a story hard to believe. But when a metaphorical narrative is understood metaphorically, it may indeed be powerfully and challengingly true.

METHOD: HOW MUCH IS MEMORY?

As I conclude these two chapters on the nature of the gospels and their language, I turn to the central methodological question of the quest for the historical Jesus. How does one make discerning historical decisions about how much is memory and how much is post-Easter testimony, about how much is history remembered and how much is metaphorical narrative?

This is sometimes relatively easy. Mainstream scholars generally see John's gospel as primarily metaphor and testimony from which it is difficult to extract historical memory with any level of confidence.

The synoptic gospels more often contain memory. But decisions about which texts do and which do not are sometimes difficult. In the rest of this chapter, I describe the two most important criteria for discerning what goes back to the pre-Easter Jesus, plus some additional considerations affecting the use of the criteria.

Two Criteria

The first criterion, *multiple attestation,* is the most objective. Stated more fully, if an element of the gospel tradition—a story or teaching or theme—is found in *two or more independent gospel sources,* at least one of which is early, it has a good claim to be memory. The word "independent" is important. For example, many stories are found in all three synoptic gospels, but this does not mean that they have triple attestation, for Matthew and Luke are not independent of Mark, but dependent upon Mark as their source for material they share in common.

The rationale for this criterion is clear. If an element of tradition is found in only one source, then it is possible that that source created it. But if it is found in two *independent* sources, then it is very unlikely that either one invented it. Rather, both sources are witnesses to its presence in the developing tradition. The likelihood that it is early is enhanced if at least one of the sources is early (and recall that our earliest sources are Q and Mark).[12] When this happens, there is a prima facie case for viewing it as going back to Jesus. In these cases, the burden of proof rests with those who would argue that the text is a post-Easter development. But if a text has only single attestation, then the burden of proof rests with those who would argue that it should be attributed to the pre-Easter Jesus.

The second criterion is *coherence.* It builds on the first one. Namely, if an element of the tradition coheres with—is consistent with—the image of Jesus that emerges from the use of the first one, then it may be regarded as memory, even if it is found in only one source. Classic examples are a number of Jesus's parables that are found only in Matthew or only in Luke. Historical scholars commonly accept most of these as going back to Jesus because their form and perspective are consistent with what else we think we know about Jesus. One might think of the first criterion as creating a "voiceprint" of Jesus. The second criterion affirms that other material in the gospels that coheres with that voiceprint can be treated as going back to Jesus.

Further Considerations

At least three considerations affect and can qualify the use of these criteria. First, if a text contains *a demonstrable tendency of the developing tradition,* then there is a good possibility that it is a post-Easter product rather than memory. This involves recognizing the tendencies of the developing tradition. Once a tendency is identified, then it becomes a factor in assessing whether the text goes back to a pre-Easter setting.

I provide two illustrations. In the previous chapter, we saw that a demonstrable tendency of the developing tradition is to add christological language to texts that do not have it. Hence historical caution requires that we see such language as the product of the community, or at least leave it in a "suspense account," that is, in a category about which we suspend judgment. But it cannot with confidence be attributed to Jesus, even if found in an early source.

A second illustration of a demonstrable tendency of the developing tradition is the placement of a brief "lesson," a short statement that seeks to crystallize meaning, at the end of a parable of Jesus. For example, in the parable of the workers in the vineyard (Matt. 20.1–16), a vineyard owner hires day laborers at different hours of the day and then, at the end of the day, pays them all the same. Matthew concludes the parable with the short statement, "So the last will be first, and the first will be last." But this has nothing to do with the meaning of the parable. It is connected to the parable only by the detail that those hired last were paid first, and those hired first were paid last. But this is not the point of the parable, which is the reaction of the workers to all of them being paid the same. The last verse looks like an addition by Matthew. Jesus may well have said it or something very much like it, but its placement here as a comment on the parable is the product of the tradition.

Another example of this second tendency is in the parable of the dishonest manager (Luke 16.1–10). The manager of a large estate is about to be fired and so he summons people who owe money to his master and reduces the amount of their debts. Three short statements follow the parable, each apparently drawing the "lesson" of the parable: "The children of this age are more shrewd in dealing with their own generation than are the children of light"; "Make friends for yourselves by means of dishonest wealth so that when it is gone, they may welcome you into the eternal homes"; and "Whoever is faithful in a very little is faithful also in much; and whoever is dishonest in a very little is dishonest also in much." Clearly, one or more of these seems to be an addition made by Luke. Thus, whenever we find a concise "lesson" attached to a parable, we need to take seriously that it may not have been part of the parable as spoken by Jesus.

A second consideration is sometimes called *environmental*. An element of tradition judged to be memory must fit into the environment, that is, the place and time of Jesus, and not only into another place or later time. An example of place: both Matthew and Luke report a saying of Jesus that speaks about wise and foolish builders, but with slightly different wording. In Matthew 7.24–27, familiar to us because of a Sunday school song, the contrast is between a wise man who built his house on rock and a foolish man who built his house on sand. When the rain came down and the flood came up, the house of the first stood and the house of the second fell. Matthew's version reflects conditions in the Jewish homeland; it speaks of building a house on the sand of a dry stream bed, a *wadi*, which during the rainy season can become a raging river.

In Luke 6.47–49, the contrast is not between building in a *wadi* or building on a rock, but between building a house with a deep foundation and building a house without a foundation. And the source of the flood is not the rain, but a river. Luke's version reflects conditions in the wider Mediterranean world. In a sense, the difference is trivial, for the meaning of the two versions is the same, and the contrast serves the same teaching purpose. But Matthew's wording is most likely earlier, and Luke has adapted the saying to another place.

An example of time: Mark 7.19 reports that Jesus "declared all foods clean." This means an abolition of the distinction between kosher and forbidden food, a distinction central to the dietary laws of the Jewish Bible. But it is very unlikely that Jesus said this. We know that whether or not Christians were to observe kosher food regulations was a major controversy for at least a few decades after Jesus's life. If Jesus had made a statement like this, it is difficult to imagine that the controversy would have lasted so long or, at least, why this saying of Jesus was not cited in the context of the controversy. Mark's statement appears to come from a time later than Jesus, either while the controversy was still going on or after it had been settled. To state the general point of the consideration again, if a story or teaching is to be seen as memory, it must fit into the environment of Jesus, that is, into the time and place of the Jewish homeland in the first third of the first century.

A third consideration concerns stories reporting *spectacular events*, such as Jesus feeding a multitude with a few loaves and two fish, walking on the Sea of Galilee, and stilling a storm. These stories are found in the synoptic gospels as well as in John. On the assumption that John is independent from the synoptics, they have double independent attestation. Does this mean that they should be accepted as historical? Should they be part of our picture of the historical Jesus? How does one make a discerning decision about whether these are memory or metaphor?

The question is not always important. One will never go wrong doing a parabolic reading of these stories as metaphorical narratives and setting aside the question of memory. Of course, some metaphorical interpretations may be judged as fanciful or as flat wrong. A metaphorical reading does not mean "anything goes" or that one metaphorical reading is as good as any other. Judgments about the presence and meaning of metaphor are affected by our understanding of the ancient context, as in our treatment of the stories of Jesus's birth. But if one is interested in the historical Jesus, then decisions need to be made about whether such stories contain historical memory. These decisions will be affected by at least two factors.

The first is whether the language of the story has obvious symbolic meaning. For example, the story of Jesus feeding a multitude in the wilderness echoes the well-known story in the Jewish Bible of ancient Israel being fed by God in the wilderness following the exodus from Egypt. As the synoptic gospels tell the story, the echo is implicit (Mark 6.30–44; Matt. 14.13–21; Luke 9.10–17). In John's version of the story (6.1–15, 25–59), the connection to Israel in the wilderness becomes explicit: "Our ancestors ate the manna in the wilderness" (v. 31). As John's story unfolds, Jesus himself becomes the "true bread from heaven" and the "bread of life." He says, "Whoever comes to me will never be hungry" and "I am the living bread that came down from heaven. Whoever eats of this bread will live forever; and the bread that I will give for the life of the world is my flesh" (vv. 35, 51). For John, the story is a metaphorical narrative about Jesus as spiritual food. And because the story is given this manifestly metaphorical meaning, there is reason to think that it is metaphor and not memory.

A second factor affecting the historical judgment about whether a story is memory or metaphor involves our sense of the limits of the spectacular, of what is possible. That is, are there some things that never happen? Our sense of the limits of the possible is a "metahistorical" factor, one that is not historical itself but that affects our historical judgment. To illustrate with a postbiblical story, St. Denis was a Christian in Paris beheaded by the Romans during a persecution in the middle of the third century. After his execution, St. Denis picked up his severed head and walked several miles to his church where he sang the Mass. Would any amount of evidence convince us that this happened? Or would most of us say, "Oh, I don't think things like that ever happen"? My point is that all of us have some sense of the limits of the possible, even though we might disagree about what those limits are.

To apply this to the gospels, does it ever happen that somebody can feed five thousand people with five loaves and two fish? Does it ever happen that somebody can walk on the sea? Does it ever happen that somebody can change a large quantity of water into wine? If I became convinced that things like this sometimes happen, I could entertain the possibility that Jesus did things like this.

But if not, then as a historian I cannot conclude that Jesus did— unless I assume that Jesus had supernatural powers unlike any other human being. But to make this assumption would be to assume that Jesus is not human like the rest of us, which is contrary to the central Christian claim that Jesus as a figure of history was fully human. And if one were to say, "Ah, but Jesus was also fully divine, and that's why he could do things like this," one might respond that a human who has unique divine powers is not human like the rest of us. Moreover, if Jesus could do things like this because he was divine, why didn't he do a greater number of spectacular deeds? There certainly was great human need.

Thus I treat the most spectacular stories in the gospels as metaphorical narratives and not as memory. I do think he performed healings and exorcisms, but I am skeptical that he walked on the sea or fed a multitude with a small amount of food or changed water into wine. I could be wrong, of course; historical judgments are always probability judgments. But in any case, I do not use these stories as historical data in my treatment of the pre-Easter Jesus. And because this statement may sound simply negative, I conclude by emphasizing once again that metaphorical narratives can be powerfully truthful, even though not literally factual.

THE HISTORICAL TASK

The writing of history is neither a science nor an art. Direct observation of the past is not possible, just as verification through experimentation is impossible. The verifiable results of science are beyond what a historian can provide. Neither is it an art, for it is not sheer imagination and creativity. It is perhaps more like a craft in which a construction is made out of existing material. It involves both data and creativity. And as with a craft, one learns how to do it by doing it. It is not a process in which one simply learns the rules and then mechanically applies them.[13]

Perhaps an even better analogy is comparing a historian's work to the work of a detective. Unless there is an eyewitness, making a case depends upon collecting evidence and then formulating a hunch that accounts for the evidence. The process involves three quite distinct stages, sometimes done by the same person and sometimes by different people. The first stage is the "street stage," the gathering of all possible evidence, and at this stage one does not yet know how much of what has been gathered is really evidence. The second stage is the analysis of the evidence, the forensic stage. The third stage is the forming of a hunch, a hypothesis, a reconstruction of what happened, which involves forming the accumulated data into a pattern.

The hunch and the evidence are reciprocally related. On the one hand, the hunch flows out of the evidence; and on the other hand, the hunch acts back on the evidence, affecting how it is seen. Some of what looked like potential evidence will be seen not to be evidence after all. A detective's work thus involves a kind of circularity. So also does the work of a historian. A historical reconstruction is generated from the data, and the reconstruction affects how the data is seen. The test of the hunch, the hypothesis, the reconstruction, is in part how well it accounts for the evidence. And the final test is what the jury makes of the reconstruction, whether it strikes them as persuasive or not.

The study of the historical Jesus is one of the most exciting intellectual and religious adventures of the last few centuries. Indeed, the quest for the historical Jesus is for some people the greatest detective story ever told. But before we embark on it, we must first see the world, the historical and cultural context, the matrix, in which Jesus lived. For a historian, context is indispensable. Words and deeds have their meaning in the historical and cultural context in which they are said and done. And so in the next chapter, we turn to the world of Jesus—the world that shaped him and that he addressed.

FOUR

The Shaping of Jesus

Jewish Tradition in an Imperial World

To a degree unusual among the world's enduring religions and scriptures, time and place—that is, history—matter for both Judaism and Christianity. Much of the Jewish Bible concerns ancient Israel's engagement with history, empires, and kingdoms: the exodus from Egypt, the time of Israel's kings, the exile in Babylon, the return, and later developments in the homeland. So also with the gospels and the rest of the New Testament. The story of Jesus and early Christianity not only occurs in a particular historical world, but directly engages it. For the Bible, history, society, and historical existence matter.

Luke locates the story of Jesus's public activity very specifically in time and place:

> In the fifteenth year of the reign of Emperor Tiberius, when Pontius Pilate was governor of Judea, and Herod was ruler of Galilee, and his brother Philip ruler of the region of Ituraea and Trachonitis, during the high priesthood of Annas and Caiaphas ... (3.1)

Tiberius had become emperor of Rome in 14 CE, and so the time was about 28 or 29 CE. The place, of course, was the Jewish homeland. Luke names its three major areas and their rulers: Judea in the south, governed by Pilate and the high-priesthood of the Jerusalem temple; Galilee in the north, ruled by Herod Antipas, son of Herod the Great; and an area north and east of Galilee, ruled by another son of

Herod the Great, Philip. All of these, as we shall see, ruled as collaborators with the Roman Empire.

SOCIAL WORLD

"The past is a foreign country: they do things differently there." So begins a British novel set in the early twentieth century.[1] Part of what makes the past foreign is the distance in time. The world was very different a half century ago when I grew up. To imagine distances of centuries and millennia is daunting. But the difference is not only about time, but about a very different *social world.*

"Social world" is an important and illuminating shorthand term. It refers to the social environment of a particular time and place. It basically means the same as "culture," understood as everything that humans add to nature. It is the social canopy under which people live. A very comprehensive term, it includes political and economic systems, codes of behavior and convention, understandings of what is real and how to live, religious traditions and practices, language, technology, and more.

The social world is what makes a time and place *that* time and *that* place. It is what distinguishes life in the Netherlands from life in Pakistan, life in Japan from life in Mexico, and so forth. Though there are natural differences between these areas (such as topography and climate), what most differentiates them—what makes them most foreign to each other—is the distinctive social world of each.

The social world in which we live pervasively shapes us. Growing up, socialization, means internalizing the understandings of life operative in our social world. It means being sufficiently shaped by our social world so that we know how to live in it.[2] This is true even for those who question it, resist it, or rebel against it, for what they reject is the shared understandings of their social world.

To apply this to Jesus, it is impossible to see his significance without setting his life and public activity in the context of his social world. It would be like trying to understand the significance of Abraham Lincoln's speeches without setting them in the context of the Civil War, or Martin Luther King Jr.'s words and deeds without locating them in the mid-twentieth-century struggle over civil rights. Words and deeds have their meaning in the cultural context, the social world, in which they are said and done.

So it is with Jesus. Seeing the cultural context in which he grew up and that he addressed is indispensable. It was shaped by two overlapping social worlds: the world of the Roman Empire and the world of Judaism. Very different from each other, they were often in conflict. In this chapter, we explore these two social worlds as the historical matrix of Jesus. These were the worlds that shaped Jesus and the worlds that he addressed.[3]

TYPES OF PREMODERN SOCIETIES

In order to imagine the very different world of Jesus, it is crucial to understand the type of society in which he lived. Our awareness of types of societies comes from social history and macrosociology. Knowing about these types provides a large framework for understanding the shape and dynamics of societies very different from ours.

The Roman world in which Jesus lived was an imperial form of *a preindustrial agricultural domination system.* This was the most common type of society from the development of agriculture about five thousand years ago until the industrial revolution of a few centuries ago. The piling up of adjectives—imperial preindustrial agricultural domination system—may be inelegant and even discouraging, but each illuminates a central feature of Jesus's world.

Before describing this type of society, it is illuminating to begin with two earlier types. They illustrate what it means to speak of types of societies as well as highlight how the development of agriculture revolutionized human life and made possible the emergence of preindustrial domination systems.

The earliest human societies were *hunting and gathering societies.* Most were also nomadic. The cultivation of crops and the domestication of farm animals had not yet happened. As a result, large concentrations of population were impossible. Humans lived in small groups, only as large as could be sustained by hunting and gathering.

There was little or no concentration of wealth. Dwellings were simple and often temporary, and life was communal. What could individual wealth mean in such a society? If it existed at all, it was limited to what you could carry on your back. This type of society lasted a very long time—for millions of years, until about ten thousand years ago.

Then the second major type of society, *early horticultural societies*, began to develop. The key transition was the beginning of cultivation, still very small-scale. Humans had not yet learned how to produce metal, and tools were limited to stone, bone, and wood—essentially to digging sticks and hoes. The plow was still thousands of years in the future. Cultivated land was basically limited to the size of garden plots (hence this type of society is called *horticultural*, not agricultural). But for the first time in human history, settled populations became possible, and the first towns emerged. They were small, typically a few hundred people and only occasionally a few thousand. An example of a large horticultural settlement is Catal Huyuk in Turkey, which had a population of about two thousand in the 5000s BCE. These were still largely communal societies in which food was produced and shared communally. Differentials of wealth and power were minor.

A third type, the one that lasted into the time of Jesus and later, began to emerge in the fourth millennium BCE: *agricultural (or agrarian) societies*. Two developments made this possible. The first was the discovery in the 3000s BCE of how to produce metal, beginning with copper, then bronze, and, in the second millennium BCE, iron. Metal tools—including the plow—replaced stone, bone, and wooden ones. The second development was the domestication of animals for agricultural work. For the first time, there was large-scale agriculture and the production of agricultural surpluses.

The development of agriculture is perhaps the most important revolution in human history. It brought about fundamental changes in human social organization. With the development of large-scale agriculture, large concentrations of settled populations became possible. Cities, not just towns, emerged. The first cities in the ancient Near East were in the great river valleys of Egypt and Mesopotamia.

The birth of cities was followed very soon by the emergence of a small wealthy and powerful class. The exact details of the process are unclear; we have no written records. But we can imagine how it may have happened. Cities required governance, and hence a governing class emerged. With their stores of food and other wealth, cities also required protection from outsiders—from nomadic tribes, social bandits, and others who looked greedily upon them. And so a protector class developed. Both governing and protector classes drew their wealth from the society, for they were not producers themselves. Over time, they (or at least the leading figures among them) became increasingly powerful and wealthy. Whether power generated wealth or whether wealth generated power is a chicken-and-egg question. In any case, the two were allied: the powerful were wealthy, and the wealthy were powerful.

The birth of cities also meant that, for the first time, armies became possible. Before there were large concentrations of population, warring took the form of small war parties, not armies. Cities often expanded into kingdoms, and kingdoms sometimes expanded to become empires.

THE PREMODERN DOMINATION SYSTEM

With the advent of cities and kingdoms, the premodern domination system was born. Societies of this type are sometimes called agrarian or preindustrial domination systems, for agriculture was the primary source of wealth.

They are called domination systems for the simple reason that one class of people—the wealthy and the powerful—ruled the society. There were the rulers and the ruled. Because this is the type of society in which the Bible emerged and in which Jesus lived, I describe it more fully.

Central Features

Four primary features help us to see the character of premodern domination systems. First, these societies were *politically oppressive*.

They were ruled by a few, typically by a monarchy and aristocracy and their associates. With their extended families, the ruling elites (as they are commonly called) were usually about 1 to 2 percent of the population. Because they commonly lived in cities, they are also commonly called urban elites. Ordinary people had no voice or power in the shaping of the society.

Second, these societies were *economically exploitative*. The wealthy and powerful acquired a high percentage of the society's annual production of wealth, typically from half to two-thirds. Because of the importance of this feature, I will soon develop it more fully.

Third, these societies were *religiously legitimated*. According to religion as developed by the elites, rulers ruled by divine right, and the social order and its laws reflected the will of God. Rulers maintained that they did not set it up this way—*God* did. Of course, religion sometimes became the source of protest against such claims. But in all premodern societies known to us the wealthy and powerful used religion to legitimate their place in the social order.

Fourth, these societies were marked by *armed conflict*, by organized violence. Elites could increase their wealth and power only by increasing agricultural production from their own people or by acquiring land and its agricultural production from another society. The ruling elites thus needed armies, whether to increase their own holdings or to defend their holdings against others. Wars were common. They were not fought for nationalistic reasons, as sometimes happens in the modern world, but were initiated by ruling elites for the sake of acquiring wealth from the agricultural lands of neighboring societies.

A Two-Class Society

Together the features of the premodern domination system produced a two-class society. To speak of only two classes is, of course, a large simplification, for there were distinctions within the two classes. But the premodern social world was a two-class society in a way that the modern Western world is not. We commonly think of at least three classes—upper, middle, and lower—and of the middle class as the largest class. But in that world, there was no "middle class" in our sense of a bulge in the middle. Rather, there was a very small class at the very top, no significant middle, and the vast majority of the population (around 90 percent) at the bottom.

The division was both political and economic. Politically, there were the rulers and the ruled. Economically, there were the wealthy and the rest of the population. Power and wealth overlapped; there were the powerful and the wealthy, and those without power or wealth.

The distinction between the two classes was above all economic. The lifestyle of the wealthiest 1 to 2 percent was extravagant, their consumption conspicuous. They dwelt in palaces and villas, financed impressive public buildings and constructed fortresses, and maintained armies. Attached to them was a subclass that served them, known as "retainers," commonly about another 5 percent of the population: government and religious officials, military officers and bureaucrats, managers and stewards, scribes and servants, and urban merchants who sold to them.

The wealth of the elites came from the primary source of wealth in preindustrial societies, namely, from agricultural production and other manual labor. The elites did not produce wealth themselves. Rather, they used their power to set up the economic system so that wealth flowed to them through taxation on agricultural production, direct ownership of agricultural land, sharecropping and tenant-farmer arrangements, slave labor and indentured labor through debt, and so forth.

The most common shorthand name for the lower class in this type of society—about 90 percent of the population—is the peasant class. It consisted mostly of agricultural workers; some owned small parcels of land and others were tenant farmers, sharecroppers, or day laborers. It also included other manual workers such as fishermen, construction workers, artisans, miners, and low-ranking servants. At the very bottom were the radically marginalized: the homeless, beggars, the lame and blind, the unclean and untouchable.

It is called the peasant class not only because it was made up largely of agricultural workers, but also because it was a rural class.

The peasant class commonly did not live in cities, except for those who were servants of the elites. Cities were relatively small; they had not yet become centers of production, as in modern times, but were primarily centers of governance and consumption. Production occurred in the rural areas. Thus the term "peasant class" names the rural class made up of agricultural and manual workers. Though rural, they did not live on farms as we think of farms, but in hamlets, villages, and towns. This type of society is also sometimes called a "peasant society," referring not simply to the vast majority of the population, but to peasants as the primary producers of wealth.

The impact of this two-class society upon peasant life was severe. Because of elite extraction of peasant production, peasants lived at a subsistence level. The powerful and wealthy were quite good at calculating how much they could extract from the peasant class without starving them or driving them into rebellion. Peasant life was consequently hard and vulnerable. A bad crop year, whether caused by drought, flood, locusts, war, or other calamities, was catastrophic. The death of a farm animal could be a major crisis. Perhaps the most dramatic way to make the point is with life expectancy in the elite and peasant classes. Infant and childhood mortality in the ancient world was high. But members of the elite who survived childhood often lived into old age—hence the biblical expression "three score and ten" as a good life span. Members of the peasant class who survived childhood had a life expectancy of about thirty years.

There is nothing unusual about this type of society. With various permutations, preindustrial domination systems persisted through antiquity into the medieval and early modern periods until the democratic revolutions of the last few hundred years. All who have traveled in the Middle East or Europe have seen the remains of these societies: tombs and temples, fortresses and castles, palaces and villas, cathedrals and monuments that go back to preindustrial times. Where did the wealth come from that made all of this possible? From the production of the peasant class, channeled into the hands of the wealthy and powerful by the domination system that they created.

And one could make a good case that, in industrial and postindustrial forms, domination systems continue to be common today. In this sense "domination systems" are normal, not abnormal, and thus can also be called the "normalcy of civilization." "Domination system" calls attention to its central dynamic: the political and economic domination of the many by a few and the use of religious claims to legitimate it. "Normalcy of civilization" calls attention to how common it is. There is nothing unusual or abnormal about this state of affairs.

Although this type of society was exceedingly common throughout the world for several millennia, biblical scholars generally, including me, took a long time to see its significance for understanding the world of the Bible and Jesus. Only about twenty-five years ago did the light it sheds begin to be emphasized in biblical scholarship. But once seen, it has the ring of truth and generates an "of course" response. It is the world of ancient Egypt and the exodus. Ancient Israel traced its origin to the liberation of its ancestors from a domination that was political, economic, and religious. After the exodus, a new kind of society was created by the Israelites, an economically much more egalitarian one lived under the lordship of Israel's God rather than under the lordship of Pharaoh. But within a few hundred years, with the rise of an Israelite monarchy around 1000 BCE, a native domination system began to be created. By the time of King Solomon, Israel's third king, a domination system was firmly in place. Israel had become a new Egypt, the Israelite king a new Pharaoh.[4] For the next thousand years, ancient Israel lived under either native or imperial domination systems. The Bible came into existence in this kind of social world. Much of it is protest against it.

AN IMPERIAL DOMINATION SYSTEM

Now that the central features of premodern agricultural domination systems have been sketched, I turn to the final adjective that describes the Roman social world of Jesus: it was an *imperial* domination system. Rome took control of the Jewish homeland in 63 BCE. For the previous hundred years, there had been a period of Jewish independence under a native ruling family known as both the Maccabees and Hasmoneans. They came to power in a successful Jewish revolt against the Hellenistic empire of Antiochus Epiphanes in the 160s BCE. But this brief period of independence under native rulers was brought to an end in 63 BCE.

An imperial domination system has major economic impact. To explain, it is important to distinguish between an *independent* and a *tributary* domination system. The first is ruled by a native elite who extract wealth from peasant production. But they do not need to pay tribute to anybody else. The second is under imperial control and must pay tribute to the empire. The native elite often remain in place, but now they must extract an additional amount of peasant production in order to pay tribute to the empire that rules them. Imperial domination systems are thus tributary domination systems.

So it was in the Jewish homeland. As in most of its territories, Rome delegated authority to native rulers whom it appointed. These native collaborators with imperial rule are commonly called client kings or client rulers. Beholden to Rome for their initial appointment, they could remain in power only so long as they pleased Rome, which included collecting and paying a large sum of annual tribute. Rome most often appointed client rulers from aristocratic and wealthy families. For the first quarter century after 63 BCE, Rome ruled through the existing Jewish aristocracy, the Hasmoneans, descendants of the Maccabees. But power struggles within the native aristocracy created persistent disorder.

Herod the Great

In 40 BCE Rome appointed a king known to history as Herod the Great, the most famous of its client kings. By birth he was only half Jewish and an Idumean. When Rome designated him "king of the Jews," he was in his early thirties and an outsider to the traditional native aristocracy. It took him three years of military campaigning to gain control of the kingdom he had been given. His actual reign thus began in 37 BCE and lasted until his death in 4 BCE. His reign and its aftermath decisively shaped the world of Jesus.[5]

Herod was gifted, extravagant, and brutal. His skills as a military leader brought him to Rome's attention. He was sufficiently clever and persuasive to get himself appointed "king of the Jews." As a client king, he managed to please Rome throughout his long reign.

He lived opulently and spent extravagantly, building elegant palaces for himself in Jerusalem and Jericho, and fortresses that were also palaces at Masada, Herodium, and Machaerus. He also built projects designed to please his Roman overlord. He constructed a new city and port on the Mediterranean coast and named it Caesarea Maritima in honor of the emperor. In Samaria, he rebuilt its major city and named it Sebaste, Greek for "Augustus." He financed buildings outside of the Jewish homeland, including temples to the emperor. He also sought to endear himself to his Jewish subjects with a magnificent rebuilding of the temple in Jerusalem. The result was acclaimed even by many non-Jews as the most splendid temple in the ancient world.

Though history calls him Herod the Great, some Jewish voices called him Herod the Monstrous. He came to power by hunting down and killing members of a Jewish resistance movement opposed to Roman rule. Soon after he became king, he executed many of the traditional Jewish aristocracy and dispossessed their families of their land. Later in his reign, Herod executed members of his own family, including three of his sons and his wife Mariamne, a descendant of the revered Jewish family of the Maccabees. Near the end of his reign, two Jewish teachers and forty of their students tore down a Roman eagle from one of the entrances to the temple in Jerusalem. Herod had the ringleaders burned to death and the rest executed. In his last days, aware that his subjects would not mourn his death, he ordered that a large number of Jewish notables be executed when he died so that the country as a whole would mourn. His order was not carried out. Herod's brutality and paranoia are reflected in Matthew's gospel. Though Matthew's story of Herod ordering the slaughter of infants under two years of age in and around Bethlehem is almost certainly legendary, it fits what we know of Herod's character.

For the peasant class, the imperial domination system administered by Herod brought a worsening of economic conditions, for at least three reasons. The first is the sheer expense of Herod's reign. Where did the wealth come from that supported the opulence of his court and his extravagant building projects? By now, the answer is obvious: from the major source of wealth in preindustrial society, namely, from the agricultural production and manual labor of peasants. Only by increasing the amount extracted from the peasant class could a reign like Herod's be supported—in addition to which he had to pay tribute to Rome. Occasionally historians have suggested that Herod's building projects indicate a time of prosperity. But what they really point to is more wealth being extracted from the peasant class.

A second development adversely affected the lives of peasants under Rome and Herod: the commercialization of agriculture. Before the Roman period, most Jewish peasant families had small parcels of land on which they produced most of what they needed in order to live: crops and vegetables, animals for food and clothing, and so forth. It was still largely a barter economy; what a family did not produce itself, it got by bartering with other villagers. Peasant life, though modest and often meager, was largely self-sufficient.

But under Rome and Herod, this way of life was undergoing rapid transition to commercialized agriculture. The development involved an increase in large estates; small peasant farms were increasingly replaced by large agricultural holdings owned by the wealthy and powerful. They acquired peasant land in more than one way. Sometimes they did it through direct appropriation. Herod created a number of royal estates for himself and also awarded large amounts of land to people he favored. The wealthy also acquired peasant land through loans and foreclosure on debt.

This development had several consequences. Fewer peasants owned land. Those who had lost their land now worked as tenant farmers, sharecroppers, or indentured slaves. The owners of the land were not interested in peasants using the land for self-sufficiency; rather, they were interested in producing crops for sale and export (hence the phrase *the commercialization of agriculture*). For peasants, land and labor were no longer the source of what they needed in order to survive. If you cultivate olives or grapes or grains for somebody else, you must get your food and clothing elsewhere. Moreover, peasants who lost their land would not automatically be employed by the new landowner as tenant farmers or sharecroppers. Some became day laborers, whose existence was even more precarious, for they could not count on being hired every day. Much of their work was seasonal. Some were reduced to begging.

Third, the commercialization of agriculture led to a monetization of the peasant economy. If you were a day laborer, you were paid in coin, which you then had to use to buy what you and your family needed. If you were a sharecropper on a large estate producing primarily one commodity, you would need to sell or barter your share of the crop in order to acquire the means to pay for your family's essentials. Many in the peasant class thus went from subsistent but self-sufficient production on their own land to being dependent on how much they earned as agricultural laborers working for large landowners.

Peasant existence, always precarious, became even more so. The two central issues of peasant life were food and debt. Because many no longer produced their own food, they had to buy it with their meager earnings. Debt was a perennial fear, which peasants did everything possible to avoid. It was not entered into for the sake of consumption, as in the modern world, but for the sake of survival. But sometimes it was unavoidable, even as it was perilous. Peasants who still owned a small piece of land risked losing it through indebtedness. For those who didn't own land, indebtedness could lead to indentured slavery, even for whole families.

Herod's Successors

When Herod died in 4 BCE, revolts broke out in all parts of the Jewish homeland, indicating how repressive and unpopular his reign had been. Rome responded by sending legions of troops from Syria. In Galilee, the legions reconquered its largest city, Sepphoris, and sold many of the survivors into slavery. Nazareth was nearby, only four miles away. Then the Roman legions continued south, reconquered Jerusalem, and crucified two thousand of its defenders as a public demonstration of the consequences of rebellion. Jesus was an infant or toddler during this time.

Rome then divided Herod's kingdom into three parts, each going to one of his sons. Peraea and Galilee went to Herod Antipas. This is the Herod of Jesus's adult life. An area north and east of Galilee went to Philip. Samaria and Judea, with its capital in Jerusalem, went to Archelaus. They were very young when they came to power: Archelaus was nineteen, Herod Antipas seventeen, and Philip sixteen. Two had long reigns: Philip for thirty-seven years, until 33 CE; Herod Antipas for forty-three years, until 39 CE.

In Galilee, Herod Antipas ruled much as his father had. Like him, he was a builder. Two cities were the costliest of his building projects. He rebuilt Sepphoris, the largest city and capital of Galilee, which had been severely damaged by the Romans in 4 BCE. Josephus described Sepphoris as "the ornament of all Galilee." In the 20s CE, Antipas built a completely new city on the western shore of the Sea of Galilee. He named it Tiberias in honor of the Roman emperor Tiberius and made it his capital. The wealth required to support Antipas's reign, to pay tribute to Rome, and to build two cities continued to make life difficult for the peasant population of Galilee.

In Jerusalem, a major change in governance occurred in 6 CE that matters decisively for the story of Jesus. After a reign of only ten years, Rome removed Herod's son Archelaus from office and replaced him with governors sent from Rome. The most famous of these was Pontius Pilate, governor from 26 to 36 CE.

Rome continued the practice of ruling through native collaborators responsible to the governor. With Archelaus gone, Rome assigned the role of client rulers to the temple authorities in Jerusalem. They included the high priest plus a group called in the gospels "the chief priests and elders." Rome appointed the high priest from the "high-priestly families," part of the traditional Jerusalem aristocracy. They were wealthy, in part because of the wealth that flowed into Jerusalem from tithes, taxes, pilgrimage, and building projects such as the temple, which Herod the Great had begun and which continued to be built in the first century. Their wealth also came from ownership of agricultural land, despite the Torah's prohibition against priests owning land. They conveniently interpreted that prohibition to mean that priests could not *work* as laborers on the land, but it did not prevent them from *owning* land.

Though the high priest was the head of the native domination system, his position was vulnerable. Not only did he owe his appointment to Rome, but he could remain in office only so long as his rule pleased Rome. Many failed. From 6 CE to 66 CE, Rome appointed eighteen high priests. Three of these served a total of thirty-nine years, with the longest tenure held by Caiphas, from 18 CE to 36 CE. This means that the remaining twenty-two years saw fifteen high priests.

Thus, early in Jesus's life, the high priest and temple authorities became the mediators of imperial rule, responsible for collecting and paying tribute to Rome and for maintaining domestic order.[6] Jerusalem and the temple, the sacred center of the Jewish world, had become the center of native collaboration with an imperial domination system.

This, then, was the imperial social world in which Jesus grew up. In the north, in Galilee, the peasant class was ruled by Rome's client king Herod Antipas. In the south, the peasant class was ruled by the temple authorities in Jerusalem, beholden to the Roman governor. In both Galilee and Jerusalem, a native domination system operated within an imperial domination system, increasing the amount of production extracted from the peasant class. Within the imperial domination system, two layers of elites, one native and one imperial, had to be supported.

Within the peasant class, there was deep discontent with this state of affairs. Jesus's social world was marked by a "spiral of violence" with four stages.[7] The first stage was the institutional and systemic violence of the domination system itself, with its injustice and oppression. Stage two involved protest and resistance by the dominated. Stage three brought counterrepression by the authorities, and stage four full-blown revolt. The spiral repeated itself a number of times between the advent of Roman rule in 63 BCE and the outbreak of the great Jewish revolt in 66 CE, which Rome brutally suppressed, including destroying Jerusalem and the temple in the year 70. Indeed, the spiral of violence did not stop then, for a second major revolt against Rome broke out in the Jewish homeland in 132 CE, only to end in defeat three years later. But this takes us beyond our time period.

GROWING UP IN A PEASANT VILLAGE

Jesus was from the peasant class. This does not mean, however, that he and his family were agricultural workers. Rather, it means that he was from the rural population, which lived under a preindustrial agrarian domination system. The tradition that his father, Joseph, was a *tekton*, a Greek word that can mean carpenter, stonecutter, or even "handyman," is probably factual; Joseph was a manual laborer. Jesus may have learned his father's craft. But being a *tekton* did not mean an economic standing better than peasants who did agricultural work. Most often, a *tekton*—a worker who was not involved in agriculture—came from a family that had lost its land. It did not imply movement up the economic ladder.

Nazareth was so small that it left no trace in written historical records. Archaeology has been able to tell us only a little. Estimates of its population range from two hundred to four hundred. Most were agricultural laborers who walked each day to the land they worked, whether their own or a landlord's. A peasant family who still owned land was better off than families who worked for others as sharecroppers, tenant farmers, or day laborers. Though the area was rocky, it was reasonably fertile. Agriculture centered around olives, grains, grapes, legumes, vegetables, and animal products. The latter included milk, cheese, eggs, wool, and skins.

The buildings of Nazareth were modest, and there may have been no public buildings at all. Peasant dwellings were humble. Excavations indicate they were generally made of unhewn stones and had dirt floors; many included a cave as part of their living space. More prosperous peasants lived in one- or two-room homes connected to one another to form a square with a shared courtyard in the middle. The village was most likely too small to have had its own market or shops, though there was probably a market day once or twice a week.

Was it large enough to have had a school to which Jesus would have gone? An earlier generation of scholars thought so. They commonly spoke of Nazareth as having a synagogue school where boys learned how to read and write, using the Torah as their primary text. This no longer seems likely. The evidence for such schools in villages in Galilee is later and probably refers to conditions a few centuries after the time of Jesus.

Nazareth was located near the top of a ridge about twenty miles inland from the Mediterranean Sea, with the Sea of Galilee another fifteen miles to the east and Jerusalem about seventy miles to the south. Four miles to the north, across the ridge, was the city of Sepphoris. Nazareth lived in its shadow. As already mentioned, in 4 BCE. Sepphoris, as a center of revolt against Roman rule, had been besieged and reconquered by the Romans.

In that part of the world, as elsewhere, memories endured. We may wonder what stories were told in Nazareth about what had happened in Sepphoris, and what may have happened in Nazareth itself. A village four miles from a city under attack by Roman legions is unlikely to have been unaffected. No doubt a variety of lessons were drawn from the memory. Some may have emphasized the futility of resistance to imperial power, leading either to pragmatic adjustment or bitter resignation. Others may have emphasized Rome's brutality and oppression, fueling a desire for further resistance, whether as instigators or sympathizers.

That Sepphoris was rebuilt during Jesus's life was a reminder of its destruction. Given that Joseph was a *tekton*, it is possible that he worked there during its rebuilding. If so, his sons—Jesus and his brothers—may also have done so. This is possible, though there is no way of saying more.

Jesus almost certainly visited Sepphoris while he was growing up. The four miles could be walked in an hour, and it is difficult to imagine a precocious boy and young man like Jesus not being curious about the city. Compared to Nazareth, it was not only large, but wealthy. As the major city and capital of Galilee, it was the home of Galilee's ruling elite until Herod Antipas built Tiberias in the 20s. It had impressive public buildings, fortified city walls, opulent homes, a large covered market with shops, paved streets, public squares with mosaic floors, and so forth. Assuming that Jesus went there at least occasionally, what did he make of what he saw? Was he intrigued? Disturbed?

As the capital, it was also the residence of Herod Antipas and the center of his administration. This is the Herod who executed Jesus's mentor John the Baptizer. In the gospels, Jesus called Herod "that fox," a very negative term better translated in English as "that skunk." The image suggests not cleverness but odor, not shrewdness but stench.

Jesus lived in Nazareth into his twenties. About these years of his life, sometimes called his "missing years," we know nothing else. People have speculated about them from ancient times. In the centuries after the four gospels were written, Christians created stories about Jesus's early life. They are rather fanciful tales. In the *Infancy Gospel of Thomas* (not the same as the *Gospel of Thomas*), Jesus as a child performs miracles. He makes sparrows out of clay and claps his hands, and they fly away. He strikes a playmate dead and then restores him to life. In the *Infancy Gospel of Matthew,* the baby Jesus points to the animals gathered around his manger, and they begin to talk. Another legend reports that Joseph of Arimathea was his uncle, and that the two of them sailed to England when Jesus was twelve, where Jesus built a simple church to honor his mother, Mary, near Glastonbury. Non-Christian legends report that he journeyed to the East, where he learned from Buddhist teachers. About all of these stories, the historical verdict is, "Not likely." But what we do know about these years is that he grew up and came to maturity in a Jewish family in a Jewish village in a Jewish social world.

A JEWISH SOCIAL WORLD

Nazareth was a Jewish village. Most likely no Gentiles lived there. Some would have been Jews for centuries, especially those who had migrated from the southern parts of the homeland during the Jewish reoccupation of Galilee in the second century BCE. Others might have become Jewish during the same period.

Thus Jesus was socialized into a Jewish social world. Its vision of life was very different from the domination system of Rome and its native collaborators. It was constituted by the sacred traditions of Judaism: its scriptures and stories, worship and festivals, prayers and practices, observances and conventions. Its foundations were practice, the Jewish Bible, and the temple in Jerusalem.

Practice

Judaism has often been described as a religion of practice. And so it was in the time of Jesus. Though there were convictions at the heart of Judaism, Judaism (then and now) does not emphasize "belief," as many forms of Christianity do. Rather, to be a Jew meant to live as a Jew.

This meant observing the Torah (the Jewish law, about which I will soon say more) and other Jewish teachings in daily life, for the Torah concerned all of life, not just what we often think of as the religious part of life. We should also not think of observing the Torah, of practice, as "works" or Judaism as a "religion of law," as Christians (especially Protestants) have commonly done. Rather, Judaism in the time of Jesus has been concisely described as *covenantal nomism* (from the Greek word *nomos*, which means "rule," "order," or "law"). It was based in the conviction that God had chosen Israel and that Israel had agreed to live in accord with God's covenant. To use a common Christian word, it thus combined grace (God's choosing of Israel) and response to grace.[8]

Jesus learned Jewish practice simply by growing up in a Jewish family in a Jewish village. He would have absorbed it just as we absorb the cultural world in which we grow up. Family, community, and daily life (as well as synagogue and scripture) were the primary agents of Jewish socialization. In his world, religion was not one of the activities of life, as it is for most people in the modern world, who learn their religion separately from and in addition to learning their culture. Rather, Judaism was the cultural canopy under which he was socialized.

These practices were based on the Torah and its interpretation and included most of life, both infrequent and frequent activities. By the former, I mean punishment of criminals, compensation for property damage, divorce and remarriage, and so forth. But it also covered daily and weekly activities. Food laws defined permissible and impermissible foods. Purity laws dealt with bodily fluids and blemishes and the means of purification. Blessings and thanksgivings were prescribed for various daily events.

Each day began and ended with the recitation of the Shema, ancient Israel's concise crystallization of its central conviction:

> Hear, O Israel: the LORD is our God, the LORD alone. You shall love the LORD your God with all your heart, and with all your soul, and with all your might. Keep these words that I am commanding you today in your heart. Recite them to your children and talk about them when you are at home and when you are away, when you lie down and when you rise. Bind them as a sign on your hand, fix them as an emblem on your forehead, and write them down on the doorposts of your house and on your gates. (Deut. 6.4–9)

Twice a day, in accord with Jewish practice, Jesus recited, perhaps chanted, these words.

One day a week was the sabbath. On this day, many activities—any that could be considered "work"—were prohibited. The prohibitions strike many modern people as burdensome, but it was not so. Instead, the sabbath was the most festive day of the week: free from labor, it was a time for eating, lovemaking, gathering in community for prayer and worship, and leisure. The sabbath remembered God as creator and the time of Eden before work began, and it remembered God as the liberator of Israel from the unremitting labor of Egypt.

The sabbath included attending synagogue. As in Jewish villages generally, Nazareth would have had a synagogue, even though probably not a synagogue building. Not only was Nazareth perhaps too small and poor to have built a synagogue, but the evidence for synagogue *buildings* in Galilee in the first century is very scant; archaeologists have found only a few traces. But the word "synagogue" does not intrinsically refer to a building, but to *an assembly*, a gathering of people for religious purposes. When the gospels refer to Jesus teaching in synagogues, these gatherings may be meant rather than buildings.

Though there was probably not yet an established order of synagogue service, these gatherings included prayer, recitation of scripture, teaching, interaction, and probably community affairs. Worship, teaching, and conversation occurred. People sat or stood facing each other rather than in rows all facing one direction, thus encouraging interaction. There would have been one or more leaders, but it would be anachronistic to think of them as rabbis in the sense of formally trained and officially designated teachers. Such institutionalization came after the time of Jesus. In his time, the word *rabbi* meant simply "teacher"; it was a term of respect, not an official role.

Festivals were also part of Jewish practice. The three major festivals recalled the events of Israel's story of its origins. Passover recalled the exodus from Egypt, Pentecost the giving of the law on Mt. Sinai, and Tabernacles the years of journeying through the wilderness to the promised land. Though these three festivals were to be celebrated in Jerusalem, it is very likely that they were also celebrated in local communities like Nazareth by those who did not (or could not) go on pilgrimage to Jerusalem. A fourth festival, Hanukkah, was a recent innovation; it celebrated the rededication of the temple in Jerusalem after its defilement by a foreign emperor in the second century BCE. Also called the Festival of Lights, it occurred near the winter solstice.

Observing these practices was understood as an obligation to God within the framework of God's gracious acts toward Israel. They also were identity markers, distinctive practices that inculcated a Jewish identity. They also mediated the reality of God by reminding the Jews of Nazareth, and Jews generally, of the presence of God in the dailiness of life.

The Bible of Jesus

In addition to practice, Jesus was shaped by the Jewish Bible. As we know the Jewish Bible, the Christian Old Testament, it has three main parts: the law (*torah*), the prophets, and the writings. But in the time of Jesus, only the first two parts had become sacred, reflected in the New Testament phrase "the law and the prophets." The canon of the third major part, "the writings," had not been finalized, though parts of it, especially the Psalms, were clearly considered to be sacred.

For the vast majority of peasants, the Bible would have been heard, not read. There is more than one reason. Literacy rates in the ancient world were low, especially in the peasant class. Moreover, biblical scrolls (like all documents) had to be produced by hand and were thus expensive. In addition, the ability to read a biblical scroll was a highly technical skill. The Bible in the time of Jesus had no chapter and verse divisions, no separation between words or sentences, no punctuation, and no vowels. Even locating a passage in a scroll would have been difficult. Though peasants might possess "peasant literacy" (the ability to sign their name and perhaps to write simple agreements), few would have had "scribal literacy." But peasants would have heard the Bible in synagogue gatherings, in story-telling, and during Jewish festivals.

Torah

The Torah is the first five books of the Bible, Genesis through Deuteronomy, sometimes called the Pentateuch, the Five Books of Moses, or "the law." But "the law" is a somewhat misleading designation, for "Torah" means more than what we mean by "law" or "laws." The word means "instruction," and as instruction the Torah includes Judaism's stories of origins as well as the laws by which Jews lived. It combines narrative and behavior, story and practice.

Torah as Narrative. As narrative, the Torah integrates a host of individual stories within an overarching macrostory. The first part of the macrostory centers on God's promise of children and land to Israel's nomadic ancestors. Children meant the continuation of life, and land was the basis of life. Abraham and Sarah are promised life and the basis of life; their offspring would become a great people living in their own land. But history presented obstacles. The first two generations of ancestors were barren until God intervened when, humanly speaking, conception and birth were impossible. In the third generation, Jacob had twelve sons who were the fathers of the twelve tribes of Israel. But then the greatest threat to the promise occurred; the ancestors were enslaved by Egypt, the empire that ruled their world.

This leads to the second and central part of the macrostory at the heart of the Torah, the exodus from Egypt under the leadership of Moses and God's covenant with Israel at Mt. Sinai. It is a story of liberation from bondage and the creation of a society very different from life under Pharaoh's domination. The third part of the macrostory returns to the theme of God's promise and fulfillment. As the Torah ends, the Hebrew tribes stand on the border of the promised land, poised to take possession of it. God's promise of descendants and land is about to be fulfilled. At the heart of the Torah is a story of oppression and liberation, bondage and freedom, and the creation of Israel as a people living in their own land under the lordship of God.

Torah and Behavior. The Torah also contains the laws by which Israel was to live. The most familiar of these are, of course, the Ten Commandments. They concern loyalty to God and laws for living together. The first speaks of God's character and lordship: "I am the Lord your God, who brought you out of the land of Egypt, out of the house of slavery; you shall have no other gods before me" (Exod. 20.2–3). The second prohibits graven images, the third prohibits swearing falsely in God's name, and the fourth commands sabbath observance. The rest are basic rules for living together as a community: honoring parents, which includes caring financially for them in their old age; no killing, adultery, stealing, or false witness; and no coveting of one's neighbor's house, property, or wife.

The laws of the Torah also include much more. They cover the details of daily life: compensation for damage to property, rules for divorce and remarriage, food laws that distinguished between clean (permissible) and unclean (forbidden) food, purity regulations about bodily emissions and blemishes, laws about tithing, criminal law, and more.

Some of these conflicted directly with life under the domination system, especially laws about land and debt. The Torah contains some of the most radical social legislation in history. Rural land could not be bought or sold in perpetuity, for it belonged to God:

"The land shall not be sold in perpetuity, for the land is mine; with me, you are but aliens and tenants" (Lev. 25.23). The intention was to guarantee that every family would keep its land or, minimally, have a chance to redeem it if lost through debt. The regulations for the sabbath year are also radical: every seventh year, all debts are to be forgiven and all indentured slaves are to be set free. The intent is clear: to prevent the growth of a permanently indebted and indentured class. Finally, in the jubilee year (every fiftieth year), all rural land was to be returned, without payment, to the original family of ownership. The jubilee regulation recognizes that a family might lose its land through foreclosure on debt, but mandates its return. Once again, the intent is clear: to prevent the growth of a permanently landless and impoverished class.

This understanding of land and debt stood in stark contrast to what was happening in the time of Jesus. Under the imperial domination system, the growth of large estates and the commercialization of agriculture meant that an increasing number of peasants were losing their land, the basis of life. Rome and its clients treated the land as if it belonged to them, not to God. Indebtedness was the way peasants could lose their land, if they still had a small plot. And if they didn't own land, indebtedness was the path to becoming indentured slaves. Thus, for most in the peasant class, securing enough food and avoiding debt were the central issues of their lives.

A passage from the Jewish tradition expresses the outrage created by this state of affairs. In it, the Romans give their account to God of all they have done for their Jewish subjects, to which God's reply is:

Imbeciles! Everything that you did, you did only for your own good. You established marketplaces to have your brothels, you built bathhouses to give pleasure to your bodies. And the gold and silver you stole from Me, for so it is written, the silver is Mine and the gold is Mine. (*Avoda Zara* 2b)

The Torah as a whole stood in tension with the domination system of Jesus's day. With its macrostory of liberation from an earlier empire and the gift of a land, it pointed to a very different vision as God's passion.

The Prophets

The tension between Torah and the domination system also runs through the other major part of the Jewish Bible in the time of Jesus, "the prophets." This includes a collection of narrative books commonly called the "former prophets" (Joshua, Judges, Samuel, and Kings) as well as books bearing the names of familiar prophetic figures (Isaiah, Jeremiah, Ezekiel, Amos, Hosea, and so forth), known as the "latter prophets." Both the former and latter prophets indicted and condemned the domination system that was established in ancient Israel with the birth of the monarchy.

The Former Prophets. Joshua, Judges, Samuel, and Kings narrate the story of ancient Israel from the settlement of the promised land until the end of the monarchy in 586 BCE, when Jerusalem was conquered and destroyed by the Babylonian Empire. Indeed, their central theme is the rise, failure, and fall of the monarchy in Israel and Judah.

The former prophets contain two very different attitudes toward the monarchy. One strand affirms kingship as a gift of God. The other sees it as the beginning of Israel's troubles. The ambivalence is in part the difference between an ideal king and actual kings. The prophets, former and latter, are not kind to actual kings. Indeed, they regularly indict them for injustice and idolatry. The two went hand in hand: injustice was the product of having lords other than the God of Israel.

The first book of Samuel expresses the ambivalence. Two contrasting stories about the emergence of kingship in Israel stand side by side, one promonarchy (9.1–10.16) and the other antimonarchy (8.4–22). According to the first, kingship comes from God. It is God who decides to give Israel a king "to save my people from the hand of the Philistines; for I have seen the suffering of my people, because their outcry has come to me" (9.16). When Samuel then anoints Saul to be the first king of Israel, he speaks of it as God's will: "The LORD has anointed you ruler over his people Israel. You shall reign over the people of the Lord and you will save them from the hand of their enemies all around" (10.1). The king will be the savior of Israel.

The antimonarchy tradition sees the advent of kingship very differently. That Israel should have a king is not God's idea, but the people's desire, a desire portrayed as a rejection of God's kingship. And so Samuel warns them of the consequences of having a king. It is a stunningly accurate description of the ancient domination system. The central feature is named with a sixfold repetition of "he [the king] will take":

> These will be the ways of the king who will reign over you: *he will take* your sons and appoint them to his chariots and to be his horsemen, and to run before his chariots; and he will appoint for himself commanders of thousands and commanders of fifties, and some to plow his ground and to reap his harvest, and to make his implements of war and the equipment of his chariots. *He will take* your daughters to be perfumers and cooks and bakers. *He will take* the best of your fields and vineyards and olive orchards and give them to his courtiers. *He will take* one-tenth of your grain and of your vineyards and give it to his officers and his courtiers. *He will take* your male and female slaves, and the best of your cattle and donkeys, and put them to his work. *He will take* one-tenth of your flocks, and you shall be his slaves. And in that day you will cry out because of your king, whom you have chosen for yourselves; but the Lord will not answer you in that day. (8.11–18)

According to this tradition, kingship brought the oppression and injustice of a domination system to Israel. The last two books of the former prophets, 1 and 2 Kings, chronicle the almost universally dismal record of the monarchy.

The Latter Prophets. The rest of the second part of the Jewish Bible consists of the words of figures we commonly think of as the prophets: three major prophets (Isaiah, Jeremiah, and Ezekiel) and twelve minor prophets (sometimes called the "Book of the Twelve").

The designations "major" and "minor" do not refer to their relative importance, but to the length of the books that bear their names. Like the former prophets, most of them focus on the monarchy, its injustice, and its fall; some of them speak after the fall, that is, during and after the exile.

These books are not narratives, but collections of oracles—short memorable and often poetic "speeches"—that the prophets, in the name of God and God's covenant with Israel, spoke against the powerful and wealthy ruling elite centered in the monarchy. An early cluster (Amos, Hosea, Micah, and Isaiah) spoke in the eighth century BCE, proclaiming God's judgment against the economic injustice, violence, and idolatry of the domination system. A second cluster proclaimed God's judgment against the ruling elite in the decades preceding Jerusalem's destruction by the Babylonians in 586 BCE.

They spoke about God's passion for economic justice and condemnation of injustice. A representative sampling illustrates their indictment of the wealthy and powerful. From Amos:

> Alas for those who lie on beds of ivory, and lounge on their couches, and eat lambs from the flock, and calves from the stall; ... but are not grieved over the ruin of Joseph [meaning "the poor"]. (6.4–6)

> They ... trample the head of the poor into the dust of the earth, and push the afflicted out of the way. (2.7)

> You ... oppress the poor, ... crush the needy. (4.1)

> You trample on the poor and take from them levies of grain. (5.11)

Speaking in the name of God so that the "I" is God, not the prophet, Amos indicted the worship of God as practiced by the elite:

> I hate, I despise your festivals, and I take no delight in your solemn assemblies. Even though you offer me your burnt

offerings and grain offerings, I will not accept them; and the offerings of … your fatted animals, I will not look upon. Take away from me the noise of your songs; I will not listen to the melody of your harps. But let justice roll down like waters, and righteousness like an ever-flowing stream. (5.21–24)

In the same century, Micah indicted the elite for their ruthless acquisition of peasant land: "They covet fields, and seize them; houses, and take them away; they oppress householder and house, people and their inheritance" (2.2). So also Micah indicted the rulers for their failure to serve the cause of justice:

Listen, you heads of Jacob and rulers of the house of Israel! Should you not know justice?—you who hate the good and love the evil, who tear the skin off my people, and the flesh off their bones? (3.1–2)

Cities, where the urban elite lived, were singled out for condemnation. About the capital cities of the Northern and Southern Kingdoms, Micah said:

What is the transgression of Jacob [the Northern Kingdom]? Is it not Samaria? And what is the high place of Judah [the Southern Kingdom]? Is it not Jerusalem? (1.5)

To Jerusalem, Isaiah said: "God expected justice, but saw bloodshed; righteousness, but heard a cry!" (5.7). About Jerusalem, Jeremiah said: "Run to and fro through the streets of Jerusalem, look around and take note! Search its squares to see if you can find one person who does justice and seeks truth" (5.1). Jeremiah even indicted the temple of God in Jerusalem: "Has this house, which is called by my name, become a den of robbers in your sight?" (7.11).

The latter prophets also include prophetic figures who spoke during and after the Jewish people's exile in Babylon. The second half of the book of Isaiah is an exquisite example of their words of encouragement and reassurance to an impoverished and virtually enslaved community living under a foreign empire. To the exiles, the prophet announced that God is doing "a new thing"—that God will bring them back from exile to their homeland. Thus these God-intoxicated critics of injustice were also voices of promise and hope. They proclaimed that God had a very different social order, a very different future, in mind. God's passion, God's dream, was justice and peace.

Together, "the law and the prophets" were the Bible of Jesus. We do not know if he knew it as a written text. As mentioned earlier, most in the peasant class did not. It is possible that a precocious and motivated youth from the peasant class could have found a way to attain scribal literacy. But whether Jesus knew the Jewish Bible only from hearing or also from reading, it is clear that it shaped him. Jesus grew up in a social world saturated with the God of the Torah and the prophets.

Together, the combination of practice and the Jewish Bible incubated lives centered in God. They also incubated a vision of life under God very different from what Jesus and his peasant contemporaries were experiencing under the two tiers of a native and an imperial domination system. And as we will see in a later chapter, he himself became a passionate critic of the domination system in the name of the God of Israel.

The Temple in Jerusalem

Jerusalem and its temple were the sacred center of the sacred geography of the Jewish social world. They had been for almost a millennium. King David had made Jerusalem the capital of the United Kingdom in the early 900s BCE. His son Solomon built the temple, understood as the dwelling place of God on earth. In the seventh century, through reforms introduced by King Josiah (one of the very few kings described as a good king in the Jewish Bible) a few decades before Jerusalem and the temple were destroyed by the Babylonians, the temple in Jerusalem became the only place where sacrifices could be offered to God. The tradition is enshrined in the book of Deuteronomy in the Torah. The role that it gave to the temple continued to be affirmed after the Jewish people returned from exile in the late 500s BCE.

Within the theology that developed around it, the temple in Jerusalem was the "navel of the earth" connecting this world to its source in God, and here (and only here) was God's dwelling place on earth. Of course, ancient Israel also affirmed that God was everywhere: heaven and the highest heaven cannot contain God, and God's glory fills the earth. But God was especially present in the temple. To be in the temple was to be in God's presence.

The temple became the center of Jewish devotion and the destination of pilgrimage. Both are movingly expressed in a collection of psalms used by Jewish pilgrims as they "went up" to Jerusalem on pilgrimage. Commonly called "songs of ascent" (Pss. 120–134), they speak of the yearning and joy engendered by Jerusalem as the city of God. One says, "I was glad when they said to me, 'Let us go to the house [the temple] of the LORD!' Our feet are standing within your gates, O Jerusalem.... Pray for the peace of Jerusalem: 'May they prosper who love you'" (122.1–2, 6). Another affirms, "When the LORD restored the fortunes of Zion [Jerusalem], we were like those who dream. Then our mouth was filled with laughter, and our tongue with shouts of joy" (126.1–2). And another: "For the LORD has chosen Zion; God has desired it for God's habitation. 'This is my resting place forever; here I will reside, for I have desired it'" (132.13–14).

The theology that developed around the temple claimed for it an institutional monopoly on access to God. Not only did temple theology affirm that God dwelled there as nowhere else, but the temple was the one and only place of sacrifice. Only there could sacrifices be offered for certain kinds of sins, and only there could certain kinds of impurities be dealt with. Doing so was the prerequisite for access to God, for entering the place of God's presence. Not all Jews accepted this claim. Jesus and his mentor John the Baptizer were among them. But the theology of the temple affirmed it.

Jerusalem and the temple had a future significance as well: it was the city of promise and hope where God's promise and Israel's hopes would be fulfilled. It had been so for centuries. From it, God's ideal king, a king like David, would rule over a restored Israel. He would be anointed by God, which is the meaning of the word "messiah" (in Greek, *christos;* in English, Christ).

Jerusalem was not only the city of Jewish hope, but the place from which God's future for the world would go forth. Seven hundred years earlier, in one of the most familiar passages from the Jewish Bible, Isaiah said:

> In days to come, the mountain of the Lord's house [Mount Zion in Jerusalem, on which the temple, the Lord's house, was built] shall be established as the highest of the mountains, and shall be raised above the hills; all the nations shall stream to it.
>
> Many peoples [the nations, not just Israel] shall come and say. "Come, let us go up to the mountain of the Lord, to the house of the God of Jacob; that he may teach us his ways and that we might walk in his paths."
>
> For out of Zion shall go forth instruction, and the word of the Lord from Jerusalem. God shall judge between the nations, and shall arbitrate for many peoples; they shall beat their swords into plowshares, and their spears into pruning hooks; nation shall not lift up sword against nation, neither shall they learn war any more. (2.2-4)

It is an extraordinary passage. Jerusalem is not only the center of Israel's future, but the world's. It will be the highest mountain that draws the nations to it: many peoples will stream to it. From it, God's instruction, God's *torah*, will go forth; they will learn God's ways and how to walk in God's paths. War shall be no more. Jerusalem will be the city of peace, of *shalom*, at the center of the world.

But Jerusalem and the temple also had a more sinister aspect. As mentioned earlier in this chapter, they became in the time of the monarchy the center of a domination system. Temple and domination system went hand in hand. Kings and high priests alike were part of the aristocracy, and the temple virtually became the chapel of the wealthy and powerful. Prophets railed against Jerusalem as the faithless city that had abandoned God's covenant and chased after other gods, oppressing the poor, widows, and orphans. Indeed, from the perspective of the prophets, Jerusalem's conquest and destruction occurred because of its injustice and idolatry. This was God's will. The Lord who brought them out of Egypt did not intend that they become rulers and ruled within a new domination system.

The sinister aspect of Jerusalem is apparent in the time of Jesus. During his lifetime, the city at the center of Jewish hope and God's destiny had become the place of collaboration with the imperial domination system. Indeed, according to a saying attributed to Jesus, the city had a reputation for slaying prophets: "Jerusalem, Jerusalem, the city that kills the prophets and stones those who are sent to it" (Luke 13.34 = Matt. 23.37). It was the city that did not know "the things that make for peace" (Luke 19.42).

To conclude this description of the Jewish social world at the time of Jesus, its two pillars, as a number of scholars have said, were Torah and temple. Torah should not be narrowly understood as "law" and temple should not be narrowly understood as "sacrifice." Rather, Torah was both story and practice; in its more expansive sense, it was the Jewish scripture as a whole, including the prophets.[9] And the temple was not only about sacrifice, but the center of devotion and hope and promise.

TWO WORLDS IN COLLISION

The collision between Roman imperial theology and domination and the Jewish social world led to a variety of Jewish responses. They ranged from active collaboration to resigned and often resentful acceptance. Some harbored hopes for an imminent dramatic divine intervention: God would soon act and set things right. Others—and these responses often overlapped—were determined to preserve Jewish identity in spite of the pressures to assimilate. Still others followed the path of violent rejection, ranging from social banditry to armed rebellion.

This is the world that shaped Jesus—the world in which he grew up and the world that he addressed. And a further factor shaped him: his experience of God and his relationship to God. God was the central reality in his life. We explore this further and decisive shaping in the next chapter.

FIVE

The Shaping of Jesus

His Experience of God

Many Christians are accustomed to thinking of Jesus *as* God. Familiar Christian language contributes to the identification. The fourth-century Nicene Creed declares Jesus to be "God from God,… true God from true God,… of one Being with the Father" and affirms that Jesus was active in the creation of the world: "through him all things were made." Moreover, in their devotion and worship, Christians address prayers to Jesus and sing hymns to Jesus as God. About the post-Easter Jesus, this language is correct: the risen, living Christ is one with God, a divine reality.

But in this chapter we focus on the pre-Easter Jesus and God. What was his relationship to God? To state its central claim in advance, *the pre-Easter Jesus was not God, but God was the central reality of his life.* So the gospels present him. The story of his adult life begins with an experience of God: "He saw the heavens torn apart and the Spirit descending like a dove on him" (Mark 1.10). He told parables about God—about God's character and passion. He taught a way of life centered in God: "You shall love the Lord your God with all your heart, and with all your soul, and with all your mind, and with all your strength" (Mark 12.30). At the heart of his ethical vision was the imitation of God: "Be compassionate, just as your Father is compassionate" (Luke 6.36). He proclaimed the kingdom of God, its presence, coming, and importance: "Strive first for the kingdom of God" (Matt. 6.33; Luke 12.31). He named the power that flowed through him as the power of God: "If it is by the Spirit of God that I cast out demons, then the kingdom of God has come to you" (Matt. 12.28; Luke 11.20).

How did God become so central to Jesus? Much is explained by his Jewish heritage. As described in the previous chapter, Jesus grew up in a Jewish world saturated with God, whose sacred scripture and practices mediated a life centered in God.

But there is an additional and crucial reason: it flowed out of his experience of God. For Jesus, God was not simply an article of belief, but an experienced reality. In this, he was like the most central figures of the Jewish Bible and tradition; the stories of Israel present them as people who had experienced God. Near the end of this chapter, I suggest that, broadly understood, the term *mystic* designates the kind of person Jesus was—someone who experienced God vividly and whose way of seeing and life were changed as result. What most shaped Jesus was the Jewish tradition and his mystical experience of God. He was, I argue, a Jewish mystic.

SPEAKING OF GOD

The notion that God can be experienced is foreign to many in the modern world. Atheists, of course, deny that such experiences are possible, and agnostics are skeptical. But even many Christians in our time find the claim strange. To a considerable extent, this is because the most common modern Western concept of God, shared by Christians as well as by many atheists and agnostics, is that the word "God" refers to a personlike being separate from the universe. Because this "superbeing" is not here, but somewhere else, "out there," beyond the universe, God is not a reality that can be experienced.

The term commonly used for this way of thinking of God—as a being separate from the universe—is *supernatural theism*. This form of theism seems orthodox to many Christians because of its familiarity. Language that speaks of God as a personlike being is common in the Bible. Perhaps the most familiar example is the opening line of the Lord's Prayer: "Our Father in heaven." But when taken as a concept of God, as the meaning or referent of the word "God," it is misleading and inadequate, for it is only half of the biblical concept of God. It speaks only of God's *transcendence*, God's beyondness.

The Bible also speaks of God's presence everywhere and in everything. This is most concisely expressed in words attributed to the apostle Paul: God is the one "in whom we live and move and have our being" (Acts 17.28).[1] Note what the language affirms: we live within God, we move within God, we have our existence within God. God is not somewhere else, but right here, all around us, the encompassing Spirit in whom everything that is, is. Though this notion sounds foreign to some Christians, it really shouldn't. Most of us heard it while we were growing up: God is everywhere, God is omnipresent. The semitechnical term for this is God's *immanence,* which means "indwelling." God dwells in everything, and everything dwells within God. For the Bible, and for orthodox Christian theology through the centuries, God is both transcendent and immanent, both *more* than the universe and *present in* the universe.

A term increasingly used to name this way of thinking about God is *panentheism.* Its Greek roots indicate its meaning: *pan* is the Greek word for "all" or "everything"; *theism* comes from the Greek word for "God," *theos;* and the middle syllable *en* is the Greek word for "in." Panentheism affirms that everything is *in* God, even as it also affirms that God is *more* than everything. Though the term is only about two hundred years old, the notion is as ancient as the language of supernatural theism.

But in recent centuries, many Christians began to think of God as only transcendent. The cause of this change was the Enlightenment of the seventeenth century. Before then, most Christians thought of God not only as more than the world, but also as present in the world. The world was shot through with the presence of God. But the Enlightenment led to a new way of thinking of the universe, as a closed-system of matter and energy operating in accord with natural laws. In effect, the Enlightenment removed God from the universe; nature became disenchanted, the world became desacralized. The notion that God is "everywhere," God's immanence, was eclipsed. Panentheism was replaced by supernatural theism.

Whether people use the term "panentheism" does not matter. But whether people think of God as only transcendent (supernatural theism) or as both transcendent and immanent (panentheism) does matter. For many people in our time, supernatural theism is the only concept of God they know, and it often leads to skepticism about God. When somebody says to me, "I don't believe in God," my first response is, "Tell me about the God you don't believe in." Almost always, it's the God of supernatural theism. Thinking that the word "God" refers to a being separate from the universe, "out there" and "not here," is a major cause of modern atheism, agnosticism, and skepticism.

The difference between these two forms of theism matters for an additional reason. For supernatural theism, God is not here and thus cannot be experienced, except perhaps in moments of supernatural intervention. This God can only be believed in, not known. We will know God only after death; in this life, we can only believe. For pan-entheism, God is here, all around us, even as God is also more than everything. It thus provides a framework for understanding what it means to speak of experiencing God.

When I was a young college teacher in my mid-twenties, an older colleague delighted in characterizing post-Enlightenment theology as "flat-tire theology"—"All the *pneuma* has gone out of it." The cleverness of his comment depended on the multiple meanings of the Greek word *pneuma:* "air," "wind," "breath," and "Spirit."[2] All the air, Spirit, has gone out of it. I understood his point, even though I thought it a bit too negative. For me, modern theology was a joy; it was insightful, challenging, liberating.

Yet I also see that my colleague's statement had a lot of truth in it. Modern theology, including modern biblical scholars and Jesus scholars, seldom takes seriously that God can be experienced and that experiences of God are foundational to the Bible as a whole.[3]

EXPERIENCES OF GOD

The religions of the world are filled with stories of experiences of God or the sacred, terms that I use synonymously and interchangeably. They have been studied by historians of religion, anthropologists, social historians, psychologists, and scholars of mysticism. A hundred years ago, in his classic book *The Varieties of Religious Experience,* the American psychologist and philosopher William James spoke of such experiences as being among the most striking and extraordinary psychological phenomena known.

James called them experiences of "the unseen" and "a more." Abraham Heschel, one of the two most famous Jewish theologians of the twentieth century, wrote about the state of "radical amazement" in which we experience a sacred reality beyond all of our categories. Martin Buber, the other most famous Jewish theologian of recent time, wrote about encountering "the You" beyond the subject-object distinction of our ordinary experience. The psychologist Abraham Maslow named them "peak experiences," and the German historian of religions Rudolf Otto wrote about experiences of the "numinous" behind or underneath phenomena, the *mysterium tremendum et fascinans*—the tremendous mystery that fills us with awe and also attracts and allures us. Huston Smith, now in his late eighties and perhaps the most widely known scholar of religion still with us, describes experiences of the sacred in the religions of the world that generated "the virtual human unanimity" that reality— "what is"—has more than one level. In addition to the visible world of our ordinary experience, there is a stupendous "more"—the sacred.[4]

To use William James's most generic term for the sacred, these are experiences of a "more." They fall into two primary categories or types: experiences of the sacred as a personlike being or beings in another level of reality; and experiences of the sacred as a presence flooding the whole of reality, including, of course, the world.

For Christians, the first type may involve experiences of God, Jesus, angels, Mary, or saints. Such experiences include visions and auditions. In visions, one sees into another reality; in auditions, one hears a voice from another reality. Probably the best-known biblical example among Christians combines vision and audition: Paul on the Damascus road *saw* a great light and *heard* the voice of Jesus addressing him (Acts 9.3–6; see also Acts 22; 26.).

The second type involves experiences of the sacred pervading this world. We see the world we ordinarily see and experience: a landscape, a room, a person, whatever is in front of us. Unlike with visions, no extra beings or realities are experienced, but there is often a visual aspect: what we see *looks different*—wondrous, radiant, glorious. To use a biblical phrase, in these moments the world is seen as "filled with the glory of God," transfigured; the radiance of God, the radiant presence of the sacred, suffuses everything. What we behold may become luminous, as if there were light shining through everything. In such moments, language and our habituated patterns of perception that domesticate reality fall away, and with eyes wide open we behold "what is" in all of its "suchness." Sometimes a visual aspect is not involved. Rather than seeing the "glory of God," we become aware of a sacred presence pervading everything.

The first type of experience leads to the language of supernatural theism, the sacred as personlike being. The second type, whether visual or a sense of a presence, leads to the language of panentheism, a "more" that is also immanent. The sacred that is experienced by some as a being or beings is experienced by others as a more than personal reality, a transpersonal reality.

Both types of experience may occur spontaneously, out of the blue, with no apparent cause. But sometimes spiritual practices—solitude, fasting, prayer, chanting, drumming, rhythmic movement, and so forth—become the occasions for such experiences. To illustrate with one practice, both types of experiences may occur during what is called "contemplative prayer" or "meditation." This practice involves entering into a state of sustained internal silence. A verse from the Psalms seems to refer to this practice: "Be still, and know that I am God" (46.10). In this state, people sometimes have visions and/or auditions and a sense of encounter with the sacred as personal being. Or they may experience a sense of descending to a deep level of the self in which the distinction between the self and the one in whom we live and move and have our being becomes very soft and permeable, sometimes even vanishing, leading to a sense of union or communion with God, or the sacred.

Both types of experience involve a subjective state, a change from ordinary everyday consciousness to a nonordinary state of consciousness. The latter is "ecstatic" in the root sense of the word, which means to be "out of" or "beyond" one's ordinary state of consciousness. Though some people regard such experiences as illusory or delusional rather than as disclosures of something real, those who have them do not. Rather, for them, these experiences have a strong noetic quality, a quality of *knowing* that leads to an ontological conviction, a conviction about reality itself. There is an overwhelming sense of having experienced something real, indeed, the ultimately real. They are experienced as revelations, not as hallucinations.

To use language from William James once again, such experiences move one from *secondhand religion* (what one has heard from others) to *firsthand religion* based on the experience of a "more." This is the contrast spoken of in the climax of the book of Job. After God displays the wonders of creation to Job, he responds: "I had heard of you by the hearing of the ear, *but now my eye sees you*" (42.5).[5]

Whatever one makes of these kinds of experiences, and whatever one thinks their ontological implications are, we need to take seriously that they happen. Moreover, the most important figures in human religious history are spoken of as people who had them. Though these experiences could be illustrated from any and all of the world's enduring religions, I illustrate them from Judaism, the most relevant tradition for the study of Jesus.

EXPERIENCES OF GOD IN THE JEWISH TRADITION

Experiences of God are central to the Jewish Bible and its major figures, beginning with the stories of Israel's ancestors in the book of Genesis. Abraham had visions, heard auditions, and entertained heavenly visitors. So also did his grandson Jacob, the father of the twelve tribes. In one, he saw a fiery ladder connecting this world to another level of reality, with angels ascending and descending on it. Afterward he exclaimed, "This is the gate of heaven" (Gen. 28.17)— that is, the doorway into another reality.[6]

Similar stories are told about Moses, the most central figure of Israel's history. He received his call to become Israel's liberator through an experience of God. He saw a bush that burned without being consumed, aflame with divine radiance, and from the bush heard the voice of God speaking to him. Later, he repeatedly ascended the sacred mountain in order to commune with God and there was given the laws by which Israel was to live. After one such encounter, we are told, his face glowed with the radiance of the holy (Exod. 34.29–35). According to his brief obituary at the end of Deuteronomy, Moses *knew* God "face to face" (34.10–12).

The books of the prophets abound with experiences of the sacred. On a mountain, alone, the ninth-century BCE prophet Elijah experienced God in a theophany. Stories are told about his traveling "in the Spirit" and as a channel for the power of Spirit as both a healer and rainmaker. At the end of his life, his disciple and successor Elishah saw him carried into the other world by "a chariot of fire born aloft in a whirlwind" (2 Kings 2.11).[7]

One hundred years later, Isaiah's call to be a prophet began with an overwhelming experience of God:

> I saw the Lord sitting on a throne, high and lofty; and the hem
> of his robe filled the temple. Seraphs were in attendance above
> him; each had six wings: with two they covered their faces, and
> with two they covered their feet, and with two they flew. And
> one called to another and said: "Holy, holy, holy is the LORD of
> hosts; the whole earth is full of his glory." (6.1–3)

So also the prophet Ezekiel's call involved experiences of the sacred: "In the thirtieth year, in the fourth month, on the fifth day of the month, as I was among the exiles by the river Chebar, *the heavens were opened, and I saw visions of God*" (1.1). In addition to visions, the prophets sometimes spoke of the Spirit descending upon them: "The spirit of the LORD *fell upon me*" (Ezek. 11.5) and "The spirit of the Lord GOD is *upon me*" (Isa. 61.1).

The Jewish tradition reports that such experiences continued into the time of Jesus. Stories are told about Jewish charismatics roughly contemporary with Jesus who were known for their intimacy with God, long hours of contemplative prayer, healings, and exorcisms. The two most famous of these charismatics were Honi the Circle-Drawer (first century BCE) and Hanina ben Dosa (first century CE).

Hanina was even called God's son by a voice from heaven: "The whole universe is sustained on account of *my son* Hanina."[8]

JESUS'S EXPERIENCE OF GOD

Jesus stands in this tradition of Jewish figures for whom God, the sacred, was an experiential reality. The data in the gospels supporting this claim are early and widespread, particular and general, direct and indirect. They are found in the earliest layers of the gospel tradition, in both Q and Mark, as well as in later layers. Texts report visions, long hours of prayer, and a sense of the presence of the Spirit in him. His language often expresses an intimacy with God. His activity as a healer and exorcist is linked to an awareness of the Spirit of God active through him. More generally, his wisdom teaching often reflects a transformed perspective and perception most compatible with an enlightenment experience of the sacred. His passion and courage as a prophet suggest an experiential grounding in God like that of the prophets of the Jewish Bible.

When did God become an experiential reality for Jesus? How early in his life did this happen? As a child? An adolescent? A young adult? According to the stories of his birth in Matthew and Luke, in which Jesus was conceived by the Spirit of God, God was "in Jesus" from his beginning. But for reasons described in Chapter 3, mainstream scholars do not see these (or the story of Jesus in the temple at age twelve) as historical accounts. And even if we did see them as historical, they would still not answer the question of when God became an experiential reality for Jesus. We don't know when this was, for the gospels report nothing historical about Jesus before his adulthood.[9]

What we do know is that sometime in his twenties Jesus left Nazareth and journeyed to a wilderness where a prophet named John the Baptizer was active. Jesus's decision to do so suggests a deepening religious passion. Why else would he leave home and family to be with a wilderness prophet?

John was an important figure in first-century Judaism. The gospels all highlight his significance, and Josephus gives more space to

John than Jesus (*Antiquities* 18.116–19). His importance did not derive from an institutional role, for he had no official standing. Indeed, he was an anti-establishment figure. According to the gospels, he dressed like Elijah, the great prophet of the Jewish Bible who brought down a kingdom. John subverted the temple's role as mediator of access to God by proclaiming a means of forgiveness— repentance and baptism—that bypassed the temple. He publicly criticized his ruler Herod Antipas, and as a result was arrested and executed.

Mark 1.4 provides a very terse description of John's mission: "John the Baptizer appeared in the wilderness, proclaiming a baptism of repentance for the forgiveness of sins." John's baptism was "for the forgiveness of sins." As such, it countered the temple's claim to be the mediator of forgiveness. John was an antitemple prophet and, as we shall see, Jesus followed him in this. Moreover, it was a baptism of *repentance,* a word that then meant something quite different from later Christian meanings of being sorry, remorseful, or penitent for one's sins. Repentance had two related meanings in ancient Judaism. It was associated with return from exile; to repent is to return, to follow "the way of the Lord" that leads from exile to the promised land. The Greek roots of the word suggest an additional meaning; to repent is to "go beyond the mind that you have"—to go beyond conventional understandings of what life with God is about.

In addition to proclaiming forgiveness apart from the temple, John's message included indictment, threat of judgment, and promise of a coming one. Indictment:

> You brood of vipers! Who warned you to flee from the wrath to come? Bear fruits worthy of repentance. Do not begin to say to yourselves, "We have Abraham as our ancestor"; for I tell you, God is able from these stones to raise up children to Abraham. (Matt. 3.7–9; Luke 3.7–8)

Against whom is the indictment directed? According to Matthew, against the Sadducees and Pharisees; according to Luke, against the crowds that came to be baptized. But it seems unlikely that John would call people who sought his baptism a "brood of vipers." It also seems unlikely that he would call the Jewish people in general (including the peasant class) offspring of vipers. More likely, it is directed against specific people, though it is impossible to be more precise.

Threat of judgment:

> Even now the ax is lying at the root of the trees; every tree therefore that does not bear good fruit is cut down and thrown into the fire.... His winnowing fork is in his hand, and he will clear his threshing floor and will gather his wheat into his granary; but the chaff he will burn with unquenchable fire. (Matt. 3.10, 12; Luke 3.9, 17)

The language is vivid: the ax is about to swing, the winnowing fork is ready to separate the wheat from the chaff, and unfruitful trees and chaff alike "will burn with unquenchable fire." It is not enough to be descendants of Abraham. Something more is called for: repentance—a path of return, the way of the Lord, "going beyond the mind that you have."

The coming one:

> The one who is more powerful than I is coming after me; I am not worthy to stoop down and untie the thong of his sandals. I have baptized you with water; but he will baptize you with the Holy Spirit. (Mark 1.7–8)

The language of a "coming one" echoes the language of the prophet Malachi, the last book of the Jewish Bible in the time of Jesus: "The messenger of the covenant in whom you delight—indeed, *he is coming,* says the LORD of hosts" (3.1).

To go to this figure, as Jesus did, was to seek out a movement of protest and renewal. His time with John was decisive. Our two earliest sources, Mark and Q, begin the story of his adult life with John, as do all four gospels. We don't know how long the two were together, but presumably Jesus became a follower of John for a period of time. John was his teacher, his mentor. Clearly, Jesus regarded him highly. About him, Jesus later said, "Truly I tell you, among those born of women no one has arisen greater than John the Baptist" (Matt. 11.11; Luke 7.28; and thus from Q). That is high praise.

What did John think of Jesus? Did he think he was the "coming one"? From Mark's point of view, the "coming one" was of course Jesus, and ever since Christians have spoken of John as the "forerunner" of Jesus. But most likely, John did not recognize Jesus as the "coming one." As noted in Chapter 2, John's recognition of Jesus as superior to him is added to Mark by Matthew. Moreover, after John was imprisoned and heard about what Jesus was doing, he sent messengers to inquire of Jesus, "Are you the one who is to come, or are we to wait for another?" (Matt. 11.3; Luke 7.19). The passage suggests that John had not thought of this possibility until then.

Thus, from a post-Easter perspective, John was the forerunner of Jesus who proclaimed Jesus's coming. But in a pre-Easter context, he was the teacher of Jesus, and Jesus was his disciple. And it was during his time with John that Jesus had his first reported experience of God.

In the Beginning: A Vision of the Spirit

John and his message made an impression on Jesus, for he decided to undergo John's "baptism of repentance for the forgiveness of sins." "In those days," Mark tells us, "Jesus came from Nazareth of Galilee and was baptized by John in the Jordan" (1.10). Then, Mark tells us, as Jesus came up out of the water:

> He saw the heavens torn apart and the Spirit descending like a
> dove on him. And a voice came from heaven, "You are my Son,
> the Beloved; with you I am well pleased." (1.11)

Mark's story of Jesus begins with an experience of God. The passage reports both a vision and an audition. Like Ezekiel some six centuries before (1.1), Jesus saw the heavens opened as if they were torn apart. Through this rent, this tear, he saw "the Spirit descending like a dove on him," language that echoes the words of an earlier Spirit-filled prophet: "The Spirit of the Lord GOD is upon me" (Isa. 61.1).[10] For Jesus the vision was accompanied by an audition. A voice from heaven declared to him, "You are my Son, the Beloved; with you I am well pleased." The phenomenon of a heavenly voice was well enough known in Judaism that it had a name, *bath qol*, which means "daughter of a sound." The metaphor perhaps suggests much the same as the voice of God speaking to Elijah in "a sound of sheer silence" (1 Kings 19.12) several centuries before.[11]

Mark presents Jesus's experience of the Spirit as private. In Mark, as noted in Chapter 2, no one else saw the heavens torn apart or the dove descend, and the voice addresses Jesus alone: "*You* are my Son, the Beloved; with *you* I am well pleased." In Matthew, as also noted in Chapter 2, the voice uses third-person language and makes a public announcement to the crowd: "*This* is my Son, the Beloved, with *whom* I am well pleased" (3.17). But in Mark, only Jesus hears the voice. The implication is that this is when Jesus became aware of being Spirit-anointed, Spirit-filled. According to Mark, this is the beginning of the story of Jesus—an experience of the Spirit of God.

About the historical factuality of Jesus's baptism by John and the vision itself, there is little reason for doubt. Unless we think that visions simply do not happen or that they are always a sign of psychosis, there is no reason to deny this experience to Jesus. However, about the words spoken by the heavenly voice, "You are my Son, the Beloved; with you I am well pleased," there is reason for historical uncertainty, simply because the words so perfectly express a post-Easter perception of Jesus's identity. As such, they may well be the product of the followers of Jesus in the years after Easter.

But how we interpret "my Son" in this passage affects the historical judgment. If "Son" is given the theological meaning that it later came to have among Christians, then the phrase must be viewed as post-Easter or at least put into a "suspense account." But if given the meaning that it has in stories of Jewish charismatics contemporary with Jesus, then it is historically possible to imagine this as part of the experience of Jesus, for they too had experiences in which a *bath qol*, a voice from heaven, declared them to be God's "son." Read this way, the words not only become historically possible, but link Jesus to charismatic Judaism.

Whatever the historical judgment concerning the voice from heaven, the story of Jesus's vision at his baptism places him in the Spirit-filled stream of Judaism. Indeed, standing as it does at the beginning of his public activity, the vision is reminiscent of the "call narratives" of the prophets. Like theirs, his ministry began with an experience of the Spirit of God.

Visions in the Wilderness

Following Jesus's baptism, both of our earliest gospel sources, Mark and Q, report that Jesus spent forty days in the wilderness. Mark's account is very brief. The Spirit that descended upon him at his baptism "immediately drove him out into the wilderness," an extraordinarily barren and arid area riven by canyons between cliffs filled with caves, rocky and sun-blasted. There he encounters Satan, who tests him: "He was in the wilderness forty days, tempted by Satan; and he was with the wild beasts; and the angels waited on him" (1.12–13). The phrase "the angels waited on him" echoes the story of Elijah (1 Kings 19.5–8) and thus associates Jesus (like the Baptizer) with Elijah.

The account in Q (Matt. 4.1–11; Luke 4.1–13) is considerably longer. It adds what may be implicit in Mark, namely, that Jesus fasted during the forty days. Prolonged fasting is a spiritual practice in many religious traditions. After several days of water only, body chemistry changes, often resulting in nonordinary states of consciousness, including visions. To do this in solitude "in the wilderness" puts this practice in a category called by anthropologists and historians of religion a "vision quest" or "wilderness ordeal." In this state, according to Q, Jesus had a series of three visions.

The two main characters in the visions are Jesus and Satan. The visions are thus not experiences of God, but of "Satan" (Mark) or "the devil" (Matthew and Luke, and thus Q). But as visions, they are experiences of another level of reality, and these can involve experiencing evil spirits. There are "diabolical" mystical experiences.[12]

Satan has a history in the Jewish tradition. In earlier parts of the Jewish Bible, he is one of the servants of God and part of the "heavenly council" gathered around God (an image of God as a king surrounded by a council of subordinates). In the first two chapters of the book of Job, Satan is God's spy and tester. But in the centuries after the exile, when the Jewish people were ruled by one foreign empire after another, the notion gradually emerged that "this world"—the world of history—is under the control of an evil power that stands opposed to God. Satan, once a servant of God, became the "devil."

I pause to consider a question that may be in the minds of some readers. Is Satan real? Is there a devil? That some people have experiences of an evil power or powers is clear. But what ontological conclusion should be drawn from such experiences? I am skeptical myself that there is an ontologically real evil power. But the personification of evil as Satan does reflect the fact that evil is "bigger" than any of us. Evil is not simply the product of free individuals making free bad choices. In many ways, the world is in bondage to evil powers. Minimally, I understand New Testament language about Satan and "principalities and powers" as a symbolic way of saying that this world often seems to be under the control of an evil power. But whatever one thinks about the ontological status of Satan, some people have visions of Satan.

Satan comes to Jesus three times. The visions are nearly identical in Matthew and Luke, though the sequence is different. Following Matthew's sequence, the first two begin with the same conditional phrase, a hypothetical phrase, "*If* you are the Son of God ..." In the vision at his baptism, Jesus had heard a voice declare to him, "You are my Son, the Beloved." In effect, Satan is saying, "Really? Then confirm it."

Satan first comes to him when Jesus had fasted for forty days and "was famished." The devil invites Jesus to "command these stones to become loaves of bread." The test: *if* you are the Son of God, feed yourself, take care of yourself, use your status and power for yourself. Jesus responds by quoting a passage from the Jewish Bible: "One does not live by bread alone, but by every word that comes from the mouth of God" (Deut. 8.3).

In the second vision, the devil takes Jesus to Jerusalem and the highest point of the temple ("the pinnacle") some three hundred feet above the valley below. There he says to Jesus, "*If* you are the Son of God, throw yourself down." Then Satan quotes the Bible: "For it is written, 'God will command his angels concerning you' and 'On their hands they will bear you up, so that you will not dash your foot against a stone.'" What does this invitation mean? To do something spectacular, something foolish, in the confidence that God will come to his rescue? Jesus refuses, seeing such an act as a testing of God and once again responds with a biblical passage: "Do not put the Lord your God to the test" (Deut. 6.16).

In the third vision, the devil takes Jesus to "a very high mountain" where he shows him "all the kingdoms of the world and their splendor." The hypothetical phrase "*If* you are the Son of God" disappears. Now the invitation is to abandon God. The devil says to Jesus, "All these I will give you if you will fall down and worship me." This is the imperial temptation: "all the kingdoms of this world and their splendor" can be yours, and it is presented as satanic. A third time Jesus responds with a passage from the Bible: "Away with you, Satan! For it is written, 'Worship the Lord your God, and serve only him'" (Deut. 6.13). Then, we are told, "The devil left him, and suddenly angels came and waited on him."

Did this happen? What should be the historical verdict on these visions? *That* Jesus spent an extended period of time in the wilderness soon after his baptism is historically highly probable. The two-fold testimony of Mark and Q is significant.

But are we to regard the Q story with its visions as based on historical memory, that is, on actual experiences of Jesus? Or as the creation of the early Christian movement? A majority of scholars think the latter more probable, even though it is in our earliest source.[13] For me, the Q story is in a historical "suspense account"—it is a text about which I suspend historical judgment because of the difficulty of making a probability judgment one way or another.

But even if the Q story is the post-Easter product of Jesus's followers, it indicates that they saw him as one who had these kinds of experiences. And if he were not this kind of person, why would they speak of him this way? We can imagine reasons why they might. For example, perhaps they wanted to present him as a divinely anointed figure by attributing visions to him, just as the stories of Moses and the prophets do. But the most plausible reason is that he was this kind of person.

After the Beginning: Jesus and the Spirit

The synoptic gospels thus inaugurate their story of Jesus's public activity with stories of visions. Throughout the rest of their portrayal of Jesus, there are multiple indicators that Jesus's message and activity were grounded in his experience of the Spirit of God. Stories about him and sayings and teachings attributed to him affirm that for Jesus, God was an experiential reality and that this was central and foundational to all that he became.

Spirit and Teaching

Early in his gospel, Mark reports that Jesus made a striking impression as a teacher very different from the scribes, the "official" teachers. His hearers "were astounded at his teaching, for he taught them as one having *authority*, and not as the scribes" (1.22). Behind the Greek word for "authority" lies the Jewish term for the power of God, *Gevurah*. Jesus spoke from the mouth of the *Gevurah*,[14] that is, from the mouth of the Spirit.

Jesus himself claimed an authority grounded in the Spirit. When representatives of the religious leaders in Jerusalem questioned him about the origin of his authority, Jesus responded with a counterquestion: "I will ask you one question; answer me, and I will tell you by what authority I do these things. Did the baptism of John come from heaven, or was it of human origin?" (Mark 11.29–30). Was the authority of John "from heaven," that is, from God? Though unexpressed, Jesus's own view is clear; implicitly he claimed the same authority as John, one grounded neither in institution nor tradition, but in the sacred, in God.

Repeated features of his teaching suggest an awareness of an authority grounded in God. Many of his sayings begin, "I say to you," in which the authority of the "I" is emphasized. Often these are prefaced in an unprecedented manner with "amen" (in recent English translations, rendered as "truly," "certainly"). As a solemn affirmation of the truth of a statement, "amen" normally came at the end of a statement, *not* before.[15] Sometimes his emphatic "I say unto you" was incorporated into a contrast with the words of the tradition using the pattern, "You have heard that it was said ..., but I say to you ..."[16] Thus the language of Jesus indicates an awareness of a tradition-transcending authority, one from the mouth of the Spirit.

Spirit and Healing

Jesus spoke of the power of the Spirit flowing through him. In the context of casting out a demon, he identified the power as the Spirit of God: "If it is by the Spirit of God that I cast out demons, then the kingdom of God has come to you" (Matt. 12.28; Luke 11.20).[17] On another occasion, after a woman had touched his garment in order to be healed, he perceived "that power had gone forth from him" (Mark 5.30).

Spirit and Presence

People who encountered Jesus sometimes experienced a spiritual presence in him. Rudolf Otto speaks of a *numinous presence* that is frequently reported in or around those who have decisive experiences of the sacred. There is a sense of "otherness" in them that evokes awe, amazement, or astonishment. There may be something authoritative about the way they speak, penetrating about the way they see, or powerful about their presence.[18] The Buddhist tradition speaks of a "Buddha field," a "zone of liberation," around the Buddha and subsequent Buddhist "saints," or *bodhisattvas;* to be in their presence was to experience something extraordinary. In the Christian tradition, the followers of St. Francis in the thirteenth century spoke of a similar presence in him. In the Jewish Bible, perhaps Moses's glowing face when he came down from the sacred mountain (Exod. 34.29–35) belongs in the same category; the Torah's characterization of him suggests that there was something "other," a numinous presence, about him.

Narrative descriptions of Jesus in the gospels suggest that Jesus had this kind of presence. We have already mentioned the report in Mark that people sensed the presence of the Spirit when Jesus taught. Later in his gospel, Mark vividly conveys the impression he made, the "cloud of the numinous" that was present around him: "And they were on the road, going up to Jerusalem, and Jesus was walking ahead of them; and they were amazed, and those who followed were filled with awe" (10.32).[19]

In what is commonly called the story of Jesus's "transfiguration," we are told that the inner core of his disciples experienced the presence of the *numinous* in him in a glorified form (Mark 9:2–4; Matt. 17:1–8; Luke 9:28–36; Matthew calls the experience a vision). Though almost certainly a purely metaphorical narrative and not memory, the story is nevertheless important and illuminating. On "a high mountain" three of Jesus's disciples saw him "transfigured before them, and his clothes became dazzling white." They saw Jesus's body and clothing suffused with light, filled with the radiant presence of God, the glory of God. Like Moses in the book of Exodus, Jesus momentarily "glowed" with the radiance of the Spirit. The story continues: "And there appeared to them Elijah with Moses; and they were talking with Jesus." Elijah and Moses were two of the great figures of the Jewish Bible who knew God.[20] Whether this happened is not decisive for its meaning. Even as a post-Easter metaphorical narrative, it associates Jesus with the two great men of Spirit of Israel's history.

That there was something "other" about Jesus was recognized even by those who did not think it came from God. Mark 3 contains a striking juxtaposition of negative perceptions of Jesus by his family and opponents. When his family heard that crowds were gathering around Jesus because of what he was doing, "they went out to restrain him, for they said, '*He has gone out of his mind*'" (3.21). Some English translations (including the widely used NRSV) obscure the meaning of the Greek text by translating the second "they" as "people," thus attributing the perception that Jesus was "out of his mind" to "people" and not to his family. But the Greek text has the word "they" (not "people") and the antecedent is clearly "his family." The verse is startling even to many people who are familiar with the gospels: the family of Jesus thought he was insane, crazed.

The next verse reports the perception of opponents, namely, scribes from Jerusalem. About Jesus, they said, "He has Beelzebul, and by the ruler of the demons he casts out demons."[21] Jesus is charged with being possessed by the devil. The scribes do not deny that he is filled with spiritual power and that he can cast out demons—but they attribute it to the "ruler of the demons." Family and opponents respond to the same phenomenon, Jesus's activity and growing popularity. But his family sees him as insane and his opponents as possessed by an evil spirit. But they both agree that Jesus's presence was other than "normal."[22]

Spirit and Contemplative Prayer

The gospels report that Jesus often withdrew into solitude for extended periods of prayer, just as stories about Moses and Elijah do. Mark reports: "In the morning, while it was still very dark, he got up and went out to a deserted place, and there he prayed" (1.35); "After saying farewell to them, he went up on the mountain to pray" (6.46). Luke reports that Jesus on occasion prayed all night (6.12).[23]

Long hours of prayer point to contemplative prayer, mentioned briefly earlier in this chapter. A kind of prayer characteristic of mystics, it is quite different from the most familiar kind of prayer (and the only kind that many Christians are aware of), which is verbal prayer. In verbal prayer, as the phrase suggests, God is addressed with words, whether out loud in public prayer or internally in private prayer. Verbal prayer is typically relatively brief, ordinarily no longer than a few minutes. As a Jew, Jesus practiced this kind of prayer when he said morning and evening prayers, synagogue prayers, prayers of thanksgiving, praise, and petition, and so forth.

Contemplative prayer is quite different. It involves lengthy periods of internal silence. Ordinary consciousness is stilled, one sits quietly in the presence of God, and its deepest levels can involve communion or union with God. This form of prayer was part of the Jewish tradition. As noted earlier, it was practiced by Jewish charismatics contemporary with Jesus. It is central to Jewish mysticism, which stretches back beyond the medieval Kabbalah to the *merkabah* ("throne") mysticism of Jesus's time and before.[24] For *merkabah* mystics, contemplative prayer was the vehicle for ascending through the heavens to a vision of the throne of God—that is, to an experience of God.

Spirit and Intimacy with God

That Jesus experienced God intimately is suggested by his use of the word *abba* to address God in prayer. *Abba* is an Aramaic word used by children to address their father. Used by young children on the babbling edge of speech, it is much like the English "papa" or "dah-dah." But it is not simply the language of children; it was also used by *adult* children to address their father. The word is relational, familial, intimate.

In Mark's gospel, Jesus addresses God as *abba* in his prayer on the night before his death: "*Abba*, Father, for you all things are possible; remove this cup from me; yet, not what I want, but what you want" (14.36). Though this is the only appearance of the word in the gospels, we need to remember that Mark was written in Greek, and so the presence of Aramaic *abba* indicates its importance. Many scholars also think that *abba* also lies behind the Greek word for "father" at the beginning of the Lord's Prayer in Luke. Matthew's version of the prayer has the more formal and familiar "Our Father in heaven," but Luke has simply "Father." Paul provides further evidence. Though he (like the gospel writers) wrote in Greek for Greek-speaking communities, he includes the word *abba* twice as language commonly used to address God by followers of Jesus (Rom. 8.15; Gal. 4.6). A strong scholarly consensus affirms that the use of *abba* goes back to Jesus himself.

In scholarship of the last half century, too much and too little has been made of *abba*. Too much: it has sometimes been claimed that the usage is unique to Jesus and therefore indicates a unique consciousness of God.[25] But, though calling God *abba* was unusual within Judaism, it was not unheard of. Particularly and strikingly, *abba* appears in stories about the Jewish charismatics whom we mentioned earlier.[26] Too little: because *abba* is known to have been used by others within Judaism, its significance for Jesus has sometimes been dismissed. But the most plausible explanation of their and Jesus's departure from conventional ways of addressing God is the experience of God as an intimate reality.

Beyond the use of *abba,* the more formal but still intimate term "father" is used for God very frequently in the gospels. Jesus speaks of God as father three times in Mark, four times in Q, four times in material found only in Luke, thirty-one times in material found only in Matthew, and over a hundred times in John.[27] On the one hand, the distribution of data indicates that the developing tradition had a strong tendency to add the term "father." On the other hand, the frequency is still remarkable. In the whole of the Jewish Bible, God is called "father" fewer than twenty times. God is much more commonly called "king" and "Lord." The point is not that the Jewish Bible sees God as remote rather than intimate or as harsh rather than loving. The notion that it does is a widespread but mistaken Christian stereotype. The point, rather, is what accounts for this sudden surge of "father" language for God in the gospels? The most plausible explanation is that the generative impulse for such language goes back to Jesus—to his experience of God as an intimate presence.[28]

Enlightened Teacher and Prophet

In addition to these stories and sayings that indicate that Jesus experienced the sacred, there are two more general features of the synoptic portrait of Jesus that point to him as one who had experienced God: his teaching of an enlightenment type of wisdom and the perception of him as a prophet.

Teacher of an Enlightened Wisdom

Experiences of the sacred generate a different way of seeing. They are experiences of illumination. As we shall see in greater detail later in this book, the wisdom teaching of Jesus reflects a transformed way of seeing very different from conventional ways of seeing. His teaching is full of images of light and darkness, blindness and seeing. The most common forms of his teaching—parables and provocative short sayings—invite a different way of seeing. Ordinary and conventional ways of seeing are a kind of blindness. He taught a way, a path, the narrow way, that led beyond the broad way of convention. In this, he was like the Buddha, who taught an enlightened wisdom that flowed out of his experience of enlightenment. Jesus saw differently—and the most persuasive explanation of why he saw differently is that he had seen differently.

Jesus as Prophet

Jesus was perceived by others to be a prophet and he spoke of himself as one. When he asked his followers, "Who do people say that I am?" Mark tells us that they responded, "John the Baptist; and others Elijah; and still others, one of the prophets" (8.27–28; see also 6.15). Moreover, Jesus referred to himself as a prophet. In the context of his hostile reception in Nazareth where he had grown up, he said, "Prophets are not without honor, except in their hometown" (Mark 6.4; see also Luke 4.24). On his final journey to Jerusalem, Jesus said, "It is impossible for a prophet to be killed outside of Jerusalem" (Luke 13.33). In the estimation of others and in his own consciousness, he was like the prophets of the Jewish Bible. As with them, his calling and passion as a prophet came out of his experience of God.

JESUS AS A JEWISH MYSTIC

In a book that I wrote twenty years ago, my shorthand phrase for Jesus as one who experienced the sacred was "Spirit person." I considered using the term "mystic," but decided not to because of the term's ambiguity in contemporary American usage. For many, "mystic," "mystical," and "mysticism" are at best vague and often have negative connotations, suggesting fuzzy thinking or something that need not be taken seriously. And even when the terms are understood to refer to experiences of the sacred, they often suggest an otherworldly orientation that has little to do with the dailiness of life. Some of the most influential theologians of the twentieth century thought of mystics and mysticism very negatively.[29] Overcoming the negative connotations of "mystic" and "mysticism "would be difficult, I thought. But since then, I have begun to speak of Jesus as a Jewish mystic rather than a Jewish Spirit person. I mean the same thing.

Much depends on how one defines mystics and mysticism. There are narrow and broad definitions. When I speak of Jesus as a Jewish mystic, I am using a broad and traditional definition: mysticism refers to the "experiential knowledge of God." The Latin phrase for this, which I cite to indicate that it is traditional, is *cognitio Dei experimentalis*.[30] A mystic knows God. To expand this broad and basic definition, William James defines mystical experience as a nonordinary state of consciousness marked above all by a sense of *union* and *illumination*, of reconnection and seeing anew.[31]

What is meant by a sense of union, of reconnection, is best understood by contrasting it to our ordinary consciousness. Ordinary consciousness is marked by a sense of separation, a distinction between the self and the rest of reality, commonly called the self-world distinction. This awareness emerges early in our lives in the birth of self-awareness, the sense of being a separate self. In this ordinary everyday consciousness, we experience ourselves as "in here" and the world as "out there." It is the world of the subject-object distinction, so common that it is built into our grammar: I (subject) see you (object). It is the world of the boundaried self, the separate self. It can be a world of deep alienation (as in the title of Sylvia Plath's book of poetry *The Bell Jar*) or a world of considerable contentment and pleasure. In either case, ordinary consciousness involves this sense of separation.

In mystical experience, this sense of separation is replaced by a sense of connection with "what is." The experience might be one of encounter, as in visions, or of communion or union, as in "eyes open" and "eyes closed" mystical experiences. In these experiences, the boundaries of the self momentarily grow soft or disappear. What we might call the "dome of the ego," that sense we have of living inside an enclosure, falls away. The dome becomes permeable and porous or may even vanish completely. Rather than experiencing separation, we experience connection. A sense of particularity (that I am a particular self) may remain in the midst of a sense of connection (experiences of "communion"), or a sense of particularity may disappear completely (experiences of "union"). But whether or not a sense of particularity remains, these are *unitive* experiences. Mystical experiences involve a sense of reconnection to what is. This is what happened to Jesus as well as to the other central figures of his tradition.

The second defining characteristic of mystical experiences according to James is that they involve *illumination,* a radically new way of seeing. Images of enlightenment—of blindness and seeing, light and darkness—abound in texts that reflect mystical experience. Job's exclamation, "I had heard of you by the hearing of the ear, but now my eye sees you" (42.5), is a classic example, as is the line from the familiar hymn "Amazing Grace": "Once I was blind, but now I see" (based on John 9.25). The consequence of Paul's mystical experience on the Damascus road was that "something like scales fell from his eyes" (Acts 9.18). He now *saw*.

To use another of James's terms, these experiences are *noetic*. Those who have them experience them as a *knowing* (which is what *noetic* means).[32] Though commonly marked by wonder, amazement, joy, and bliss, they are experienced not simply as an emotional state, but as a knowing: one knows something one didn't know before. What is known is not a new bit of information, a new item of knowledge, but "the Real," the sacred, another level of reality, or, to use the most common Western word for what is known, God.

This understanding of mystical experience is the basis for my definition of mystics. Mystics are people who have vivid and typically frequent experiences of the sacred and whose lives are decisively changed as result. Not everybody who has such experiences is a mystic. Some do not integrate the experiences into their lives, whether because of their infrequency or for some other reason. But all mystics have such experiences.

Mystics have, to use the broad traditional definition, an "experiential knowledge of God." Mystics also know something more; namely, they know the immediacy of access to God. Not immediacy in the sense of "ease," as if access to God is easy, but that God is accessible to experience apart from mediators, that is, apart from institution and tradition. Mystics stand in an unbrokered relationship with God. They do not intrinsically become anti-institution or antitradition— but they know that no institution or tradition has a monopoly on access to the sacred. For this reason, mystics have often been distrusted and sometimes persecuted by the official representatives of the religious traditions in which they have lived.

Though some mystics have led cloistered lives with little direct connection to the world, there is nothing intrinsically "otherworldly" about mysticism. Many mystics have become more deeply involved in the life of the world because of their mystical experiences. The most famous activists and reformers in the history of Christianity (and in other religions) have had mystical experiences. The experience of the sacred became the basis of their lives, the ground of their conviction, the source of their insight and courage.

Mystical experience not only changes the way mystics see. It also empowers, for mystics have experienced a reality, a ground, greater than themselves and the world. Empowerment begets courage and often leads to passionate protest against the way things are and advocacy of another vision of how things can be.[33] For these mystics, the world has a positive value; it is the good creation of God, and not simply to be escaped. Rather, it is filled with the glory of God. It is where we live—but it needs to be changed.

It is in this sense of the word "mystic" that I see Jesus as a Jewish mystic. What the gospels report about him fits this profile very well. He not only experienced God, but it was the ground of his vocation, activity, and teaching. He spoke and taught from the Spirit, he healed from the Spirit, and he became a passionate advocate of God's passion for justice. Jesus as a Jewish mystic also stood in the tradition of the Jewish Bible with its passion for justice. The God whom he experienced was not a "generic" sacred, but the God of Israel, the God of the law and the prophets.

Jesus as a Spirit-filled Jewish mystic standing in the tradition of the Jewish prophets is perfectly crystallized in the inaugural scene of Jesus's public activity in Luke's gospel. Inaugural scenes in the gospels are important—each gospel writer uses the opening scene of Jesus's public activity to state what he sees Jesus and his mission to be most centrally about. Jesus's first words portray him as in touch with God: "The Spirit of the Lord is upon me, because the Lord has anointed me ..." The rest of the passage emphatically speaks of a prophetic vocation and task: "... to preach good news to the poor. The Spirit of the Lord has sent me to proclaim release to the captives and recovery of sight to the blind, to let the oppressed go free, to proclaim the year of the Lord's favor" (4.18–19). The language comes from the book of Isaiah (61.1–2; 58.6), thus locating Jesus in the prophetic stream of the Jewish Bible.

Although Luke's inaugural scene is almost certainly his creation and construction and not a memory of Jesus's first public appearance, it succinctly summarizes what we find in the synoptic gospels.[34] From Jesus's vision at his baptism and his visions in the wilderness and continuing onward through his public activity, his life and mission were marked by a deep experiential relationship with the Spirit of God, with the sacred.

CONCLUDING COMMENTS

Jesus as a Jewish mystic—as one anointed by the Spirit, filled with the Spirit—is the germ, the generative impulse, for familiar Christian language about him. It is but a short step from "the Spirit of the Lord has anointed me" to speaking of Jesus as the "Messiah." "Messiah" (Hebrew *mashiah*, Greek *christos*, English "Christ") means "the one anointed by God." So also the Christian affirmation that Jesus is the "Son of God" has its embryo in Jesus's experience as a Jewish mystic, as seen in his calling God *abba*. *Abba* is a parental metaphor whose male correlate is "son"; if God is *abba*, Jesus is "son." Of course, it would not have been "Son of God" in the later Christian theological and ontological sense, or the "only begotten Son" who is "of one substance with God," the second person of the Trinity, who combined two natures in one person.[35] Such language is post-Easter. But the germ of christological language lies in the pre-Easter Jesus as a Jewish mystic.

I return to the question of Jesus and God with which this chapter began. Was Jesus—the pre-Easter Jesus—God? No. Did he experience God? Was he a Spirit-filled Jewish mystic who stood in the tradition of Moses and the prophets? Yes. And so we turn now to the public activity of Jesus, a Jewish mystic.

SIX

The Big Picture

The Synoptic Profile of Jesus

Jesus began his public activity soon after the visions reported at his baptism and in the wilderness. Mark tells us it was "after John had been arrested," which might be simply be a chronological marker but is more likely a causal indicator. With his mentor imprisoned, Jesus "came to Galilee, proclaiming the good news of the kingdom of God" (Mark 1.14–15).

A question of language: what term shall we use for Jesus's public activity? We need one that encompasses his message, deeds, and purpose. Common phrases such as "the ministry of Jesus" and "the message of Jesus" are too narrow. "Ministry" suggests what a pastor or priest does. "Message" suggests that Jesus was primarily a teacher and/or preacher. Of course, he was that, but to construe his primary activity as verbal is too narrow. Even "mission" often has a narrowly religious connotation, as when we speak of missionaries who seek to convert individuals from one religion to another. "Public activity"— the phrase I have used thus far—also has shortcomings; it is very general and too bland.

But if "mission" is understood more broadly, it works quite well. *The Oxford English Dictionary* includes among its definitions of the word "a sending or being sent to perform some function or service" and this "for the production of a temporal effect." When "for the production of a temporal effect" is included, mission intrinsically has within it a purpose or aim. Thus mission is activity with a purpose. Mission involves a concentrated commitment, a dedicated devotion, purposeful activity. Mission and vocation are thus quite similar, for a vocation involves calling, activity, and purpose.

In this sense, we might speak of the mission or vocation of Moses or Jeremiah or St. Francis or Martin Luther King or Gandhi or Dorothy Day. For all of these, mission and vocation were religious, even as they were more than what is often meant by "religious." In what follows, I refer to the public time of Jesus's life as his mission, and, for the sake of variety of language, occasionally as his public activity or vocation, always understanding these terms as including his message, deeds, and purpose as a Spirit-filled Jewish mystic.

In this chapter, I describe the "big picture" of Jesus as found in the synoptic gospels. "Big picture" may be an inelegant phrase; by it, I mean "the whole" of their story of Jesus and his mission, a "profile." I begin with it for more than one reason. It may not be familiar to some readers. Moreover, it is important to see the whole before we focus on its parts, as we shall do in subsequent chapters. And some readers who know the gospels quite well may not be aware of how much the synoptic profile of Jesus differs from the profile in John's gospel. Often the synoptic gospels and Jesus are seen through a Johannine lens.

I use the synoptic gospels to generate the "big picture" because they are based on our earliest sources, Q and Mark. Though Matthew, Mark, and Luke differ from one another in significant ways, their portraits of Jesus share a common pattern and features. I do not presume that they are primarily memory, as if the purpose of Mark, Matthew, and Luke was simply to report "what happened." As post-Easter documents written in the last third of the first century, they contain memory even as they reflect and integrate several decades of early Christian experience and thought.

Moreover, it is clear that their presentation of Jesus's mission is not chronological but topical. For example, the second and third chapters of Mark are a collection of conflict stories, but there is no reason to think that these conflicts happened in sequence, one right after another. As another example, the fourth chapter of Mark is a collection of parables, but there is no reason to think that Jesus hadn't told a parable before then, or to think that he told this collection of parables one after another in this sequence. Only their most basic framework is chronologically historical: Jesus's mission began in Galilee and ended in Jerusalem.

Jesus's public activity was brief. In the synoptics, everything can fit into one year. It begins in Galilee and ends with his execution at the next Passover. John's gospel suggests a longer period of time, but only three or four years at the most. Given Jesus's subsequent importance, the brevity of his public life is remarkable. The central figures of other religions had much longer periods of public activity. According to Jewish tradition, Moses's mission as the liberator and lawgiver of Israel lasted forty years. The Buddha taught for fifty years after his enlightenment experience, and Muhammad carried out his mission for a quarter of a century after he began receiving revelations from Allah. In comparison, the mission of Jesus is like a meteor flashing through the night sky.

And so we turn to the way the synoptic gospels present "the whole," their profile of Jesus. It is the earliest way of telling Jesus's story, and it has a distinctive pattern as well as central features.

THE THREEFOLD PATTERN OF THE SYNOPTIC PORTRAIT

I begin with the synoptics' pattern, their narrative framework. They present the story of Jesus in three major sections. The first is an extended period of activity in Galilee. The third is Jesus's final week in Jerusalem. Separating and connecting the first and third parts is the story of Jesus's journey from Galilee to Jerusalem.

I note in passing that this pattern is very different from the one in John's gospel, where Jesus journeys back and forth between Galilee and Jerusalem several times, with his activity more or less divided between Galilee in the north and Judea in the south. In this respect, John *may* be more historical. It is not only possible but perhaps likely that Jesus went to Jerusalem more than once during the period of his public activity. But in the synoptics, most of Jesus's activity is concentrated in Galilee, climaxing with a single journey to Jerusalem and his last week.

And so we turn to the synoptic pattern of Galilee, journey, and Jerusalem. Because Mark provides the narrative framework for both Matthew and Luke, I describe how Mark tells the story as a whole, with occasional comments about what Matthew and Luke add to it.

Galilee

After Jesus's inaugural visions, the Galilean period of his mission begins. In a sentence, Mark (followed by Matthew and Luke) presents Jesus proclaiming the kingdom of God as a healer, exorcist, teacher, and prophet. Mark's portrait of Jesus's time in Galilee includes:

- The message of the coming of the "kingdom of God," Mark's advance summary of Jesus's message (1.15). There is virtual unanimity among scholars that this was central to Jesus's mission and message.

- Healings and exorcisms. These comprise the largest share of the Galilean narrative. There are many stories of specific healings and exorcisms, and several summary statements that Jesus attracted crowds because of his growing reputation as a healer.

- Teaching. Jesus teaches in a variety of settings: in synagogues, by the Sea of Galilee, in the town of Capernaum (which seems to have been his "headquarters"). He teaches with parables and short memorable sayings. His teaching (and his mission as whole) was directed primarily to the peasant class.

- Sea and bread miracles. In Mark, Jesus twice stills a storm on the Sea of Galilee and twice feeds a multitude with a few loaves of bread.

- Calling and sending disciples. Jesus extends his own activity by calling twelve to be disciples and sends them out on a mission of proclamation and healing.

- Conflict. Three chapters (2, 3, and 7) are filled with stories of Jesus in verbal conflict with critics about forgiveness, meals, fasting, the sabbath, purity, and the source of his power.

Matthew and Luke augment Mark's narrative of the Galilean period by adding significant amounts of Jesus's teaching, most of it from Q. For example, Matthew adds the three-chapter-long Sermon on the Mount (Matt. 5–7) at the very beginning of Jesus's mission. Luke adds a shorter collection, often called the Sermon on the Plain, that includes some of the same material. Both also add much more teaching. Thus they greatly expand the picture of Jesus as teacher, even as they follow Mark's narrative framework.

The climax of the Galilean period is Peter's affirmation, "You are the Messiah," that is, "You are the Christ" (Mark 8.29). As noted in Chapter 2, Jesus's christological status is not part of his own message in Mark or the synoptics. Peter's affirmation occurs in private—only Jesus and the disciples are present. Now the story turns toward Jerusalem.

Journey to Jerusalem

Immediately after Peter's affirmation, Mark introduces the theme of Jesus's journey to Jerusalem with the first of the three anticipations of Jesus's execution and resurrection that structure this section (8.31; 9.31; 10.33–34). The last one is the most detailed:

> See, we are going up to Jerusalem, and the Son of Man [a common way that Jesus refers to himself in the synoptics] will be handed over to the chief priests and the scribes, and they will condemn him to death; then they will hand him over to the Gentiles; they will mock him, and spit upon him, and flog him, and kill him; and after three days he will rise again.

Going to Jerusalem is about confrontation with the temple authorities ("the chief priests and scribes") and imperial authority ("the Gentiles"), followed by crucifixion and resurrection. Though Mark includes one exorcism and one healing in this part of his gospel, it is dominated by teaching, whose subject matter is primarily about discipleship, which means following Jesus on this journey. And, as noted in Chapter 3, the story of Jesus's journey is framed at the beginning and end by stories of blind men being given their sight. To have one's eyes opened is to see the meaning of this journey.

Mark's story of the journey is not quite three chapters long. Matthew makes some minor changes and expands it slightly by adding a few parables. But Luke greatly expands it to about ten chapters (9.51–19.27). He introduces his journey story with the solemn words, "Jesus set his face to go to Jerusalem," or, as in the King James translation, "He steadfastly set his face to go to Jerusalem." Luke's additional material is primarily teaching, including some of Jesus's most famous parables. Set in the context of the journey section, they are teachings "on the way."

Jerusalem

The third part of the synoptic pattern brings Jesus to Jerusalem at the season of Passover, the annual festival that drew the greatest number of Jewish pilgrims to the city to remember and celebrate ancient Israel's liberation from Egypt at the time of the exodus. The story of Jesus's last week in Jerusalem consumes almost 40 percent of Mark's gospel. It is dominated by conflict, teaching, and of course Jesus's arrest, trial, execution, and resurrection. No healings or exorcisms occur. This week will be treated in greater detail later. For now, I note the following components of this part:

- Prophetic acts. The week begins with two provocative prophetic actions. Jesus enters the city riding on a colt that symbolizes a kingdom of peace rather than a kingdom based on violence and power. The next day, Jesus performs a prophetic act in the temple and indicts it as "a den of robbers." As a result, the temple authorities resolve to find a way to kill him.

- Conflict with authorities. The week continues with a series of verbal conflicts between Jesus and the temple authorities. They seek to discredit him with the crowd or to trap him into making an incriminating statement so they can arrest him.

- Passover meal. Jesus shares a final meal with his followers, after which he is betrayed and arrested.

- Crucifixion. His execution was the result of collaboration between the temple authorities and Roman imperial authority. Crucifixion was an imperial form of execution that made a public statement: "This is what happens to those who defy us." Matthew and Luke follow Mark's story quite closely with a few additions. Only Luke reports the charges brought against Jesus (23.1–2) and that he was also taken before Herod Antipas (23.6–12). Only Matthew includes the scene of Pilate washing his hands of the blood of Jesus and "the people as a whole" shouting out, "His blood be on us and our children" (27.25). Over the centuries, this brief scene has been a major source of Christian anti-Jewish attitudes with horrific consequences for Jewish people.[1]

- Resurrection. "On the third day" (actually, less than forty-eight hours after Jesus's death), Jesus's tomb is found empty (Mark). Matthew and Luke also have the story of the empty tomb, and each adds stories of Jesus appearing to some of his followers.

CENTRAL FEATURES OF THE SYNOPTIC PORTRAIT

On several of the central features of the above pattern of the synoptic portrait of Jesus, I now comment more fully. Some are apparent from the outline above, and others are less obvious. Together they help us to see "the whole."

Not About "Heaven"

I begin with a negative point. Jesus's mission and message were not about "heaven," not about how to attain a blessed afterlife. Though

Jesus, like many of his Jewish contemporaries, affirmed an afterlife, it was not his primary concern. Because many Christians as well as non-Christians tend to see Jesus and Christianity within the framework of what happens after death, it seems important to realize at the outset that this was not what his mission was about. It wasn't about what you must believe or how you must behave in order to attain heaven. Rather, his mission was about the character of God, the way of centering in God, and the kingdom of God, all of which will be developed in subsequent chapters.

Our impression that it was about how to get to heaven is in part the product of centuries of emphasis upon an afterlife within Christianity, both as a sanction against wrong behavior and as hope in the face of death. It is also due to two familiar phrases in the gospels, Matthew's "kingdom of heaven" and John's "eternal life."

But Matthew's "kingdom of heaven" does not mean a kingdom *in* heaven, in another world beyond death. Rather, it is Matthew's substitute for the phrase "kingdom of *God*" in passages that he uses from Mark and Q. Matthew most often changes "kingdom of God" to "kingdom of heaven" not because he's thinking of an afterlife, but because of a common Jewish reverential practice of avoiding using the word "God" as much as possible. And the kingdom of God, the kingdom of heaven, is *for the earth*, as the Lord's Prayer in Matthew affirms. It is about the transformation of life in this world.

So also John's phrase "eternal life" does not mean what we commonly mean by heaven. The Greek phrase translated as "eternal life" or "everlasting life" means "the life of the age to come." And for John, the life of the age to come—eternal life—is already available. As John 17.3 puts it, "This is eternal life: to know God." Note the present tense. The life of the age to come—eternal life—consists of knowing God in the present. This emphasis is characteristic of mystics and thus consistent with seeing Jesus as a Jewish mystic. That this may continue beyond death is not denied, but the emphasis is not on how to enter a blessed place beyond this life.

An Itinerant Mission to the Jewish Peasant Class

Jesus's mission was primarily to the peasant class. The synoptic gospels never report that he went to a city, except for Jerusalem. There is no mention of his taking his mission to Sepphoris or Tiberias, the two largest cities of Galilee, despite their proximity to the areas in which he was active. Rather, his activity was in the villages, towns, and countryside of Galilee, rural areas populated primarily by peasants. From the peasant class himself, he directed his mission and message to peasants, and most of his followers came from among them.

The gospels do report that some wealthy and powerful people were also attracted to Jesus. All mention that Joseph of Arimathea, a member of the Jerusalem elite, was a sympathizer. Luke reports that women of means provided financial support for Jesus and his followers: "Joanna, the wife of Herod's steward Chuza, and Susanna, and many others, who provided for them out of their resources" (8.3). Luke also mentions that a wealthy tax collector named Zacchaeus became a follower (19.1–10). In John's gospel, a member of the ruling class named Nicodemus was attracted to Jesus. Nevertheless, it is clear that Jesus's mission was primarily to peasants, those most exploited by the imperial domination system and its native collaborators.

His mission was marked by itinerancy, by which I mean simply that he went from place to place. He did not settle down in a permanent location and have people come to him, as he might have. In recent scholarship, Jesus's itinerancy has sometimes been understood to signify "homelessness" as a lifestyle that he advocated and embodied. But Jesus doesn't seem to have been "homeless" in the sense of having no place to return to. The gospels sometimes refer to him being "at home" in Capernaum, a fishing town on the Sea of Galilee. The implication is that itinerancy was not about homelessness, but about mission. He sought to reach as many of the peasant class in Galilee as possible.

And Jesus went to the *Jewish* peasant class. Twice Matthew makes explicit what is implicit in Mark and Luke: the mission of the pre-Easter Jesus was to Jews. Matthew reports that Jesus said to his disciples as he sent them out on a mission in the midst of his mission, "Go nowhere among the Gentiles, and enter no town of the Samaritans, but go rather to the lost sheep of the house of Israel" (10.5–6). Matthew also says that Jesus similarly restricted his own mission: "I was sent only to the lost sheep of the house of Israel" (15.24).[2] Though all three synoptic gospels report a few contacts with Gentiles and Luke and John mention contact with Samaritans, it is clear that the historical Jesus saw his mission to be primarily to Jewish peasants living within the traditions of Judaism. Jesus did not intend to start a new religion, but to do something within Judaism. This does not mean that Christianity as a religion open to Gentiles is a mistake. But it does mean that a mission to Gentiles is post-Easter, as the New Testament itself makes clear.

Mighty Deeds: Healings and Exorcisms

A remarkably high percentage of the synoptic story of Jesus's mission in Galilee concerns what are commonly called his "miracles," though the term "miracle" with its modern connotation of supernatural intervention into a world governed by natural laws does not occur.[3] Rather, in the gospels, they are called "mighty deeds" or "deeds of power." Most of them were healings and exorcisms, which are referred to in a large number of individual stories and in summary statements. The gospels consistently distinguish between the two; not all healings were exorcisms, and not all maladies were attributed to evil spirits. So we consider them in sequence.

Healings

The synoptics contain thirteen stories of particular healings. The conditions include fever, leprosy, paralysis, withered hand, bent back, hemorrhage, deafness and dumbness, blindness, dropsy, severed ear, and a sickness near death or paralysis.[4] Given the nature of the gospel narratives, I shall not treat the question of the precise event behind each account, but will simply note the impression the stories create. Even though we are not dealing with "newspaper account" material, we are in touch with how Jesus's very early followers, still in contact with the living oral tradition, saw him.

The stories create a vivid impression of a charismatic healer at work. Sometimes Jesus healed by word. He said to the man with the withered hand, "Stretch out your hand," and the hand was restored (Mark 3.5). Most often touching was also involved. When a leper came to him, Jesus was moved with compassion, touched him, and the leprosy left him (Mark 1.40–42). Sometimes he used physical means in addition to touching, as in the case of a deaf man. Jesus "put his fingers into his ears, and he spat and touched his tongue. Then looking up to heaven, he sighed, and said to him, 'Ephphatha,' that is, 'Be opened.' And immediately his ears were opened, his tongue was released, and he spoke plainly" (Mark 7.32–35).[5] Of special interest here is the Aramaic word *ephphatha*, "Be opened." In context, it clearly refers to the opening of the man's ears, but may also have the connotation of the *heavens* opening up: "Looking up into heaven, he said, 'Be opened.'" Through the opening from heaven, healing power flowed.

Like the Jewish charismatic Hanina ben Dosa, Jesus healed at a distance.[6] A Roman centurion entreated Jesus to heal his servant who was lying paralyzed in the centurion's home some distance away. Seeing the centurion's faith, Jesus said, "Go; let it be done for you according to your faith." The text concludes: "And the servant [at home] was healed in that hour" (Matt. 8.5–13; Luke 7.1–10).

Words attributed to Jesus also refer to his healings in summary form. To messengers sent to him by John the Baptizer, he said, "Go and tell John what you hear and see: the blind receive their sight, the lame walk, lepers are cleansed, the deaf hear, the dead are raised, and the poor have good news brought to them" (Matt. 11.4–5; Luke 7.22, and thus Q). The list of *types* of healings (the blind see, deaf hear, lame walk, and so forth) is largely drawn from Isaiah 35.5–6, which refers to the coming age of God's deliverance. The Q saying concludes with an echo of Isaiah 61.1, which links it to the coming of the Spirit. Thus it is not clear whether the list was meant to be a citation of the categories of Jesus's healings or whether it was a way of saying that the coming age and the outpouring of the Spirit had begun.

To attempt to explain *how* these healings happened is beyond our purpose and probably impossible. They are sometimes seen as "faith healings," made possible because the diseased persons had faith that they would be healed. This understanding makes possible a psychosomatic explanation that stretches but does not break the limits of the modern worldview. But it doesn't work as a comprehensive explanation. Though some stories mention faith, others do not. Indeed, in a few, the faith of the healed person could not be a factor.

Rather, within the thought world of the synoptic stories, Jesus's healings were the result of "power." The Greek word commonly used for Jesus's mighty deeds is *dunamis*, which means "power," most often used in the plural. As mentioned earlier, his healings were "mighty deeds," "deeds of power." *Dunamis*, power, is sometimes used in the singular to refer to one of the central qualities of God, as in "the *power* of God" or "the *power* of the Most High." It can even be used as a name for God: "You will see the Son of man seated at the right hand of the *Power*" (Mark 14.62). The mighty deeds of Jesus were understood by the gospel writers as power from the Power.

In the book of Acts, written by Luke and thus reflecting a synoptic point of view, this power is directly associated with the Spirit of God: "But you will receive *power* when the Holy Spirit has come upon you" (Acts 1.8). Luke also makes the connection in his gospel: "Then Jesus, filled with the *power of the Spirit*, returned to Galilee" (4.14). The mighty deeds of Jesus were seen as the product of the power that flowed through him as a Spirit-filled mystic.

Exorcisms

Jesus's exorcisms were also the result of the power of the Spirit: "If it is by the Spirit of God that I cast out demons, then the kingdom of God has come to you" (Matt. 12.28; Luke 11.20). According to the synoptics, Jesus exorcised evil spirits from many who were possessed. Mark has four stories of exorcisms, sometimes vividly narrated:

- A man "with an unclean spirit" in Capernaum (1.21–28)

- A demoniac living among tombs inhabited by a host of demons named Legion (5.1–20)

- The daughter of a gentile woman (7.24–30)

- A boy convulsed by an unclean spirit that dashed him to the ground and caused him to foam at the mouth and be unable to move (9.14–29)

In addition, summaries mention multiple exorcisms: "He cast out many demons" (Mark 1.34); Jesus "went throughout Galilee, proclaiming the message in their synagogues and casting out demons" (Mark 1.39); "Those who were troubled with unclean spirits were cured" (Luke 6.18).

Even more than extraordinary cures, possession and exorcism are alien to the modern world. Though we may have heard reports of them from faraway places, they are foreign to our experience. Moreover, the notion of "possession" by a spirit from another level of reality does not fit into the modern worldview. Yet possession and exorcism are widely attested. The gospels mention exorcists other than Jesus: Pharisaic exorcists, an unnamed exorcist who expelled demons in Jesus's name even though not a follower of Jesus, and Jesus's own disciples.[7]

Possession and exorcism are also attested in many other cultures. Cross-cultural studies report a number of typical traits. "Possession" occurs when a person falls under the control of an evil spirit or spirits. Such people are inhabited by a presence that they (and others) experience as other than themselves. In addition to having two or more "personalities," they exhibit bizarre and often destructive or self-destructive behavior. Convulsions, sweating, and seizures are common. Unusual strength and uncanny knowledge are sometimes also reported.[8]

Within the framework of the modern worldview, we are inclined to see possession as a prescientific diagnosis of a condition that must have another explanation, perhaps as a psychopathological state that includes among its symptoms the delusion of believing oneself to be possessed. Perhaps a psychopathological explanation is possible, though this is not decisively clear.[9] Social conditions may also be a factor; some data from anthropology and social psychology suggest that conditions of political oppression, social deprivation, and rapid social change (all of which characterized the Jewish homeland in the first century) are correlated with increased frequency of possession.[10]

But whatever the modern explanation might be, and however much psychological or social factors might be involved, we need to recognize that Jesus and his contemporaries (and people in premodern cultures generally) thought that people could be possessed by a spirit or spirits from another plane. Their worldview took for granted the actual existence of such spirits.[11] Perhaps the shared convictions were in part responsible for the phenomenon. In any case, the participants—possessed, exorcist, onlookers—did not simply *think* of these as cases of possession and exorcism, but *experienced* them that way.

Jesus's healings and exorcisms attracted crowds. People flocked to him. "They brought to him all who were sick or possessed with demons. And the whole city was gathered around the door" (Mark 1.32–33). As a healer, "his fame spread,… and great crowds followed him" (Matt. 4.24–25). "People came to him from every quarter" (Mark 1.45). "And he told his disciples to have a boat ready for him because of the crowd, so that they would not crush him; for he had healed many, so that all who had diseases pressed upon him to touch him" (Mark 3.9–10). Indeed, it was his reputation as a healer and exorcist that generated an audience for him as a teacher.

Teaching: Stories and One-Liners

Mark's story of the Galilean period is about evenly divided between Jesus's "deeds of power" and his teaching. Because Matthew and Luke both add large amounts of teaching to Mark, they emphasize Jesus's activity as teacher even more. Indeed, "teacher" is the most common title used for Jesus in the gospels.[12] In this chapter, I treat the *mode* of Jesus's teaching, *how* he taught, the *manner* of his teaching. In subsequent chapters, I will describe *what* he taught, the *content* of his message.

It is helpful to imagine the settings in which Jesus taught. The gospels report several: synagogue gatherings, meals, outdoors in the countryside and beside the Sea of Galilee, village squares or courtyards, and during his final week in Jerusalem in the open-air courts of the temple. With the possible exception of synagogue gatherings, all of these were informal settings, and even village synagogue gatherings had a degree of informality. Interaction and dialogue were common.

In these settings, Jesus taught in a distinctive way. He used primarily storytelling (*parables*) and short memorable sayings (his great "one-liners"). Less colloquially, the latter are often called *aphorisms*. The use of storytelling and memorable one-liners was not unique to Jesus. But it was distinctive and characteristic, and it discloses something about both him and his message.

It is illuminating to contrast these forms of teaching with other forms used by teachers in the time of Jesus. These included "laws" or "rules," usually based on an exposition of Torah, that used the form of "You shall" or "You shall not." But we seldom find this form in Jesus's teaching. So also, though Jesus sometimes referred to the Jewish Bible, he did not use the form of extended commentary on scripture. Neither did he use the most common form of prophetic speech, "Thus says the Lord," or "Hear the word of the Lord." Nor did he use the form of long abstract discourses, except in John's gospel (and most scholars do not think these go back to Jesus). When there are extended blocks of teaching in the synoptic gospels, such as the Sermon on the Mount, they are made up of memorable short sayings that have been collected together.

Thus Jesus's use of parables and aphorisms was deliberate as well as characteristic. And so we turn to how these forms of teaching worked and what they disclose about Jesus's manner of teaching.

Parables: Storytelling

Parables are made-up stories, fictional narratives, and their meaning does not depend upon their factuality. How many there are in the gospels is difficult to discern, for there are disagreements about whether some texts are parables or another form of speech. But most scholars classify thirty to forty texts as parables.[13]

The parables of Jesus range from extended stories with multiple characters and scenes to very short stories. Indeed, the shortest are basically one-liners:

> The kingdom of God is like yeast that a woman took and mixed in with three measures of flour until all of it was leavened. (Matt. 13.33; Luke 13.20–21)

> The kingdom of God is like treasure hidden in a field, which someone found and hid; then in his joy he goes and sells all that he has and buys that field. (Matt. 13.44)

> The kingdom of God is like a merchant in search of fine pearls; on finding one pearl of great value, he went and sold all that he had and bought it. (Matt. 13.45–46)

But even these very short ones are narratives—in them something happens.

The longer parables are more fully developed stories. They include some of the best known of Jesus's teachings, such as the prodigal son, the good Samaritan, workers in the vineyard, the unmerciful servant, the talents, and the wicked tenants.[14]

Parables work by being good stories. They draw the audience into the narrative. They need to be good stories not only to avoid being tedious, but because fanciful or unrealistic details would get in the way of the audience's entering the story. They may describe surprising behavior, and often do, but not behavior that leaves the realm of the credible.

Parables invite the audience to make a judgment. Implicitly, the parables begin or end with, "What do you think?" The question is made explicit at the beginning of a parable in Matthew 21.28.[15] Even the very short parables do this: *how* is the kingdom of God like a woman leavening flour, *how* is it like a merchant in search of fine pearls, *how* is it like a man who finds treasure in a field?

The Greek roots of the word parable are illuminating; they mean "to cast alongside." A parable is a story cast alongside of life for the sake of leading the audience to see something differently. They engage the hearers and are thus intrinsically interactive. As C. H. Dodd, the best-known British New Testament scholar of the twentieth century, put it seventy years ago, they leave "the mind in sufficient doubt about [their] precise application to tease it into active thought."[16]

It is important to realize that Jesus told his parables many times. It is impossible to imagine that an itinerant teacher like Jesus would use good stories like the prodigal son or the good Samaritan only once. This realization has two immediate implications. First, what we have in the gospels are "plot summaries" of stories told many times and probably at varying lengths, depending upon the occasion. The longest parable, the prodigal son, is just over five hundred words in English and takes about four minutes to read aloud. But it is easy to imagine the story being expanded into greater length by adding details about the prodigal son's life in exile, his journey of return, and his homecoming to his father's joy and his older brother's bitterness. So also with the other parables. Even some of the very short ones can be seen as plot summaries of stories that could be elaborated, though some may always have been provocative one-liners. The second implication is that the gospel context of a parable is only one possible context. We need to imagine each parable told in many contexts and not restrict it to the meaning that we discern in its particular gospel context.

Parables are an interactive form of teaching. As already noted, they tease the mind into active thought and engage the listener in the question, "What do you think?" But, additionally, they probably not only led hearers to think privately to themselves about their meaning, but also provoked interaction among the hearers and between the hearers and Jesus. After hearing the parable of the workers in the vineyard, what do you think of the vineyard owner who pays all of his day laborers the same wage at the end of the day, regardless of how long they have worked? Good guy or bad guy? Generous or unjust? It is easy to imagine a spirited discussion.

Or in the parable of the good Samaritan, what do you think of a priest and Levite who pass by a man who has been beaten up and lies half dead on the road from Jerusalem to Jericho? Is it just what you would expect from a priest and Levite because you don't think much of official religious functionaries? Or do you see their ethical dilemma? They were obligated to help, but also obligated to avoid contact with a corpse (the man is specifically described as "half dead") and thus perhaps fulfilling an obligation rather than being heartless. And what do you think of an obligation like that when it gets in the way of being compassionate?

Or in the parable of the prodigal son, what do you think of a son who asks for his inheritance while his father is still alive and then squanders it in a foreign land? What do you think of a father who welcomes home a son like that by treating him so extravagantly? And what do you think of an older brother who resents what has happened? And what is the story about?

We should not imagine Jesus's hearers sitting in reverent silence after Jesus had finished a parable (and perhaps not even during the telling). I do not mean that they would have been rowdy or rude or restive. But the informal settings—a meal, a village square or courtyard, in the open air by the sea—as well as the manner of his teaching meant that interactive conversation and dialogical interchange almost certainly happened. Of course, we should not imagine Jesus telling a story and then saying, "Now I'm going to put you in small groups for ten minutes and then we'll come back together to process what you've come up with." But we do need to imagine interaction around the question, "What do you think?"

The parables of Jesus disclose two characteristics of his teaching. First, they do not depend upon scripture to make their point, even as many or most of them reflect a mind shaped by the Jewish Bible and tradition. But they do not provide commentary on, and thus depend on, an authoritative text. Did Jesus tell nonscriptural stories rather than comment on scripture because he couldn't expect a thorough knowledge of scripture in his primarily peasant audience? Or because he wanted them to use their common sense, their judgment, over against the theology and social vision of the elites? Or because he had a metaphoric mind? More than one, or all of these?[17]

Second, as a way of teaching, the parables are invitational rather than imperatival. Most of them are invitations to see differently rather than stories that say, "Do this." There are a few of the latter, but not many.[18] But most of them invite his hearers to engage major questions such as their perception of the character of their God, the conditions of their lives, and how then to live. They appeal to the imagination, meaning the images by which people live their lives (and not the imagination as fantasy or daydreaming).

Short Sayings: Aphorisms

The other most frequent form of Jesus's teaching consisted of memorable short sayings, commonly called aphorisms. "Aphorism" is an umbrella term that covers all of the short sayings of Jesus, including beatitudes ("Blessed are you who are poor," Luke 6.20), directives ("You cannot serve God and wealth," Matt. 6.24), analogies to nature ("Consider the lilies of the field," (Matt. 6.28), and pronouncements about the way things are ("The sabbath was made for humankind, and not humankind for the sabbath," Mark 2.27). The gospels attribute over a hundred of these to Jesus.

It is illuminating to compare them to their close relative, the proverb. In one way, they are alike. Both are short memorable sayings that suggest how to live. But they are quite different in origin and function. Proverbs commonly express the folk wisdom, the conventional wisdom, of a culture—what everybody knows or should know. They are most often anonymous, the product of generations of experience and reflection. They are distillations of how to live, expressions of the wise way, the way of convention, in contrast to the way of foolishness and folly.

Aphorisms on the other hand express the fresh insight of a particular individual and often function to overturn or subvert conventional wisdom. They are surprising, arresting, and thought-provoking. In subsequent chapters, I will explore their meaning. For now, I simply provide some examples of Jesus's aphorisms, in addition to those mentioned above:

Let the dead bury their own dead. (Matt. 8.22; Luke 9.60)

The eye is the lamp of the body. (Matt. 6.22; Luke 11.34)

Why do you see the speck in your neighbor's eye, but do not notice the log in your own eye? (Matt. 7.3; Luke 6.41)

Can a blind person guide a blind person? Will both not fall into a pit? (Luke 6.39; Matt. 15.14)

No good tree bears bad fruit, nor again does a bad tree produce good fruit; for each tree is known by its own fruit. Figs are not gathered from thorns, nor are grapes gathered from a bramble bush. (Luke 6.43–44; Matt. 7.16–18)

You strain out a gnat but swallow a camel! (Matt. 23.24)

Call no one your father on earth, for you have one Father—the one in heaven. (Matt. 23.9)

You are the salt of the earth; but if salt has lost its taste, how can its saltiness be restored? (Matt. 5.13; Luke 14.34)

No one after lighting a lamp puts it under the bushel basket, but on the lampstand, and it gives light to all in the house. (Matt 5.15; Luke 11.33)

As with the parables, we need to imagine all or most of these spoken many times. An itinerant teacher does not use memorable one-liners like these only once. Thus the literary context in each gospel is not the only context in which they were heard or should be interpreted.

Moreover, we need to imagine their being spoken one at a time or, at the most, a few at a time. It is instructive to read the sayings brought together in Luke's Sermon on the Plain (6.20–49) and Matthew's much longer Sermon on the Mount (5.1–7.27) and to ask whether we can imagine all of these being spoken one right after another in a single oral discourse. Though we can imagine a few of them being spoken in sequence, we cannot imagine Jesus saying all of either Luke's or Matthew's sermon in a single discourse. It is too much for any audience to take in. No gifted teacher would do that. There never was a "Sermon on the Mount" or a "Sermon on the Plain," even though most of the sayings are based on things Jesus did say. Rather, the two sermons are collections of individual sayings spoken many times on different occasions.

How should we imagine Jesus using these short sayings? Did he speak them as one-liners without elaboration and leave them hanging in the air for his hearers to consider? Though this may occasionally have happened, it seems more likely that he would have elaborated on them. They may have functioned as "oral texts" for a longer teaching. The term "gist" is helpful here. We all know what it means to remember the "gist" of a story or a joke. Jesus's short sayings as reported in the gospels are "gist"—crystallizations of things he said many times and then expanded upon.

In function, Jesus's aphorisms are very much like his parables—provocative and invitational forms of speech. They provoke thought, lead people to reconsider their taken-for-granted assumptions, and invite them to see life differently. In the next two chapters, we consider their content—the vision of God and life to which Jesus invited his hearers.

Meals: Eating Together

At the center of Christian worship throughout the centuries stands a meal, variously known as the Eucharist, the Mass, the Lord's Supper, or Communion.[19] As a sacrament of bread and wine presupposing the death and resurrection of Jesus, it is manifestly a post-Easter development. Yet it has its roots in the pre-Easter meal practice of Jesus. Meals—not ritual meals, but the sharing of food and drink in company—were one of the central features of his mission. Many passages refer to meals, some are set in the context of meals, some are teachings about meals, and some refer to conflicts about meals.[20]

I begin by noting that the synoptic portrait of Jesus links meals to both healing and teaching. Meals and healing are connected in the earliest layer of the developing tradition and have multiple independent attestation.[21] I invite another episode of historical imagination, a speculative enterprise, but one that helps us to envision what this might have looked like "on the ground." How might we imagine the connection between meals and healing in Jesus's mission?

One scenario begins by imagining that Jesus heals somebody in a village. What is the likely response, beyond amazement and gratitude? He (and those with him) would be invited to a meal. It is the classic ancient way of expressing gratitude and hospitality. Most likely, the meal would include not only the extended family of the healed person, but other villagers as well—a healing was big news. In a slightly different scenario, Jesus's reputation as a healer meant that when he arrived in a hamlet or village, many were eager to see him and hear him and probably would do so in the hospitality context of a meal. Thus, even without Jesus healing anybody on any particular occasion, a meal would be the result.

The connection to teaching follows directly. At these village meals, or before or after them, people would listen to what Jesus had to say. His activity and reputation as a healer drew an audience. Of course, not all of his teaching was done in the context of meals, but some of it was.

Eating together—sometimes called "commensality" or "table fellowship"—had an additional significance in the world of Jesus. Meals in the mission of Jesus were not simply prompted by his healings and occasions for teaching. Nor were they simply about sustenance, though they were that. To say the obvious, food is the material basis of life, and it is important to realize that meals—real food with real people—were central to Jesus's mission. The Lord's Prayer contains a petition for daily bread, indicating the centrality of food, of material sustenance, in Jesus's vision of the kingdom of God. But more than sustenance was involved. Not less, but more.

There were two reasons why eating together had symbolic significance. First, in the ancient Mediterranean world in general and the Jewish homeland, sharing a meal was a form of social inclusion, and refusing to share a meal was a form of social exclusion. Meals reflected the social boundaries of a group. As a recent study puts it:

> It would be difficult to overestimate the importance of table fellowship for the cultures of the Mediterranean basin in the first century of our era. Mealtimes were laden with meanings that greatly exceeded individuals' consumption of food. Biblical exegetes owe a debt of gratitude to cultural anthropologists who have discerned that eating practices encode far-reaching messages about appropriate patterns of social relations among participants. In the words of conceptual path breaker Mary Douglas, "The message is about different degrees of hierarchy, inclusion and exclusion, boundaries and transactions across the boundaries."[22]

Eating together was "symbolic of friendship, intimacy and social unity." When meals included people beyond the extended family, they almost invariably reflected the social boundaries and stratifications of the society.[23] Elites ate with elites (still true most of the time in modern Western societies). Within the peasant class, we may imagine that meal practice was less rigid. But even there, some people would be excluded. Moreover, offering meal hospitality to a stranger was a significant act.

Meals had a second significance within the Jewish homeland. For at least two groups, the Pharisees and Essenes, meal practice had become a symbol of what God wanted Israel to be. Both practiced "closed commensality" grounded in an understanding of God's command in Leviticus 19.2: "You shall be holy, for I the LORD your God am holy." They understood holiness to mean purity. The meals of the Essenes were restricted to those who had completed a rigorous novitiate and required purification beforehand. Pharisaic meal practice was restricted to those who kept the same laws of purity that applied to priests while officiating in the temple. This higher degree of purity created sharp social boundaries around Pharisaic commensality.[24] For both groups, meal practice embodied in microcosm a macrocosmic vision of what an Israel faithful to God looked like.

This realization is essential for understanding the strong criticism that Jesus's meal practice drew. Several times the gospels report the criticism, consistently the same: "Why does he eat and drink with tax collectors and sinners?" (Mark 2.16); "He has gone in to be the guest of one who is a sinner" (Luke 19.7); "This fellow welcomes sinners and eats with them" (Luke 15.2); "Look, a glutton and a drunkard, a friend of tax collectors and sinners!" (Matt. 11.19; Luke 7.34).[25]

Within a Christian perspective that views *all* people as sinners, the accusation that Jesus eats with "sinners" brands the critics as hypocrites who exempt themselves from the category. But the term had not yet been theologized and universalized. Rather, like the term "tax collectors," "sinners" referred to a group of people— namely, to people who were insufficiently observant from the vantage point of those making the accusation. What sinners and tax collectors had in common was that they were marginalized groups, with the "worst" of them seen as outcasts and untouchables. The accusation is that Jesus's meal practice included people whose presence discredited him. We will return to this issue in a later chapter. For now, the point is that the meal practice of Jesus was sufficiently central and public that it became a source of controversy and conflict.

Conflict: Controversy and Crucifixion

The mission of Jesus provoked conflict. This is one of the central features of the gospels. To say the obvious, he was executed by the authorities. But conflicts began long before his final fatal week in Jerusalem. They occur throughout the whole of his public activity, in Galilee and Jerusalem. Immediately after Mark describes the beginning of Jesus's mission, his second and third chapters report a series of criticisms from opponents. Chapter 7, still in the Galilean period, reports another set of conflicts. In Galilee, the opponents are scribes (a literate class attached to the elites) and/or Pharisees (a renewal group who emphasized purity).

The conflicts concerned frequent practices of Jesus, such as healing on the sabbath, eating with disreputable people, and inadequately observing regular fasts and the laws of purity. Sometimes conflict was generated by particular boldly provocative actions, as in his entry into Jerusalem followed by his disruption of the temple at the beginning of the last week of his life.

There, in Jerusalem, the conflict became deadly. The opponents are no longer Pharisees, but are the "chief priests, elders, and scribes."[26] In this context, the scribes were learned employees (retainers) of the chief priests and elders. The chief priests (including the high priest) were the heads of aristocratic priestly families, and the elders were the heads of other wealthy and powerful families. Centered in the temple, they were the native elites who collaborated with and administered Roman imperial rule.

A persuasive portrait of Jesus must account for the conflicts his mission generated. His opponents were not simply bad people who couldn't stand a nice guy. Most were sincere and devout, living in accord with their vision of God's will for Israel. Even the authorities responsible for his arrest and execution can be seen as doing the best they could, given their difficult responsibility of keeping order and placating Rome. When we see Jesus's opponents as simply bad or evil people, we not only malign them, but risk missing the passionate edginess of Jesus.

Something Greater Than Solomon

A final point in this treatment of central features of the synoptic profile is that Jesus spoke of what he was doing as of crucial importance. The sayings are early, found in Q material. At least some, and perhaps all, go back to Jesus.

The first refers to the prophetic and wisdom tradition of Israel. Jesus affirmed that something greater than Jonah, the most successful of Israel's prophets, and something greater than King Solomon, fabled for his wisdom, was happening:

> The people of Nineveh ... repented at the proclamation of
> Jonah, and see, something greater than Jonah is here!... The
> queen of the South ... came from the ends of the earth to listen
> to the wisdom of Solomon, and see, something greater than
> Solomon is here! (Matt. 12.41–42; Luke 11.31–32)

Another early saying also refers to the past and contrasts it to the
present time:

> Blessed are the eyes that see what you see! For I tell you that
> many prophets and kings desired to see what you see, but did
> not see it, and to hear what you hear, but did not hear it. (Luke
> 10.23–24; Matt. 13.16–17)

And yet another uses language from Isaiah, where the prophet
speaks of a time when God will deliver Israel from exile and oppression (35.5–6). To messengers sent to Jesus from the imprisoned John
the Baptizer to ask if Jesus is "the one who is to come," Jesus responds:

> Go and tell John what you hear and see: the blind receive their
> sight, the lame walk, the lepers are cleansed, the deaf hear, the
> dead are raised, and the poor have good news brought to them.
> (Matt. 11.4–5; Luke 7.22)

The claim that Jesus was doing something of great significance is
"old hat" to Christians—by which I mean that it's so familiar so as to
be unremarkable. Of course, what he was doing was important: this
was the savior of the world, the Word become flesh, the incarnation
of God's only son, the sacrifice for sin that makes forgiveness possible, the beginning of Christianity, the "one true religion." But as we
have seen, his mission and message were not about himself or dying
for the sins of the world or the creation of a new religion. These notions are all post-Easter developments. This does not mean that they
are wrong—but it does mean that the sense of crucial importance
that sounds throughout these sayings from the synoptic gospels must

be about something other than Jesus's identity as the Son of God and the saving purpose of his death.

A FIVE-STROKE PROFILE AND A SUMMARY

I conclude this chapter on seeing the "big picture" of Jesus's mission with two compact and complementary summaries. The first is a five-stroke sketch, or profile, of Jesus. The profile arises out of the historical study of the gospel texts, even as it also provides a framework for ordering or organizing the traditions in the gospels that we have good reasons to think of as historical. To some extent, the sketch summarizes what we have already seen, but it also provides a framework for the fuller picture of Jesus's mission that will be developed in subsequent chapters. The pre-Easter Jesus was:

1. *A Jewish mystic.* As explained in Chapter 5, God was an experiential reality for Jesus, and his experience of the sacred is the most persuasive explanation of what else he became.

2. *A healer and exorcist.* His activity must have been remarkable; more healing and exorcism stories are told about him than about any other figure in the Jewish tradition.

3. *A wisdom teacher.* Jesus used the classic forms of wisdom (parables and aphorisms) and taught the classic subject matter of wisdom: what God is like, what life is like, and "the way."

4. *A prophet.* Like the canonical Jewish prophets, he was a radical critic of the domination system in the name of God and God's passion for justice. Perhaps more than anything else, this led to his execution.

5. *A movement initiator.* Even though Jesus's mission was brief, a movement came into existence around him during his lifetime. Small and embryonic, including both followers and sympathizers, it embodied his vision of the character and passion of God.

My second summary is a brief narrative. The occasion was a television interview before which I was told that I would have a minute and fifteen seconds to answer the question, "What was Jesus like?" This is what I said:

> Jesus was from the peasant class. Clearly, he was brilliant. His use of language was remarkable and poetic, filled with images and stories. He had a metaphoric mind. He was not an ascetic, but world-affirming, with a zest for life. There was a sociopolitical passion to him—like a Gandhi or a Martin Luther King, he challenged the domination system of his day. He was a religious ecstatic, a Jewish mystic, for whom God was an experiential reality. As such, Jesus was also a healer. And there seems to have been a spiritual presence around him, like that reported of St. Francis or the present Dalai Lama. And as a figure of history, Jesus was an ambiguous figure—you could experience him and conclude that he was insane, as his family did, or that he was simply eccentric or that he was a dangerous threat—or you could conclude that he was filled with the Spirit of God.[27]

We turn now to a more detailed exploration of the mission and message of Jesus.

SEVEN

God

God's Character and Passion

God and God's kingdom were at the center of Jesus's life and mission. In this chapter, I treat his perception of God. What did he think God was like—what was God's *character*? And what was God's *passion*—what was God's will, yearning, desire? These two themes, the character and passion of God, run throughout Jesus's message as a teacher and his activity as a healer, prophet, and movement initiator.

JESUS AS TEACHER

To say that Jesus was a teacher does not say much, for there are varieties of teachers and teaching. There is teaching that conveys information, knowledge. This is the primary purpose of schoolteachers, from the elementary to university level: to communicate information about their subject matter.[1] There is moral teaching that focuses on right and wrong behavior, whether general principles, such as seeking the greatest good, or commandments about particular behaviors, or both. But neither of these expresses what it means to say that Jesus was a teacher.

Rather, Jesus was a teacher of wisdom. Wisdom is not about knowledge or information. Neither is wisdom primarily about commandments or rules, even though it speaks about a way of life. Rather, wisdom is a genre of teaching with typical forms and typical content. Its characteristic forms are short sayings and stories, as treated in the previous chapter. Its content, its subject matter, focuses on the most central questions of life:

- What is real, and what is reality like? What is its character? In a religious context in which the reality of the sacred is affirmed, the question becomes, what is the character of the sacred, the character of God?

- How do we typically live? What are we like? What is our "condition"?

- What is "the way"? How shall we live?

The questions are related; how we see reality pervasively shapes our sense of the way we should live. Thus wisdom teachers teach a way of life grounded in a perception of reality. Because it is so grounded, the way is commonly spoken of not simply as *a* way, but as *the* way. The image of "the way" is common to wisdom teachers worldwide. In ancient Israel, we see it in the books of Proverbs, Job, and Ecclesiastes and in some "wisdom" psalms.[2] It is central to wisdom teachers in other traditions, such as the Buddha and Lao Tzu.

Wisdom teachers fall into two primary categories. The first is teachers of "conventional wisdom." This kind of wisdom, as the term "conventional" suggests, is the wisdom of a culture—a body of directives and practical guidance grounded in the experience of generations. Its classic form is the proverb, which has been defined as a short sentence founded upon long experience and containing a truth. In the Bible, the classic embodiment of conventional wisdom is much of the last two-thirds of the book of Proverbs.[3]

Conventional wisdom covers everything from etiquette to family roles to general values such as industry, diligence, and discipline. Its central message consists of variations on a theme:

- Follow this way—the wise way, the right way—and your life will go well.

- You reap what you sow. The wise and righteous will flourish, and the foolish and wicked will wither.

- Often the corollary is those whose lives turn out badly have themselves to blame.

There is value and truth in conventional wisdom. All cultures need ways of behavior that people can count on in each other, ranging from not stealing and not killing and not testifying falsely to stopping at stop signs. We could not live together in groups without a consensus about acceptable behavior. Furthermore, there are ways of living that often lead to misery and ways that are more likely to lead to a good life. How our lives turn out is to some extent the result of virtues such as industry, discipline, and prudence.

But there is also a second kind of wisdom, one that challenges the taken-for-granted cultural consensus of conventional wisdom. A counterwisdom, a subversive or alternative wisdom, it is what we find in Job and Ecclesiastes as well as in the teachings of the Buddha and Lao Tzu. All taught a way that undermined conventional wisdom as the ultimate truth about reality and how to live.

Jesus was this kind of wisdom teacher. As with other great wisdom teachers, his counterwisdom was grounded in his perception of "what is." For Lao Tzu, "what is" was the "Tao," the "Tao that cannot be named"; the wise way was to live in accord with the Tao. For the Buddha, "what is" was "suchness," "isness," beyond all of our concepts, and we live in harmony with suchness by letting go of our grasping. For Jesus, "what is" was the God of Israel who, like the Tao and suchness, was beyond all images and yet known in experience. What Jesus said about God, about reality and its character, was grounded not in convention, not in socialized conviction, but in his experience of the sacred. Jesus taught a counterwisdom because of his experience of God. Because of that experience, he saw differently.

All of Jesus's teaching was directed to his contemporaries living in a first-century Jewish world. He had no other audience in mind. In this sense, there is no such thing as the "timeless" teaching of Jesus. Yet there is a timeless quality to much of what he said, and therefore also a timeliness, simply because his counterwisdom stood in tension not only with his social world, but also with the conventional wisdom of any time.

Jesus did not systematically divide his teaching into various topics. Perhaps his mind didn't work that way, or perhaps he didn't live long enough to do so. If he had lived into his eighties, as the Buddha did, would he have systematized it? It is, of course, an idle question. Nevertheless, though he didn't divide his teaching into themes, we can see that his parables and aphorisms revolved around the great themes of wisdom: the character of God/reality, the human condition (how we typically live), and "the way" of centering in God and living in accord with God's character. We begin with the first of these themes.

THE CHARACTER OF GOD

Ideas matter. Though we often think of them as less real than the "real world," our ideas profoundly shape our lives. Of the ideas that affect us, perhaps most fundamental is our image of the character of reality—of what is real and what reality is like. Deep within all of us is an image or picture of reality, whether consciously articulated or not, that more than anything else shapes how we live. We may "image" reality as indifferent, as threatening and destructive, or as nurturing and life-giving. How we see the character of reality fundamentally affects our response to life.[4]

We who are products of modern Western culture tend to image reality as ultimately indifferent. According to the worldview that emerged in the Enlightenment, reality is made up of tiny bits of stuff, of atoms and subatomic particles in constant motion, of matter and energy in interaction with each other. In a somewhat well known colloquial expression, reality is a vast "cosmic soup."[5] As such, it is indifferent to human purposes and hopes—it simply is.

I do not mean that all of us see "what is real" this way or to disregard public opinion polls that show that most Americans affirm the existence of God.[6] But unless transformed by convincing experience, belief in God in our time is commonly added on to this more basic picture of reality as inanimate and impersonal. God becomes the one who will rescue us from an indifferent universe beyond death or, alternatively, the source of personal meaning in a universe otherwise bereft of meaning and the presence of God.

This deep sense of an indifferent universe and cosmic loneliness has been one of the central themes of art, music, movies, and literature over the last century, including fiction and poetry as well as philosophical and theological works. With stark clarity and humorous hyperbole, a scene from Woody Allen's movie *Manhattan* expresses it. The main character (Allen himself) is trying to pick up a young woman who is staring at a modern abstract painting in an art gallery. He starts a conversation: "Nice painting." Without taking her eyes away from it, she says:

> It restates the negativeness of the universe; the hideous, lonely emptiness of existence, the nothingness; the predicament of man forced to live in a barren, godless eternity like a tiny flame flickering in an immense void with nothing but waste, horror, and degradation forming a useless bleak straitjacket in a black absurd cosmos.[7]

Though a caricature, there is a measure of this apprehension in most of us. An image of reality as indifferent easily shades into one that is threatening and destructive. The way of life that flows out of this ranges from despair to denial to seeking to secure ourselves as best we can in the midst of an indifferent and ultimately destructive reality. How we see the character of reality affects how we respond to life.

Of course, in the world of Jesus, the question was not whether God was real. Rather, the question concerned God's character. Most basically, what was God like? And what was God's passion, God's consuming desire? What did God want for and from Israel?

The Prodigal Son

With good reason, Jesus's story of the prodigal son (Luke 15.11–32) is perhaps his best-known parable; only the good Samaritan is a serious rival. Also for good reason, scholars have suggested titles for the story that emphasize the father, for the focus is as much on him as on the prodigal: "the father and his two sons," "the waiting father," "the loving father," "the compassionate father." This well-known story illustrates how parables work as a form of wisdom teaching, introduces central themes of Jesus's wisdom teaching, and highlights the character of God.

In its literary context in Luke, the parable of the prodigal son defends Jesus's inclusive meal practice. It is the third in a series of parables that answer his critics' charge, "This fellow welcomes sinners and eats with them" (15.2). In this context, the parable justifies Jesus's meal practice by analogy to what a father would do when the son he thought was lost and dead comes home—he would celebrate with a feast. Implicitly, in Luke's context, Jesus's meal practice with undesirables is a celebration of the return of the "lost."

But given the virtual certainty that Jesus told this parable many times, we need to imagine its meaning as an oral story in the context of his mission as a whole, not simply in the particular literary context provided by Luke.

The story unfolds in three scenes. As mentioned briefly in the previous chapter, we can easily imagine each scene expanded in different tellings. What we have in Luke is a plot summary, with economical details. Scene one, the prodigal's journey into exile:

> There was a man who had two sons. The younger of them said to his father, "Father, give me the share of the property that will belong to me." So he divided his property between them. A few days later the younger son gathered all he had and traveled to a distant country, and there he squandered his property in dissolute living. When he had spent everything, a severe famine took place throughout that country, and he began to be in need. So he went and hired himself out to one of the citizens of that country, who sent him to his fields to feed the pigs. He would gladly have filled himself with the pods that the pigs were eating; and no one gave him anything.

The description of the son's plight uses a central image from the Jewish Bible: exile. The younger son "traveled to a distant country," a gentile land. There, like the Jewish people in exile, and like Adam and Eve living their lives "east of Eden," he lived a great distance from home. To be in exile is to be separated from that to which one belongs. Details of the story underline the depth of his descent: after he squandered his money, famine struck the foreign land and he fell into need and poverty—and yet no one gave him anything. His hunger became so desperate that he became a swineherd working for a Gentile. A Jewish son could have fallen no further.

The description would have evoked reflection, perhaps interaction. What do you think of a son who acts that way? Is he so utterly irresponsible that his desperate plight is only what he deserved? Or do you understand him? Do you feel sorry for him? Suppose you had left your father's house and gone to a far country, and that you ended up not only living among Gentiles, but working for a Gentile, and that you even became a swineherd. Can you still return home? And how will you be received? Is this a story about a particularly foolish son? Or is this a story about all of us?

Scene two, the son's return from exile and the father's welcome:

> But when he came to himself he said, "How many of my father's hired hands have bread enough and to spare, but here I am dying of hunger! I will get up and go to my father, and I will say to him, 'Father, I have sinned against heaven and before you; I am no longer worthy to be called your son; treat me like one of your hired hands.'" So he set off and went to his father. But while he was still far off, his father saw him and was filled with compassion; he ran and put his arms around him and kissed him. Then the son said to him, "Father, I have sinned against heaven and before you; I am no longer worthy to be called your son." But the father said to his slaves, "Quickly, bring out a robe—the best one—and put it on him; put a ring on his finger and sandals on his feet. And get the fatted calf and kill it, and let us eat and celebrate; for this son of mine was dead and is alive again; he was lost and is found!" And they began to celebrate.

The prodigal "comes to himself" and undertakes a journey of return. He has his *mea culpa*, his "I have sinned against heaven and before you," all ready. But his father sees him a long way off and, filled with compassion, races to his son, embraces him, and kisses him before his son can speak his *mea culpa*. Indeed, he virtually ignores his son's confession as he orders his servants to fetch the best robe, a ring, and sandals and to prepare a festive meal celebrating the son's return. The father's behavior is joyfully extravagant. Again, the "teasing of the mind into active thought" is close at hand. What do you think of a father who acts that way? A bit over the top? A lot over the top? More than you would do? Just what you would do? Should he at least have given the son a reprimand and put him through a probationary period? And are we supposed to think God is like this? Do you think God is like this? But the story is not yet over.

Scene three, the dutiful son's reaction:

> Now his elder son was in the field; and when he came and approached the house, he heard music and dancing. He called one of the slaves and asked what was going on. He replied, "Your brother has come, and your father has killed the fatted calf, because he has got him back safe and sound." Then he became angry and refused to go in. His father came out and began to plead with him. But he answered his father, "Listen! For all these years I have been working like a slave for you, and I have never disobeyed your command; yet you have never given me even a young goat so that I might celebrate with my friends. But when this son of yours came back, who has devoured your property with prostitutes, you killed the fatted calf for him!" Then the father said to him, "Son, you are always with me, and all that is mine is yours. But we had to celebrate and rejoice, because this brother of yours was dead and has come to life; he was lost and has been found."

The older, dutiful son hears the sound of music and dancing. When he learns the reason for celebration, he refuses to join in. Filled with a sense of unfairness, he remains outside. So his father goes to him and listens to his complaint. The parable then ends with the father's simple justification of the celebration: "We had to celebrate and rejoice, because this brother of yours was dead and has come to life."

The statement includes an implicit invitation to the older son, left hanging in the air: will he be able to see this and join the celebration?

Again, the mind is teased into thought and the audience into interaction. What do you think of the older son's reaction? Understandable? Should life be the way he thinks it should be? Is he right that filial faithfulness is about duty and the fulfilling of conventional obligations? Or is he a jerk? Is he unable to see what parental compassion involves? And what do you think? Will he join the celebration, or will he let his feelings of resentment and sense of unfairness keep him outside?

The parable thus invites reflection on more than one theme. But at its center is an invitation to see the character of God in a particular way: God is like the father who yearns for his son's return from exile. When he sees him coming, he is "filled with compassion" and then joyously celebrates his homecoming. His compassion extends to his dutiful son as well: he goes outside to invite him to join the celebration. For the dutiful son to do so would, of course, involve seeing very differently; he would have to let go of his most basic vision of the way life should be. The parable invites a different way of seeing by inviting reflection about the character of God and the kind of life that follows from seeing God's character in a particular way. The themes interlock.

A few scholars have suggested that this parable is autobiographical, that Jesus spoke from his own experience of having been a prodigal.[8] About this, one can say only that it is an interesting possibility. But it does raise a useful question: why did Jesus see God as a compassion-filled parent? One could argue that he deduced it from his understanding of the Jewish Bible or from thinking about God. But it seems more likely to have come from his experience—not from being a prodigal, but from his experience of God as compassionate.

Parents and Children

As in the preceding parable, Jesus used the relationship of parent to child as an image of God's character in a short saying attested by both Matthew and Luke (and thus from Q):

> Is there anyone among you who, if your child asks for bread, will give a stone? Or if the child asks for a fish, will give a snake? If you then, who are evil, know how to give good gifts to your children, how much more will your Father in heaven give good things to those who ask him! (Matt. 7.9–11; Luke 11.11–13)

Like parables and aphorisms often do, the saying invites reflection. As parents, you know your desire to give good things to your children. Do you imagine that God is any different? God's character is like that of parents who give good gifts to their children.

Birds and Lilies

In another of Jesus's well-known teachings reported in both Matthew and Luke, he invited his hearers to look at the world of nature as a disclosure of God's character. Again, themes interlock: how we see God's character affects our response to life. The subject is worry, anxiety.

> Do not worry about your life, what you will eat or what you will drink, or about your body, what you will wear. Is not life more than food, and the body more than clothing? Look at the birds of the air; they neither sow nor reap nor gather into barns, and yet God feeds them. Are you not of more value than they? And can any of you by worrying add a single hour to your span of life? And why do you worry about clothing? Consider the lilies of the field, how they grow; they neither toil nor spin, yet I tell you, even Solomon in all his glory was not clothed like one of these. But if God so clothes the grass of the field, which is alive today and tomorrow is thrown into the oven, will God not much more clothe you—you of little faith? Therefore, do not worry, saying, "What will we eat?" or "What will we drink?" or "What will we wear?" For it is the Gentiles who strive for all these things; and indeed God knows that you need all these things. But strive first for the kingdom of God and God's jus-

tice, and all these things will be given to you as well. (Matt. 6.25–33; Luke 12.22–31)[9]

The appeal is simple and challenging. Look around you—see how God feeds the birds and clothes the lilies. The invitation is to see God as life-giving, generous, lavish. Not even the richest of Israel's kings was so gorgeously adorned as the lilies. Jesus saw reality as characterized by a cosmic generosity.

The alternative to seeing reality this way is worrying, being anxious. Worry (underlined by being mentioned four times in this brief passage) and "little faith" go together. In this context, little faith is the failure to see God's character disclosed in the feeding of birds and the clothing of lilies. Worry and faith are opposites, for faith is trust in the generosity of God. Do not worry. Instead, "strive first for the kingdom of God and God's justice."

The same perception of God's character is sounded in a much briefer passage: "God makes the sun rise on the evil and the good, and sends rain on the righteous and on the unrighteous" (Matt. 5.45).[10] God provides sunlight and rain, the basis of food and life, to all. Again, Jesus invited his hearers to see in nature—looked at attentively from a certain perspective—a glimpse of the divine nature. Like earlier figures in the Spirit-filled stream of Judaism, he saw the earth "filled with the glory of God," shot through with God's radiant presence. God's character is marked by compassionate generosity.

Character and Imperative: Imitating the Compassion of God

In one of his most concise sayings, Jesus speaks of compassion not only as the primary quality of God, but also as the primary quality of a life lived in accord with God. In remarkably few words, theology and ethics are combined: "Be compassionate, just as your Father is compassionate" (Luke 6.36). Found in slightly different form in Matthew 5.48, the passage affirms an ethic known as *imitatio dei*, "imitation of God."[11] The ethical imperative is to live in accord with God's character. As the fuller context in both Luke and Matthew indicates, this means imitating the God, who "is kind to the grateful and the wicked" (Luke) and "makes the sun rise on the evil and the good and sends rain on the righteous and unrighteous" (Matt.).

Several English translations of this saying do not use the word "compassionate," which is a better translation, but "merciful": "Be merciful, just as your Father is merciful."[12] "Merciful," however, is quite archaic. How often do we use the word in everyday language, outside of a church context? "Mercy" and "merciful" have quite different connotations in English from "compassion" and "compassionate." "Mercy" and "merciful" imply a situation of wrongdoing: mercy can be shown to someone who deserves punishment. In a religious context, mercy implies a situation of sin, as in the expression, "God, be merciful to me, a sinner." Though God has the right to punish, the sinner appeals for God to be merciful. In this context, "mercy" is a virtual synonym for "forgiveness."

The meaning of "compassion" is quite different. It is both a feeling (the roots of the English word mean "to feel with," to feel the feelings of another) and a way of acting that flows out of that feeling. Of course, in a situation of wrongdoing, compassion can be the motive for forgiveness. But compassion is a much broader term, applying to contexts in which there is no question of wrongdoing or forgiveness. We may feel compassion toward victims of famines, hurricanes, wars, illness, accidents, injustice, and so forth. In these contexts, it would be odd to speak of mercy or being merciful. Rather, we are to be compassionate as God is compassionate.

The centrality of compassion in the ethical teaching of Jesus is underlined in the parable of the good Samaritan (Luke 10.29–37). In this famous story, a priest and Levite pass by a man beaten by robbers, but a Samaritan stops to help; he bandages his wounds, brings him to an inn, takes care of him, and then leaves money with the innkeeper for his continuing care. At the end of the parable, Jesus asks, "Which of these three, do you think, was a neighbor to the man who fell into the hands of the robbers?" The answer: "The one who showed him *compassion*."[13] It is not about showing mercy to a person who has committed a wrong, but about being compassionate to a victim. Then Jesus said, "Go and do likewise."

The Servant Who Lacked Compassion

God's character as compassionate and the imperative to be compassionate are central to a parable Jesus told about a king and his hugely indebted servant (Matt. 18.23–34). In this story, we see that compassion is not simply a "soft" virtue. It can have an edge and involve passionate judgment. Scene one:

> A king wished to settle accounts with his slaves. When he began the reckoning, one who owed him ten thousand talents was brought to him; and, as he could not pay, his lord [the king] ordered him to be sold, together with his wife and children and all his possessions, and payment to be made. So the slave fell on his knees before him, saying, "Have patience with me, and I will pay you everything." And out of pity for him, the lord of that slave released him and forgave him the debt.

"Servant" might be a better term than "slave," for this is obviously a high-ranking servant of considerable means. The enormous amount of his debt, ten thousand talents, indicates this (even though he cannot repay it). A talent was the largest monetary unit of the time, equivalent to six thousand denarii, the plural of denarius, the daily wage of a common laborer. One talent thus equals about twenty years of wages. Ten thousand talents amounts to two hundred thousand years of wages for one worker, or a year's wages for two hundred thousand workers. Indeed, the debt is hyperbolic: a talent was the largest unit of money, and "ten thousand" was the largest number used in calculations.[14] But the king "out of pity"—the word can also mean "compassion"—releases him from his debt. The king's compassionate act invites reflection about the character of God—is this what God is like?

But the parable is about more than God's compassion. It continues in scene two:

> But that same slave, as he went out, came upon one of his fellow slaves who owed him a hundred denarii; and seizing him

by the throat, he said, "Pay what you owe." Then his fellow
slave fell down and pleaded with him, "Have patience with me,
and I will pay you." But he refused; then he went and threw
him into prison until he would pay the debt.

Though shown compassion by the king, the servant does not show
compassion for a fellow servant owing him a much smaller debt,
even though he uses the same language that the higher-ranking servant had just used. Instead, the latter has him imprisoned.

Scene three:

When his fellow slaves saw what had happened, they were
greatly distressed, and they went and reported to their lord all
that had taken place. Then his lord summoned him and said to
him, "You wicked slave! I forgave you all that debt because you
pleaded with me. Should you not have had mercy [compassion]
on your fellow slave, as I had mercy [compassion] on you?"
And in anger his lord handed him over to be tortured until he
would pay his entire debt.

The story that began with the king's compassion ends with his
harsh judgment against the servant who did not act compassionately.
The message is the same as Luke 6.36: "Be compassionate, just as
God is compassionate." Jesus called people to imitate, participate in,
collaborate with the compassion of God. But the invitation comes
with a threat, a sanction: if you are not compassionate, God's compassion will become fierce. Living in accord with the character of
God is the only way life will work.

Compassion and Judgment: Sheep and Goats

Compassion and judgment are combined in a well-known parable
about the last judgment (Matt. 25.31–46). Though the word "compassion" does not appear in the parable, it is about deeds of compassion. In it, all the nations of the world are gathered before the "Son
of Man" (later in the parable called the "king") seated "on the throne

of his glory." People are then separated as a shepherd separates sheep from goats at the end of the day. The criteria for separation, for judgment, are whether they fed the hungry, gave drink to the thirsty, welcomed the stranger, clothed the naked, took care of the sick, and visited those in prison. To those who did, the king says, "Just as you did it to one of the least of these who are members of my family, you did it to me." And to those who did not: "Just as you did not do it to one of the least of these, you did not do it to me." Living compassionately has consequences, just as lack of compassion does.

I include this parable even though mainstream scholars are uncertain or doubtful that it goes back to Jesus. I am among the uncertain. But I include it because of its familiarity and importance to Christians. Whether it goes back to Jesus or not, it at the least tells us how his followers saw the centrality of compassion and its relation to judgment.

Among the reasons for scholarly uncertainty is that it is found only in Matthew. This is not decisive, however, as several parables found only in Matthew or Luke are commonly thought to originate with Jesus. A more important reason is that in Matthew it is clearly a parable about the "second coming" of Jesus: "When the Son of Man comes in his glory, and all the angels with him, then he will sit on the throne of his glory. All the nations will be gathered before him." For Matthew, the Son of Man is Jesus. Moreover, Matthew sets this story in the context of his version of Jesus's "apocalyptic discourse" concerning signs of the end, judgment, and the importance of being ready (Matt. 24–25). Immediately preceding it are two other judgment parables that, in this context, are second-coming parables, the wise and foolish virgins (25.1–13) and the talents (25.14–30).

Most mainline scholars (including me) do not think that Jesus spoke about his second coming. To suppose that he did would require imagining that he tried to teach his followers about a second coming when they had not yet understood his "first coming" very well, including not really understanding that he was going away, that is, that he would be killed. The synoptics consistently portray his disciples as "not getting it."

So if this parable is intrinsically about the second coming of Jesus, it is unlikely to go back to him. However, it is quite easy to imagine the gist of the story being told in a context other than the second coming. If we imagine the story without the opening line about the "Son of Man" coming "in his glory" and sitting on "the throne of his glory," it becomes a story about a king judging his subjects on the basis of deeds of compassion being done (or not done) to *all* of his subjects, including the "least."

Of course, it is still a parable about God's judgment—but it need not be a story about the second coming of Jesus as the Son of Man. If the gist of this story does go back to Jesus, it raises some interesting questions. Did Jesus speak about a final judgment? Other passages in the gospels suggest that he did. For example, a passage in both Matthew and Luke (and thus Q, and early) speaks of the long-dead queen of Sheba (a contemporary of King Solomon) and the people of ancient Nineveh rising "at the judgment" and condemning "this generation" (Luke 11.31–32; Matt. 12.41–42). Many others also do.

Granted that Jesus used language about a final judgment, did he believe in a last judgment with eternal consequences—that some people would go to hell? The harshest examples of such language in the gospels are almost all in Matthew. The threats include casting persons into the "outer darkness" or the "furnace of fire," where "there will be weeping and wailing and gnashing of teeth" (e.g., 8.12; 13.42). Given that this is characteristic of Matthew's point of view, it is unlikely that these passages go back to Jesus. But some judgment passages do.

It is possible that Jesus did believe in a final judgment in which some people would go to hell. It is also possible, at least equally so, that the afterlife was not a central concern of Jesus and that he used the language of a final judgment to reinforce the importance of acting compassionately. We can imagine the language working this way: you who believe in a final judgment—what do you think the basis, the criterion, will be? His own answers to that question, as reported in the gospels, subvert and undermine widely accepted notions of his time (and perhaps every time). The judgment will not be based on membership in a group, or on beliefs, or on rule keeping, but on deeds of compassion. But whatever Jesus believed about rewards and punishments in a final judgment, his mission and message were much more concerned about life in this world than about our fate beyond death.

An Ambiguous Parable: A Generous Landlord?

I conclude this section with a parable often seen as a disclosure of God's character, but one that may have a quite different meaning. I do so in part because the parable may belong in this category, and therefore should be treated here, but also to illustrate how some parables may have been heard (and intended) differently from our accustomed way of hearing them.

In this parable, commonly called the workers in the vineyard (Matt. 20.1–15), Jesus tells a story about a landowner who hires workers early in the day to work in his vineyard and agrees to pay them each a denarius, the usual daily wage. (These were day laborers, who were among the most marginalized of the peasant class. They did not even have the security of other landless workers such as tenant farmers and sharecroppers, for their work was seasonal and sporadic. Though a family could survive on a daily wage of a denarius, day laborers could not count on getting work every day.) Then, at 9 AM, noon, 3 PM, and 5 PM, the vineyard owner hires more. At the end of the day, he pays them all the same, a denarius, even though some have worked the whole day and others for only an hour. Those hired early in the day complain. The landlord has the last word as he addresses them:

> I am doing you no wrong; did you not agree with me for the usual daily wage? Take what belongs to you and go; I choose to give to the last the same as I give to you. Am I not allowed to do what I choose with what belongs to me? Or are you envious because I am generous?

Imagining this as an oral story told a number of times, the parable invites reflection. What do you think of a vineyard owner who behaves this way?

The most common interpretation sees this parable as a story about the character of God. God is like the vineyard owner who gives everybody what they need, whether they have worked a little or a lot. God does not reward us on the basis of our work. Indeed, especially in Protestant circles, the story is often understood as a parable of radical grace. Heard this way, it points not only to the generosity of God, but also to our tendency to find this unfair. God is the generous employer, but we begrudge such generosity, just as the older brother in the story of the prodigal complained about his father's generosity. As a parable about God, it subverts the notion that God orders life on the basis of rewards for work done.

The above interpretation is certainly possible, and most scholars have seen it this way. But recently a very different interpretation has been suggested. It begins with a question. How would the peasant audience to whom Jesus spoke have heard this story about a large landowner and day laborers? Would they have heard the behavior of the landowner as pointing to what God is like? Or would they have heard it as an indictment of how wealthy landowners behave? We can easily imagine the latter, because this is what these landowners were like. The peasant audience might have thought: "They get our land"—often through foreclosure on debt—"and turn us into tenant farmers, sharecroppers, and day laborers. Then they try to get by with as few workers as possible, and that's why they don't hire more in the morning. Then when they need more, they accuse those of us who haven't been hired yet of being lazy." (In the parable, the owner says to the laborers he hires late in the day, "Why are you standing here idle all day?" as if it's their fault that they aren't working.) "Then they pay everybody the same wage, barely enough for survival, and expect to be seen as good-hearted, generous people. Talk about arrogance!"[15]

Heard this way, the parable is not a story about God; it invites critical reflection about the domination system, indeed indicts it. Of course, it is not just a story about the outrageous way landowners behave. It is told "in the name of God"—that is, it is part of Jesus's mission and message. But rather than being a story *about* God, it raises consciousness about the domination system.

Perhaps Jesus could have intended it both ways, though this is a bit difficult to imagine. But these two ways of hearing it do share something in common. Namely, it is either a story about God's generosity or a story that indicts an unjust and ungenerous domination system in the name of God. It is a story about God as compassionate or about a system that lacks compassion.

The Associations of Compassion

In Hebrew (the language of the Jewish Bible) and Aramaic (the language of Jesus), the word translated into English as "compassion" has rich metaphorical associations. It is the plural of a noun that in its singular form means "womb." Sometimes the association with womb is explicit: a woman feels compassion for the child of her womb (1 Kings 3.26); a man feels compassion for his brother, who comes from the same womb (Gen. 43.30). Compassion is located in a particular part of the body, the loins. In women, this means, of course, in the womb. In men, it is located in the bowels, and this explains the otherwise rather odd biblical expression of bowels being moved with compassion.[16]

Compassion, with its associations with the womb, is also used of God in the Jewish Bible. God is often spoken of as "gracious and compassionate."[17] The word lies behind the phrase from the King James Bible, "the tender mercies of God."[18] It appears in a passage from Jeremiah; God is the speaker:

Is Ephraim [Israel] my dear son? My darling child?
For the more I speak of him, the more I do remember him.
Therefore my womb trembles for him;
I will truly show motherly compassion upon him. (Jer. 31.20)[19]

God's womb (!) trembles, and God vows to show "motherly compassion" upon Israel.

Thus Jesus's perception of God's character as compassionate, as womblike, is rooted in the Jewish tradition. A striking and evocative image, it has rich associations; it is life-giving, nurturing, embracing, caring. Like a womb, God is the one who gives birth to us and nurtures us. As a mother loves the children of her womb and wills their well-being, so God loves us and wills our well-being. Compassion as what a mother feels for the children of her womb can also have a fierce dimension. When a mother sees her children being threatened or abused, she can become passionate in their defense. For Jesus, God's character had this dimension as well, as we shall soon see.

And we are to be compassionate. As we have seen, the central imperative in the teaching of Jesus is to live in accord with God's character: "Be compassionate, as God is compassionate." As an ethic, an *imitatio dei*, its associations are rich. We are to feel for others as a mother feels for the children of her womb and act in accord with those feelings. We are to feel for others as God feels for all of God's children and act accordingly.

Jesus's perception of God's character and an ethic based upon the imitation of God continued in the post-Easter context of early Christianity. Though their most common word for God's character is "love" rather than "compassion," the meaning is the same. The first letter of John is a sustained meditation on God's love and the life of faithfulness to God as the imitation of God's love. "God is love, and those who abide in love abide in God" (4.16). "Beloved, let us love one another, because love is from God; everyone who loves is born of God and knows God" (4.7). "Beloved, since God loved us so much, we also ought to love one another" (4.11).

So also, Paul names the primary Christian virtue as love. In his magnificent exposition of "the gifts of the Spirit," the fruit of a life centered in God, the climax is one of the most familiar verses in the New Testament: "Faith, hope and love abide, these three; and the greatest of these is love" (1 Cor. 13.13). It is grounded in God's character as love, as disclosed in the life and death of Jesus: "God proves his love for us in that while we still were sinners Christ died for us" (Rom. 5.8).

In another very familiar verse, the author of John's gospel speaks of God's love for the world: "For God so loved the world ..." (3.16). For John, Jesus is the revelation of God's love, and so the *imitatio dei* becomes an *imitatio Christi*, an imitation of Jesus. The Jesus of John's gospel says, "I give you a new commandment, that you love one another. Just as I have loved you, you also should love one another" (13.34). The symmetry between the message of Jesus and the testimony of the post-Easter community is striking: love one another because the character of God as known in Jesus is love.

GOD'S PASSION: JUSTICE

We move from how Jesus saw the character of God to how he saw the passion of God. God's character and passion are not separate, but closely related, just as they are in people. Our passion—our dedicated devotion, our consuming interest, our concentrated commitment—is a major indicator of our character, indeed, flows out of our character. So it is in Jesus's teaching about God. God's character and passion, what God is like and God's will for the world, go hand in hand.

God's passion is justice. God's character and God's passion go together, for the simple reason that justice is the social form of compassion. As the social form of compassion, justice is about politics, not in the modern sense of electoral politics, but in the sense suggested by the root of the English word. It comes from the Greek word *polis*, which means "city." Politics is about the shape and shaping, the structure and structuring, of the city and, by extension, of human communities more generally, ranging from the family to society as a whole.

In this sense, the Jewish Bible is pervasively political. It is a central dynamic, beginning with the story of the exodus from Egypt and the creation of a new form of community under the lordship of God in the rest of the Pentateuch. It continues in the prophetic critique of the injustice of the monarchy and the experience of the Jewish people after the exile under one imperial power after another. I emphasize the political significance of God's compassion because compassion can be heard as primarily an ethic for relationships between individuals, or as something added on to society as charity for those who need help, as in the phrase familiar in our time "compassionate conservatism." But it is not so in the Bible or for Jesus. Rather, justice is the political form of compassion, the social form of love, a compassionate justice grounded in God as compassionate.

In the mission of Jesus, we see God's passion for justice above all in the central place of the kingdom of God. Jesus was passionate about God's kingdom (hereafter sometimes called "the kingdom" for short). And Jesus's passion for God's kingdom was grounded in God's passion for the kingdom.

But what Jesus meant by the kingdom of God divides contemporary Jesus scholarship. Indeed, it is the primary division. Some scholars argue that Jesus was convinced that the kingdom would come in the near future by means of a dramatic intervention by God, a position called "imminent eschatology" or "apocalyptic eschatology." Other scholars argue that Jesus's language about the kingdom is to be understood in a different framework, one that involves human collaboration with God. Because of the importance of this question for glimpsing the pre-Easter Jesus, we will return to it in Chapter 9. For now, I leave unaddressed whether Jesus thought the kingdom would come through supernatural intervention in the near future or whether his kingdom language is to be understood differently. Here, in the context of the kingdom of God as God's passion, I cite three points about which there is widespread agreement among scholars on both sides of the division.

First, God's kingdom was *for the earth*. As noted earlier, it is not about heaven. Second, "kingdom of God" was a *political* as well as *religious* term, to distinguish between two aspects of life that were not separable in the Jewish world of Jesus. The Torah and the prophets were about both religion and politics. Nor were they separable in the larger world of the Roman Empire. As noted in Chapter 3, Roman imperial theology combined religion and politics: its theology of the emperor as divine and as son of God legitimated the political order that Rome saw itself as having brought to the world. Moreover, Rome referred to itself not as an "empire," but as a "kingdom." In this context, Jesus's use of kingdom language would have had a political edge and meaning. His hearers knew about the kingdom of Herod and the kingdom of Rome. But Jesus spoke about a kingdom other than Rome and its client kings.

As a political-religious metaphor, the kingdom of God referred to what life would be like on earth if God were king and the kingdoms of this world, the domination systems of this world, were not. To say that "kingdom" is a political term does not imply that Jesus thought it would be brought about by a political process, whether electoral (which he didn't imagine) or by political reform or revolution. He did not simply imagine a different set of rulers and a modified system. But minimally, his use of the phrase "kingdom of God" subverted and negated the kingdoms of his day by affirming a different king and kingdom—what life would be like on earth if God were Lord and the lords of this earth were not. Most simply, his use of the word "kingdom" challenged the kingdoms of this world.

Third, the kingdom of God was not only for the earth, but involved a *transformed world*. It is a blessed state of affairs, a utopia brought about by God, God's dream for the earth. Imaginative descriptions from Jewish sources near the time of Jesus portray an earth transformed by God into a world of plenty. One speaks of "life without care" in which "springs of wine, honey and milk" flow on an earth that will "bear more abundant fruits spontaneously." Moreover:

> The earth will belong equally to all, undivided by walls or fences.... Lives will be in common and wealth will have no division. For there will be no poor man there, no rich, and no tyrant, no slave. Further, no one will be either great or small anymore. No kings, no leaders. All will be on a par together.[20]

It means the end of injustice and violence. Everybody will have enough, and nations will not make war on nations anymore.

Whatever else scholars might add to this list, most (all?) would agree that the phrase "kingdom of God" pointed to that kind of world, a blessed state of affairs, a utopia, to be brought about God. Some would argue that Jesus's language about the kingdom included more than this, such as the resurrection of the dead and being united with them in a great banquet: "Many will come from east and west and will eat with Abraham and Isaac and Jacob in the kingdom of God" (Matt. 8.11; Luke 13.28–29). But they would agree that the kingdom is about a transformed earth, however it was to be brought about.

The primary disagreement is thus not about the *content* of what the kingdom would be like, but *how* and *when* Jesus thought this would happen. Did he expect God to do this, and soon? Did he expect God to do it with or without us—that is, regardless of human response it was going to happen? Or did he expect us to do it with God? That is, what is the response he sought from those who heard him? To *prepare* for what God was soon going to do, namely, the imminent arrival of the kingdom? Or to *collaborate* with its coming, to *participate* in it, to *embody* it? I will return to the how and when questions in a later chapter.

For now I emphasize that the phrase "kingdom of God" names God's passion for the earth—God's will, God's promise, God's dream. That it involves justice for those oppressed and exploited by the domination system is illustrated by two very familiar portions of the gospels, the Lord's Prayer and the Beatitudes.

The Lord's Prayer is a prayer for the coming of God's kingdom *on earth:* "Your kingdom come *on earth,* as it is in heaven." As John Dominic Crossan memorably puts it: heaven's in great shape—earth is where the problems are. "Your kingdom come on earth as it is in heaven" is immediately followed by petitions for daily bread and forgiveness of debt: "Give us this day our daily bread," and "Forgive us our debts as we also have forgiven our debtors" (Matt. 6.11–12).

Bread and debt were the two central survival issues in peasant life. Bread symbolized food, enough food, always an issue for peasants living at a subsistence level. Indebtedness was the way peasants could lose their land, if they still had some. If they were already landless, they could lose their freedom: unpaid debt could result in imprisonment or being sold into indentured servanthood. We are, of course, accustomed to hearing this petition as asking for the forgiveness of sins. But two of the three versions of the Lord's Prayer in early Christian documents (Matthew and the *Didache*) use the words "debt" and "debtors," and the third (Luke) has "sins" in one line and "indebted" in the second. True, the word "debt" could have the metaphorical meaning of "sin" in first-century Judaism, but "debt" and "debtors" most likely had their literal meanings as well. The coming of God's kingdom is about bread for the world and freedom from debt. It is good news for the poor.

The connection between the kingdom of God and the well-being of the poor and hungry is also found in the Beatitudes (blessings) at the beginning of the Sermon on the Plain in Luke:

Blessed are you who are poor, for yours is the kingdom of God.
Blessed are you who are hungry now, for you will be filled.
Blessed are you who weep now, for you will laugh. (6.20–23)

In the kingdom of God, the poor will be blessed, the hungry filled, and those who weep will laugh. Given the context, "you who weep" probably does not refer to grief and bereavement, but to the daily sorrow caused by the privations of life in the peasant class. In the kingdom, there will be laughter and joy, not weeping and sorrow.

That Luke understands these statements in a material way is confirmed by the "woes" that immediately follow:

Woe to you who are rich, for you have received your consolation.
Woe to you who are full now, for you will be hungry.
Woe to you who are laughing now, for you will mourn and weep.
Woe to you when all speak well of you, for that is what their ancestors did to the false prophets. (6.24–26)

The rich, full, laughing, and well-regarded were obviously those who were doing well within the present state of affairs. The coming of the kingdom would be good news for the poor and hungry, but not for them. It would involve a great reversal of the way things were.

Matthew's version of the Beatitudes in the Sermon on the Mount also sets them in the context of the kingdom of God, although his wording is slightly different. Rather than Luke's "Blessed are you who are poor, for yours is the kingdom of God," Matthew has, "Blessed are the poor *in spirit*, for theirs is the kingdom" (5.3). Rather than Luke's "Blessed are you who are hungry," Matthew has, "Blessed are those who hunger and thirst *for righteousness*" (5.6).

The differences have sometimes been attributed to Matthew's "spiritualization" of the Beatitudes so that they no longer refer to materially poor and hungry people. But this need not be the case. "Poor in spirit" almost certainly does not refer to well-to-do people who are nevertheless spiritually poor, but to people whose material poverty has broken their spirit.[21] Moreover, "righteousness" in the Bible and Matthew often does not mean personal rectitude, as it most often does in modern English, but justice. "Those who hunger and thirst *for righteousness*" likely means "those who hunger and thirst *for justice.*" The meaning of Matthew's wording is thus similar and perhaps identical to what we find in Luke, for it is the poor and hungry who yearn for justice. In short, like the Lord's Prayer, the Beatitudes confirm that the kingdom of God is both religious and political: it is *God's* kingdom, and it is a *kingdom on earth* that involves a transformation of life for the poor and hungry.

And just as Jesus spoke of imitating God's compassion, so he spoke of participating in God's passion. At the end of the passage in which Jesus spoke of our worry about food and clothing, he said: *"Strive first for the kingdom of God and God's justice,* and all these things will be given to you as well" (Matt. 6.33; Luke 12.31). God's character as compassion and God's passion as the kingdom of God were at the center of Jesus's mission. They were Jesus's passion as well. Indeed, as we shall see, his passion for the kingdom led to his execution. He risked and gave his life for it.

EIGHT

Wisdom

The Broad Way and the Narrow Way

We turn to Jesus's teaching about "the way," the second primary focus of wisdom teachers. In addition to speaking about the character and passion of God, Jesus spoke about a way, a path of transformation leading from how we ordinarily live our lives to a different way of being.

In this, he is like the other great wisdom teachers of the world's religions. The image of a *way*, indeed *the* way, is at the center of their message. Indeed, it is often used to name their teaching. The title of a collection of sayings attributed to a sixth-century BCE Chinese wisdom teacher is *The Way of Lao Tzu*. So also in Buddhism; "the way" is the climax of the four "noble truths." So also in Christianity; its first name was those "who belonged to *the Way*" (Acts 9.2).

Like other wisdom teachers, Jesus spoke of two ways. There is a common way, the one followed by most people, and an alternative way. There is the broad way and the narrow way, the foolish way and the wise way, the way of death and the way of life. The two ways are the one "which most of us follow and which consists in 'making the best of a bad job,' and the 'way of the saints.'"[1] The first is to be left behind, and the second embarked upon. In familiar phrases from Robert Frost and Henry David Thoreau, the alternative way is the "road less traveled," which involves marching to the beat of "a different drummer."

The importance of following another way reflects a perception of human life shared by Jesus and other great wisdom teachers; namely, there is something wrong with our lives as most commonly lived.

The ailment afflicts rich and poor, the satisfied and the suffering, the contented and the miserable. Though there are satisfactions in life, especially for the more fortunate, our lives are nevertheless marked and marred by suffering and grasping, anxiety and self-preoccupation, bondage and exile, blindness and convention, and feelings of unworthiness and insignificance. To use common Christian language, human life is "fallen," not what it is meant to be. The sense that there is something wrong is felt internally and seen externally—in injustice and wars and all the other suffering that we inflict upon one another.

The great wisdom teachers teach that there is a way out of this state of affairs, the dis-ease of common human life. To use a medical metaphor, the two ways involve a diagnosis and a cure, a description of the malady and a prescription for transformation. As William James put it over a hundred years ago, the "common nucleus" to which the religions of the world "bear their testimony unanimously" consists of two elements, a perception of "an uneasiness" and "its solution."[2] In this chapter, we explore Jesus's teaching about the problem and the cure, his perception of how we typically live our lives and "the way" that leads beyond this condition.

WAYS WITHIN JUDAISM

Judaism was about "the way," as it still is. The image is central to the Jewish Bible. There is the way of the exodus, the way through the sea, the way of Torah, the way of return from exile, the way of wisdom, the way of life. "Choose life, not death" runs through the Jewish tradition.

Within the world in which Jesus grew up and lived, "the way" of Judaism was variously understood. There is nothing unusual about this in the world's religions. Buddhism is about "the way," and yet there are quite different understandings about what this means. Christianity throughout its history has spoken of "the way," even as the Christian path has been seen in many and diverse ways, as exemplified in contemporary American Christianity as well as in other times and places.

The majority of Jesus's contemporaries followed the way of "common Judaism"—living within the framework of Jewish tradition and convention. Many no doubt did so devoutly. There were also intensified forms of Judaism. The way of the Pharisees intensified the Jewish way by emphasizing purity in the midst of life. The way of the Essenes also emphasized purity, but thought it could be achieved only by withdrawal from the world. There was also the way of violent resistance, whose adherents are often but anachronistically called "Zealots."[3] All were motivated by loyalty to God, and each was grounded in a perception of God's character and passion, God's nature and will.

THE JEWISH WAY OF JESUS

In this context, Jesus spoke of another way, one that was also deeply Jewish, even as it was an intensification of Judaism. Just as the way of the Pharisees was different from the way of the Essenes, so the way of Jesus was different from both, even though all were Jewish. Thus Jesus's teaching about the way involved not only affirmation of another way, but sometimes also criticism of the other ways. But even more often, the way that is criticized is a broader way, one shared by the other ways and by most ways before or since.

Jesus named the two ways the broad way and the narrow way, the wide gate and the narrow gate. The first leads to destruction and the second leads to life:

> Enter through the narrow gate; for the gate is *wide* and the road is easy that leads to *destruction*.... The gate is *narrow* and the road is hard that leads to *life*. (Matt. 7.13–14; see also Luke 13.23–24)

He also spoke of them as the wise way and the foolish way. The first is like building one's house upon rock, and the second like building one's house upon sand:

> Everyone then who hears these words of mine and acts on them will be like *a wise man who built his house on rock*. The rain

fell, the floods came, and the winds beat on that house, but it did not fall, because it had been founded on rock. And everyone who hears these words of mine and does not act on them will be like a *foolish man who built his house upon sand.* The rain fell, and the floods came, and the winds blew and beat against that house, and it fell—and great was its fall! (Matt. 7.24–27; Luke 6.47–49)

In Matthew, this parable concludes the Sermon on the Mount; in Luke, it concludes the Sermon on the Plain. Its position in both gospels at the end of a collection of teaching suggests that the collection as a whole is about the two ways.

THE BROAD WAY

We begin with Jesus's perception of the broad way. Strikingly, it was not the way of obvious wickedness—not the way of murder, stealing, extortion, brutality, abuse, corruption, and so forth. Though Jesus certainly didn't approve of these, they did not constitute the broad way. Indeed, the broad way was not even what people commonly think of as "sinful," as specific acts of disobedience to God (such as gluttony, drunkenness, adultery, and so forth). The teaching of Jesus in this respect (as well as many others) differs markedly from preaching that emphasizes the "hot sins," as some of today's evangelists do.

Rather, the broad way is the way most people live most of the time. It is not that most people are "wicked," but that most live lives structured by the conventions of their culture, by taken-for-granted notions of what life is about and how to live, by what "everybody knows." Every culture has its conventions, indeed, is virtually defined by its conventions. Growing up involves internalizing the conventions of one's culture. Thus we do not simply live in a world of convention; rather, convention lives within us. Our lives are structured, even driven, by the central conventions of our culture. We learn to value what our culture values, pursue what our culture tells us to pursue, and see as our culture sees. In short, we commonly live in a world of conventional wisdom.

We begin with the primary metaphors Jesus used to express his perception of the common way of life from which we need deliverance. There are compelling reasons for affirming that all of these metaphors go back to Jesus, even as they are also important in early Christianity. This language is both grounded in the message of Jesus and of central significance for his post-Easter followers.

Blind Though Sighted

Blindness is a frequent metaphor in the teaching of Jesus. There are sighted people who are blind: "You have eyes and fail to see" (Mark 8.18; see also 4.12). Several sayings refer to this condition. As an itinerant oral teacher, he spoke most (and probably all) of these many times. Blind though sighted was a major theme of his message.

He spoke of the blind leading the blind, and the futility of doing so: "Can a blind person guide a blind person? Will not both fall into a pit?" (Luke 6.39; Matt. 15.14). The saying obviously refers to sighted people. There is a smaller group (those who guide) and a larger group (those they seek to guide). Those who guide are presumably teachers or leaders; it is difficult to imagine a different referent. They could be local teachers, leaders of other movements, or official leaders such as the temple authorities and their scribes/ teachers. They are called "blind." But blindness applies not only to them, but also to the ones they seek to guide. It was a widespread condition.

Jesus spoke of people having not merely specks, but logs in their eyes. "Why do you see the speck in your neighbor's eye, but do not notice the log in your own eye?... First take the log out of your own eye, and then you will see clearly to take the speck out of your neighbor's eye" (Luke 6.41–42; Matt. 7.3, 5). The saying suggests not only impaired vision, but blindness to impaired vision.

There are healthy and unhealthy eyes: "The eye is the lamp of the body. So, if your eye is healthy, your whole body will be full of light; but if your eye is unhealthy, your whole body will be full of darkness" (Matt. 6.22–23; Luke 11.34). The health of the eye—how we see— makes all the difference. A healthy eye is like a lamp, and when our eye is healthy, we see clearly. But when our eye is unhealthy, we grope in the dark.

There are people who can see signs of the weather but who are blind to the signs of the times:

> When you see a cloud rising in the west, you immediately say, "It is going to rain"; and so it happens. And when you see the south wind blowing, you say, "There will be scorching heat"; and it happens. You know how to interpret the appearance of earth and sky, but why do you not know how to interpret the present time? (Luke 12.54–56; Matt. 16.2–3)

The passage is both an indictment and an invitation. It indicts some (his audience in general or a particular group?) as blind to what is happening, even as it invites them to look again, to see anew.

Looking—seeing anew—is not only about seeing the signs of the time, but also about seeing the character of God. Seeing is the central image of Jesus's sayings about the birds and the lilies: "Look at the birds of the air.... Consider the lilies of the field" (Matt. 6.26, 28; Luke 12.24, 27). Look and see how God feeds them and clothes them.

Indeed, the very forms of Jesus's teaching—parables and aphorisms—are invitations to a different way of seeing. Their function is to bring about a radical perceptual shift.

The metaphor of blindness and seeing is not only prominent in the teaching of Jesus, but also found in stories about his giving sight to blind people. There are three, two in Mark and one in John. They clearly have a metaphorical meaning, even as one or more may well be based on historical memory. But they are told for their more-than-historical meaning. As we have already seen in Chapter 3, Mark's stories of Jesus healing the blind man of Bethsaida and blind Bartimaeus (8.22–26; 10.46–52) frame the central section of his gospel, whose theme is following Jesus on "the way" that leads to his death and resurrection.[4] To be given one's sight, to see, means seeing and following Jesus as "the way."

John's story of Jesus healing a blind man functions in much the same way. It becomes the occasion for the Jesus of John to say, "I am the light of the world" (9.5).[5] The meaning of the healing is that, as the "light of the world," Jesus brings people out of darkness into light and gives sight to the blind. He brings *enlightenment*, a religious metaphor that many people associate primarily with Asian religions. But enlightenment is central to John's gospel and to early Christianity more generally. John announces it in the magnificent and thematic prologue to his gospel: Jesus is "the true light, which enlightens everyone," who "was coming into the world" (1.9). Our condition is blindness, being "in the dark," unable to find a way. The solution is to regain our sight, to see again, to have our eyes opened, to come into the light, to be enlightened.

Dead Though Alive

Just as Jesus spoke of sighted people who were blind, so he spoke of living people who were dead. In what has been called Jesus's most radical saying, he said, "Let the dead bury their own dead."[6] Obviously, he spoke this about people who were alive; they are the "dead" who bury the dead. In both Luke and Matthew, it is set in the context of Jesus calling people to follow him:

> To another Jesus said, "Follow me." But he said, "Lord, first let me go and bury my father." But Jesus said to him, "Let the dead bury their own dead." (Luke 9.60; Matt. 8.22)

Within Judaism, the duty to bury one's father was one of the most sacred obligations, overruling even sabbath laws. For Jesus to say that following him meant disregarding that obligation was radical.

But it seems unlikely that Jesus said this saying only once and only in the context of a would-be follower wanting to bury his father first. It is difficult to imagine that he used a brilliant one-liner like this only once. It is magnificent: "Let the dead bury their own dead." The meaning is clear—there is a way of living that amounts to living in the land of the dead. And the saying also affirms that it is possible to leave the land of the dead. Like so many of Jesus's sayings, it both indicts and invites.

Death as a metaphor for a way of living also appears in the parable of the prodigal son. Twice the prodigal's father describes the prodigal as having been dead: "This son of mine was dead," "This brother of yours was dead" (Luke 15.24, 32). To say the obvious, the prodigal was alive while he lived in a foreign land. Yet his life in exile is spoken of as the equivalent of being dead. One can be dead even though alive.

Just as the metaphor of blindness is found both in Jesus's teaching and in narratives about him, so is the metaphor of death. It is central to the story of the resurrection of Lazarus in John's gospel (11.1–44). Of course, the *story* is about a "real" death and a "real" bringing back to life of a dead person; within the narrative world of the story, Lazarus was not only in a tomb, but had been dead for four days. But like many of the stories in John, it is symbolic, a purely metaphorical narrative. Very few, if any, mainline scholars affirm that it is history remembered. Christians who interpret the gospels literally and factually disagree, of course. For them, the story reports a historical event, one of the most spectacular miracles attributed to Jesus. But whatever one thinks about the factuality of the story, the way it is told points to a more-than-historical meaning. To that meaning we now turn.

The theme of the story, its primary affirmation, is one of the famous "I am" sayings attributed to Jesus and found only in John's gospel: "I am the resurrection and the life" (11.25). Just as John used the story of the healing of the blind man as the occasion for Jesus to say, "I am the light of the world," so he uses this story as the occasion for Jesus to say, "I am the resurrection and the life."

The saying is part of an interchange between Jesus and Martha, the sister of Lazarus. Martha meets Jesus near the village where Lazarus has died. As the interchange unfolds in John 11.23–25, note the pattern:

Jesus makes a statement: "Your brother will rise again."

Martha takes the words literally and misunderstands: "I know that he will rise again in the resurrection on the last day."

Jesus corrects her misunderstanding: "I am the resurrection and the life."

This pattern is also found in John's story of Nicodemus and Jesus (3.1–10):

Jesus makes a statement: "No one can see the kingdom of God without being born anew" (or "born again," or "born from above"—all are possible translations).

Nicodemus takes the words literally and misunderstands: "How can anyone be born after having grown old? Can one enter a second time into the mother's womb and be born?"

Jesus corrects his misunderstanding: "You must be born of the Spirit."

The structure of the narrative shifts the meaning from literal to metaphorical.

So also in the story of Lazarus. The dialogue shifts from the literal to the metaphorical and from the future to the present. Martha spoke of the resurrection as future, as "on the last day." Jesus's response shifts to the present tense: "I am the resurrection and the life." Martha thought of the resurrection as a future event at the end of time; but Jesus's response corrects her misunderstanding and speaks of resurrection as a present reality. The metaphorical meaning is clear: Jesus is "the resurrection and the life" who brings life to the dead, just as he is "the light of the world" who brings sight to blind.

In a metaphorical sense Lazarus is "Everyman," dead and bound in a tomb. The story ends with the dramatic scene of Lazarus coming out, still wearing the clothing of death: "The dead man came out, his hands and feet bound with strips of cloth, and his face wrapped in a cloth." Jesus speaks the last words: "Unbind him, and let him go" (11.44). As "the resurrection and the life," Jesus calls people forth from their tombs, gives them life, and sets them free. Whatever one thinks about whether this story "really happened," something like this is its more-than-historical meaning. Jesus is the resurrection and the life—not at the last day, but already.

Of course, this story, like most of John's gospel, goes beyond anything Jesus himself said or did. It is John's post-Easter testimony to Jesus, reflecting the experience of his community. They had been brought from death to life through Jesus, just as they had been brought from darkness into light. Their use of this imagery not only is consistent with the message of Jesus, but confirms that these were central metaphors for those who stood closest to Jesus in time.

Exile

The metaphor of exile is deeply embedded in the gospels. A universal and archetypal image of the human condition, it is also grounded in the historical experience of ancient Israel. In the sixth century BCE, Jerusalem and the kingdom of Judah (later known as Judea) were conquered by the Babylonian Empire. Some of the Jewish people were taken into exile in Babylon, several hundred miles across a desert wilderness from their homeland. There they lived in impoverished conditions of virtual slavery for almost half a century. The literature of the period is filled with lament, sorrow, and a yearning for home. Then the great prophet of the exile, whose words are found in the second half of the book of Isaiah, announced in some of the richest language in the Bible that God had prepared a "way of return." Soon they did return home. The experience of exile and return imprinted itself indelibly in Jewish memory.

Exile is also central to the story of Adam and Eve in the opening chapters of Genesis. They begin their lives in paradise, in the Garden of Eden, the place of God's presence. But then they are exiled from the garden and must live their lives "east of Eden" (Gen. 3.24). It is a powerful metaphor for the human condition. We live our lives in exile, separated from that to which we belong, that which we hold dear, that which we remember but do not often experience, that which we yearn for. It is a condition of estrangement.

The centrality of exile imagery in the gospels is pointed to by the prominent use of language about "the way." "The way" is the way of return from exile. As already noted, Mark's gospel begins by quoting the prophet of the exile: "The voice of one crying out in the wilderness—'Prepare the way of the Lord, make his paths straight'" (Mark 1.3, citing Isa. 40.3). Indeed, the second half of the book of Isaiah, all dealing with the exile, is the most frequently echoed portion of the Jewish prophets in the gospels.

The metaphor of exile is also central to the parable of the prodigal son (Luke 15.11–32). The younger son "traveled to a distant country," where he fell into privation and servitude. There he yearns for home, and finally embarks on the journey back to his father's farm. It is a story of exile and return.

Bondage

Like exile, the metaphor of bondage is grounded in Israel's history, even as it is also a more universal image for the human condition. It is the central theme of ancient Israel's primal narrative in the Torah, the story of bondage to Pharaoh and liberation by God. As an image of the human condition, it referred and refers to both "external" bondage to systems of political and economic oppression and "internal" bondage, whether created by convention or commitment.

The image is central to Luke's report of Jesus's "inaugural address," his advance summary of what was most central to the mission of Jesus, a passage treated already in the context of Jesus as a Jewish mystic. As Luke tells the story, Jesus has returned to Galilee after his vision quest in the wilderness. On a sabbath in the synagogue in his home village of Nazareth, Jesus finds a passage from the book of Isaiah and uses it to announce his mission:

> The Spirit of the Lord is upon me, because he has anointed me to bring good news to the poor. He has sent me to proclaim release to the captives and recovery of sight to the blind, to let the oppressed go free, to proclaim the year of the Lord's favor. (4.18–19, citing Isa. 61.1–2; 58.6)

Though most mainline scholars see the setting and perhaps the story as a whole as Luke's creation, most also agree that it is a very appropriate summation of Jesus's mission and message.

The passage combines a number of metaphors. The words from Isaiah come from the time of the Jewish *exile*. It speaks of sight to the *blind*. *Bondage* is the dominant metaphor, as indicated by the number of lines devoted to it: Jesus's mission is "to proclaim release to the captives," "to let the oppressed go free." So also the emphasis on "good news to the poor": they are the captives and oppressed. The poor were not simply the impoverished at the bottom of an otherwise prosperous society, but were poor primarily because of systemic economic exploitation. The final line, "the year of the Lord's favor," also connects to economic deprivation. It alludes to the jubilee year, which involved restoration of all agricultural land to the original families of ownership (Lev. 25.8–12). Whether Luke (or Jesus) meant the language of jubilee literally is uncertain and perhaps unlikely, but the echo of the language fits the theme of "good news to the poor." Jubilee, whether understood literally or metaphorically, is about liberation from poverty, captivity, and oppression.

Like exile, bondage is a pervasive image in the gospels, found in narratives about Jesus as well as in the message of Jesus himself. Poor people—perhaps the peasant class as a whole, and certainly the majority—are spoken of as in bondage, as we have just seen. Possessed people are in bondage to demons. In one case, the demons are named "Legion" (Mark 5.9), an allusion to the Jewish people's bondage to Rome.

The language of bondage also appears in healing stories. In Luke 13.10–17, Jesus heals a woman crippled for eighteen years, bent over, unable to stand up straight. Jesus says to her, "Woman, you are set free from your ailment." Then he is criticized for doing this on the sabbath. His response uses the language of bondage and freedom and implies that the sabbath itself is about liberation: "Ought not this woman, a daughter of Abraham whom Satan bound for eighteen long years, be set free from this bondage on the sabbath day?" Freed from her bondage, the woman "stood up straight."

A story of Jesus healing a paralyzed man belongs to the same metaphorical family. To a paralytic brought to him lying on a mat, Jesus said, "Stand up and take your mat and walk" (Mark 2.9; see also John 5.8). In the more familiar words of an earlier translation, "Rise, take up your bed and walk." The metaphorical meaning of the two stories is clear. Jesus frees people from being bent over by bondage so they can stand up straight again, from paralysis so they can walk again.

The language of bondage and liberation continues in Paul. In his letter to the Galatians, he wrote, "For freedom Christ has set us free. Stand firm, therefore, and do not submit again to a yoke of slavery" (5.1). The context is slavery to "the law"—not the Jewish law as Torah, but a more universal understanding of law as a system of requirements from which people need to be liberated in order to be in relationship to God as known in Jesus.

These metaphors embedded in and shaping the message of Jesus are provocative, to say the least. The broad way, our most common way of living, involves being blind though sighted, dead though alive, in exile though perhaps at home, in bondage though perhaps living in the land of the free. The diagnosis is challenging. It invites reflection. Is this the way things are? Are we blind, dead, in exile and bondage? And if this is the way things are, what then?

The broad way as Jesus saw it, and as mentioned earlier, is not the path of gross wickedness, not the way of obvious sinfulness. It afflicts most of us most of the time, the fortunate and the unfortunate, the privileged and the unprivileged, the righteous and the unrighteous. Perfectly respectable people are caught within it. Indeed, following the broad way is most often not the result of a conscious and free decision; rather, we fall into it. It is the result of seeing our lives through the lens of convention. It is our common lot, now as well as then.

Jesus's perception of the way of convention as the broad way was also central to the most influential philosophical teacher of wisdom in Western culture. Just as Jesus is the most important religious figure in the history of the West, so Socrates (469–399 BCE) is the most important philosophical figure. What has become one of his best-known sayings is, "The unexamined life is not worth living." If we do not examine our lives, if we do not submit them to critical reflection, we are doomed to live our lives as the conventions of our culture dictate.

To state the same diagnosis with arresting phrases used by a contemporary writer, normal adult consciousness—the way we are because of our socialization within a culture—is marked by "mass hypnosis" and "consensual paranoia." Mass hypnosis is displayed in our living in a trancelike state, valuing what our culture values, and pursuing our culture's image of the good life. Consensual paranoia is evident because we fear what our culture fears.[7] This is our common state, and if we do not become conscious of it and examine it, we will live within it.

Jesus and Socrates are different in important ways, yet they also share much in common. Both were mystics; both challenged the life of convention; and both were executed by the authorities. Socrates was put to death on the charges of impiety (refusing to accept conventional understandings of life and the sacred) and corrupting others to think likewise. The charges go hand in hand. It is striking that the two most revered figures of Western religion and philosophy were executed by the powers that ruled their worlds.

How should we honor them? Should we build memorials to them? Jesus spoke of this in one of his "woe" sayings:

> Woe to you! For you build the tombs of the prophets whom your ancestors killed. So you are witnesses and approve of the deeds of your ancestors; for they killed them, and you build their tombs. (Luke 11.47–48; Matt. 23.29–31)

Figures like Socrates and Jesus and the prophets are safely entombed in antiquity. But what if they are not simply to be revered as exceptional figures from the past, but to be followed in the present?

In addition to using this collection of metaphors to characterize the common human condition, Jesus undermined the central concerns of the conventional wisdom of his time. His subversion of convention continues in his teachings about family, wealth, honor, and purity.

Lords of Convention: Family, Wealth, Honor, and Purity

Family

Kinship—the extended family—had a significance in the world of Jesus difficult for those of us in contemporary American culture to imagine.[8] The family was extended rather than nuclear, multigenerational rather than consisting primarily of parents and children. People lived in extended families throughout their lifetime rather than growing up and leaving home. The family was also an authoritarian patriarchal structure; authority was vested in men, especially in the father.

The extended family was the primary social and economic unit. It meant everything:

> It not only was the source of one's status in the community but also functioned as the primary economic, religious, educational, and social network. Loss of connection to the family meant the loss of these vital networks as well as loss of connection to the land.[9]

The family was the basic unit of economic production and thus the source of material security (or insecurity). It was also the primary source of identity. Genealogies mattered. A man was known as son of his father. A woman was known as daughter of her father until she married, when she became known as wife of her husband. People were embedded in kinship and, not surprisingly, loyalty to family mattered greatly. Family was the primary in-group to which one gave one's allegiance. Like all in-groups, it also constrained one's allegiance.

In this social context, Jesus's sayings about family and kinship were strikingly radical. In our time, a common form of Christianity emphasizes "family values" as central to the Bible and Jesus. But Jesus frequently called for a break from the family and the obligations and security that went with it.

He spoke of following him as involving "hating" one's family: "Whoever comes to me and does not *hate* father and mother, wife and children, brothers and sisters … cannot be my disciple" (Luke 14.26). The passage is softened somewhat (but only somewhat) by the fact that "hate" can be an idiom in Hebrew and Aramaic meaning "to love less" or "to put in second place." Matthew's version of the saying reflects this idiomatic meaning: "Whoever loves father or mother more than me is not worthy of me; and whoever loves son or daughter more than me is not worthy of me" (10.37). But even the softer form calls for a following of Jesus that transcends family obligations.

Jesus relativized the significance of his own family. When a crowd sitting around him tells him that his "mother and brothers" are looking for him (Mark 3.32), Jesus replies:

"Who are my mother and my brothers?" And looking at those who sat around him, he said, "Here are my mothers and my brothers! Whoever does the will of God is my brother and sister and mother." (Mark 3.33–35)

He negates his blood family as he speaks of a new family marked by a common loyalty to God.

Becoming a disciple meant leaving family. In Mark's account of Jesus calling his first disciples:

Jesus saw James son of Zebedee and his brother John, who were in their boat mending the nets. Immediately he called them; and they left their father Zebedee in the boat with the hired men, and followed him. (1.19–20)

So also in Luke. An unnamed person who wishes to follow Jesus says to him, "I will follow you, Lord; but let me first say farewell to those at my home." Jesus responds, "No one who puts a hand to the plow and looks back is fit for the kingdom of God" (9.61–62).

Another saying refers to division within families brought by his mission:

> Do not think that I have come to bring peace to the earth; I
> have not come to bring peace, but a sword. For I have come
> to set a man against his father, and a daughter against her
> mother, and a daughter-in-law against her mother-in-law.
> (Matt. 10.34–35; Luke 12.51–53)

The first line is sometimes quoted out of context to portray a Jesus
who endorses war: "I have not come to bring peace, but a sword." But
in context, it unmistakably refers to the sword of division that cuts
family ties. Interestingly, the division is generational, son against father,
daughter against mother, daughter-in-law against mother-in-law.

Yet another saying may negate patriarchal family authority: "Call
no one your father on earth, for you have one Father—the one in
heaven" (Matt. 23.9). As a personal aside, in the pre-ecumenical Lutheran milieu in which I grew up, I was told that this verse explains
why we called our clergy "pastor" and not "father," as the Catholics
and Episcopalians did. Did they not know that Jesus prohibited calling someone "father"? Needless to say, that was an ahistorical reading
of the text. But in its first-century historical context, this verse may
mean that because God is your Father, you are to have no other fathers. Its meaning would thus be parallel to language about God's
lordship: because God is Lord, you are to have no other lords. If so, it
is a marvelous example of using patriarchal language for God (God
as father) to subvert all earthly patriarchy.[10]

Do these sayings about family mean a complete rejection of family
by Jesus? It seems highly unlikely. That Jesus spoke of loving our
neighbor and even loving our enemies makes it impossible to imagine that his final word about family was simply negative. But his
teaching clearly affirms that embeddedness in family and its conventions can hold one in bondage and prevent responding to the message of centering in God and God's passion. He saw the conventional
patriarchal family as a constricting institution that demanded a loyalty inconsistent with loyalty to God. To give primary allegiance to it
locked one into the world of convention. Indeed, freedom from the
constricting structures of the patriarchal family was a major reason
that early Christianity was especially attractive to women.[11]

Wealth

Wealth and possessions were central to the conventional wisdom of the time, as they are in most times and places. Obviously, it was good to be wealthy, for wealth provided both comfort and security. It was also a source of identity, a sign that one had lived right. Though Jewish voices did speak of the "unrighteous wealthy," wealth was commonly seen as a blessing from God that flowed from following the path of wisdom. In the minds of at least some, wealth was a sign of God's favor. Sayings in the book of Proverbs, part of the conventional wisdom of ancient Israel, can be understood this way: "In the house of the righteous there is much treasure, but trouble befalls the income of he wicked" (15.6); "The reward for humility and fear of the LORD is riches and honor and life" (22.4); "A slack hand causes poverty, but the hand of the diligent makes rich" (10.4); "An idle person will suffer hunger" (19.15b); "Misfortune pursues sinners, but prosperity rewards the righteous" (13.21).[12]

The inference, drawn in many cultures by those with wealth and sometimes by those without, is close at hand: if you're prosperous, it's because you have lived right; if you are impoverished, it's your own fault. The wealthy deserve their wealth, just as the poor deserve their poverty.

Yet Jesus regularly criticized wealth in both sayings and stories. For Christians today who are affluent or who aspire to affluence, these are among the most challenging teachings in the gospels. He pronounced woes upon the rich and blessings upon the poor (Luke 6.20–26). He told unfavorable stories about the pursuit of wealth: "Be on your guard against all kinds of greed; for one's life does not consist in the abundance of possessions" (12.15). Then he told a parable:

> The land of a rich man produced abundantly. And he thought to himself, "What should I do, for I have no place to store my crops?" Then he said, "I will do this: I will pull down my barns and build larger ones, and there I will store all my grains and my goods. And I will say to my soul, 'Soul, you have ample

goods laid up for many years; relax, eat, drink, and be merry.'"
But God said to him, "You fool! This very night your life is
being demanded of you. And the things you have prepared,
whose will they be?" So it is with those who store up treasures
for themselves but are not rich toward God. (Luke 12.16–21)

With good reason, this passage is commonly called the parable of the
rich fool. Folly and wealth, not wisdom and wealth, go together.

Another parable (Luke 16.19–31) starkly contrasts the lavish life
of a rich man and his chilling indifference to a beggar at the gate of
his villa:

There was a rich man who was dressed in purple and fine linen
and who feasted sumptuously every day. And at his gate lay a
poor man named Lazarus, covered with sores, who longed to
satisfy his hunger with what fell from the rich man's table; even
the dogs would come and lick his sores.

Both die. Lazarus "was carried away by the angels to be with
Abraham"; he goes to "the bosom of Abraham," as an older translation puts it. The rich man goes to Hades; tormented and in agony, he
longs for a drop of water to cool his tongue. He beseeches Abraham
to send Lazarus to warn his brothers so that they will change their
lives and avoid his fate. Abraham replies: "They have Moses and the
prophets; they should listen to them." The rich man thinks that won't
be enough, so he beseeches Abraham again: "But if someone goes to
them from the dead, they will repent."

Abraham's final words in the parable are: "If they do not listen to
Moses and the prophets, neither will they be convinced even if someone rises from the dead." The point is obvious. The law and the
prophets, the Jewish scriptures, should be enough to reveal God's passion for the poor. If you don't "get it" from that, neither will you "get
it" even if someone rises from the dead. Wealth and obduracy, riches
and hardness of heart, most often go together—then and now.

In an aphorism using the language of slavery, Jesus spoke of
wealth as a source of bondage for those who seek it:

> No one can serve two masters; for a slave will either hate the
> one and love the other, or be devoted to the one and despise
> the other. You cannot serve God and wealth. (Matt. 6.24; Luke
> 16.13)

Like the noun "slave," the verb "serve" refers to slavery. In the ancient world, slaves were understood not to have their own will;
their will was under the control of their master. Thus the first sentence of the saying states an obvious truth: no one can be a slave to
two masters. The second sentence applies the obvious truth to
wealth, or "mammon," to use a word familiar from older translations.
"Mammon" does mean wealth, but more broadly refers to the material basis of life. Thus it refers not only to the wealthy, but to all for
whom wealth is a central concern. Jesus saw mammon, wealth, as a
slavemaster that prevents centering in God.

The stark contrast between serving God and serving wealth appears
in another saying in which Jesus spoke of the foolishness of storing
up treasure on earth and the wisdom of storing up treasure in God:

> Do not store up for yourselves treasures on earth, where moth
> and rust consume and where thieves break in and steal; but
> store up for yourselves treasures in heaven, where neither moth
> nor rust consumes and where thieves do not break in and steal.
> For where your treasure is, there your heart will be also. (Matt.
> 6.19–21; Luke 12.33–34)

The "heart" is the self at its deepest level, and whatever the heart
treasures most is where one's loyalty will be.

In a well-known story reported in all of the synoptic gospels, a
rich man asks Jesus, "What must I do to inherit eternal life?" In
Matthew, the man is also spoken of as young, and in Luke as a ruler.
Hence it is often called the story of the rich young ruler. But in Mark
10.17–31, the earliest version of the story, he is simply rich.

For us, his question about "eternal life" suggests that he is asking,
"What must I do to go to heaven?" But in the first century, "eternal

life" meant the "life of the age to come," and as the story unfolds, it is equated with the "kingdom of God" (Mark 10.23; Matt. 19.23; Luke 18.24). The question is thus about entering the kingdom of God.

To the rich man, Jesus says, "You know the commandments," and then names some of them: "You shall not murder,... commit adultery,... steal,... bear false witness,... defraud; Honor your father and mother." The man says, "Teacher, I have kept these since my youth." Jesus accepts his claim; the man seems to have led a conventionally good life. Then Jesus says to him: "You lack one thing; go, sell what you own, and give the money to the poor; and you will have treasure in heaven; then come, follow me." The man is "shocked." This is what following Jesus means? He cannot do it; he "went away grieving, for he had many possessions." His wealth held him in bondage, preventing him from following this teacher to whom he was attracted.

After he leaves, Jesus says to his disciples, "How hard it will be for those who have wealth to enter the kingdom of God." They are perplexed, and so he adds, "It is easier for a camel to go through the eye of a needle than for someone who is rich to enter the kingdom of God." Is it because wealth is wicked? Or because wealth is a snare? In either case, it is an indictment of what has been valued greatly by the conventional wisdom of most cultures, or at least the fortunate within them.

Jesus himself was apparently without possessions, and he commanded his disciples to be likewise.[13] He and they may have practiced a form of "holy poverty."[14] Yet it is not clear that Jesus opposed wealth in principle. At least a few wealthy people were attracted to his vision, including some women who supported him and his disciples.[15] The early Christian movement also attracted some people of means, disenchanted elites disillusioned by the life of wealth and privilege. They might be role models for affluent Christians today. Nevertheless, Jesus clearly saw the desire for wealth as one of the primary distractions and preoccupations in life, as a consuming and blinding passion, despite the value assigned to it by conventional wisdom.

Honor

Honor was a central concern in the world of Jesus. To some extent the product of birth, family, and wealth, it was sustained by social recognition. It was not just social status, but also the *regard* one felt entitled to in virtue of that status.

> Honor is the value of a person in his or her own eyes (that is, one's claim to worth) *plus* that person's value in the eyes of his or her social group. Honor is a claim to worth along with the social acknowledgment of worth.[16]

Much behavior was therefore dictated by the desire to acquire, preserve, or display honor and to avoid its opposite, shame. Honor and shame are still major motivators of behavior in much of the Middle East as well as elsewhere.

Jesus ridiculed the concern with honor. He mocked those who sought social recognition:

> Beware of the scribes, who like to walk around in long robes, and to be greeted with respect in the marketplaces, and to have the best seats in the synagogues and places of honor at banquets! (Mark 12.38–39; see also Luke 11.43 = Matt. 23.6)

Noticing how guests chose the places of honor at a banquet, he counseled the opposite: "When you are invited, go and sit down at the lowest place." He concluded the teaching with, "For all who exalt themselves will be humbled, and those who humble themselves will be exalted" (Luke 14.7–11; see also Matt. 18.4; 23.12; Luke 18.14). Those who seek honor will be shamed, and those who do not care about shame will be honored.

He chastised religious practices—giving alms, fasting, praying—motivated by the desire for honor:

> Whenever you give alms, do not sound a trumpet before you.... Whenever you fast, do not look dismal, like the hypo-

crites, for they disfigure their faces so as to show others that they are fasting.... But when you fast, put oil on your head and wash your face, so that your fasting may be seen not by others but by your Father who is in secret. (Matt. 6.2, 16–18)

So also with prayer. One should not pray in public so as to be "seen by others"; "whenever you pray go into your room and shut the door and pray ... in secret" (6.5–6).

Purity

A fourth concern structuring the conventional wisdom of Jesus's social world was purity and its opposite, impurity (sometimes also referred to as cleanness and uncleanness). It is important to realize that purity and impurity have broad anthropological and cross-cultural meanings as well as more particular meanings in the world of Jesus. In their broad sense, "purity rules have a place for every-thing and everyone, with everything and everyone in its place." It is a system of cultural classification and borders: "between clean and un-clean, there must be a line."[17] In this broad sense, all cultures have purity rules, even as their content varies greatly.

Purity in the world of Jesus was concerned with particular mat-ters: food and meals, corpses, bodily emissions (semen, menstruation, discharges), childbirth, bodily blemishes and imperfections. Impurity could also be acquired from contact with people who were in a state of impurity.

Impurity and sin were not the same. Some actions that violated the purity rules were clearly wrong and thus sinful, such as eating forbidden foods. But some sources of impurity were unavoidable. For example, an emission of semen made a man impure, but it was not sinful. Childbirth and menstruation made women impure, but nei-ther was a sin. Contact with a corpse created impurity, but relatives were still obligated to prepare the dead for burial. When impurity was acquired, it was removed through a number of means, including passage of time, ritual washing, and sacrifices, in various combina-tions. Not all impurities required all three.[18]

But though sin and impurity were not the same, impurity was to be avoided when possible. Moreover, as already mentioned, it was contagious; it could be acquired from those who were impure. Furthermore, impurity clung. If not dealt with, it remained. Impurity thus had social consequences. Jews who were chronically nonobservant of the rules of purity and purification would be in a perpetual state of impurity, as would those who were only occasionally observant. Those generally but not always observant were in an ambiguous group, depending upon who was evaluating them.

How seriously Jews in the peasant class were concerned with their own purity or the purity of their fellow villagers is difficult to know. But we do know that purity mattered greatly to some of Jesus's contemporaries. Two of the most devout Jewish groups, the Essenes and the Pharisees, intensified purity rules. The biblical basis was Leviticus 19.2, an *imitatio dei* that named God's central quality as holiness: "Speak to all the congregation of the people of Israel and say to them: *You shall be holy, for I the LORD your God am holy.*" Both Pharisees and Essenes understood God's holiness as purity: to be holy as God is holy meant to be pure as God is pure.

Because the Essenes had withdrawn to the wilderness, they had little influence on public life. Scholars disagree about how much influence the Pharisees had. But textual and archaeological evidence both indicate a widespread concern with purity in the Jewish homeland. Hundreds of immersion pools (*miqvaoth*) used for purification have been unearthed in both Galilee and Judea. Some were in homes of the wealthy; others were for public use.

Purity was also central to the temple in Jerusalem, the spatial center of the purity system. In the sacred geography of Judaism, the "holy of holies" was the center of a series of concentric circles of descending degrees of required purity. Those in charge of the temple or active in the temple as priests and Levites and ordinary Jews entering the temple area were obligated to be in a state of purity.

The purity rules of ancient Judaism strike many modern people as somewhere on the spectrum from bizarre to puzzling and, at best, unimportant and irrelevant. To be sure, they are obviously the product of a particular time and place and reflect a particular society's ideas about the boundaries between pure and impure. The vast majority of Christians and many modern Jews regard them as no longer applicable. I know of no Christians who avoid planting two kinds of seed in the same field or wearing clothes made of two kinds of cloth or who practice ritual immersion after intercourse or menstruation, even though these are commanded in the Bible.[19]

Yet the particular purity rules of Judaism were part of the world of Jesus. Moreover, as we have seen, impurity had social consequences: it was contagious and it clung. Thus the categories of pure and impure were attached to individuals and groups. Impure individuals mentioned in the gospels include lepers (people with skin conditions, but not the illness known in our world as Hansen's disease) and a woman with a perpetual flow of blood. The prodigal son had made himself impure by becoming a swineherd. Groups seen as impure included those possessed by demons; though not mentioned in purity laws, they are regularly referred to as having an "unclean spirit." Samaritans were impure. Most likely, many of "the poor" were also impure, especially the destitute and those on the edge of destitution. Though I am aware of no statement that says they were impure, to be radically impoverished made observance of rules about purity and purification very difficult.

In this context, Jesus's sayings about purity are as radical as his teachings about family, wealth, and honor. In a social world that saw purity as the product of following particular behaviors, Jesus affirmed that purity was the product of what people were like on the "inside." Most of his sayings on this topic are set in the context of conflict with Pharisees. This is not surprising, for they were the group in public life most committed to the intensification of purity.

That purity is about the "inside" and not the "outside" is expressed in a concise aphorism in Mark. The verse uses the term "defile," part of the same linguistic family as "pure" and "impure," "clean" and "unclean": "There is nothing outside a person that by going in can defile, but the things that come out are what defile" (7.15). As with most and perhaps all of his short sayings, Jesus is likely to have said this on many occasions.

In Mark, the extended context is Pharisaic criticism of Jesus's followers for not washing their hands before eating:

Now when the Pharisees and some of the scribes who had come from Jerusalem gathered around Jesus, they noticed that some of his disciples were eating with defiled hands, that is, without washing them.... So the Pharisees and the scribes asked him, "Why do your disciples not live according to the tradition of the elders, but eat with defiled hands?" (7.1–2, 5)

The issue, of course, is not hygiene but purity. Jesus's critics say that eating with unwashed hands brings impurity. His response, "There is nothing outside a person that by going in can defile, but the things that come out are what defile," denies that impurity is a contagion that one contacts from the outside. Rather, impurity is the product of what is inside. What is inside is, of course, "the heart" (Mark 7.21).[20]

In a world to a large extent structured by purity laws, this aphorism was subversive. It is like saying in a racially segregated society that race is a matter of what people are like on the inside, not on the outside. A familiar Beatitude in the Sermon on the Mount makes the same point: "Blessed are *the pure in heart*, for they will see God" (Matt. 5.8).

The contrast between "outside" and "inside" appears in a Q saying as well. Luke sets it in the context of Jesus being invited to dine with a Pharisee who then was "amazed to see that he [Jesus] did not first wash before dinner" (11.38; it is the same issue as in Mark 7). Jesus responds, "You Pharisees clean the *outside* of the cup and of the dish, but *inside* you are full of greed and wickedness" (Luke 11.39; Matt. 23.25).

Whether the indictment—"you are full of greed and wickedness"—was true of all Pharisees is beside the point. No doubt some were good, even saintly; indeed, we know the names of some Pharisaic "saints." But what is criticized is the preoccupation with an understanding of purity that emphasizes the "outside."

Yet another criticism of Pharisees makes use of purity language. They were concerned with corpse impurity, that is, avoiding becoming impure through proximity to a corpse. Jesus turns this concern against them. In a Q saying, he charges that their influence is defiling, like a grave that has not been marked: "Woe to you! For you are like unmarked graves, and people walk over them without realizing it" (Luke 11.44; Matt. 23.27).[21]

In addition, purity issues are at the center of criticism of Jesus's inclusive meal practice, one of the most prominent features of his activity. Twice his critics are named as Pharisees (Mark 2.15–16; Luke 15.1–2): "Why does he eat with tax collectors and sinners?" and "This fellow welcomes sinners and eats with them."

The same criticism is found in a saying of Jesus in Q that refers to unnamed persons who criticized both him and his mentor John:

> John the Baptist has come eating no bread and drinking no wine, and you say, "He has a demon"; the Son of Man has come eating and drinking, and you say, "Look, a glutton and a drunkard, a friend of tax collectors and sinners!" (Luke 7.33–34; Matt. 11.18–19)

The issue was not *what* Jesus ate (not whether he ate forbidden food), but *with whom* he ate: tax collectors and sinners.[22] These were people whose presence defiled those who ate with them. Yet Jesus did eat with them. Though these were real meals, they also had symbolic meaning. His meal practice was an enacted parable of a different understanding of purity and a much more inclusive vision of the kingdom of God. For Jesus, purity, not impurity, was contagious.

Thus his teaching about purity, like his teaching about family, wealth, and honor, challenged conventional convictions concerning what life was about and how it should be lived. His parables and sayings cover the gamut of first-century Jewish life in the homeland. As snapshots of typical behavior, they disclose Jesus's diagnosis of the human condition and the conventions of his time, the "broad way." He saw his contemporaries as preoccupied with their concerns, limited in their vision, captive to their convictions, and embedded in convention. What was true then seems still to be the way things are for most of us most of the time.

THE NARROW WAY

The other way that Jesus taught—the narrow way, the alternative way, the road less traveled—is conceptually simple and easy to state, even as it is existentially challenging. It has been implicit and some-times explicit in the material we have considered in this chapter.

Centering in God

In a phrase, the way of Jesus consists of a radical centering in God. This is, of course, the foundation of Judaism. When asked what the greatest commandment was, Jesus quoted the Shema from Deuter-onomy, the core of the daily prayers of Judaism: "You shall love the Lord your God with all your heart, and with all your soul, and with all your mind, and with all your strength" (Mark 12.30).

The same imperative is found in Jesus's aphorism about the im-possibility of serving two masters:

> No one can serve two masters; for a slave will either hate the one and love the other, or be devoted to the one and despise the other. You cannot serve God and wealth/mammon." (Matt. 6.24; Luke 16.13)

Serve God—center in God—or you will serve another lord. *That* will put you in exile and bondage and make you blind.

It is the meaning of his parable about the wise man who built his house on the rock and the foolish man who built his house on sand. What is the "rock"? Given the contexts in which Matthew and Luke set this saying, the rock was the teaching of Jesus in the Sermon on the Mount and the Sermon on the Plain. But if we assume that Jesus told this parable more than once, as seems very likely, he would have said it in more contexts than the ones Matthew and Luke set it in.

For Jesus himself, the "rock" was God. "Rock" is an image for the sacred in the Jewish Bible. God is "the Rock" of Israel (Deut. 32.15); "The LORD is my rock" (Ps. 18.2); "a rock of refuge" (Ps. 31.2); God alone "is my rock" (Ps. 62.2); and "Look to the rock [God] from which you were hewn" (Isa. 51.1).

But it is not enough to say that the "rock" is God, for the rock is not just any understanding of God, but the rock is God *as Jesus had come to know God*, the God whose character is compassion and whose passion is justice. This is the rock on which Jesus invited his hearers to build. To build on anything else is to build upon sand.

Repentance

A second image for the narrow way is an imperative: "Repent." The word is found in the gospels less often than we might expect, given its importance in popular Christianity throughout the centuries. But it is part of Mark's advance summary of Jesus's message: "The time is fulfilled, and the kingdom of God has come near; *repent*" (1.15).

The word means something quite different from what it means to many Christians, for whom the verb "repent" and the noun "repentance" mean to feel sorrow and contrition about one's sins and turning from sin to God. Many of us who grew up Christian acquired this understanding in childhood. To repent meant "to feel really, really bad about what a sinful person you are."[23]

But this is not what it means in the gospels. There it has two meanings. The first is grounded in the Jewish experience of exile in Babylon, of separation from Jerusalem and the holy land as the place of God's presence. *To repent* means "to return," and in particular to return from exile. Thus it intrinsically belongs to the same linguistic family as the image of "the way": "the way" is the path of repentance, the path of returning to God through a deep centering in God.

A second meaning is suggested by the roots of the Greek word used in the gospels. Of course, Jesus taught in Aramaic, either all of the time or most of the time. But given that we have his teaching only in Greek, the meaning of the Greek term matters. At the very least, it suggests what the authors of the gospels had in mind when they say he used this word. The Greek roots of "repent" mean "*to go beyond the mind that you have.*" To repent is to see again, to go beyond the mind that is the product of convention, to acquire a new mind, a new way of seeing.

Thus the word "repent" combines *to return from exile* and *to think/ see anew*. It means to return from a condition of estrangement and exile to the presence of God. And it means to acquire a new way of seeing and thinking that goes beyond the conventions of culture. Both meanings involve centering in God—in God as Jesus spoke of God.

Dying and Rising

A third image of the narrow way is the path of dying—more fully, of dying and rising, death and resurrection. This image was central to Jesus's post-Easter followers. Paul speaks of dying and rising with Christ as the way of becoming "in Christ" (Rom. 6). He speaks of himself as having undergone the path: "I have been crucified with Christ; it is no longer I who live, but Christ who lives in me" (Gal. 2.19–20). So also in John's gospel in a famous passage, to be born again means to die to an old way of being and to be born into a new way of being, one centered in the Spirit of God (3.1–10).

Did Jesus himself also use the language of dying and rising, the path of death and resurrection, as a metaphor for the way that he taught? Given that speaking of the way of Jesus as the path of death and resurrection has an obvious setting and meaning after Easter, a response to this question is both tentative and problematic.

What we can say is that Mark and Q, our two earliest gospel sources, report that he did. According to Mark 8.34, Jesus said, "If any want to become my followers, let them deny themselves and *take up their cross* and follow me." In the Jewish homeland in the first century, taking up one's cross was an image for death. It did not yet mean patiently bearing whatever burden might befall one, as when we sometimes speak of "our cross" in life as a physical difficulty or even a troublesome in-law. Rather, taking up one's cross referred to the Roman practice of requiring a person condemned to be crucified to carry the horizontal crossbeam to the place of execution, where the vertical post was permanently fixed in the ground. To take up one's cross was to embark upon the path of death.

In Mark, the context of this saying is the narrative of following Jesus "on the way." The verses immediately after it amplify the imagery of losing one's life:

> For those who want to save their life will lose it, and those who lose their life for my sake and for the sake of the gospel will save it. For what will it profit them to gain the whole world and forfeit their own life? (8.35–36)

If language about taking up one's cross were found only in Mark, historical prudence would require seeing it as most likely a post-Easter creation. But it is also found in Q, probably put into written form in the 50s of the first century: "Whoever does not *carry the cross* and follow me cannot be my disciple" (Luke 14.27; Matt. 10.38). In both Luke and Matthew, the context is division among families, which suggests a metaphorical meaning to carrying one's cross: it means to die to the world of convention. In Luke, the saying is followed by teaching about the cost of discipleship (14.28–33). The cost is one's life.

Thus, as both Mark and Q report Jesus's message, the narrow way is the path of death. But death is not annihilation; rather, it is entry into a new way of life. Together, death and resurrection as an image of the way means dying to an old identity and way of being and being born into a new identity and new way of being, one centered in God. Whether or not Jesus himself explicitly spoke of the way as the path of dying and rising, the notion is implicit in his message: centering in God is the way that leads to life.

CENTERING IN GOD AS BELOVING GOD

We return to "centering in God" as a concise phrase for the narrow way. It is the best shorthand phrase I know of for crystallizing the way of Jesus. It is what we see in his teaching. And it is what we see in his life—he was radically centered in God. God was for him, as a Jewish mystic, an experiential reality. His centering in God, in the one in whom he lived and moved and had his being, was the source of his wisdom, compassion, courage, and, as we will see in the next chapter, his challenge to the domination system. In him, mysticism, empowerment, and resistance came together.

Thus it should not surprise us that his followers began to speak of *him* as the way. By the end of the first century, the Jesus of John's gospel says, "I am the way, and the truth, and the life" (14.6). Because this verse has sometimes been understood to mean that only people who believe in Jesus (namely, Christians) can be saved, it is troublesome for many today, both within the church and outside it. Is it really possible that nobody other than Christians can be saved? That the God of the universe has chosen to be known in only this one way? But within John's incarnational theology, the verse need not mean this. Incarnation means embodiment, becoming flesh. For John, just as Jesus is the Word of God become flesh and the wisdom of God become flesh, so he is "the way" become flesh. For John, what we see in Jesus is the way—the incarnation, the embodiment, of a life radically centered in God. *This*—the way we see in Jesus—is the way.[24]

The phrase "centering in God" needs to have the particular content provided by Jesus's life and teaching. The way of Jesus was intrinsically linked to his perception of God's character and passion. Without this realization, centering in God has little content. Without this, the phrase can become an abstraction and understood quite conventionally as well as diversely. Most of Jesus's contemporaries would have said they were centering in God. Some of them no doubt did. So also most Christians today would say they are centering in God, or at least trying to. But there is a difference between centering in God and centering in ideas about God, just as there is a difference between *following* the way and *believing* in the way. The latter often becomes religion as convention, as a set of beliefs and behaviors learned from others. Our beliefs about God rather than the reality of God often become what we center in.

To center in God means to love God with heart, soul, mind, and strength. It means to belove God. How do we belove? What does it mean to belove God? It has multiple resonances: to yearn for, to pay attention to, to commit to, to be loyal to, to value above all else. For

Christians, this was the central meaning of the word "believe" until its meaning became distorted by the collision between Christianity and modernity. But until a few centuries ago, to believe meant to belove.

And to belove God, to center in God, has an additional crucial meaning. To belove God means to love what God loves. What does God love? The answer is in one of the most familiar Bible verses, John 3.16: "God so loved the world ..." In the next chapter, we will explore what God's love for the world meant for Jesus.

NINE

Resistance

The Kingdom and the Domination System

The Bible is both personal and political. I did not always see it this way. I grew up in a church that saw little connection between Christianity and politics. They were two different realms, one belonging to God and the other to Caesar. The notion that there could be a conflict between the two was quite foreign. But over the decades of my adult life, the perception that the Bible is political as well as personal has deepened into a conviction.

This twofold affirmation means something simple and basic. The Bible is personal. It is about our relationship to God *as persons*. This relationship is the path of personal transformation—the way of return from exile, sight to the blind, liberation from bondage; it is the way to new beginnings, the way to a life centered in God. Beloving God makes all the difference in our lives as persons.

The Bible is political. It is about God's passion for a different kind of world—one in which people have enough, not as the result of charity but as the fruit of justice, and in which nations do not war against one another anymore. God's passion is for a world very different from domination systems, large and small, ancient and modern, systems so common that they can be called the normalcy of civilization.

The theme runs through the Bible. As seen in Chapter 4, at the center of the Torah is the story of the ancient Israelites' liberation from Egypt and the creation of a very different form of community, in covenant with the God who had brought them out of the land of bondage. The second major section of the Bible, the Prophets, treats the rise and fall of the monarchy and its betrayal of God's passion for justice and peace. To affirm that the Bible is political is simply to recognize this emphasis. Once seen, it seems self-evident.[1]

So also the way of Jesus was both personal and political. It was about personal transformation. And it was political, a path of resistance to the domination system and advocacy of an alternative vision of life together under God. His counteradvocacy, his passion for God's passion, led to his execution. The way of the cross was both personal and political.

In this chapter, we explore how Jesus's message and activity challenged the domination system of his time and place. I begin with a brief review of its central features, more fully described in Chapter 4:

1. Rome ruled the Jewish homeland through native collaborators from the elite class. When Jesus began his mission, Galilee had been ruled for about thirty years by Herod Antipas. Judea and Samaria were ruled by the temple authorities and Jerusalem aristocracy, under a high priest appointed by Rome. He and the other temple authorities were responsible for satisfying both Rome and their Jewish subjects. Though the authorities in Jerusalem did not have political jurisdiction in Galilee, they sought to have religious jurisdiction, not through overt authority but through influence. They had a stake in how Galilean Jews behaved—an economic stake in whether they paid tithes to the temple and a political stake in whether they were restive and prone to rebellion.

2. As in preindustrial agrarian societies generally, the system created and ruled by the powerful and wealthy served their financial interests and was economically oppressive to the rest of the population. This has been "the way things are" in most societies since the Neolithic revolution of the fourth millennium BCE, which created large-scale agriculture, cities, city-states, kingdoms, and empires.

3. There are compelling reasons to think that conditions in the peasant class were worsening. Herod the Great and his sons

spent lavishly not only on their regal lifestyle, but on massive building projects, including whole cities, all of which required a larger and larger extraction of peasant agricultural production. Rome's client rulers in both Galilee and Jerusalem also needed to extract wealth from peasant production to pay the annual tribute to Rome. The economic consequences for the peasant class were severe. Though life had always been hard, a peasant family that had land could normally produce enough for its own sustenance. But more and more peasant families were losing their land and entering a more desperate kind of poverty. To be landless meant living on the edge of destitution, and often over the edge.

JEWISH RESPONSES TO THE DOMINATION SYSTEM

Jewish responses to the domination system covered a wide spectrum.[2] Some practiced the way of accommodation, especially the temple authorities, the wealthy, and their retainers. Their social roles required cooperation with Rome and the implementation of Roman rule, even as they also needed to satisfy their Jewish subjects enough to keep them politically quiet. This was often not easy; they had a tough job.

Accommodation was not simply an upper-class phenomenon, however. Many in the rest of the population also accommodated themselves to Roman rule, but for a different reason. Their motivation was not participation in privilege, but resignation to "this is the way things are," a status quo enforced by imperial power and the threat of imperial violence.

At the other end of the spectrum was the way of violent resistance. The two hundred years from the imposition of Roman rule in 63 BCE until the last major Jewish revolt in 132–35 CE were marked by periodic outbreaks of armed resistance. These outbreaks would not have happened if there were not a significant number of Jews sufficiently desperate and resentful to take up arms against Rome and its client rulers. The path of violence was never far beneath the surface.

There was also the way of nonviolent resistance, in both passive and active forms. The passive form included intensified loyalty to the distinctive practices of Judaism. In diverse ways, Pharisees and Essenes and many practitioners of common Judaism followed this path. Loyalty to tradition was a form of defiance, a refusal to assimilate to a non-Jewish way of life. Though some may have followed this way without seeing it as resistance, it nevertheless was, just as intensified loyalty to the Catholic Church was in Ireland under British rule and, more recently, in Poland under Soviet rule.

There was also the way of active nonviolent resistance. Josephus and Philo provide two vivid examples from around the time of Jesus. In the late 20s while Pilate was governor, imperial troops carried standards with images of the emperor into Jerusalem. A large number of Jews (Josephus says they "flocked together in crowds") gathered in protest in front of Pilate's residence in Caesarea, where they remained for five days. When ordered to leave or be killed by Pilate's soldiers, Josephus tells us: "The Jews, as by concerted action, flung themselves in a body on the ground, extended their necks, and exclaimed that they were ready rather to die than to transgress the law."[3] Pilate decided not to act.

Just over a decade later, in 40 CE, another episode of massive Jewish nonviolent resistance occurred in response to the plan of the Roman emperor Caligula to have a statue of himself erected in the Jerusalem temple. Josephus reports that "many tens of thousands" of Jews came together to stop the action. Though Josephus's numbers are often hyperbolic, clearly many protesters were involved, as Philo also reports. According to Josephus, "The Jews assembled with their wives and children" in front of Petronius, the Roman official charged with implementing the plan, "and presented themselves, their wives and children, ready for the slaughter."

Philo, writing almost contemporaneously with the event, reports it in greater detail. The protesters divided themselves into six companies, three male and three female: old men, young men, and boys; aged women, younger women, and virgins. Their statement to Petronius made their intention clear:

> We are, as you see, without any arms.... And if we cannot pre-
> vail with you in this, then we offer up ourselves for destruction,
> that we may not behold a calamity more terrible and grievous
> than death.... We willingly and readily submit ourselves to be
> put to death.[4]

Petronius responded by delaying the plan, which then was abandoned after Caligula was assassinated back in Rome.

These episodes not only illustrate that active nonviolent resistance
was a strategy used in the Jewish homeland, but imply both organization and leadership. Protests involving large crowds coming together and behaving in a highly disciplined manner do not happen
spontaneously.[5]

Jesus was, as we shall see, among those advocating and practicing
active nonviolent resistance to the domination system. Public criticism, then as now, was a form of resistance. Like some of the prophets of the Jewish Bible, he performed symbolic acts that challenged
the symbols of power. He seems also to have taught specific strate-
gies of nonviolent resistance. Indeed, his resistance to the way things
were and his counteradvocacy of the kingdom of God led to his execution.

THE LAST WEEK

We begin with the last week of Jesus's life, for it provides a series of
epiphanies of his challenge to the domination system. The word
"epiphany" means "disclosure" or "revelation." The great epiphany—
his execution by imperial authority—occurred at the end of the week,
which I treat in the next chapter. Here I focus on the beginning of
the week that has come to be known as Holy Week.[6]

The place and time are significant: Jerusalem during the week of
Passover. Jerusalem was not just any city, and Passover was not just
any week. The city was, as we have seen, central to the sacred geography of Judaism. It was the holy city, the home of the temple, the
place God had chosen to dwell on earth, the focus of Jewish devotion
and the destination of pilgrimage. In the first century, it also had a

230 JESUS

more sinister aspect; it had become, as it had been at times in the past, the center of the native domination system.

Passover, the most important of the annual Jewish festivals, celebrated the exodus of the early Israelites from Egypt. It drew hundreds of thousands of pilgrims to Jerusalem. Because this remembrance of Jewish liberation had sometimes been the occasion for riots and revolts, it was Roman practice to reinforce the imperial garrison stationed adjacent to the temple with additional troops. Passover brought not only a great number of Jews to the city, but also a greater imperial presence.

In or around the year 30, Jesus was among those who came to Jerusalem for Passover. As the gospels tell the story, his journey to the holy city was not simply the routine journey of a pilgrim, but deliberate and intentional. Indeed, in the synoptic gospels, this is the only time in the course of his public activity that he went to Jerusalem.

The gospels provide a more detailed account of Jesus's last week than of any other portion of his life. Earlier in the gospels, indications of time are general and vague. But for his final week, our earliest gospel Mark (largely followed by Matthew and Luke) provides a day-by-day and sometimes hour-by-hour narrative. In this chapter, I treat Sunday through Tuesday as epiphanies of Jesus's challenge to the domination system.

Sunday

At the beginning of the week of Passover, now called Palm Sunday by Christians, Jesus entered Jerusalem on a young donkey at the head of a procession made up of followers who had come with him from Galilee. Approaching the city from the east, he rode the donkey down the Mount of Olives as his followers cheered and chanted, "Hosanna! Blessed is the one who comes in the name of the Lord! Blessed is the coming kingdom of our ancestor David! Hosanna in the highest heaven!" (Mark 11.1–10).

Why did Jesus ride a donkey into Jerusalem? The question is the key to understanding what this act meant. Some answers are trivial and can be dismissed easily. Because he was tired or had sprained his ankle. Because on a donkey's back, he would be up higher so people could see him better. Another answer is not so trivial because some see it as the explanation: it was foreordained, predicted by prophecy. It had to happen this way.

But it was not the fulfillment of a prediction. Rather, it was what scholars of the Jewish Bible call a "prophetic act." Prophetic acts were provocative public deeds performed for the sake of what they symbolized, and they are called *prophetic* acts because they are associated with the prophets of ancient Israel. For example, Isaiah walked naked through the streets of Jerusalem over a period of three years to warn its inhabitants about what would happen if they made an alliance with Egypt—they would be carried off naked as the spoils of war (Isa. 20).

Jeremiah smashed a pottery jar in front of the senior priests and elders of Jerusalem and said, "Thus says the LORD of hosts: So will I break this people and this city, as one breaks a potter's vessel, so that it can never be mended" (19.11). Other prophetic acts of Jeremiah are reported in Jeremiah 13 and 27–28. In a public square, Ezekiel portrayed Jerusalem on a brick and laid siege to it with a toy army. There, also in public, he ate starvation rations to symbolize the famine and privation that would come upon a city under siege (Ezek. 4). Prophetic acts were ancient "street theater"—actions performed in public to draw a crowd and to convey a message.

So also Jesus's mode of entering Jerusalem was a prophetic act. As Mark tells the story, it was deliberate, planned, prearranged; Jesus set it up in advance. He tells two of his followers, "Go into the village ahead of you, and immediately as you enter it, you will find there a colt [of a donkey] that has never been ridden; untie it and bring it. If anyone says to you, 'Why are you doing this?' just say this, 'The Lord needs it and will send it back here immediately'" (Mark 11.2–3). They do so, bring the young donkey to Jesus, and he rides it into Jerusalem.

What did it mean? The meaning is implicit in Mark and explicit in Matthew. Jesus's action was based on a passage from the prophets that spoke of a humble king who would enter Jerusalem on the colt of a donkey. He would be a king of peace who would banish chariots, warhorses, and battle bows from the land and command peace to the nations (Zech. 9.9–10). By riding into Jerusalem on a young donkey, Jesus enacted his message: the kingdom of God of which he spoke was a kingdom of peace, not violence.

The meaning of Jesus's mode of entry is amplified by the realization that two processions entered Jerusalem that Passover. The other procession was an imperial one. On or about the same day, the Roman governor Pontius Pilate rode into the city from the opposite side, the west, at the head of a very different kind of procession: imperial cavalry and foot soldiers arriving to reinforce the garrison on the Temple Mount. They did so each year at Passover, coming to Jerusalem from Caesarea Maritima, the city on the Mediterranean coast from which the Roman governor administered Judea and Samaria.

Imagine the scene as Pilate's procession entered the city, a panoply of imperial power. Weapons, helmets, golden eagles mounted on poles, sun glinting on metal and gold. The pounding of horse hooves, the clinking of bridles, the marching of feet, the creaking of leather, the beating of drums, the swirling of dust. The eyes of the silent onlookers, some curious, some awed, some resentful.

Jesus (as well as the authors of the gospels) would have known about Rome's policy of sending reinforcements to the city at Passover. His decision to enter the city as he did was what we would call a planned political demonstration, a counterdemonstration. The juxtaposition of these two processions embodies the central conflict of Jesus's last week: the kingdom of God or the kingdom of imperial domination. What Christians have often spoken of as Jesus's triumphal entry was really an anti-imperial entry. What we call Palm Sunday featured a choice of two kingdoms, two visions of life on earth.

Monday

On the next day, Monday, Jesus performed a second prophetic act in Jerusalem. As Mark tells the story:

Jesus entered the temple and began to drive out those who were selling and those who were buying in the temple, and he overturned the tables of the money changers and the seats of those who sold doves; and he would not allow anyone to carry anything through the temple. He was teaching and saying, "Is it not written, 'My house shall be called a house of prayer for all the nations'? But you have made it a den of robbers." (11.15–17)[7]

Commonly called the "cleansing of the temple," though the phrase is not in the gospels, this episode would best be called, as we will see, the "indictment of the temple."

The event occurred in the court of the temple, a very large open area of about twenty-four acres bordered by columned porticoes. The temple building itself was small by comparison. Somewhere within the open courtyard, pilgrims could purchase animals for sacrifice and change money into the proper coinage for paying the temple tax. This is the activity that Jesus disrupted: he drove out the sellers and the buyers and overturned the tables of those changing money and the seats of those selling sacrificial doves. Then, Mark tells us, Jesus would not allow anyone to carry anything through the temple. Not surprisingly, all of this drew a crowd, and then Jesus taught.

If we visualize the scene historically, we cannot easily imagine that Jesus did this all by himself. Presumably some of his followers helped him. We also need to imagine it as limited in scope and duration. If Jesus and his followers had taken control of the whole temple court and held it for hours, the imperial troops stationed on the porticoes and garrisoned in the adjacent Fortress Antonia would have intervened. So we need to imagine that the disruption was brief (a few minutes? an hour?) and in a limited area. From a distance, it could look like a minor disturbance that was soon over with.

What did this act mean? Why did Jesus do this? It is inadequate to refer to it as his "temple tantrum," as if he were suddenly filled with anger at what he saw there, surprised that such things were going on. Rather, the act looks very intentional. Though Mark doesn't tell us it was planned, as the entry on Sunday was, it seems highly unlikely that Jesus simply decided to do it on the spot. It was deliberate, thought out in advance.

Also inadequate is perhaps the most common reading of the story at the popular level, which says that commercial activity—selling and buying and changing money—should not be going on in a place of worship. For many, naming the story as the "cleansing of the temple" means that Jesus sought to purify the temple by ridding it of money changers and vendors. But this interpretation does not work historically. The sellers of sacrificial animals and the money changers were not illicit or corrupt, but traditional; they provided a necessary service for the functioning of the temple. If you were a pilgrim who had traveled many miles (and some came hundreds of miles), it was much more convenient to purchase your sacrifice in Jerusalem than to carry it with you from home. Moreover, there is evidence that prices and exchange rates were closely regulated, so the issue was not that pilgrims were being fleeced by sharp merchants.

Was the issue sacrifice itself? That God doesn't want animal sacrifices? We have no reason to think that Jesus opposed animal sacrifice, though it is easy to imagine that he was indifferent about it. But the meaning of the temple act does not seem to be that the killing of animals in the name of God should stop.

Fortunately, we do not have to guess about its meaning. As Mark tells the story, Jesus interpreted the act himself, as prophets who performed prophetic acts in the Jewish Bible often did. His disruptive act became the occasion for him to teach. This may be the reason that he, and presumably his followers, would not allow anyone to carry anything through the temple—this was a time for paying attention to what Jesus had to say.

> Jesus was teaching and saying, "Is it not written, 'My house shall be called a house of prayer for all the nations'? But you have made it a den of robbers."

Jesus's interpretation of his action combines two passages from the Jewish Bible. The first is from Isaiah 56.7, which says the purpose of the temple is to be "a house of prayer for all the nations."

The second echoes Jeremiah 7.11, part of what is called Jeremiah's "temple sermon." Standing in the gate of the temple, Jeremiah said, "Do not trust in these deceptive words: 'This is the temple of the LORD, the temple of the LORD, the temple of the LORD'" (7.4). He warned that it would be destroyed unless those who worshiped there began to practice justice:

> If you truly amend your ways and doings, if you truly act justly one with another, if you do not oppress the alien, the orphan and the widow, or shed innocent blood in this place, and if you do not go after other gods to your own hurt, then I [God] will dwell with you in this place. (7.5–7)

Then, still speaking in the name of God, Jeremiah said, "Has this house [the temple], which is called by my name, become *a den of robbers* in your sight?" The phrase in Hebrew suggests not just thievery, but robbing with violence. In what sense had the temple become "a den of robbers," a cave of violent ones? In Jeremiah, the meaning is apparent: it was "a den of robbers" precisely because it had become the center of an oppressive system that did not practice justice, but exploited the most vulnerable in society. It was an indictment of the powerful and wealthy elites of his day, centered in the monarchy and temple. Their everyday injustice made them robbers, and they thought of the temple as their safe house and place of security.

Thus, when Jesus called the temple "a den of robbers," he was not referring to the activity of the money changers and sellers of sacrificial animals. Rather, he indicted the temple authorities as robbers who collaborated with the robbers at the top of the imperial domination system. They had made the temple into a den of robbing and violence. Jesus's action was not a cleansing of the temple, but an indictment of the temple. The teaching explains the act. Indeed, it was the reason for the act.

It was the kind of deed that could get one in trouble, and it did. The temple authorities decide that Jesus must die: "And when the chief priests and the scribes heard it, they kept looking for a way to kill him." But they do not take action immediately. Why not? "They were afraid of him, because the whole crowd was spellbound by his teaching" (Mark 11.18). The crowd, the people, were with Jesus. The implication is that they too resented the role that the temple played in the imperial system.

Tuesday

Tuesday is filled with verbal battles between Jesus and the authorities. It is a long day in the gospels. More verses are devoted to it than to any other day in Jesus's final week. Three episodes will illustrate the issues. The events all occur in the court of the temple in the presence of a crowd. More is meant, however, than the fact that the temple court was always thronged with thousands of pilgrims during Passover Week. Namely, the exchanges between Jesus and the authorities would have drawn a crowd. There were onlookers to these encounters or, to coin a word, onhearers.

By What Authority?

The first episode unfolds as Jesus walks in the court of the temple (Mark 11.27–33). Representatives of the authorities (Mark names them as "the chief priests, the scribes, and the elders") ask him, "By what authority are you doing these things? Who gave you this authority to do them?" "These things" refers to his anti-imperial entry on Sunday and his anti-temple indictment on Monday. They hope to trap Jesus into making a response that will create trouble for him.

Jesus skillfully evades their question. He makes a bargain with them: "I will ask you one question; answer me, and I will tell you by what authority I do these things." His question to them: "Did the baptism of John come from heaven?" That is, was it from God? "Or was it of human origin? Answer me." The question poses a conundrum for them, and they confer with each other: "If we say, 'From heaven,' he will say, 'Why then did you not believe him?' But shall we say, 'Of human origin'?" Because the crowd is present, they do not want to say the latter, for "they were afraid of the crowd, for all regarded John as truly a prophet." Lamely, they respond: "We do not know." Their lack of an answer fails to meet the terms of the bargain and sets up Jesus's response: "Neither will I tell you by what authority I am doing these things." He has kept his part of the bargain, even as he has not answered their question. Hoping to trap him, they end up silenced and looking foolish.

Vineyard and Tenants

In the second episode, Jesus takes the initiative. With the crowd and the authorities still present, he tells a parable about a vineyard owner who leases his vineyard to tenants (Mark 12.1–12). When harvest time comes, the owner sends a servant to collect his share of the produce. But the tenants beat him and send him away with nothing. He sends another servant, with the same result, and another, whom they killed; he sends still more, some of whom are beaten and some killed. Finally, he sends his son, imagining that the tenants will respect him. But they see this as their chance to take complete possession of the vineyard: "This is the heir; come, let us kill him, and the inheritance will be ours." So they kill him.

Then Jesus asks, as Isaiah asked after telling a similar parable seven centuries earlier (Isa. 5.1–7), "What then will the owner of the vineyard do?" The answer is obvious: "He will come and destroy the tenants and give the vineyard to others."

What did this mean? What is the vineyard? Who are the tenants? As in Isaiah, the vineyard is Israel. And the tenants who want to keep all the produce of the vineyard for themselves? Again the answer is obvious: the wealthy and powerful who exploit the vineyard. So Mark understands it as he concludes his report of the parable: "When they [the representatives of the temple authorities] realized that *he had told this parable against them*, they wanted to arrest him." But they do not, for "they feared the crowd." The crowd continues to be with Jesus.

This parable is often called the parable of the wicked tenants, and, of course, they are wicked; they beat and kill the servants and son of the vineyard owner. But their motivation is that they want all of the produce of the vineyard for themselves, and thus the parable would be better called the parable of the greedy tenants. The authorities are the greedy tenants. It is the same indictment as on Monday in the temple act: they have made the temple into a den of robbers.

Render unto Caesar?

The third episode (Mark 12.13–17) contains a well-known saying of Jesus, most familiar in the language of an earlier translation: "Render unto Caesar the things that are Caesar's, and to God the things that are God's." It has often been understood as a doctrinal pronouncement about the relationship between the religious realm and the political realm. In the first, we are to give our allegiance to God; and in the second, we are to give our allegiance to Caesar, that is, to temporal authority.

The result of this understanding among most Christians has been political quietism, a process that began in the fourth century when the Roman Empire embraced Christianity.[8] Since then, Christians have generally seen themselves as obligated to obey both civil authority and God. This understanding reached its horrendous zenith and nadir in the twentieth century in Nazi Germany, where the majority of both Protestants and Catholics saw no conflict between being loyal to Hitler and being Christian.

In the United States, though in a less virulent way, many Christians see this saying as the basis of our notion of separation of church and state. For them, the political realm and the religious realm are not and should not be related. There is no connection between being a follower of Jesus and one's politics.[9]

But this is not what the passage meant in Mark's story of Jesus's final week. The episode is part of the continuing effort of the authorities to trap Jesus. "Then they [the temple authorities] sent to him some Pharisees and some Herodians to trap him in what he said." Though Herodians are mentioned a couple of times in the gospels, we know nothing about them except their name, which suggests that they were supporters of Herod and his sons, part of the ruling class. With them are "some Pharisees."

These representatives of the authorities begin obsequiously: "Teacher, we know that you are sincere, and show deference to no one; for you do not regard people with partiality, but teach the way of God in accordance with truth." Then they ask the trap question: "Is it lawful to pay taxes to the emperor, or not? Should we pay them, or should we not?"

The question is skillfully posed. If Jesus were to respond that, yes, it's fine to pay taxes to the emperor, he risked discrediting himself with the crowd, many of whom resented imperial rule. If he were to say no, people shouldn't pay taxes to the emperor, then he could be charged with sedition, a capital offense.

Jesus's response is even more skillful. He asks his interrogators for a coin, specifically a denarius, a Roman coin that had an image of the emperor as well as his title "son of God." They produce one. He looks at it and asks, "Whose head is this, and whose title?" Of course, he already knows that, but by asking he makes his questioners respond in the presence of the crowd. They answer, "The emperor's." Already Jesus has discredited them; they are carrying a coin with a graven image that heralded the emperor as divine. Jesus concludes the exchange: "Give to the emperor the things that are the emperor's, and to God the things that are God's." His words mean: it's the emperor's coin—go ahead, give it back to him; and give to God what is God's.

What did this mean? Were they to pay taxes to the emperor or not? The statement leaves the question unanswered. Like Jesus's response to the question about his authority, it is a nonanswer to a question intended to trap him, not a doctrinal statement about civil and religious authority.

But suppose we were able to ask an additional question: "Jesus, what belongs to God?" I'm certain he would say, "Everything." Everything we know about him indicates that he shared a central affirmation of the Jewish Bible: "The earth is the LORD's and all that is in it" (Ps. 24.1).[10] And what belongs to the emperor? Nothing.

Verbal encounters with representatives of the authorities continue during the rest of Tuesday. Throughout, the opposition is not between Jesus and the people, "the crowd," but between Jesus and the authorities. The people are his allies, or at least sympathizers, and the authorities are afraid to take action against Jesus in their presence.

JESUS AS PROPHET

These scenes from the first few days of Passover Week are epiphanies of an opposition to the domination system that runs throughout the gospels. In these episodes as well as earlier in his mission, Jesus resembles the prophets of the Jewish Bible, especially those who challenged the monarchies of ancient Israel in the decades before their destruction. With public words and public acts, they protested the way the rulers, generally with the collaboration of those in charge of the temple, ignored God's passion for justice by exploiting the poor. They warned that their rule would come to an end because they had abandoned the covenant God had made with the people of Israel, a covenant mandating loyalty to God and God's passion for justice. The rulers had gone after other gods, especially the gods of power and wealth. Idolatry and injustice went together.[11]

Jesus not only resembles the Jewish prophets, but may have thought of himself as one. In Mark, after his rejection in Nazareth where he had grown up, he said, "Prophets are not without honor, except in their hometown, and among their own kin, and in their own house" (6.4). In Luke, while on his final journey to Jerusalem, he said, "It is impossible for a prophet to be killed outside of Jerusalem" (13.33). Moreover, the gospels report that some of his contemporaries thought of him as a prophet.[12]

But whether or not Jesus thought of himself as one, the category of prophet provides a lens through which to see a significant portion of his mission and message. To avoid a possible misunderstanding, I mention that there is a widespread modern meaning of the words "prophet" and "prophecy" that is very different from what the terms mean in the Bible. For many people today, prophecy is about the distant future, and a prophet is one who has been given supernatural knowledge of that future.

Popular Christianity has contributed to this impression. Many Christians believe, or think they should believe, that the primary role of the Jewish prophets was to predict the coming of the Messiah, that is, Jesus. Some passages in the New Testament, especially in Matthew, reinforce this notion. Some Christians also believe that biblical prophecy refers to events still to happen, especially events preceding the second coming of Jesus. Web sites and "prophecy conferences" in some churches focus on how biblical prophecies may be coming to pass in our time, as if the prophets of the Bible were talking about events thousands of years later than their time.

But all of this, it must be said, is a misunderstanding of what a biblical prophet was. Did the prophets speak about the future? Yes, sometimes. But they spoke about a short-range future, one that would flow out of present circumstances. Moreover, their statements about the future were most often conditional. They said to those they indicted: if you keep doing what you are doing, this is what will happen; but if you change your ways, the future may be different. When they did speak of a long-range future, they spoke in general and marvelously metaphorical language about God's dream for a world of justice and plenty and peace. And they spoke against the powers who stood in the way of this dream, who indeed betrayed the dream of God.

We turn now to other passages in the gospels in which Jesus challenged the domination system of his day. Like his prophetic predecessors, from whom he seems to have learned much, he indicted the powerful and wealthy in the name of God and God's passion for justice, God's dream.

Threats Against Jerusalem

Jesus's indictment of the temple authorities by his prophetic act on Monday of Passion Week is amplified by a number of other passages that warn of a coming destruction of the city. In the judgment of a considerable number of scholars, these warnings do not go back to Jesus, but were created within early Christianity near or after 70 CE, when Jerusalem was conquered and destroyed by the Romans. Some may have been shaped by the events of 70, but some are found in both Mark and Q as well as in Luke, thus making a case in favor of some of them going back to Jesus.

We begin with a saying in both Matthew (23.37–38) and Luke (13.34–35) and thus Q. Matthew places it in Jerusalem during the last week; Luke places it earlier, as part of Jesus's journey to Jerusalem. Luke's context (13.31–33) is striking. It reports an earlier plot to kill Jesus. Some Pharisees warn him that Herod Antipas, who had recently executed John the Baptizer, wants to kill Jesus. This is one of the few occasions in the gospels when Pharisees are presented as sympathetic to Jesus. They say to him, "Get away from here, for Herod wants to kill you." Jesus's response is full of contempt for the ruler of his land; he calls Herod "that fox," the first-century equivalent of "that skunk."

Then, in one of the passages just cited in which Jesus refers to himself as a prophet, Jesus says, "I must be on my way, because it is impossible for a prophet to be killed outside of Jerusalem." In this context, the Q threat to Jerusalem follows:

Jerusalem, Jerusalem, the city that kills the prophets and stones those who are sent to it! How often have I desired to gather your children together as a hen gathers her brood under her wings, and you were not willing! See, your house is left to you, desolate. (Matt. 23.37–38; Luke 13.34–35)

It is a strong indictment. As the center of the domination system historically as well as during Jesus's time, Jerusalem kills and stones the prophets. The "I" who desired to gather Jerusalem's children could be Jesus or God; in prophetic oracles, the "I" is often God. The "house" is the temple. The desolation of the house, the temple, refers to its abandonment by God, just as the prophet Ezekiel spoke of God leaving the temple and the city, thus making it vulnerable to destruction (Ezek. 10).

In Mark, in addition to the indictment of the temple on Monday, Jesus issues another warning on Tuesday. In Mark 13.1–4, at the beginning of a chapter filled with ominous portents of what is to come, some of Jesus's followers say as they are leaving the temple, "'Look, Teacher, what large stones and what large buildings!' Their wonder was well founded; the temple and the walls of the temple platform looked impregnable. Some of the stones were forty feet long, ten feet high, and fourteen feet thick and weighed five hundred tons. Jesus's response warns of what will happen: "Do you see these great buildings? Not one stone will be left here upon another; all will be thrown down."[13]

In a vivid passage, Luke reports that Jesus wept as he looked at the city from the top of the Mount of Olives, a view familiar to those who have been to Jerusalem in our time:

> If you, even you, had only recognized on this day the things that make for peace! But now they are hidden from your eyes. Indeed, the days will come upon you when your enemies will set up ramparts around you and surround you, and hem you in on every side. They will crush you to the ground, you and your children within you, and they will not leave within you one stone upon another, because you did not recognize the time of your visitation from God. (19.41–44)

Like the Jewish prophets before him, Jesus laments the future he sees for the city. It did not know the "things that make for peace." As often in the New Testament, the word "peace" does not mean simply absence of conflict, but has the meaning of the Hebrew word *shalom*, wholeness and well-being, in a comprehensive sense; *shalom* is God's dream of a world of justice, plenty, and peace. But Jerusalem, the center of native collaboration with imperial domination, no longer knew the "things that make for *shalom*."[14]

Like prophetic indictments in the Jewish Bible against Jerusalem and the temple, these should not be understood as God's judgment against Judaism, the Jewish people, or temple worship. Rather, they are judgments against the rulers on behalf of the people whom they dominated. The issue was that Jerusalem, the holy city, the city of God, had become the center of an oppressive domination system.[15] *That* is why Jesus called it a robbers' den.

The Rulers and the Wealthy

Jesus's prophetic indictments were directed against the rulers of his own people. But his message shows an awareness of the prevalence of domination systems in the larger world. He said to his followers, "You know that among the Gentiles those whom they recognize as their rulers lord it over them, and their great ones are tyrants over them." And then he turned this into a lesson on how his vision differed from the normalcy of cultures. To those who followed him he said, "But it is not so among you" (Mark 10.42–43).

Jesus's prophetic perspective also shaped his statements about wealth. In the previous chapter, we treated many of these in the context of his criticisms of conventional wisdom, the "broad way." There the issue was wealth as a lord that seduced people away from centering in God.

But his indictments of the wealthy were also critiques of the domination system. In his world, how did people become rich? Only by collaborating with and perpetuating the domination system. The well-to-do were not ordinary people who had worked hard to acquire an education or a skill or to start a business that brought significant financial rewards. Rather, wealth in premodern societies was the product of being in a small elite class in a massively exploitative system. Wealth was acquired through inheritance or by allying with the rulers. Peasants knew this. How did the wealthy become wealthy? By taking their land and much of their production. In Jesus's world, the wealthy were not innocent, but complicit.

Jesus also indicted the retainers who served the interests of the ruling elite. About scribes employed by the wealthy and powerful, he said: "Beware of the scribes, who like to walk around in long robes, and to be greeted with respect in the marketplaces, and to have the best seats in the synagogues and places of honor at banquets!" Why should one beware of them? Because they paraded their status? If they had been modest, would they have been okay? No. Rather, the passage continues, because "they devour widows' houses" (Mark 12.38–40). How do they devour widows' houses? Presumably by foreclosing on them because of indebtedness.

He indicted lawyers, scholars of the law, who served the elite: "Woe also to you lawyers! For you load people with burdens hard to bear, and you yourselves do not lift a finger to ease them" (Luke 11.46; Matt. 23.4). What were these burdens? Through the lens of the Protestant Reformation's emphasis upon grace versus law, the burdens have often been understood to mean "works of the law," as if Judaism were marked by an insistence upon earning one's righteousness through obedience to the minutiae of the law. But this is to project a Reformation controversy back into the gospels. Rather, the "burdens hard to bear" imposed by the lawyers on the people referred to their role in the system of economic oppression.

Jesus also indicted those Pharisees who insisted on meticulous tithing but who neglected justice. Tithes functioned as taxes on agricultural production, and the payment of tithes served the interests of the temple in particular. At least some of the Pharisees extended the application of the tithes beyond what was required in the Torah. About this, Jesus said:

> Woe to you Pharisees! For you tithe mint and rue and herbs of all kinds, and neglect justice and the love of God; it is these you ought to have practiced, without neglecting the others. (Luke 11.42; Matt. 23.23)

Tithing is not opposed outright. But it is contrasted to the weightier matters of the law: justice and the love of God. "These you ought to have practiced."

In an earlier chapter, we saw that Jesus pronounced blessings on the poor and woes upon the wealthy. Why? Because the poor were especially virtuous, and the wealthy lacked personal virtue? If the wealthy followed the Ten Commandments, would that have been enough? But the issue does not seem to be personal goodness. Rather, the kingdom of God, God's dream for the world, will bring blessing for those burdened by the domination system and woe for its perpetrators and beneficiaries. The kingdom of God is about a great reversal of the way things are.

Finally, I note that some of Jesus's wisdom forms of speech functioned as prophetic indictments. The parable of the good Samaritan (Luke 10.25–37) does not simply teach that we, like the Samaritan, should act as a neighbor to those who need help. It also indicts the priest and Levite who pass by. Why did they pass by? Jesus's audience would have known the reason. The priest and Levite were obligated to avoid corpse impurity. Because the wounded man might have been dead (he is described as "half dead"), they pass by. Their loyalty to purity prevented them from acting compassionately.

Other parables defend Jesus's inclusive meal practice. These were real meals, but also prophetic acts that symbolized his vision of the kingdom of God as including outcasts and marginalized people. In Luke 15.1–32, the parables of the lost sheep, the lost coin, and the prodigal son are all set in the context of defending Jesus against the charge, "This fellow welcomes sinners and eats with them."

It is possible that one of Jesus's most puzzling parables also fits into this category. Commonly called the parable of the talents, it is found in somewhat differing forms in Matthew 25.14–30 and Luke 19.11–27. A talent is a very large unit of money (the use of the word has often led to the misunderstanding that the parable is about the "talents" we have, e.g., musical, intellectual, athletic, or entrepreneurial gifts). The parable tells the story of a wealthy man (Matthew) or a ruler (Luke) who goes away and entrusts large sums of money to three different slaves. When he returns, he rewards the first two slaves, each of whom has made money with the money entrusted to him. But the third servant has simply preserved the money given to him by hiding it in the ground. The master judges him harshly: "You wicked and lazy slave! You knew, did you, that I reap where I did not sow, and gather where I did not scatter? Then you ought to have invested my money with the bankers, and on my return I would have received what was my own with interest" (Matt. 25.26–27; Luke 19.22–23).

The judgment on the third slave is harsh: "Take the talent from him, and give it to the one with ten talents. For to all those who have, more will be given; and they will have an abundance; but from those who have nothing, even what they have will be taken away." It gets worse: "As for this worthless slave, throw him into the outer darkness, where there will be weeping and gnashing of teeth" (Matt. 25.28–30; Luke 19.24–27).

The reason this parable is puzzling is because the wealthy owner or ruler has most often been understood as God. Is this the way God acts? Rewarding those who use money to make money in a society such as Jesus lived in? Reprimanding the third slave for not at least investing the money to get interest on it—a violation of the law against usury? Taking away from those who have nothing even what little they have? Or is the key to this parable the realization that the wealthy owner does not represent God? That the parable is instead an indictment of the wealthy? Perhaps the parable is saying, this is the way the domination system works—the wealthy get wealthier, and those who have nothing have even what little they have taken away from them.[16]

NONVIOLENT RESISTANCE

Much of what has already been treated fits into the category of nonviolent resistance. Public criticism of authorities is a form of nonviolent resistance (unless, of course, it advocates violence). The anti-imperial entry and antitemple indictment are acts of nonviolent resistance, just as symbolic deeds from the recent American past are. Examples from the civil rights movement include sit-ins at lunch counters, freedom rides on integrated buses, and demonstrations in many cities. Other examples include pouring duck blood on selective service files during the Vietnam era or denting the nose cone of an intercontinental missile. And because some Christians have occasionally used Jesus's prophetic act in the temple as a justification for violent action, it is important to underline that minor property damage in a symbolic act is very different from lethal violence against persons.

In addition, there is an extended passage in Matthew's Sermon on the Mount, most of it from Q, that counsels nonviolent resistance. More than any other New Testament scholar, Walter Wink has made the rest of us aware of this reading of Matthew 5.38–41, 43–45, and I am indebted to him.[17] For ease of commentary, I number the statements in the passage:

248 JESUS

1. You have heard that it was said, "An eye for an eye and a tooth for a tooth." But I say to you, Do not resist an evildoer.

2. But if anyone strikes you on the right cheek, turn the other also.

3. And if anyone wants to sue you and take your coat, give your cloak as well.

4. And if anyone forces you to go one mile, go also the second mile.

5. You have heard that it was said, "You shall love your neighbor and hate your enemy," but I say to you, Love your enemies and pray for those who persecute you, so that you may be children of your Father in heaven; for he makes his sun rise on the evil and on the good, and sends rain on the righteous and on the unrighteous.

There is a habitual conventional way of reading this cluster of sayings as commending passive acceptance of wrongdoing: don't resist somebody who beats you; go the extra mile; don't insist on your own rights. Colloquially, be a doormat—let people walk all over you. Moreover, it has most commonly been understood to refer to personal relationships, not to the political realm. Most Christians have not thought of this passage as prohibiting participation in war or capital punishment. Official violence is okay. But all of this, Wink persuasively argues, is a misunderstanding of the passage whose effect is to domesticate it politically. The powers that be are pleased with the doormat reading.

The first statement begins by citing the law of retribution, "An eye for an eye and a tooth for a tooth." A principle found three times in the Jewish Bible,[18] it sounds barbaric to modern ears, but actually put limits on retaliation: one may not take more than an eye for an eye, a tooth for a tooth. This is followed by a contrasting saying of Jesus that is often mistranslated, as it is in the NRSV, the version quoted above: "But I say to you, Do not resist an evildoer." But the Greek verb translated "resist" most often means "resist with violence." Thus, rather than counseling nonresistance to an evildoer, which would imply doing nothing in the face of evil, the verse really says, "Do not resist an evildoer *with violence*."[19] As the following statements of the text make clear: resistance, yes; violence, no.

The next three statements provide specific examples of nonviolent resistance. The second statement says: "But if anyone strikes you on the right cheek, turn the other also." The specification of the right cheek and the awareness that people in that world used their right hand to strike somebody provide the key for understanding the saying. How can a person be hit on the right cheek by a right-handed person? Only by a backhanded slap (act it out and see for yourself). In that world, a slap with the back of a hand was the way a superior struck a subordinate. The saying thus presupposes a situation of domination: a peasant being backhanded by a steward or official, a prisoner being backhanded by a jailer, and so forth. When that happens, turn the other cheek. What would be the effect of that? The beating could continue only if the superior used an overhand blow—which is the way an equal struck another equal. Of course, he might do so. But he would be momentarily discombobulated, and the subordinate would be asserting his equality even if the beating did continue.

The third statement, "If anyone wants to sue you and take your coat, give your cloak as well," imagines a setting in which a person is being sued for his outer garment because of nonpayment of debt (and only a very poor person would have only a coat to offer as collateral). In that world, peasants commonly wore only two garments, a long tunic and an outer garment that also served as a blanket. The effect of giving up the inner garment as well the outer would, of course, be nakedness. The act would not only startle the creditor, but would also shame him, for nakedness shamed the person who beheld the nakedness. Moreover, it would be a symbolic statement: look what this system is doing to us, stripping us naked.

The fourth statement, about going the "second mile," refers to a known practice of imperial soldiers. Soldiers were allowed to compel peasants to carry their considerable gear for one mile, but no more. The reason for the restriction was that soldiers had been abusing the option by forcing peasants to carry their gear all day (or even longer). The result was not only popular resentment, but peasants ending up a day's journey (or more) from home. And so the restriction was introduced, and soldiers faced penalties for violating it, some of them severe. In this setting, what are you to do when an imperial soldier requires you to carry his gear for a mile? Do it—and then keep going. The situation, Wink suggests, is almost comical—imagine an imperial soldier wrestling a peasant to get his gear back while the peasant says, "No, no, it's fine. Let me carry it another mile."

Wink argues persuasively that we should not think of these as "rules," as what one should do every time these cases happen. It is difficult to imagine Jesus intended "turn the other cheek" as a rule to be followed every time one was beaten, for it would not take long for the person inflicting the beating to realize, "Oh, it's the old turn-the-other-cheek trick." Rather, they are meant as creative examples of nonviolent resistance whose purpose is to spark the imagination to create more.

The fifth statement begins with a more general statement: "Love your enemies and pray for those who persecute you." In the context of the preceding statements, it means loving enemies while at the same time *also* nonviolently resisting them.

Jesus's advocacy of nonviolent resistance was a way different from the other main responses to the domination system. He rejected the path of compliance, whether the way of elite collaboration or peasant resignation. Indeed, he criticized the former and sought to empower the latter. But he also rejected the path of violent resistance and took his stand among those who practiced nonviolent resistance.

Did he reject violent resistance because he saw the futility of it—that it would simply result in another slaughter of peasants by the military power of empire? He was certainly aware of what had happened in Sepphoris and Galilee when Rome suppressed the revolts of 4 BCE. Or did he reject violence for more than strategic and prudential reasons?

The ending of the fifth statement suggests that his position was not simply prudential, but grounded in his perception of God's character. The reason for loving enemies? "So that you may be children of your Father in heaven," who "makes the sun rise on the evil and on the good, and sends rain on the righteous and on the unrighteous." That is the way God is. Love of enemies and nonviolent resistance are grounded in God's character and passion. God's character is nonviolent; therefore be nonviolent. God passion is justice, therefore be passionate about justice. Resist injustice. And do so nonviolently.

Thus Jesus opposed the domination system. His warnings to Jerusalem and his prophetic criticism of the wealthy and powerful and their retainers together with his teaching about nonviolent resistance are of a piece with the epiphanies at the beginning of Passover Week. We turn now to how this opposition is related to the "kingdom of God."

THE KINGDOM OF GOD

Near the end of Chapter 7, I introduced the kingdom of God in the context of how Jesus saw God's character and passion. There I argued that Jesus saw the kingdom as God's passion. For Jesus as a Spirit-filled Jewish mystic who knew God, the kingdom was his passion as well. We now return to this topic.

The kingdom of God was at the center of Jesus's mission. Mainstream scholars are virtually unanimous that Mark's advance summary of Jesus's message is correct: "The time is fulfilled and the kingdom of God has come near" (1.15). A generation ago, a scholar wrote:

> Ask any hundred New Testament scholars around the world, Protestant, Catholic or non-Christian, what the central message of Jesus was, and the vast majority of them—perhaps every single expert—would agree that his message centered in the kingdom of God.[20]

The statement remains true today.

But what did Jesus's message about the kingdom of God, its coming, and its nearness *mean*? How and when did he think the kingdom would come? What did his followers understand him to mean? Here the unanimity among contemporary scholars becomes a deep division. Before describing the division, I review and amplify the points about which there is general agreement.

First, the kingdom of God is not about heaven. Rather, it is for the earth, as the Lord's Prayer makes clear: "Your kingdom come *on earth*." It is about a transformed world, a world of justice and plenty and peace, where everybody has enough and where, in the striking phrase from the prophet Micah, "No one shall make them afraid" (4.4).

Second, the phrase uses both political and religious language. "Kingdom" in the first century was a political term. Jesus's hearers knew about Herod's kingdom and Rome's kingdom (the word Rome used for what we call its empire). Jesus could have spoken about the *community* of God, or the *family* of God, or the *people* of God. But he didn't. Instead, he spoke about the *kingdom*. The usage had to be deliberate, intended to contrast the kingdom of God with the kingdoms of this world.

It is the kingdom of *God.* It's not just about politics, but is the way the world would be if God were king, and the kings and domination systems of this world were not. It is God's dream, God's passion, God's will, God's promise, God's intention for the earth, God's utopia—the blessed place, the ideal state of affairs. As the Beatitudes in both Luke and Matthew affirm, it is good news for the poor and bad news for the wealthy and powerful. It is a reversal of the way things are. No wonder the common people heard Jesus gladly.

We turn now to the disagreement, which involves introducing the semitechnical term "eschatology." Though not a biblical term, it has come to be used widely in biblical scholarship. Its Greek root, *eschaton,* means "end" or "last" or "final." Eschatology thus means the end of things, the last things, the final things, the ideal state of affairs.[21] Though sometimes equated with the "end of the world," it is important to realize that biblical eschatology is not about the end of the space-time world, not about the disappearance or vanishing of the earth, but about the transformation of this world.[22]

The division within contemporary Jesus scholarship concerns the questions of *how* and *when* Jesus thought this would come about. Today's scholars are divided between those who understand the kingdom of God within the framework of "imminent eschatology" and those who don't.

Imminent Eschatology

The claim that Jesus's message about the kingdom is to be understood within the framework of imminent eschatology[23] goes back over a century to Johannes Weiss and Albert Schweitzer.[24] When did Jesus think the kingdom would come? Soon, very soon. How did he think it would come? God would do it. In the twentieth century, this understanding became dominant within Jesus scholarship, with a few exceptions.[25] In the last twenty-five years, the exceptions have become a chorus, though a number of influential scholars continue to affirm imminent eschatology.[26] My impression is that the discipline today is about evenly divided.

Imminent eschatology is shorthand for an understanding of the kingdom of God in which it is seen as:

- *Imminent:* Jesus believed it would happen soon, within his generation.

- *Inevitable:* Its coming was not conditional—it was going to happen.

- *Interventionist:* God would do it by supernatural intervention. How else could it happen soon?

- *Unmistakable:* Its coming would be so dramatic and obvious that nobody could doubt that it had happened.

Imminent eschatology has considerable persuasive power. Otherwise it would not have been embraced by so many scholars. Elements in the gospels and the New Testament cited in its support include:

- Jesus's immediate predecessor and most important post-Easter follower both believed they were living in the "end times." The preaching of John the Baptizer sounds like imminent eschatology, and Paul believed that Jesus's second coming was at hand.[27] Because Jesus is in the middle between these two who held imminent expectations, it is thus plausible to think that Jesus had this expectation too. Moreover, imminent eschatology is found not just in Paul but in most of the New Testament, including, of course, the book of Revelation, whose author expected the events he wrote about to happen soon. Indeed, he says so seven times.

- Some gospel sayings speak of the coming of the "Son of Man" in contexts of judgment. Mark 13.24–27 refers to the sun and moon being darkened, stars falling from the skies, and the Son of Man coming on the clouds of heaven to gather the elect from the four corners of the earth. It is followed by 13.30: "Truly I tell you, this generation will not pass away until all these things have taken place." (See also Mark 8.38; 14.62; Luke 12.8–9.)

- Some kingdom sayings speak of it as future (including the Lord's Prayer) and as near. Indeed, Mark 9.1 refers to it as coming "with power" during the lifetime of some of Jesus's hearers: "Truly I tell you, there are some standing here who will not taste death until they see that the kingdom of God has come with power."

- The vivid sense of crisis running through the mission and message of Jesus is understood to flow from his conviction that "time is short" and therefore the need to repent is urgent.

In short, imminent eschatology means that Jesus expected a dramatic supernatural intervention by God in the very near future that would establish the kingdom of God.

It follows, of course, that Jesus was wrong. Scholars who hold this view cover a religious spectrum, ranging from skeptics and agnostics to committed Christians. It has very recently been treated under the title "The History of a Delusion."[28] Those who are Christian have most often suggested ways of dealing with and integrating Jesus's mistake, some of them quite powerful.[29] For them, affirming that

Jesus was deeply mistaken about the imminence of the kingdom of God does not mean the end of Christianity. I agree. The validity of Christianity does not depend upon whether Jesus had a mistaken eschatology. That is not what is at stake. But what is at stake is how we see Jesus as a historical figure.

Rethinking Imminent Eschatology

I am among those who understand Jesus and his message of the kingdom of God within a different framework. It has not always been so. In my first years of graduate school, I was persuaded that imminent eschatology was the most compelling paradigm within which to see Jesus. I suppose this was to be expected; the dominant scholarly voices in the discipline saw it this way, and I was learning the discipline. This is not the place to describe the process by which I came to a different understanding.[30] Instead, I describe the result, generally shared by scholars who disagree with what was the dominant understanding.[31]

First, we agree that there are many passages in the gospels and New Testament that affirm imminent eschatology. But we see these as passages about the "second coming" of Jesus. When Paul and Revelation and other parts of the New Testament proclaim that the "end is near," they consistently associate it with the return of Jesus. In the gospels, the sayings about the coming of the Son of Man in the near future also seem clearly to refer to the second coming of Jesus.

So we agree with advocates of imminent eschatology that this expectation is prominent in the New Testament (and that it was mistaken). But we think the texts that speak of this are "second coming of Jesus" texts, and we do not think that Jesus spoke of his own second coming. Rather, we think the conviction that Jesus would come again emerged in the post-Easter community. The Jesus whom the rulers of this world had executed and who had been vindicated by God would soon come again to complete what he had begun.

Second, there is much in the gospels that does not fit within the framework of imminent eschatology, or does not fit very well. This includes the great diversity among the kingdom sayings. Some do speak of the kingdom as future, such as the petition in the Lord's Prayer, "Your kingdom come." The kingdom is not yet—it is still to come. But there are very few that speak of it as imminent, as Mark 9.1, quoted above, does. We think it likely that Mark 9.1 and Mark 1.15 (and much of Mark 13, including 13.30) are the products of intensified eschatological expectation generated by the Jewish revolt of 66–70 CE with its climax in the destruction of Jerusalem and the temple. This catastrophic event within a Jewish worldview shared by Mark and other early Christians intensified the sense that the "end" must be near.

But there are many other kingdom sayings that do not fit very well. I list, with minimal exposition, the categories of kingdom sayings:

- The kingdom is present in Jesus's exorcisms. "If it is by the spirit of God that I cast out demons, then the kingdom of God has come to you" (Matt. 12.28; Luke 11.20).

- The kingdom can be experienced now. When asked by some Pharisees when the kingdom would come, Jesus said, "For in fact, the kingdom of God is among you" (Luke 17.20). The same affirmation is found in two sayings in the *Gospel of Thomas* (3; 113). In both cases, *Thomas* reports that Jesus is correcting a misunderstanding. In *Thomas* 3, the issue is, *where* is the kingdom? In the sky? In the sea? No. "Rather the kingdom is within you and it is outside you." Both within and without—but not somewhere else. In *Thomas* 113, the issue is *when* the kingdom will be. Sometime else? No. "Rather, the kingdom of the Father is already spread out on the earth, and people aren't aware of it." It already is—but we are blind to it.[32] The *Thomas* sayings reflect a mystical understanding of the kingdom.

- The kingdom can be sought and found. It can be stumbled upon, as in the parable of treasure found in a field (Matt. 13.44). It can be searched for, as in the parable of the merchant in search of fine pearls (Matt. 13.45). So also the saying "Search, and you will find; knock, and the door will be opened for you" is about the kingdom (Luke 11.9; Matt. 7.7).

- The kingdom grows. It is like a seed growing secretly under the ground (Mark 4.26–29), like a mustard seed (Mark 4.30–32), like yeast in flour (Luke 13.20–21; Matt. 13.33).

- The kingdom is about bread and debt forgiveness, food and new beginning (the Lord's Prayer).

- The kingdom can be entered. Some sayings in this category can be understood within the framework of imminent eschatology. For example, "Whoever does not receive the kingdom of God as a little child will never enter it"(Mark 10.15) and "How hard it will be for those who have wealth to enter the kingdom of God" (Mark 10.23) can be understood to mean entering the kingdom *when it comes* (though they need not be understood that way). But others speak of entering in the present or the possibility of doing so. For example: "Tax collectors and prostitutes are going into the kingdom of God ahead of you" (Matt. 21.31); "You are not far from the kingdom of God" (Mark 12.34). To some of his critics, Jesus said, "You lock people out of the kingdom of God. For you do not go in yourselves, and when others are going in, you stop them" (Matt. 23.13; Luke 11.52). The implication is that it is possible to enter now.

In addition to these kingdom sayings, there is much else in the gospels that does not fit the hypothesis of imminent eschatology very well. This includes much of Jesus's wisdom teaching about God and the way. What was its meaning and purpose? Was it about preparation for the coming kingdom? About how to be ready? Were his criticisms of convention about the loyalties that can leave one unprepared for the final judgment? Were his indictments of the wealthy and powerful primarily an announcement that God was going to judge them soon? Was his good news for the poor the message, "Don't worry, God's going to fix everything soon"? Or was his message to the poor about empowerment and resistance? Was his inclusive meal practice with marginalized people primarily an affirmation that the kingdom, when it comes, will include these? Or was it an affirmation of a different vision of life now?

It seems to many of us that the framework of imminent eschatology excludes more of the gospel data than it accounts for. And the test of a hypothesis is its explanatory power. How much does it explain? How much of the data can it accommodate?

I add one more consideration, a question addressed to those who are persuaded by imminent eschatology. Do you see it as *primary* for Jesus, or as *secondary*? It is an important question. "Primary" would mean that it was the animating conviction driving his mission. He believed the kingdom of God as God's imminent, inevitable, unmistakable intervention was at hand, and this conviction shaped his message and mission as a whole. It would mean that Jesus was saying, in effect, God's going to act soon, so get ready. God is soon going to intervene and destroy the temple, disinherit the wealthy, bless the poor, and bring about the great eschatological reversal. And that's why you should abandon everything—family, possessions, status— and center in God. That's why it doesn't matter whether one pays taxes to Caesar or not. That's why concerns with purity don't matter. How can any of these concerns matter if the *eschaton,* the final judgment with eternal consequences, is at hand?

Seeing imminent eschatology as "secondary" would mean that, in addition to his activity and message as a wisdom teacher, healer, and prophet, Jesus also thought that God would soon act. It was one of the things he believed, but not the central conviction driving his mission. It would mean that Jesus was passionate about his message, and also believed that God might very well act decisively in the near future.

If one affirms imminent eschatology to be secondary and not primary, the differences between seeing Jesus within the framework of imminent eschatology and an alternative framework are not so great.[33] But seeing imminent eschatology as primary excludes much of his mission and message and risks making it as vapid as the message of many since who have announced, "The end is at hand— repent."

Participatory Eschatology

Giving a name to the alternative eschatology is difficult. Calling it "nonimminent eschatology" is accurate, but defines it negatively by what it isn't. The phrase might even suggest that Jesus thought the kingdom had the other features of imminent eschatology, but simply lacked imminence. In other words, Jesus thought the kingdom was inevitable and that God would bring it about by dramatic supernatural intervention sometime, but simply didn't set a timetable for it; it might be soon or take thousands of years. I do not think that is the alternative. There is an urgency in Jesus's mission and message that cannot be accounted for by saying, "Well, maybe all of this is thousands of years in the future."

Perhaps we might call it "participatory eschatology" or "collaborative eschatology." The key to understanding what I mean by this phrase is the question, did Jesus expect God to do this "alone"? That is, that regardless of human response, God was going to do this? As I understand scholars who advocate imminent eschatology, at least in its primary form, the answer is (and needs to be) "yes." This is *non*-participatory eschatology: God is going to act decisively soon, with or without us.

Participatory eschatology is the opposite of this. It means that Jesus called people to respond and participate in the coming of the kingdom. There is much in the gospels that indicates that Jesus did this—that he called people, and his followers in particular, to participate in his passion, which was also God's passion: the coming of the kingdom.

In the middle of his mission, Jesus sent his followers out to do what he was doing (Luke 10.4–9; Matt. 10.8–11; Mark 6.7–13.) He commissioned some of them to heal, cast out demons, share meals with those to whom they went, and proclaim the kingdom—exactly what he was doing.[34]

Jesus called people *to follow him*. Following him suggests something quite different from what a primary emphasis upon imminent eschatology suggests. What would it mean to follow somebody whose message is primarily about the nearness of the end? The proper response to such a message would be to believe it (or not), and then to do what one needed to do to be ready. But this is not an obvious meaning of the word "follow." Following suggests participation—following Jesus on the way of personal transformation of which he spoke. And it meant following the way of the cross, the way that led to Jerusalem and confrontation with the domination system.

And Jesus spoke of striving for the kingdom of God: "Strive first for the kingdom of God and God's justice" (Matt. 6.33; Luke 12.31). Did this mean, strive to be ready for the kingdom when it comes? Or strive to realize the kingdom and God's justice? The latter seems the more obvious meaning.

Does participatory eschatology mean that Jesus thought the kingdom of God, God's dream, would come about through human political achievement? By no means. I do not imagine that he thought that. It is always *God's* kingdom, *God's* dream, *God's* will. And it involves a deep centering in the God whom Jesus knew. So did he think God would bring in the kingdom without our involvement? I do not imagine this either. Indeed, the choice between "God does it" or "we do it" is a misleading and inappropriate dichotomy. In St. Augustine's magnificent aphorism, "God without us will not; and we without God cannot."

Jesus's message about the kingdom of God, it seems to me, is not that complicated. God's will for the earth, God's passion for this world, is very different from what we see around us. To his hearers he said, "Can you see that?" And he sought to open the eyes of the blind, to set free the captives and oppressed, to proclaim the jubilee of God. This is participatory eschatology.

TEN

Executed by Rome, Vindicated by God

Jesus's confrontation with the domination system during his last week in Jerusalem moves toward its climax. As we turn to the story of his final days, it is important to recall our characterization of the gospels in Chapter 3. Namely, they combine memory and metaphor, the story of Jesus remembered with the story of Jesus in metaphorical narrative. The metaphorical meaning of language is its more-than-literal, more-than-factual meaning. Metaphor refers to the surplus of meaning that language can carry.

The story of Jesus's death was remembered and told because of its more-than-historical meaning, even as it contains historical memory. In addition, as we will see, there are elements in it that are "purely" metaphorical. But even the parts that are probably historical were told because of their surplus of meaning. Combined with the stories of Easter, which will also be treated in this chapter, they were for his followers the most central stories they knew.

Mark, our earliest gospel, continues his day-by-day account of Jesus's last week. On Friday, it becomes hour by hour. With occasional and relatively minor variations, Matthew and Luke follow Mark's narrative. John's story is quite different, and some of the differences will occasionally be noted.[1]

THE LAST DAYS

Wednesday begins with the temple authorities continuing to seek a way to arrest Jesus. They want to do so in private, for they perceive the crowd to be sympathetic to Jesus and they fear a riot (Mark 14.2). Later that day, Judas, one of Jesus's disciples, provides the opportunity. He meets with the authorities and agrees to betray Jesus in a suitable place (Mark 14.10–11).

Mark provides no reason for the betrayal, though Judas's motive has been speculated about from ancient times. John's gospel implies that he did it for money; he speaks of Judas as a thief who stole from the money held in common by Jesus's followers (12.6). John also says that Satan made him do it (13.2, 27), as does Luke (22.3). In the recently discovered *Gospel of Judas*, written in the second century, Jesus orders Judas to make arrangements with the authorities for his death. Rather than Judas being a betrayer, he was the one disciple Jesus could trust to do this.[2] But scholars do not think this gospel tells us anything about the historical Jesus or the historical Judas. Other suggestions for his motivation have occasionally been made. Judas was perhaps afraid that they would all be arrested and punished, perhaps killed, and wanted to escape that fate by allying himself with the authorities. Judas was disappointed with the kind of kingdom he now realized Jesus was advocating and decided to turn Jesus over. Judas may have felt betrayed. But about all of this we must simply say that we do not (and cannot) know.

On Thursday, Jesus has a final meal with his followers. In the synoptic gospels, it is a Passover meal celebrating ancient Israel's liberation from Egypt. (In John's gospel, it is not; the Passover meal is the *next* evening, and the lambs to be eaten at that meal are killed at the same hour that Jesus dies in John).[3] In the course of the meal, Jesus speaks of the bread and wine as his body and blood. The words vary slightly in the various accounts, but the gist is clear. About the bread, Jesus said, "This is my body"; about the wine, he said, "This is my blood of the covenant."[4] A historical judgment about whether this language goes back to Jesus or is the product of the post-Easter community's ritualization of Jesus's meal practice is very difficult. Judas departs early.

The meal over, they leave the city and go to a garden called Gethsemane at the foot of the Mount of Olives just east of the walls of Jerusalem. There, in the dark, Judas arrives with a group of armed men.

In the synoptics, they are sent by the temple authorities and are presumably temple police (Mark 14.32–50). In John, the arrest party includes a large number of imperial soldiers as well.[5] Jesus's disciples flee.

Then Jesus is taken to a hearing before the temple authorities, presided over by Caiaphas, the high priest. Witnesses testify against Jesus, but they fail to agree. Their testimony includes garbled statements about Jesus threatening to destroy the temple. The high priest takes over. Having failed to find two or three witnesses whose testimonies agreed with each other, he asks Jesus directly: "Are you the Messiah, the Son of the Blessed One?"

Mark 14.62 reports Jesus's response. It begins with a terse, "I am." The Greek behind the English "I am" is ambiguous. It can be translated either as an affirmation ("I am") or as an interrogative ("Am I?"). Matthew and Luke both understand it as ambiguous. Matthew has, "You have said so" (26.64). Luke has, "You say that I am" (22.70).

Jesus's response continues: "And 'you will see the Son of Man seated at the right hand of the Power,' and 'coming with the clouds of heaven.'" This was enough for the high priest. He declares the statement to be blasphemy and asks his council, "What is your decision?" They condemn Jesus to death. Then the guards spit on him, blindfold him, and beat him.

For more than one reason, there is great historical uncertainty about this scene before the high priest and his council. First, it reports a meeting of the high priest's council at night on the day of the most important Jewish festival of the year. Trials were forbidden at night and on such days, but even if this meeting is understood as an "informal" hearing or kangaroo court, it is difficult to imagine.[6] Second, if it did happen, how did the followers of Jesus know *what* had happened at it? They had all fled. It is, of course, possible to imagine that someone who was there talked about what had happened, and the report reached Christian ears.

Yet a third reason is that the high priest's question and Jesus's response sound remarkably like a post-Easter Christian confession of faith. "Are you the Messiah, the Son of the Blessed One?" Are you the Christ, the Son of God? These are classic post-Easter affirmations about Jesus. Jesus's response sounds like a reference to his resurrection and second coming: "You will see the Son of Man seated at the right hand of the Power" echoes Psalm 110.1, one of the texts used by early Christians to express their conviction that God had raised Jesus to God's right hand. "Coming with the clouds of heaven" echoes Daniel 7.13–14, a text that also uses "Son of Man" language and that is associated in the New Testament with the expectation of Jesus's second coming (as in Mark 13.24–27). The symmetry is almost too good to be factual—Jesus was condemned for what amounts to an early Christian confession of faith. Jesus is the Messiah, the Son of God, who will come again on the clouds of heaven.

THE CRUCIFIXION

As dawn breaks on Friday, the temple authorities convey Jesus to Pilate. Jesus appears before him in the courtyard of the palace of the late Herod the Great, where the Roman governors stayed when they were in Jerusalem. Pilate looks at Jesus and asks, "Are *you* the King of the Jews?" We should probably hear mockery in his voice—you, a prisoner, bound, beaten, and bloodied, the king of the Jews? Jesus's response is nondeclarative: "You say so." Then Jesus remains silent (15.1–5). Refusing to respond to authority shows courage and suggests contempt. Indeed, Jesus does not speak again in Mark's gospel until the moment of his death.[7]

This is followed by a curious episode involving Barabbas, a prisoner awaiting execution as a Jewish insurrectionist. It is curious because it reports an implausible practice that at Passover Pilate customarily released whatever prisoner the crowd asked for. It seems an unlikely procedure for an imperial governor of a rebellious territory to follow. But as Mark tells the story, Pilate offers the "crowd" a choice between Jesus and Barabbas. They choose Barabbas and shout for Jesus's crucifixion (15.6–14).

This is a different crowd from the one that had listened to Jesus with delight during the week and whom the authorities feared. We have no reason to think that those in *that* crowd had changed their minds. Rather, *this* "crowd" (presumably a small group) had access to the courtyard of Pilate's residence (Herod's palace). The authorities didn't let just anybody in.

The Barabbas episode may be explained by the historical context in which Mark wrote, namely, near 70 CE and the Roman reconquest and destruction of Jerusalem and the temple. By then it was clear that the "crowd" had chosen the path of armed insurrection (Barabbas) that led to the catastrophic revolt of 66–70, rather than the path of nonviolence (Jesus).

So Pilate issues the order to have Jesus crucified. He is flogged. Soldiers mock him as a would-be king; they dress him in a purple cloak and a crown of thorns and salute him: "Hail, King of the Jews!" Then they hit him, spit upon him, strip him, and take him out to be executed.

In a single sentence, Mark reports the crucifixion: "It was nine o'clock in the morning when they crucified him" (15.25). Mark doesn't narrate the details of what this kind of death entailed, which were well known to people in the Jewish homeland, who had often witnessed this form of imperial execution. Two others are crucified with him. Though called "bandits" in the English translation of Mark 15.27, the Greek word is the term commonly used for those engaged in armed resistance against Rome—"terrorists" or "freedom fighters," depending upon one's point of view. They join their voices to those mocking Jesus. Only in Luke (23.40–43) is one of them described as repentant.

At noon, darkness comes over the whole land and lasts until Jesus's death three hours later. It is idle to wonder if this was an eclipse of the sun; eclipses never last more than a few minutes. Moreover, if it were an eclipse, it would simply be a coincidental natural phenomenon. Nor does it help to suggest that this was a special darkness created by God. To see the darkness as something that happened risks missing the point.[8]

Rather, the darkness is metaphor. Ancient authors often associated highly significant events on earth with signs in the sky. Darkness is an archetypal symbol associated with suffering, mourning, and judgment. Such usage appears in the Jewish Bible. In Exodus

10.21–23, one of the plagues involved "darkness over the land." In the prophets, darkness is associated with mourning and God's judgment. In a reproach to Jerusalem from the sixth century BCE, Jeremiah refers to the sun setting at midday (15.9). Texts of judgment in Zephaniah 1.15 and Joel 2.2 refer to a day of "darkness and gloom." In a passage that threatens judgment upon Israel in the eighth century BCE, Amos says in the name of God, "I will make the sun go down at noon and darken the earth in broad daylight" (8.9).

Given this background, the darkness from noon to three o'clock is best understood as symbolism. How many resonances of meaning Mark intended is unclear, but it is reasonable to imagine a combination of grief and judgment. The cosmos itself joins in mourning, even as the darkness symbolizes judgment upon the rulers who crucified the "Lord of glory," to use a phrase from Paul.

At three o'clock, Jesus dies. His last words are the opening line of Psalm 22: "My God, my God, why have you forsaken me?" (Mark 15.34). They are the only words spoken by Jesus from the cross in Mark and Matthew. Luke and John each add three more statements, thus producing what Christians know as "the seven last words."[9]

Then Mark narrates two events that provide interpretive comments about the death of Jesus. The first is the tearing of the temple curtain: "And the curtain of the temple was torn in two, from top to bottom" (15.38). Like the darkness, this event is to be understood symbolically and not as history remembered. The curtain separated the holiest part of the temple sanctuary—the "holy of holies"—from the rest of the temple building. It was the place where God was most particularly present and so sacred that only the high priest was permitted to enter it, and only on one day of the year. To say that the curtain was torn in two has a twofold meaning. On the one hand, it is a judgment upon the temple and the temple authorities. On the other hand, it is an affirmation: the tearing of the curtain, the veil of separation, means that God is accessible apart from the temple. So Jesus had taught, and so he knew from his experiences of God as a Jewish mystic.

In the second event contemporaneous with Jesus's death, the centurion in command of the soldiers who had crucified Jesus exclaims, "Truly this man was God's Son" (15.39). He is the first human in

Mark's gospel to call Jesus "God's Son"; not even Jesus's followers do so. That this exclamation comes from a centurion is very significant. Recall that, according to Roman imperial theology, the emperor was "Son of God" as well as Lord, Savior, and the one who had brought peace on earth. But now a representative of Rome affirms that *this* man, executed by the empire, is the Son of God. In the exclamation of the centurion, empire testifies against itself.

From a distance, some women watch. They had followed him and provided for him in Galilee. Mark tells us there were "many other women who had come up with Jesus to Jerusalem." They included Mary Magdalene, and Mary the mother of James the younger and of Joses, and Salome (15.40–41). They will be at the tomb on Sunday morning.

WHY DID IT HAPPEN?

Why did it happen? Why did Jesus's life end this way? Those of us who grew up in the church do not come to this question without a preunderstanding. The most widespread one is that Jesus died for the sins of the world. In her reflections on growing up Christian, Roberta Bondi, a contemporary Christian scholar, speaks for many of us: "If you had asked me in fourth grade, 'Why was Jesus born?' I would have been glad to answer, 'It was because of sin. Jesus was born in order to pay the price for our sin by suffering and dying on the cross.'"[10] His death was central to God's plan of salvation: he had to die in order to atone for our sins. It was necessary.

Called "substitutionary atonement" or "substitutionary sacrifice," this understanding of Jesus's death continues to be bedrock for most conservative Christians, even as it is being set aside or relativized by many in mainline denominations. The cover of a recent issue of a well-known conservative-evangelical magazine proclaims "No Substitute for the Substitute," heralding an article titled "Nothing but the Blood." In it, the author criticizes some evangelical scholars for weakening the claim that Jesus's death was a substitutionary sacrifice and affirms that what is at stake is "nothing less than the essence of Christianity":

> If we have any assurance of salvation, it is because of Christ's Atonement; if any joy, it flows from Christ's work on the Cross.... Apart from Christ's atoning work, we would be forever guilty, ashamed, and condemned before God.[11]

The author concludes the article with advice given by a father to his son Chad: "This is what I hold out to my young son as the hope of his life: that Jesus, God's perfect, righteous Son, died in his place for his sins. Jesus took all the punishment; Jesus received all the wrath as he hung on the Cross, so people like Chad and his sinful daddy could be completely forgiven."[12]

This understanding is part of a larger, familiar theological package in which all of us are sinners. In order for God to forgive sins, a substitutionary sacrifice must be offered. But an ordinary human being cannot be the sacrifice, for such a person would be a sinner and would be dying only for his or her own sins. Thus the sacrifice must be a perfect human being. Only Jesus, who was not only human but also the Son of God, was perfect, spotless, and without blemish. Only his substitutionary death makes our forgiveness possible.

Many people think this is the orthodox and thus "official" Christian understanding of Jesus's death, including many who have difficulty with it, whether within the church or outside of it. Hence it is important to realize that it is not the only Christian understanding. Indeed, it took over a thousand years for it to become dominant.

In fully developed form, it first appears in a book written in 1097 by Anselm, archbishop of Canterbury. It gradually became central in medieval Christianity and then in much of the theology of the Protestant Reformation. There it was foundational for the notion of radical grace: through Jesus's death, God has abolished the system of requirements by taking care of whatever you think separates you from God. Ironically and over time, it became for many Protestants the primary requirement in a new system of requirements: we are made right with God by believing that Jesus died as our substitute. Radical grace became conditional grace. And conditional grace is no longer grace.

But seeing Jesus's death primarily within the framework of substitutionary atonement goes far beyond what the New Testament says.

Strikingly, Mark's story of Jesus's death says nothing about a substitutionary sacrifice. In the other gospels, it is only if one reads them within the framework of substitution that one finds the notion there.

Of course, some New Testament authors, including Paul, use sacrificial imagery. But it is one of several images they use to speak of the meaning of Jesus's death. The others include:[13]

- The cross as the domination system's "no" to Jesus (and Easter as God's "yes" to Jesus and "no" to the powers that killed him).

- The cross as revelation of the path of transformation: we are transformed by dying and rising with Christ.

- The cross as revelation of the depth of God's love for us. It is not the story of a human sacrifice required by a judging God, but a parable of God's radical grace.

In all of these, the notion of substitution is absent. Moreover, it is important to realize that the language of sacrifice does not intrinsically mean *substitution*. This is true in ordinary language as well as in the Bible. In our everyday use of the word, we speak of soldiers sacrificing their lives for their country, and of Martin Luther King Jr. and Gandhi and others sacrificing their lives for the causes about which they were passionate. In *this* sense, was Jesus's death a sacrifice? Yes. But affirming this does not thereby imply that they and he died as a substitute for somebody else.

In the Bible, sacrifice is most commonly associated with a gift and a meal. The giving of a gift and the sharing of a meal are the classic means of bringing about reconciliation when rupture has occurred, whether with a person or God. The giving of a gift to God makes it sacred, which is the root meaning of the word "sacrifice," "to make sacred." To say that Jesus's death was a sacrifice means that his death has become sacred for us. As the language of the Eucharist in liturgical churches puts it, "Christ our Passover has been sacrificed for us; therefore, let us keep the feast." Exactly. The Passover lamb was not a substitution, but food for the journey. Christ our Passover has been made sacred for us; therefore, let us share the meal of his body and blood.

To be candid at the risk of being offensive, I see the notion of substitutionary atonement as bad theology and bad history. I do not mean to mock people who think this way or to imply that thinking this way precludes being Christian. Millions of Christians have believed in substitutionary atonement and have been good Christians. Being Christian is not primarily about getting our beliefs right. Rather, I am inviting people who believe or think they are supposed to believe in substitutionary atonement to think again, to reconsider, to see again.

I think it's bad theology because it elevates one understanding of Jesus's death above all others and makes it normative. Moreover, it says something both limiting and negative about God. It limits God by saying God can forgive sins only if adequate payment is made. Is God limited in any way? Is God limited by the requirements of law? It is negative in that in it God demands a death—somebody must die. It implies that the death of Jesus, this immeasurably great and good man, was God's will, God's plan for our salvation.

In its emphatic form, the substitutionary atonement leads to what Dallas Willard, an evangelical author, vividly calls "vampire Christians"—Christians interested in Jesus for his blood but little else.[14] But, as he and I agree, the cross is about discipleship. Discipleship, following Jesus, is not about believing a correct atonement theology. It is about following the way of the cross—commitment to the path of personal transformation as symbolized by the cross, and commitment to the path of confrontation with domination systems, equally symbolized by the cross.

In his book *The Cost of Discipleship*, written in Germany in the late 1930s, Dietrich Bonhoeffer, one of the martyred saints of the twentieth century, said, "When Christ calls a man he bids him come and die."[15] He did not then know (though he may have intuited it) that the path of discipleship, the way of the cross, would involve for him not only personal transformation but also a fatal confrontation with the powers that ruled his world. It would cost Bonhoeffer his life: he was executed by Nazi Germany. The way of the cross is about discipleship, not believing in the blood of Jesus as a substitute for our own.

I think it's bad history because it presumes that Jesus's death was part of the plan of God. But this is not a historical explanation, not an answer to the question, "Why was Jesus killed?"

EXECUTED BY ROME

That Jesus was crucified tells us that he was executed by Rome, the empire that ruled his world. It was an imperial form of execution, not a Jewish one. We do not know if the temple authorities had the power to impose capital punishment. According to John 18.31, they did not. But if they did have that power, the mode of execution would have been stoning. To say the obvious, Jesus was crucified, not stoned.

Crucifixion made a statement. There were other forms of Roman capital punishment, such as beheading. Rome reserved crucifixion for two categories of people: chronically defiant slaves and others who challenged Roman rule. What they shared in common was refusing to accept established authority.

Crucifixion was designed to be brutal and very public. Victims were nailed and sometimes also roped to a cross. Death was normally slow and excruciating (a word that comes from the Latin word for "cross"). The victim was naked and most often took several days to die. Death resulted from a combination of exposure to heat and cold, exhaustion, and respiratory failure. It was as public as possible. Victims were hung up near a city gate or other prominent place where many people would pass by. To imagine a different scenario, Jesus could have been killed in a back alley or a prison cell if the authorities had simply wanted to get rid of him. But he was crucified precisely because it made a public statement; it said this is what we do to people who oppose us. It was state-sponsored terrorism, imperial terrorism, torture and death as deterrent.

It has become a cliché among Jesus scholars to say that the most certain fact we know about him is that he was crucified. But it is an important cliché. Jesus was executed. He didn't simply die; the authorities killed him. For a sketch of the historical Jesus to be persuasive, it must account for this.

DID IT HAVE TO HAPPEN?

Was the death of Jesus foreordained? Did it have to happen, because of divine necessity, because of prophecies in the Jewish Bible, or both? In the decades after his death, his followers sometimes spoke of Jesus's death as foreordained by God and as God's providential purpose (see, for example, I Pet. 1.18–20 and Luke 24.26–27). These are, of course, retrospective and retrojective interpretations: they look back on the death of Jesus and see a purpose in it and they retroject this purpose back into the story.

This easily generates the inference that Jesus's death had to happen. But this is not a necessary inference. Consider the story from the Jewish Bible about Joseph and his brothers, the fathers of the twelve tribes of Israel. Envious of Joseph, they sell him into slavery and he ends up in Egypt. There, over a long period of time, he rises to a position of authority second only to Pharaoh. Then, because of a famine in their land, his brothers come to Egypt seeking food. They do not know what has happened to Joseph or even if he is still alive.

Joseph meets with them and, when they learn who he is, they are afraid, understandably so. Their brother whom they sold into slavery is now in a position of power and can do to them whatever he wants. But rather than being vengeful, Joseph says:

> Do not be distressed, or angry with yourselves, because you sold me here; *for God sent me* before you to preserve life…. *God sent me* before you to preserve for you a remnant on earth, and to keep alive for you many survivors. So it was not you who sent me here, *but God*. (Gen. 45.5–8)

The storyteller of Genesis affirms a providential purpose in Joseph's being sold into slavery: "*God sent me*—it was not you who sent me here, *but God*."

Does this mean that it was God's will that his brothers sold him into slavery? No. It is never the will of God to sell a brother into slavery. Did it have to happen this way? No. It could have happened differently. His brothers were not foreordained to do this. Rather, the story affirms that God can use even the evil deed of selling a brother into slavery for a providential purpose.

Applying this story to how we might see Jesus's death, was it the will of God? No. It is never the will of God that a righteous man be crucified. Did it have to happen? It might have turned out differently. Judas might not have betrayed Jesus. The temple authorities might have decided on a course of action other than execution. Pilate might have let Jesus go or decided on a punishment other than death. But it did happen this way. And like the storyteller of Genesis, early Christians looking back on what did happen ascribed providential meanings to Jesus's death. But this does not mean that it had to happen.

Yet, though not required by divine necessity, the execution of Jesus was virtually a human inevitability. This is what domination systems do to people who challenge them, publicly and vigorously. It happened often in the ancient world. It had happened to Jesus's mentor John the Baptizer, executed by Herod Antipas not long before. Now it happened to Jesus. Within a few more decades, it would happen to Paul, Peter, and James. We should wonder what it was about Jesus and his movement that so provoked the authorities at the top of the domination systems of their time.

But Jesus was not simply an unfortunate victim of a domination system's brutality. He was also a protagonist filled with passion. His passion, his message, was about the kingdom of God. He spoke to peasants as a voice of religious protest against the central economic and political institutions of his day. He attracted a following, took his movement to Jerusalem at the season of Passover, and there challenged the authorities with public acts and public debates. All of this was his passion, what he was passionate about—God and the kingdom of God, God and God's passion for justice.

Jesus's passion got him killed. His passion for the kingdom of God led to what is called his passion in a narrower sense, namely, his suffering and death. But to restrict Jesus's passion to his suffering and death is to ignore the passion that brought him to Jerusalem. To think of Jesus's passion as simply what happened on Good Friday is to separate his death from the passion that animated his life. Did Good Friday have to happen? As divine necessity? No. As human inevitability? Virtually.

Good Friday is the collision between the passion of Jesus and the domination system of his time. What killed Jesus was nothing unusual. There is no reason to think that the temple authorities were particularly wicked people. We might have enjoyed their company. Moreover, as empires go, Rome was better than most. There was nothing exceptional or abnormal about it; this is simply the way domination systems behave. So common is this dynamic that, as suggested earlier, it can be called the normalcy of civilization.

This realization generates an additional reflection. According to the gospels, Jesus did not die *for* the sins of the world. The language of sacrificial substitution is absent from their stories. But in an important sense, he was killed *because* of the sins of the world. The injustice of the domination system killed him, injustice so routine that it is part of civilization's normalcy. Though sin means more than this, it includes this. Jesus was executed because of the sins of the world.

Jesus's passion was the kingdom of God. It led him to oppose the domination system of his time. The cross of Jesus, the central symbol of Christianity, was political. His death also has religious significance. But any understanding that negates the political meaning of his death on the cross betrays the passion for which he was willing to give his life. His passion was God and the kingdom of God—and it led to his execution by the "powers that be." The domination system killed him.

EASTER: VINDICATED BY GOD

Of course, the story of Jesus does not end with his execution. His followers affirmed that God had raised him from the dead. Easter is so central to the story of Jesus that, without it, we wouldn't even know about him. If his story had ended with his crucifixion, he most likely would have been forgotten—another Jew crucified by the Roman Empire in a bloody century that witnessed thousands of such executions. Perhaps a trace or two about him would have shown up in Josephus or in Jewish rabbinic sources, but that would have been all.

But what is Easter about? On one level, the answer is obvious: God raised Jesus. Yes. And what does it mean to say this? Is it about a spectacular miracle—the most spectacular miracle there's ever been, and thus a testimony to the power of God? Is it about God demonstrating that Jesus was indeed his Son—that Jesus was who he said he was? Is it about the promise of an afterlife—that death has been defeated? All of these? Or something else?

Those of us who grew up Christian have a preunderstanding of Easter, just as we do of Jesus's death. It commonly combines the stories of Easter from all the gospels into a composite whole and then sees them through the filter of Christian preaching and teaching, hymns and liturgy. In its most common form, this preunderstanding sees the stories as historically factual reports. Reading the stories carefully discloses differences in details, but these are seen as the product of multiple witnesses. As we all know, witnesses of an event can differ about the details (think of diverging testimonies about an auto accident), but still be reliable witnesses to the basic factuality of the event (the accident really happened).

This common preunderstanding includes at least three claims. First, the tomb of Jesus was empty. Second, this was because God had raised Jesus from the dead (and not because somebody stole the body or because his followers went to the wrong tomb). Third, Jesus appeared to his followers after his death in a form that could be seen, heard, and touched.[16]

This way of seeing the Easter stories affirms what might be called their *public factuality;* that is, anybody who was there would have experienced what is reported. You or I (or Pilate) would have seen the empty tomb and the risen Jesus talking to Mary Magdalene, appearing to his disciples, inviting Thomas to touch the wounds in his body, eating breakfast with them on the shore of the Sea of Galilee, and so forth. Public factuality means that the events could have been photographed or videotaped, had these technologies been available then. For many Christians, the historical factuality of the Easter stories is so central that, if it didn't happen this way, the foundation and truth of Christianity disappear.

But focusing on the public factuality of the Easter stories risks missing their meanings. They have a more-than-factual significance. When they are claimed to be factual reports, the question of faith most often becomes, "Do you believe they happened?" Debates occur about whether the tomb was really empty and whether the testimony of the witnesses can stand up to rigorous historical inquiry. Easter faith becomes believing that these utterly unique and spectacular events happened on a particular Sunday and for a few weeks afterward a long time ago. The factual question dominates, and the meaning question often remains unasked.

And so we turn to the question of meaning. What did Easter mean to the early followers of Jesus? To state my conclusion in advance, for them, including the authors of the New Testament, Easter had two primary meanings. First, the followers of Jesus continued to experience him after his death. They continued to know him as a figure of the present, and not simply as a figure from the past. Indeed, they experienced him as a divine reality, as one with God. Second, Easter meant that God had vindicated Jesus. As Acts 2.36 puts it, "This Jesus whom you crucified, God has made him both Lord and Messiah." Easter is God's "yes" to Jesus and God's "no" to the powers that killed him. Jesus was executed by Rome and vindicated by God. To put these two meanings as concisely as possible, Easter meant "Jesus lives" and "Jesus is Lord."

PAUL: OUR EARLIEST WITNESS

We begin with Paul rather than the gospels for the simple reason that his letters were written before the gospels. Perhaps all of his genuine letters were written in the decade of the 50s.[17] He is our earliest witness to the risen Jesus. Though he does not have any Easter *narratives* (stories of Easter are found only in the gospels), the post-Easter Jesus was utterly central to him. Indeed, Paul experienced him.

"I Have Seen the Lord"

In 1 Corinthians 9.1, Paul exclaims that he has "seen the Lord." In the same verse, he asks rhetorically, "Am I not free? Am I not an apostle?" Paul's apostleship and his freedom are grounded in an experience of the risen Jesus.[18] Later in the same letter he includes himself in a list of those to whom the risen Jesus appeared:

> Jesus appeared to Cephas [the Aramaic name of Peter], then to the twelve. Then he appeared to more than five hundred brothers and sisters at one time, most of whom are still alive, though some have died. Then he appeared to James [the brother of Jesus], then to all the apostles [for Paul, a group larger than the twelve]. Last of all, as to one untimely born, he appeared also to me. (15.5–8)[19]

In Galatians, he refers to an experience of Jesus: "God ... was pleased to reveal his son to me" (1.15–16).[20] Moreover, his letters are filled with language that indicates that he was a "Christ mystic," one for whom the risen Christ was an experiential reality.[21]

But when and how did Paul experience the risen Jesus? It happened in his famous Damascus road experience, which occurred at least a few years after what we call Easter Sunday. As described three times in the book of Acts,[22] Paul saw a great light and heard the voice of Jesus. Those traveling with Paul did not share the experience, indicating that it was a private and not a public experience. It was what is commonly called a vision. It is possible, perhaps even likely, that Paul thought of the appearances of the risen Jesus to others as also visions. In the list in the passage from 1 Corinthians above, he uses the verb "appeared" four times, for their experience and for his own.

Some Christians are uncomfortable with the thought that experiences of the risen Jesus were visions. They were "only" visions, "just" visions? We who have been shaped by modern Western culture tend not to think very highly of visions. We commonly think of them as hallucinations that have little or nothing to do with the way things are, as subjective experiences that are far less important than "real" seeing.

But not all visions are hallucinations. They can be disclosures of reality. To the comment, "You mean it was *just* a vision," the proper response is that anybody who has had one would never say, "It was just a vision." Moreover, to anticipate the gospel stories, visions can involve not only seeing and hearing, but even a tactile dimension, as dreams sometimes do. Thus a story in which Jesus invites his followers to touch him or is seen to eat does not intrinsically point away from a vision.

Paul's experience of the risen Jesus changed his life. Prior to his Damascus road experience, he was Saul the Pharisee, a zealous persecutor of the movement that had come into existence around Jesus.[23] After his experience, he became a "Christ mystic" and the most important apostle of the Jewish mystic Jesus.

"Jesus Is Lord"

Paul's experience of Jesus as a living reality had a crucial corollary. It generated the conviction not only that "Jesus lives," but that God had vindicated Jesus, said "yes" to the one who had been executed by the authorities and whose movement Paul was persecuting. It meant "Jesus is Lord." This conviction sounds throughout his letters. Paul's most common way of speaking of Jesus, it can be seen as the earliest Christian "confession of faith."

"Jesus is Lord" is the climax of an early Christian hymn in Philippians 2.5–11, possibly written by Paul and in any case used approvingly by him. The first part of the hymn speaks of Jesus's life and crucifixion. Paul introduces it with the words, "Let the same mind be in you that was in Christ Jesus,"

> who, though he was in the form of God, did not regard equality with God as something to be exploited, but emptied himself, taking the form of a slave, being born in human likeness. And being found in human form, he humbled himself and became obedient to the point of death—even death on a cross.

To have "the same mind" means to do likewise, to be "obedient to the point of death—even death on a cross." For Paul, this is what it meant to follow Jesus.

The second part of the hymn affirms that God has vindicated Jesus, exalted Jesus, by giving him "the name that is above every name":

> Therefore God also highly exalted him and gave him the name that is above every name, so that at the name of Jesus every knee should bend, in heaven and on earth and under the earth, and every tongue should confess that Jesus Christ is Lord, to the glory of God the Father.

Every knee in the three-story universe of the ancient imagination—in heaven, on earth, and under the earth—shall bow, and every tongue "confess that Jesus Christ is Lord."

This affirmation put Paul on a collision course with Rome. "Jesus is Lord" was an anti-imperial statement. It denied the central claim of imperial theology: if Jesus is Lord, then Caesar is not. Imperial power had crucified the "Lord of glory" (1 Cor. 2.8). But God exalted Jesus, raised Jesus, vindicated Jesus, and bestowed upon him "the name that is above every name."

One additional comment as we leave Paul: he does not mention an empty tomb. What to make of this is unclear. Is it without significance? Possibly. Paul may have known about and believed that the tomb of Jesus was empty, but found it unnecessary to mention this in letters written to people whom he had taught in person. Or perhaps its absence from Paul's letters means that he hadn't heard a story about an empty tomb. In either case, Paul's conviction that God had raised Jesus was not based upon eyewitness reports of an empty tomb, but on his own experience of the risen Jesus. Such an experience makes the question of whether the tomb was empty irrelevant. For Paul, the risen Jesus was very real; Paul experienced him, and the experience changed his life.

THE GOSPEL STORIES OF EASTER

Exploring the meanings of the gospel stories of Easter involves asking the question, what kind of stories are they? Are they intended as historical reports, as history remembered, and thus to be believed (or doubted and disbelieved)? Is their purpose to report publicly factual events that even disinterested witnesses would have seen if they had been there? Or do they use the language of parable and metaphor to express truths that are much more than factual? Are they history or parable?

The model for the second option—seeing them as parable, as metaphorical narratives—is the parables of Jesus. Christians agree that the truthfulness of Jesus's parables is not dependent upon whether they are historically factual. Nobody is concerned about whether there really was a Samaritan who came to the rescue of a man who had been robbed and beaten by bandits or whether there really was a father who lavishly welcomed home his prodigal son. Nobody would say that these stories aren't true just because they didn't happen.

The obvious point is that parabolic narratives can be true—truthful and truth-filled—independent of their factuality. To worry or argue about the factual truth of a parable misses its point. Its point is its meaning. And "getting a parable" is getting its meaning—and often there's more than one. Moreover, parable and parabolic language can make truth claims, as the story of the prodigal son does: God is like a father who is overjoyed at his son's return from exile in a far country. God is like that.

Seeing the Easter stories as parables need not involve a denial of their factuality. The factual question is left open. A parabolic reading affirms: believe whatever you want about whether the story happened this way—now let's talk about what the story means. If you believe the tomb was empty, fine. Now, what does this story mean? If you believe that Jesus's appearances could have been videotaped, fine. Now, what do these stories mean? And if you're not sure, or even quite sure they didn't happen this way, fine. Now, what do these stories mean?

A parabolic reading insists that *the importance of these stories lies in their meanings*. An empty tomb without meaning ascribed to it is simply an odd, even if exceptional, event. Only when meaning is ascribed to it does it take on significance. This is the function of parable and parabolic language. Parable can be based on an actual event (there could have been a Samaritan who did what the character in Jesus's parable is reported to have done), but it need not be. Indeed, it may be that the most important truths can be expressed only in parable.

In any case, asking about the parabolic meaning of biblical stories, including the Easter stories, is always the most important question. The alternative of fixating on whether they report literally factual happenings leads one astray.[24] And so, as we turn to the stories of Easter in the gospels, I highlight their meaning as parable, as truth-filled stories. I leave open the question of how much of this happened, even as I affirm that their truth does not depend upon their public factuality.

The First Easter Story

Though Paul's letters contain the earliest testimony to the post-Easter Jesus, the earliest *story* of Easter is in Mark. It begins with the women who saw Jesus's death and burial going to the tomb to anoint Jesus's body:

When the sabbath was over, Mary Magdalene, and Mary the mother of James, and Salome bought spices so that they might go and anoint Jesus. And very early on the first day of the week, when the sun had risen, they went to the tomb. They had been saying to one another, "Who will roll away the stone for us from the entrance to the tomb?" When they looked up, they saw that the stone, which was very large, had already been rolled back. As they entered the tomb, they saw a young man, dressed in a white robe, sitting on the right side; and they were alarmed. But he said to them, "Do not be alarmed; you are looking for Jesus of Nazareth, who was crucified. He has been

raised; he is not here. Look, there is the place they laid him.
But go, tell his disciples and Peter that he is going ahead of you
to Galilee; there you will see him, just as he told you." So they
went out and fled from the tomb, for terror and amazement
had seized them; and they said nothing to anyone, for they
were afraid. (16.1–8)

For more than one reason, Mark's narrative should surprise us.
First, it is very brief, only eight verses. Matthew's Easter narrative
has twenty verses, Luke's has fifty-three, and John's has fifty-six, divided into two chapters. Second, Mark does not report an appearance of the risen Jesus; appearance stories are found only in the other
gospels. Third, Mark's story ends very abruptly: "So the women went
out and fled from the tomb, for terror and amazement had seized
them; and they said nothing to anyone, for they were afraid." Full
stop. End of gospel. The ending is not only abrupt, but puzzling. According to Mark, the women do not tell anybody. His ending was
deemed unsatisfactory as early as the second century, when a longer
ending was added.[25]

I briefly note some changes that Matthew and Luke make as they
incorporate Mark's text into their stories of Easter. My purpose is
not to engender skepticism, but to continue reflection about the *kind*
of stories these are.

Matthew adds two details. First, he explains how the stone got
moved; there is an earthquake, and an angel whose appearance was
like lightning and whose clothing was white as snow rolls away the
stone from the entrance to the tomb (28.2–3). Second, Matthew
alone mentions the presence of guards at the tomb (27.62–66; 28.4).
Later, Matthew tells us that the guards report what they have seen to
the chief priests and elders, who bribe them to say that Jesus's disciples stole the body while they were asleep (28.11–15).

Both Matthew and Luke change the ending of Mark's story, but
in different ways. Matthew reports that the women *did* tell the disciples: "They left the tomb quickly with fear and great joy, and ran to
tell his disciples" (28.8). So does Luke (24.9). In addition, Luke
changes the angelic commission given to the women. In Mark (and

Matthew), the women are to tell the disciples to *go to Galilee* where they will see the risen Jesus. But in Luke, the risen Jesus appears only in and around Jerusalem; he has no Easter stories set in Galilee. And so Luke replaces the command to go to Galilee with: "Remember how Jesus told you, *while he was still in Galilee,* that the Son of Man must be handed over to sinners, and be crucified, and on the third day rise again" (24.6–7).

Mark's Story as Parable

As we now reflect on what Mark's story means as parable, recall that doing so does not require a denial of the story's factuality. It simply sets the factual issue aside. As a parable of the resurrection, the story of the empty tomb is powerfully evocative:

- Jesus was sealed in a tomb, but the tomb could not hold him; the stone has been rolled away.

- Jesus is not to be found in the land of the dead: "He is not here. Look, there is the place they laid him." Luke's comment on Mark's story underlines this meaning: "Why do you look for the living among the dead?" Jesus is among the living.

- Jesus has been raised. As the angelic messenger tells the women this, he explicitly mentions the crucifixion: Jesus "who was crucified" by the authorities "has been raised" by God. God has said "yes" to Jesus and "no" to the powers who killed him. God has vindicated Jesus.

- His followers are promised: "You will see him."

And perhaps, as some scholars have suggested, the command to "go to Galilee" means, "Go back to where the story began, to the beginning of the gospel." And what does one hear at the beginning of Mark's gospel? It is about "the way" and the kingdom.

Appearance Stories in the Other Gospels

The other three gospels all have "appearance stories" in which the risen Jesus appears to his followers. Strikingly, none is found in more than one gospel—striking because in the pre-Easter part of the gospels, the same story is often found in two or more gospels. But not so for appearance stories. Each evangelist has his own, suggesting that this is the way the story of Easter was told in the community for whom each wrote. Matthew has two, Luke has two, and John has four.[26] I will treat one from each gospel as I continue to illustrate what it means to hear the Easter stories as parables of the resurrection.

The Great Commission

The story in Matthew 28.16–20 fulfills the promise of an appearance in Galilee. It happens on the "mountain" to which Jesus had told the disciples to go (28.16). Mountains matter in Matthew. Jesus speaks the Sermon on the Mount on a mountain (of course), he is transfigured on a mountain, and now he gathers his disciples one last time on a mountain.

The appearance itself is mentioned only in a subordinate clause, followed by the disciples' response of both adoration and uncertainty: "When they saw him, they worshiped him; but some doubted" (28.17). It is interesting that Matthew reports that uncertainty was possible even for those to whom Jesus appeared. But of course, this is not the primary meaning of the story.

Then the risen Jesus speaks what has come to be known as the "Great Commission":

> All authority in heaven and on earth has been given to me. Go therefore and make disciples of all nations, baptizing them in the name of the Father and of the Son and of the Holy Spirit, and teaching them to obey everything that I have commanded you. And remember, I am with you always, to the end of the age. (28.18–20)

Much is packed into this short passage. First, God has given "all authority in heaven and on earth" to the risen Jesus. The implicit but obvious contrast is to the authorities who crucified him. Jesus is lord of heaven and earth—they are not. Second, Jesus's followers are to "make disciples of all nations." A disciple is one who follows the way of Jesus, not simply a believer. They are to go to "all nations." According to Matthew, Jesus before his death restricted his mission to Israel alone; but now his followers are to take his message to the "nations," meaning the Gentiles as well as the Jews. They are to teach them "to obey everything that I have commanded you." Following Jesus is about obedience, not belief.

Third, the risen Jesus says, "I am with you always." These are the final words in Matthew's gospel, and they take us back to the beginning of his gospel. They echo a theme announced in Matthew's story of Jesus's birth, where Jesus is identified as "Emmanuel," which means "God is with us" (1.23). Now the Emmanuel theme sounds again: *"I am with you* always, to the end of the age." The risen Jesus is Emmanuel, God's abiding presence. The risen Jesus is "God with us."

The Road to Emmaus

The story in Luke 24.13–35 of the risen Jesus encountering two of his followers as they walk from Jerusalem to a village named Emmaus (pronounced ee-may´-us) is the longest Easter narrative. The two are joined by a stranger whom we as the readers know to be the risen Jesus. But they don't recognize him. The stranger asks them, "What are you discussing with each other?" They say to him, "Are you the only stranger in Jerusalem who does not know the things that have taken place there in these days?" And so they tell him about Jesus, their hopes for him, and his crucifixion. The three walk together for some hours, and the stranger talks to them about Moses and the prophets. But they still don't recognize him.

As they draw near Emmaus, the stranger begins to leave. In wonderfully evocative words, they implore him to stay: "Stay with us, because it is almost evening and the day is now nearly over." Stay with us, for night is falling. Abide with us, fast falls the eventide, to echo a well-known hymn. So he stays. As they sit at table, the stranger takes bread, blesses it, breaks it, and gives it to them. Then, we are told, "Their eyes were opened, and they recognized him." Then what happens? "He vanished from their sight."

If I were to use one story to make the case that the Easter stories are parables of the resurrection, this is the one I would use. It makes great sense as a parabolic narrative, whereas imagining that it is speaking about events that could have been videotaped is exceedingly difficult. Moreover, the story is marvelously suggestive. The risen Jesus opens up the meaning of scripture. The risen Jesus is known in the sharing of bread. The risen Jesus journeys with his followers, even when they don't know it. This story is the metaphoric condensation of several years of early Christian experience into one parabolic afternoon. Whether the story happened or not, Emmaus always happens.[27] Emmaus happens again and again—this is its truth as parabolic narrative.

Jesus Appears to Thomas

Commonly called the story of "doubting Thomas," John 20.24–29 follows the story of Jesus appearing to the disciples in a house with the doors locked on the evening of Easter Sunday (20.19–23). Thomas is not with them. As Jesus appears among them, he says "Peace be with you." Then he shows them the wounds in his hands and side. When the disciples tell Thomas, "We have seen the Lord," he does not believe them. He says, "Unless I see the mark of the nails in his hands, and put my finger in the mark of the nails and my hand in his side, I will not believe." This sets up the appearance to Thomas a week later:

> His disciples were again in the house, and Thomas was with them. Although the doors were shut, Jesus came and stood among them and said, "Peace be with you." Then he said to Thomas, "Put your finger here and see my hands. Reach out your hand and put it in my side. Do not doubt but believe." Thomas answered him, "My Lord and my God!" Jesus said to

him, "Have you believed because you have seen me? Blessed are those who have not seen and yet have come to believe."

This story explicitly makes the two primary claims about Easter found in Paul, the gospels, and the New Testament as a whole. The disciples exclaim, "We have seen the Lord!" Jesus lives; he is not a figure of the past, but of the present. And Thomas exclaims, "My Lord and my God!" It is the classic post-Easter Christian confession of faith: Jesus is Lord.

A final note: Thomas is often presented as a negative role model in Christian preaching and teaching. While I was growing up, the only thing worse than being a "doubting Thomas" was to be a "Judas." We should believe, not be skeptical or inquisitive. Don't be a doubting Thomas. Indeed, I have heard a conservative Christian apologist describe Thomas's sin as refusing to accept the apostolic witness of the other disciples.

But unless we inflect the closing words of the story with an accusatory tone of voice, there is no condemnation of Thomas. Thomas desired his own firsthand experience of the risen Jesus, and his desire was granted; Jesus appeared to him. The closing words of Jesus can be read without condemnation: "Have you believed because you have seen me? Blessed are those who have not seen and yet have come to believe." They simply affirm that those who believe without firsthand experience of the risen Jesus are also blessed, but they do not condemn those who, like Thomas, hunger and thirst for such an experience.

THE RISEN JESUS

As I conclude this exposition of Easter, I return once more to the question of history or parable. As is apparent, I find these stories to be powerfully true as parables of the resurrection. It does not matter to me as a Christian whether any of them describe events that you or I could have witnessed. It does not matter to me whether the tomb was empty.

But I am aware that a historical question can still be asked: what happened? What I am confident of is this. The followers of Jesus had experiences of him after his death that convinced them that he continued to be a figure of the present. Almost certainly some of these experiences were visions; it would be surprising if there weren't any. I have no difficulty believing Paul's statement, "I have seen the Lord," or the exclamation of the disciples, "We have seen the Lord." I think many did.

I also think there were nonvisionary experiences of the risen Jesus. Though not narrated in the New Testament, they are implicit. I think his followers felt the continuing presence of Jesus with them, recognized the same Spirit that they had known in him during his historical life continuing to be present, and knew the power they had known in Jesus continuing to operate—the power of healing, the power to change lives, the power to create new forms of community.

And I think these kinds of experiences have continued among Christians ever since. I do not think experiences of the risen Jesus were confined to the forty days between Easter and the ascension of Jesus. The "forty days" are referred to only in Acts 1.3, and it is clear that the author is not speaking about calendar time, for the same author in Luke 24.50–53 reports that Jesus ascended on the evening of Easter day. Moreover, Paul's experience of the risen Jesus on the Damascus road occurred at least a few years after the "forty days" between Easter and Jesus's ascension.

For me, the truth of the claim "God has raised Jesus" is grounded in these kinds of experiences. Not all Christians have had such an experience, but some have. Moreover, it is not necessary to have one in order to be Christian. Jesus's words to Thomas remain true today: "Have you believed because you have seen me? Blessed are those who have not seen and yet have come to believe."

What kind of existence does the risen Jesus have? Does the risen Jesus exist as a body? If he does, it is a very strange kind of body. The risen Jesus is no longer a figure of flesh and blood. Even if one takes seriously that one could touch him, as is suggested in some of the Easter stories, it would be ridiculous to imagine that the risen Jesus has a flesh-and-blood body. How much would he weigh? How tall would he be? Does he still have to eat? These are ridiculous questions—which is exactly my point. According to the Easter stories themselves, the risen Jesus is not confined by time and space, but enters locked rooms, journeys with his followers without being recognized, appears in both Galilee and Jerusalem, vanishes in the moment of recognition, and abides with his followers always, "to the end of the age."

If the risen Jesus exists as a body, it is a body so radically different from any meaning we give to the word "body" that it seems misleading to use the term. Paul himself seems to recognize this. He affirms that Jesus exists as a body, but then immediately speaks of it as a "spiritual body" and explicitly contrasts it to a "physical body" of flesh and blood (1 Cor. 15.35–50). What is a "spiritual body"? It seems idle to me to try to assign meaning to the notion by speaking of a "glorified body" or "transformed physicality," as if these phrases make the matter more intelligible. We should leave it in the language of paradox as Paul does—a "spiritual body"—and simply admit that the risen Jesus transcends our categories of body, flesh, and blood. Epistemological humility and ontological modesty are called for.

And there is one more thing to say about the experiences that lie at the heart of Easter. They carried with them the conviction that God had vindicated Jesus. Easter is not simply about people experiencing a person who has died. The Easter stories are not "ghost stories" (see Luke 24.37–43). Rather, they are stories of vindication, of God's "yes" to Jesus. God has exalted Jesus, raised him to God's right hand, made him Lord. And lest we forget how Jesus died, the Easter stories in both John and Luke remind us that the risen Jesus still carries the wounds inflicted by the empire that killed him.

There is continuity between the post-Easter conviction that God has vindicated Jesus and the message of the pre-Easter Jesus. "Jesus is Lord" is the post-Easter equivalent of Jesus's proclamation of the kingdom of God. God is king, and the kings of this world are not. Jesus is lord, and the lords of this world are not. And just as Jesus's passion for the kingdom led him to oppose the imperial domination system, so his followers' passion for the lordship of Christ led them to defy the lordship of Caesar. And just as his passion cost him his life, so their passion cost many of them their lives.

But Easter means that the powers of this world do not have the last word. As Colossians puts it, "God disarmed the rulers and authorities and made a public example of them, triumphing over them in the cross" (2.15). How did this happen? "They crucified the Lord of glory" (1 Cor. 2.8) and thereby disclosed their own blindness and moral bankruptcy. Indeed, this understanding of the death and resurrection of Jesus as God's "defeat of the powers" was the dominant understanding for the first thousand years of Christianity. To use the ancient Latin phrase, Easter is about *Christus Victor*—God in Christ triumphed over the powers that enslave and afflict the whole of creation.[28]

THE WAY OF JESUS: THE WAY OF THE CROSS

Christianity's single most important symbol is the cross. Catholic and Orthodox and some Protestant Christians make the sign of the cross. We sing, "In the cross of Christ I glory, towering o'er the wrecks of time" and "Beneath the cross of Jesus, I feign would take my stand." Many of us wear a cross. Crosses are found in most churches. In Protestant churches, the cross is most often empty, pointing to the resurrection. In Catholic churches, Jesus is most often on the cross, still bearing the suffering and wounds inflicted by the powers that rule this world. But in whatever form, the cross symbolizes that the death and resurrection of Jesus are at the center of Christianity.

The cross is both personal and political. To begin with the personal, the death and resurrection of Jesus, Good Friday and Easter seen together, are the central Christian image for the path of personal transformation. This path involves dying to an old way of being and being reborn into a new way of being.

All of the major witnesses of the New Testament testify to this. This is "the way" at the center of Mark's gospel. After Jesus speaks for the first time about his impending death and resurrection, he says, "If any want to become my followers, let them deny themselves and take up their cross and follow me" (8.34). Matthew and Luke not only take this over from Mark, but Luke adds the word "daily" (9.23) to make sure we get the point.

This is the path of transformation that Paul had experienced: "I have been crucified with Christ; it is no longer I who live, but it is Christ who lives in me" (Gal. 2.19–20). The old Paul had died, and a new Paul "in Christ" had been born. It is the path Paul affirms for all Christians when he writes about baptism as a ritual enactment of dying and rising, death and resurrection (Rom. 6.1–11). The result is a new self, a new creation: "If anyone is in Christ, there is a new creation" (2 Cor. 5.17).

It is "the way" at the center of John's gospel. The Jesus of John's gospel speaks explicitly about being "born again." In another passage, he says that unless a grain of wheat falls into the earth and dies, it cannot bear fruit (12.24). For John, what we see in Jesus is the only way. Dying and rising, being born again, is the path of personal transformation.[29]

This path, this way, is also at the center of Jesus's own wisdom teaching. With aphorisms and parables, he invited his hearers into a radical centering in God that involved dying to an old way of life. He himself knew that deep centering in God. In all likelihood, it flowed out of his mystical experience of God.

So there is a powerful personal meaning to Good Friday and Easter. The followers of Jesus are invited into the journey that leads through death to new life. Personal transformation is utterly important. Without it, we remain within the world of our socialization, a world marked by limited vision, anxiety, preoccupation, confused loyalties, unhealed wounds, exile, and bondage.

But the cross is also political. And if we do not see this, we risk betraying the passion for which Jesus was willing to give his life. The New Testament, the gospels, and Jesus do not simply speak of dying, but crucifixion. Suppose, to use a counterexample, Jesus had jumped off a high building to illustrate that the path of transformation is dying. To say the obvious, this would have involved a death. But dying and rising with Christ is not just dying and rising—it is dying and rising with the one who was crucified by the rulers of this world.

The way of Jesus involves not just any kind of death, but specifically "taking up the cross," the path of confrontation with the domination system and its injustice and violence. His passion was the kingdom of God, what life would be like on earth if God were king and the rulers and systems of this world were not. It is the world that the prophets dreamed of—a world of distributive justice in which everybody has enough, in which war is no more, and in which nobody need be afraid. It is not simply a political dream, but God's dream, a dream that can be realized only by our being grounded ever more deeply in the God whose heart is justice. Jesus's passion got him killed. But God has vindicated Jesus. This is the political meaning of Good Friday and Easter.

Most of us are familiar with the question, "Do you accept Jesus Christ as your personal Lord and Savior?" It is a crucially important question, for the lordship of Jesus is the path of personal transformation for Christians. But taking seriously the way of the cross means that there is an equally important question, identical except for one word: "Do you accept Jesus Christ as your *political* Lord and Savior?"

To take Jesus seriously is to follow him. To follow him is to participate in his passion. And his passion was God and the kingdom of God. The way of the cross leads to life in God and participation in the passion of God as known in Jesus.

Epilogue

Jesus and American Christianity Today

With Easter, the body of this book—the mission and message of the pre-Easter Jesus and his transformation into the post-Easter Jesus—comes to a close. In this more personal epilogue, I give myself permission to speak about why and how this way of seeing of Jesus matters to me as a Christian and its implications for seeing and living the Christian life today.

As I do so, I will be more overtly personal than I have been thus far—*overtly* because I recognize that the previous part of the book is also personal in that it is written from my perspective. It is the only place from which I can write—I can write only about how I see things. This is true of all authors and all books, obviously so in books of history and religion, but true also of scientific books. No one sees from an impersonal objective place outside of history. We all see from our place in space and time. In this sense, we—all of us—are intrinsically provincial.

I also think that through effort and grace, we are able partially to transcend our time and place so that we are not simply imprisoned by the parameters of our provinciality. But the notion that there is a "purely" objective place from which to see (and think and write) is fantasy. No one sees *sub specie aeternitatis,* from the vantage point of the eternal. Such vision belongs only to God.

I recall a memorable passage in a book about the work of a historian that I read in graduate school some forty years ago. In it, the author compares history (understood as what happens in time, and thus including both past and present) to a moving procession.

History is like a parade. It is easy for historians to imagine that they are in a reviewing stand, watching the parade pass by, observing it as spectators. But, the author continues, there is no reviewing stand; the historian is always part of the procession. We see from within the procession, and the procession is constantly moving. As it does so, it winds, twisting and turning, so that our angle of vision on the past is constantly changing.[1]

This is true for all of us, of course. It applies as we look back on our personal history from our present place in life. It also applies to our lives within culture. Not only does our place within culture continue to shape us, but what happens within our culture's life can affect our view of the past. It can distort it. It can also illuminate it by calling our attention to aspects of the past that we have overlooked or forgotten, not seen or neglected. So if an "objective point of view" means pure objectivity, a place outside of the historical process and our personal development, none of this book is objective.

In a softer sense of the word "objective," I trust that it is. Namely, I have sought to avoid what we might call *uncritical subjectivity*, which has two common and virtually opposite forms. One is the easy-going tolerance of difference that sees all views as valid because they're all subjective and that it's all a matter of "where you're coming from." The other form of uncritical subjectivity fails to recognize its own subjectivity and thus thinks its view is "the way things are." One is completely relative, the other is dogmatically certain.

The only way to avoid uncritical subjectivity is through critical thinking, not only about the views of others but also about one's own. This is what I have sought to do in this book: apply critical thinking to our ancient sources for knowing about Jesus, using the methods of mainstream historical scholarship as they have developed over the past few centuries, putting my position in critical dialogue with those of other scholars, and making a "public argument." A public argument is one presented for public examination and assessment. It does not simply mean saying in public, "This is the way I see things," full stop. A public argument includes *why* one sees things this way; it provides reasons for the perspective and the conclusions to which it leads—and all of it subject to public examination and evaluation: does it make sense?

Whether to call this a softer form of objectivity or to use a term like "intersubjectivity," I leave undecided. The latter term means simply that an argument makes sense to the extent that it is persuasive to others. This does not mean that "truth" is the function of majority opinion; the majority can be and too often has been wrong, in matters both trivial and great. But it does mean that being able to show how and why one reaches the conclusions that one does is a way of moving beyond uncritical subjectivity.

There is an additional aspect of my subjectivity. I do not write in a cultural or personal vacuum. This is an elaboration of the previous point: we all see from where we are. In my case, I have been shaped primarily by a North American cultural context and to a lesser extent a European one, the parts of the world with which I have had the most connection.

It is also a fresh point. I am not a dispassionate observer of what I see happening in American culture and American churches today, not a disinterested reporter of different ways of seeing Jesus and their impact on being Christian in America. Given that I am both Christian and American, this is not an impersonal matter. Rather, it matters very much. I am not neutral about Jesus and the state of the church in the United States. I have perceptions and passion about it.

PERCEPTIONS OF CHRISTIANITY TODAY

Foundational to my perception is that, as described in Chapter 1, we live in a time of a deeply divided Christianity. Unlike fifty or a hundred years ago, the divisions are not primarily denominational. Rather, the major division is between what I there called "an earlier Christian paradigm" and "an emerging Christian paradigm," between a belief-centered way of being Christian and a transformation-centered way of being Christian. To use conventional labels, the division is between conservative and progressive Christians. The former are commonly called evangelical Christians, both by themselves and others. The latter are found mostly in mainline denominations. In the Catholic Church, the issues are somewhat different, but the division exists there too.

The division is most pronounced at the two ends of the spectrum, of course. There it is so great that I sometimes refer to our time as "A Tale of Two Christianities." There is also a large group of Christians in the middle of the spectrum, undecided and uncertain about what is happening in the church, or combining elements of both visions, or in transition. Our time of two Christianities may not be the best of times and the worst of times, but there are encouraging signs as well as much to be dismayed about. I begin with dismay.

Dismay: The Christian Right

The most publicly visible Christianity in the United States today is a hardened form of the earlier Christian paradigm. As in common usage, I will call it the "Christian right." I trust that this is not dismissive name-calling or excessive stereotyping. I am simply seeking to name it, not to intensify a polarization that already exists.

It is called the "Christian right" because it is both theologically and politically conservative. Theologically, in harder or softer forms, the Christian right affirms biblical inerrancy and literal interpretation. Politically, it supports the political right with varying degrees of conviction.

The Christian right is found primarily among evangelical Christians, a broad and somewhat imprecise category that includes most fundamentalist, conservative evangelical, and Pentecostal Christians. Not all are part of the Christian right; there are important exceptions.[2] But most—probably 80 percent or more—identify with the Christian right.

It is the most visible and vocal form of Christianity in America today. The evidence of its visibility is obvious. The Christian right dominates Christian radio and television. It includes almost all of the "megachurches," mostly new congregations with ten thousand or more members. It receives the most media attention. And it is the most politically involved. Often and correctly called the electoral base of the political right as a whole, it is assiduously courted by the secular wing of the political right.

The issues for which the Christian right is most publicly and visibly known are familiar:

- It is against evolution. It campaigns for including "intelligent design" in public school curriculums. Without the Christian right, there would be no controversy about the teaching of evolution. Interestingly, there is no such controversy in other historically Christian countries. It is an American phenomenon.

- It is against abortion. Its preferred term is "pro-life," but this means primarily the beginning-of-life and end-of-life issues of abortion and euthanasia.[3] For the most part, it does not apply a "pro-life" ethic to what happens during life. It generally approves of capital punishment and war and generally opposes the notion that government should provide a safety net that supports and nourishes life. That, it feels, should be left up to individuals and charities.

- It is against homosexuality, which it views as a sinful lifestyle choice. It strongly opposes what it sees as a pervasive "gay agenda" at work in our culture.

- It is known for its emphasis on "values," but its values focus quite narrowly on questions related to sexuality, including gender. Abortion and homosexuality have just been mentioned. In addition, it favors teaching sexual abstinence in publicly funded programs, is ambivalent about contraception because it might contribute to immorality, and protests against excessive sexuality in movies and television (but generally not against violence or consumerism). It is concerned about gender roles within the family and within the church, including whether or not women can be ordained as clergy.

- It supports the civic affirmation of Christianity (or of what it often calls "the Judeo-Christian tradition"), including prayer in public schools and the Ten Commandments in public places.

Its political influence extends beyond these issues. In addition to its very visible and vocal advocacy of these causes, it generally supports the political right on other major matters. The stakes are high because of America's role in the world and Christianity's role in America.

We live in a time of the American Empire. To say that we are the empire of our time is no longer a left-wing claim, but an affirmation embraced by conservative advocates and architects of our imperial power. I add that empire is not necessarily about territorial expansion; we probably have no such ambitions. But empire is about the use of superior military and political power to shape the world in one's own interests, and to do so as unilaterally as possible.

Our cultural context raises an acute and urgent question: what does it mean to be a Christian and a citizen of the empire? It is, of course, an ancient question as well, central to the Bible, Jesus, and early Christianity.

The answer of the Christian right is clear: it supports American imperial policy and the used of armed force to enforce that policy. The demographic group providing the highest percentage of support for going to war in Iraq was white evangelicals (over 80 percent). They continue to be its largest group of supporters—in spite of the fact that Christian moral teaching, Catholic and Protestant, forbids starting a war and has done so for over sixteen hundred years. Before then, Christians were pacifists. Since then, Christian teaching has permitted going to war as a last resort of self-defense—but not preemptive war, a "right" that our government now claims.

Given this long tradition of Christian teaching about war, why were the streets of America not thronged with millions of Christians in the months leading up to the war saying, "We must not do this— it violates all Christian teaching about the conditions under which we may go to war"? The most persuasive answer is because of the imperial captivity of much of the church in the United States.

On the environment, most of the leaders of the Christian right are either silent or advocates of a God-given human dominion over nature. The result is a neglect of environmental regulation, and often opposition. Many ridicule the evidence for global warming, thereby encouraging their followers to discount what scientists are saying about the problem.[4]

On government and economic policy, most see government as at best "a necessary evil" and embrace the "smaller government, lower taxes" rhetoric of the secular political right. As a result, they support economic and tax policies that benefit the wealthiest among us. This is occurring in the context of a growing gap between the wealthy and the rest of our population over the last twenty-five years, especially the poor but also much of the middle class.[5] Much of the Christian right supports an economic and tax policy sharply in contrast to the Bible's passion for a more just distribution of God's earth.

Again, I emphasize that this is not a description of evangelical Christianity as a whole, but of the Christian right in particular. Not all evangelicals see things this way. Indeed, all of the points I have just made are made by evangelical authors critical of much of what is happening within their own tradition.[6]

Among them is Jim Wallis, author of the important best-seller *God's Politics*. Near the beginning of that book, he poses a question: how did the religion of Jesus become pro-rich, pro-war, and only pro-American? For Christians, it is a provocative question that should haunt us in what often seems to be a Christ-forgetting country.

The visibility of the Christian right has an additional consequence: many people outside of the church have a very unfavorable image of Christianity. Some examples from my own experience are:

- The majority of my students at Oregon State University grew up outside of the church, this state being one of the least "churched" areas in the country (and perhaps even number one on that list). Most of them have a very negative view of Christianity. In surveys, they regularly characterize Christians as anti-intellectual, literalistic, self-righteous, judgmental, and bigoted. It is not difficult to discern where they got this impression.

- Several midlife professionals have told me that they're embarrassed to tell their colleagues at work that they go to church because of the assumptions they think their colleagues will make. As one of them said to me, "It's such a conversation stopper."

- My wife and I know many people who are on a religious journey, a spiritual path, but who think of Christianity as the last place they would look to find something of value.

- As a friend said to me, "The greatest obstacle to Christian evangelism in our time is Christian evangelists."

The purpose of the preceding section of this epilogue has not been to rant or insult or enflame, but to describe the effects of the most visible and vocal form of contemporary Christianity in American life and the American church today. I recognize that there are many good and gentle people in congregations of the Christian right who love God and Jesus. But their theological and political attitudes are shaped by the most visible and vocal among them. This is what I am dismayed about.

I am also concerned that what I have said may sound judgmental. I am mindful that Jesus said: "Do not judge, so that you may not be judged. For with the judgment you make you will be judged" (Matt. 7.2; Luke 6.37). Ultimate judgment about everything is God's business, not ours. But Jesus did not say, "Do not discern." Indeed, much of his message was about discernment, about seeing what was going on. To his contemporaries, as well as to us, he said: you know how to forecast the weather—why can't you see the signs of the times? (Luke 12.54–56; Matt. 16.2–3).

Encouraging Signs: Emergent and Emerging Christianity

I turn now to the encouraging signs. One has already been mentioned: there is ferment and self-criticism within a stream of evangelical Christianity. It is a movement beyond the hardened forms of much of evangelicalism to a place that might be called "postevangelicalism"—a position that brings evangelical passion and devotion with it, even as it seeks to move beyond the polarizing "conservative–liberal" conflicts of modernity. Not only evangelical intellectuals but some evangelical congregations are embracing this. This wing of evangelicalism is often called the "emergent church."

Parallel to the above, a second encouraging development is happening in mainline denominations, which I and others call an "emerging Christianity." It is a "neotraditional" form of Christianity. Both the prefix and the noun are important. "Neo" recognizes that it's recent, new; we haven't seen exactly this form before. "Traditional" recognizes that it's not simply new; rather, it is a reclaiming, a retrieval, a recovery, a "seeing again" of the most central elements of the Christian tradition.

It has taken root not only in seminaries, where some of its ingredients have been present for a century or so, but in many congregations. Sometimes called "emerging congregations," they commonly share several characteristics:[7]

- They are committed to adult theological reeducation as a way of reclaiming the richness of the Bible and the Christian tradition. Such reeducation is necessary because most of us grew up with a form of the earlier paradigm of Christianity that stopped making sense to us. But rather than abandoning the Bible and tradition, emerging Christianity is reclaiming it as the basis of Christian identity and formation.

- They are communities of practice, teaching and encouraging the spiritual practices of the Christian tradition. This involves a robust affirmation of the reality of the sacred, a "rediscovery" for Christians who had become skeptical about God because of difficulties created by the earlier paradigm. Spiritual practices—daily practices such as contemplative prayer, other forms of prayer, reading the Bible or devotional classics, reminding ourselves of the presence of God in the dailiness of life; and corporate practices such as worship and embodying compassion—are the way that we live more deeply into God. Practice is about paying attention to our relationship to "what is," the sacred, God.

- They are communities of intention and commitment; to be part of them involves taking the Christian path seriously. They are welcoming communities open to anybody who wants to be there. But to become a member rather than a visitor or kindred spirit involves an intentional commitment, a covenant, to move more deeply into a relationship with God as known in Jesus.

- These communities often take seriously the role of beauty as a mediator of the sacred. The good, the true, and the beautiful, to name an ancient triad, are all affirmed as sacraments of the sacred. The way worship is done—music, the words and movement of the liturgy, the visual aspects—matters.

- They are communities that emphasize compassion, justice, and peace as the central virtues of the Christian life. This is a major result of the recovery of the Bible's passion for justice and peace. They seek to take seriously God's passion for the world. On the political spectrum, most are politically progressive, with some more moderate and some more radical. Though still a minority within the American church as a whole, they are more numerous now than a decade ago. These Christians *as Christians* are beginning to contest the Christian right's recent near monopoly in politics.

In a phrase, what is happening within these mainline congregations is a movement from *convention* to *intention* as the animating motive for being part of a church. It is something relatively new in Western Christianity. For centuries, and in the United States until a few decades ago, there was a conventional expectation that everybody would be a member of a church (and perhaps this applied to synagogues too). So long as this cultural expectation remained in place, mainline denominations did well numerically; they provided a perfectly respectable and safe way of being Christian. Nobody would ask you to do anything too weird.

This expectation no longer exists in most parts of the United States, and as a result membership in mainline denominations has declined sharply over the last forty years. The "good news" in this decline is that, very soon, the only people left in mainline congregations will be the ones who are there for intentional and not conventional reasons. This creates the possibility for the church once again to become an alternative community rather than a conventional community, living into a deepening relationship with a Lord other than the lords of culture. This is exciting.

JESUS IN OUR CONTEXT

In this division and conflict within American Christianity, Jesus plays a major role for an obvious reason, his status for Christians. For all Christians (indeed, this is the defining quality of a Christian), Jesus is the decisive revelation of God—of God's character and passion. Thus how we tell the story of Jesus matters, because in him we see the character and passion of God. And so we return to the theme of the first chapter.

The Jesus of the Christian right commonly combines all or most of the following ways of telling his story: Jesus as dying Savior, as a divine being unlike us, as judge at the second coming, and as teacher of a rigorous personal morality. It emphasizes the literal-factual meaning of language about Jesus (even as it is commonly selective in what it emphasizes).

The emerging Christian paradigm, with its historical-metaphorical approach to the gospels and the Bible as a whole, leads to a quite different way of telling the story. To use my own sketch as an example, put summarily and concisely: the pre-Easter Jesus was a Jewish mystic, healer, wisdom teacher, and prophet of the kingdom of God; he proclaimed the immediacy of access to God and the kingdom of God; he challenged the domination system, was executed by the authorities, and then vindicated by God. Easter is the beginning of the post-Easter Jesus. In the decades after Easter his followers spoke of Jesus and his significance with the most exalted language they knew: Son of God, Messiah, Lord, Light of the World, Bread of Life, and so forth. This language is the community's testimony to him.

My sketch is, of course, but one possible sketch. There are many other contemporary scholarly sketches, ranging from the wildly improbable to the equally plausible. Some people find the diversity within historical Jesus scholarship to be discouraging and some damning—if so little certainty is possible, then maybe the whole enterprise of trying to glimpse the historical Jesus is a mistake. Luke Timothy Johnson, a respected and gifted mainstream scholar and severe critic of historical Jesus scholars (including me), argues that the "real Jesus" is intrinsically more than the historical Jesus.[8] I agree with him. The real Jesus includes the post-Easter Jesus of Christian experience and tradition, and thus also the canonical Jesus—the Jesus we meet on the surface level of the New Testament. This is the Jesus who has shaped the lives of millions of people. I agree with all of this.

But I do not think we should, or need to, separate the real Jesus so sharply from the pre-Easter Jesus. For me, the real Jesus, to connect his phrase to my language, includes both the pre-Easter and the post-Easter Jesus. Both matter. And it is possible to glimpse at least a bit of the pre-Easter Jesus. What we can see is, at the minimum, interesting, and for many, of great value.

The sketch I have developed in this book is very compatible with the emerging Christian paradigm, and I intend it not just for interested readers, but as a contribution to emerging (and emergent) Christianity. Beneath all the possible disagreements about the details of my sketch is what I see as bedrock, that Jesus was a person radically centered in God, empowered by that relationship, and filled with God's passion for the world—a passion that led to his execution and vindication. Of course, the details also matter, for the details give flesh and blood to the bones that make up a sketch.

THREE LITTLE PHRASES

Thus the Jesus of the earlier paradigm and the Jesus of the emerging paradigm are quite different from each other. They lead to very different ways of telling his story. In Chapter 1, I described some of the differences and the ways they change our vision of the Christian life. Here I return to that theme with three familiar phrases.

"What Would Jesus Do?"

The question "What would Jesus do?" first became famous over a hundred years ago in a best-seller written in 1897 by Charles Sheldon called *In His Steps: "What Would Jesus Do?"* About a decade ago, it became famous once again, mostly among young evangelical Christians. WWJD even had its own jewelry.

It's a good question, an important question. And our answer to that question depends upon what we think Jesus was like. Which Jesus? The Jesus who tells us about the importance of believing in him so that we can be with him forever? The Jesus who will soon come again to judge the world? If so, then what Jesus would do is to try to convert people to believing in him. The Jesus who teaches a rigorous personal morality? If so, I suspect the answer would be following a code of moral purity, much of it having to do with sex.

I do not know how the question was answered in circles that emphasized WWJD. My point is the more general one: our image of Jesus shapes our answer to that question. To use the image of Jesus I have sketched, what would Jesus do in our context? He might once again disrupt the temple—the unholy alliance between religion and empire. I think he would teach the wrongness and futility of violence in human affairs. He would be passionate about compassion and justice as the primary virtues of a life centered in the God whom he knew. And of course, he would teach the importance of a deep centering in God. Without such centering, Jesus's vision ceases to be Jesus's vision.

"Jesus Loves Me—This I Know"

The words are familiar. Many of us sang them when we were children. And, in a story I have heard several times, they were Karl Barth's summary of the Christian gospel. Barth (1886–1968) was one of the two most influential theologians within mainline Protestantism in the twentieth century. He wrote voluminously, including a ten-volume intellectually brilliant and dense systematic theology several thousand pages long. In his seventies, during his only lecture tour of the United States, he was asked at a press conference if he could sum up his theology in a brief simple statement. He said, "Jesus loves me—this I know." I don't know whether Barth was asked to say more about what he meant. I do know that the statement is more provocative, challenging, and radical than I was able to appreciate as a child.

It poses a question: suppose we take "Jesus loves me—this I know" as one way of stating the foundation of the Christian life. And so? Then what? It is a question worth pondering. If one can say from the depth of one's being, "Jesus loves me—this I know," what follows? What does it mean to you, what does it mean to us? If I know, if we know, that Jesus loves us, what then?

What follows is loving Jesus back. And how do we love Jesus back? By loving what Jesus loved. And what did Jesus love? Once again, how we tell his story is decisive.

"For God So Loved the World"

We all know the opening words of perhaps the best-known verse in the New Testament, John 3.16. I quote it in its most familiar version, including its masculine pronouns for God:

> For God so loved the world that he gave his only Son, so that everyone who believes in him may not perish but may have eternal life.

Familiar as this verse is, it has surprises. I parse it phrase by phrase. The first phrase affirms "God so loved *the world*"—not Christians in particular, or the elect, or the church, but *the world*. God's passion is the world. Christians have often been fearful of loving the world, for they have sometimes confused it with "worldliness." But loving the world doesn't mean getting lost in the world. It means loving the world—the creation—as God loves the world.

How much does God love the world? So much "that he gave his only Son." In John, this phrase does not refer to Jesus's death on the cross as substitutionary atonement for sin, but to the incarnation as a whole. God loves the world so much that God incarnate in Jesus became part of it, vulnerable to it, partaking of it. To love the world means to love the world as God in Jesus loved the world, to give one's life for it.

"Everyone who believes in him [Jesus]"—here, as most often in the New Testament, believing does not mean believing in doctrines about Jesus, but "beloving," the beloving that is a combination of commitment, loyalty, faithfulness, allegiance to the beloved, and trust in the beloved. The result? That they "may not perish but may have eternal life." As noted in an earlier chapter, "eternal life" in John's gospel does not mean an afterlife, but "the life of the age to come." Already in the present, we may experience the life of the age to come by centering in God as known in Jesus. Jesus is now, already, "the resurrection and the life," to use another of John's phrases, the way from death to life.

Central to the verse is the affirmation that the well-being of the world is God's passion. This is the reason for the incarnation, the reason "God gave his only Son": Jesus exists for the sake of the world. To love the world as God loves the world is to love the world as Jesus loved the world. And how did Jesus love the world? Once again, how we tell the story of Jesus matters, for it shapes our answer to that question.

A VISION OF THE CHRISTIAN LIFE

The first title I suggested for this book was *An Emerging Jesus for an Emerging Christianity*. It got rejected, and that's okay. The reason I suggested the title is the central claim of this book: how we see Jesus affects how we see Christianity—it shapes what we think the Christian life is most centrally about. And thus an emerging Jesus—a Jesus seen within a historical-metaphorical paradigm—and an emerging vision of Christianity go hand in hand.

I turn now to the vision of the Christian life that flows out of this way of seeing Jesus. I have already said some things about this, of course, both explicitly and implicitly. So here I will be very concise:

- This vision of life is deeply centered in God, the sacred. So it was for Jesus. So it is in all of the enduring religions of the world. What makes Christianity Christian is centering in God *as known in Jesus*.

- Two transformations are at the center of this life. For want of better language, I call them the personal and the political. The Christian life is about personal transformation into the likeness of Christ (from one degree to another, as Paul puts it); and it is about participation in God's passion for the kingdom of God. The personal and the political are brought together in "the way of the cross"—an image of personal transformation and confrontation with the domination systems of this world.

- It is a way of being Christian in which beliefs are secondary, not primary. Christianity is a "way" to be followed more than it is about a set of beliefs to be believed. Practice is more important than "correct" beliefs. Beliefs are not irrelevant; they do matter. But they are not the object of faith. God is the "object" of commitment—and for Christians, God as known in Jesus.

- It is a life of deep commitment and gentle certitude. Deep commitment, because it involves one's whole being. Gentle certitude, because it is gentle, soft, regarding particular verbal formulations of Christianity, including precise doctrinal statements. These are always human products. They are to be valued as such and to be reformulated when necessary. Depth of commitment and dogmatic certainty about a particular set of beliefs are not the same thing.

In all of this, church matters. By "church" I mean local congregations, local communities of Christians, as well as the church aggregate. The church has more than one central function.

Churches are to be communities of transformation. This means being communities of resocialization. Most of the readers of this book have been socialized into modern Western culture, and most of us into American culture in particular. To be Christian is to be re-

socialized into a different understanding of reality and way of life—
to live in relationship to another Lord and vision, to be shaped by
the Bible and Jesus. Being Christian doesn't mean being anti-
American, but it does mean that Christian identity and loyalty
matter more than national identity and loyalty. When there is a conflict, Jesus is Lord. The church is the community that proclaims, in-
cubates, and nourishes the lordship of Christ.

Another central function of the church is that it exists for the sake
of the world. It does not exist for its own sake. It is grounded in God
who "so loved the world," not God who so loved the church and
Christians in particular. The church is to be a mediator, an instru-
ment, of God's passion for the world's well-being.

And the church is the community that remembers and celebrates
Jesus. Without such communities, the memory of Jesus would disappear. The saying that the church is always one generation away from
vanishing is true.

So it is important to be part of a Christian community—not because it's a requirement for salvation, but because of the church's role
as a community of transformation into an identity in Christ. God
does not need the church. But Christians do. God can get along
without the church. But we cannot.

CONCLUDING COMMENTS

In a very important sense, the vision of life at the heart of Christianity is not complicated. We have sometimes made being Christian
complex by indulging our desire for excessive precision and certitude.
But what it means to be Christian can be expressed with great economy and simplicity. Jesus did so: "Love the Lord your God with all
your heart, soul, mind, and strength; and love your neighbor as yourself."

One of my favorite modern ways of putting the great simplicity is
a memory shared by my mentor and friend Huston Smith, a story of
his mother's influence on his own religious vision. As I recall the
story (and I am confident that I have the gist of it right, even if not
the exact words, like the followers of Jesus), his mother's summation

of her faith was, "We are in good hands; therefore, let us take care of one another." It's hard to put it better.

Of course, I am not suggesting that we reduce Christianity to a message that can be put on a greeting card. The Christian tradition—its scriptures, its history, its intellectual tradition, its worship and practices, its wisdom, its music and art, its saints, its lives filled with compassion and sometimes justice—is an extraordinarily rich tapestry, and we impoverish ourselves if we do not pay attention to its detailed particularity. But being Christian is not complicated. At its center is Jesus, whose passion was God, the way, and the kingdom.

AN UNENDING CONVERSATION

We are all part of an unending conversation. It is an image of human life, a parable of our lives, powerfully and insightfully developed by the twentieth century American scholar Kenneth Burke. Being born is like entering a parlor where there's already a conversation going on. The conversation began long before we were born, and it will continue long after we're gone. The conversation is about life itself—about what is real, what's worth paying attention to, how we should live, and what "this" is all about. When we have listened long enough to have some idea of what the conversation is about, we join it ourselves. Then, in Burke's words, "The hour grows late, you must depart. And you do depart, with the discussion still vigorously in progress."[9]

Of course, life is about more than "talk." But the unending conversation is not just about talk. It is not just intellectuals or chatty types who become involved in this. Everybody does, however articulately or inarticulately, explicitly or implicitly. We all live in relationship to the conversation.

So also for those of us who are Christians. We are all involved in an unending conversation about Jesus. It has gone on from the time of his first followers—a conversation that includes memory, testimony, significance, meaning, application, praise, prayer, and, of course, difference and conflict. The terms of the conversation change over time and from one cultural setting to another. The title of an illuminating book by one of the twentieth century's scholarly giants makes the point: *Jesus Through the Centuries*.[10] How Christians think and talk about Jesus changes, even as there are some constants.

Indeed, for Christians, the unending conversation about Jesus is the most important conversation there is. He is for us the decisive revelation of God—of what can be seen of God's character and passion in a human life. There are other important conversations. But for followers of Jesus, the unending conversation about Jesus is the conversation that matters most.

Notes

CHAPTER ONE

1. Coauthored by Jerry Jenkins and Tim LaHaye. In addition to the twelve-volume series, there are now a couple of "prequels."

2. Richard Fox, *Jesus in America* (Sam Francisco: HarperSanFrancisco, 2003); Stephen Prothero, *American Jesus* (New York: Farrar, Straus & Giroux, 2003).

3. In passing, I note that it is difficult to know what to make of this statistic. Clearly, 84 percent of our population are not passionately committed to Jesus, which is what affirming him to be the "Son of God" should entail. Perhaps agreeing with the statement means much the same as agreeing with the statements "Muhammad is the prophet of Allah," "Moses is the lawgiver of Israel," and "The Buddha is the Enlightened One." Yes, that's who Jesus is, that's who they are.

4. Robert Capon, *Hunting the Divine Fox* (New York: Seabury, 1974), p. 90.

5. Barbara Rossing, *The Rapture Exposed* (New York: Basic Books, 2004). The notion of the "rapture" originated with John Nelson Darby in the 1800s.

6. Tim LaHaye and Jerry Jenkins, *Glorious Appearing* (Wheaton, IL: Tyndale, 2004), pp. 225–26.

7. Sam Harris reports the poll in *The End of Faith* (New York: Norton, 2005), p. 230: 22 percent of American Christians said they are "certain" that Jesus will return in the next fifty years, and another 22 percent think he "probably" will.

8. Jefferson completed his work on Jesus in his retirement. It was finally published in 1904 as *The Life and Morals of Jesus of Nazareth, Extracted Textually from the Gospels*.

9. I also use the astronomical analogy in my *The Heart of Christianity* (San Francisco: HarperSanFrancisco, 2003), p. 5, and I apologize to readers familiar with it from that book. But the notion is so important that it seems essential to repeat it in this book. In *Heart,* I use the notion to describe the conflict between two different visions of Christianity and the Christian life in our time.

10. C. S. Lewis, *Mere Christianity* (San Francisco: HarperSanFrancisco, 2001; first published in 1952), p. 52.

11. For a fuller development of this point, see my *The Heart of Christianity,* pp. 25–41, and two books by Wilfred Cantwell Smith: *Belief and History* (Charlottesville, VA: University Press of Virginia, 1977) and *Faith and Belief* (Oxford: Oneworld, 1998).

12. For an engrossing book that integrates this controversy with Galileo's personal life, see Dava Sobel, *Galileo's Daughter* (New York: Penguin, 2000).

CHAPTER TWO

1. John Meier, *A Marginal Jew: Rethinking the Historical Jesus*, vol. 1 (New York: Doubleday, 1991), p. 1.

2. In the same poll that disclosed that over 80 percent of Americans identify themselves as Christians, only 48 percent could name the gospels. The extent to which this reflects lack of involvement or the shallowness of Christian education is difficult to know.

3. From Josephus, *Jewish Antiquities*, book 18, as reconstructed and translated by Meier in *A Marginal Jew*, vol. 1, p. 61. The full text of Josephus also calls Jesus the "Messiah" and affirms his resurrection. For centuries, historians have been certain that the full text does not go back to Josephus, but is the product of Christians who amended Josephus as they copied and preserved his manuscript. But most historians think that the "core" of the passage, as presented above, goes back to Josephus himself. For Meier's persuasive case, see pp. 56–88 of his book.

4. One of the Nag Hammadi documents. For the *Gospel of Thomas*, see Stevan Davies, *The Gospel of Thomas* (Woodstock, VT: Skylight Paths, 2002); and Stephen Patterson, *The Gospel of Thomas and Jesus* (Sonoma, CA: Polebridge, 1993).

5. A small number of mainline scholars argue that Matthew (and not Mark) is the earliest gospel. The best-known advocate of this position is W. R. Farmer, *The Synoptic Problem*, 2d ed. (New York: Macmillan, 1976). See also D. L. Dungan, *A History of the Synoptic Problem* (New York: Doubleday, 1999). A slightly larger (but still small) group of scholars are skeptical about the existence of Q. But both of these views are very much minority positions. My impression is that over 90 percent of mainline scholars accept the two-document hypothesis: the priority of Mark and the existence of Q. Scholars sometimes also speak of two other "sources" that are designated "M" and "L." M refers to material found *only* in Matthew, and L to material found *only* in Luke. But it is misleading to think of M and L as "sources" if by that one means written documents. Rather, M and L designate the "leftovers" in Matthew and Luke—that is, material that is left over after material from Mark and Q has been identified. It is unlikely that the leftovers come from a written source. Rather, some of M and L is oral tradition used by only one evangelist, whether because the others chose to leave it out or didn't know about it. Some of M and L may have been created by the authors of Matthew and Luke.

6. Available in a number of versions. The most widely used is *Gospel Parallels*, ed. Burton H. Throckmorton Jr., 5th ed. (Nashville, TN: Thomas Nelson, 1992).

7. An earlier generation of scholars referred to the first as the "historical Jesus" or the "Jesus of history" and the latter as the "Christ of faith."

8. Of course, we don't know the height and weight of Jesus. But I have heard that this was the average size of an adult male in the time of Jesus.

9. I owe this observation about Matthew to Mark Allan Powell, *Jesus as a Figure of History* (Louisville, KY: Westminster John Knox, 1998), p. 4. The book is highly recommended as a balanced introduction to contemporary Jesus scholarship.

10. *Celtic Daily Prayer*, ed. Andy Raine and John T. Skinner (London: Marshall Pickering, 1994), p. 12.

11. There is a strong consensus among mainstream scholars that Jesus did not speak of himself as he does in John. Thus we best understand John's "I am" statements by hearing them as third-person statements about Jesus. Rather than imagining that Jesus himself said, "I am the Light of the World," we should imagine John saying about Jesus, "Jesus is the Light of the World." And, because of the modern Western tendency to think that if a statement isn't literally factual, then it isn't true at all, I underline that as a Christian I affirm that Jesus *is* the Light of the World, even as I do not think that Jesus said this about himself. So also, I am skeptical that Jesus proclaimed himself the "Son of God" or the "Messiah," but I nevertheless think these affirmations are true. They are the post-Easter testimony of early Christian communities, and as a Christian I agree with them—this is who Jesus is for me.

12. Günther Bornkamm, *Jesus of Nazareth* (New York: Harper & Row, 1960), p. 56.

13. The purpose of considering the historical question of whether christological language goes back to Jesus's pre-Easter life is not to create skepticism about the gospels and Jesus. A skeptical response is most often a product of literalism. Skeptical literalism exists in a "worried" form: if Jesus didn't say he was the Messiah and the Son of God, then maybe he's not, and maybe the gospels and the Bible can't be trusted. This is often the reaction of Christians who see Jesus within the literal paradigm when they first encounter a historical approach to the gospels. Skeptical literalism also exists in an "in your face" form: Jesus didn't talk like this, and so all of this language is misleading and false, the product of early Christian exaggeration, perhaps even delusion. This is the "debunking" approach. But the reaction of skeptical literalism in both forms is captive to modernity. Both are based on "factualism," the identification of truth with factuality.

14. Albert Nolan, *Jesus Before Christianity* (Maryknoll, NY: Orbis Books, 1978), p. 117.

CHAPTER THREE

1. The twelve disciples in Mark are in this story models of "failed" discipleship. None of them "get it." Judas will betray Jesus, Peter will deny Jesus, and the rest will flee. But the point remains: this is a story about the meaning of discipleship, even though the original disciples didn't "get it" at the time.

2. John's account of Jesus's public activity begins with chap. 2; all of chap. 1 is prologue.

3. Denise Levertov, *The Stream and the Sapphire* (New York: New Directions, 1997), p. 6.

4. The two most important recent studies of the birth stories are Raymond Brown's 700-page *The Birth of the Messiah* (New York: Doubleday, 1977; rev. ed., 1993),

and Robert J. Miller's 300-page *Born Divine: The Births of Jesus and Other Sons of God* (Santa Rosa, CA: Polebridge, 2003). Because of its shorter length and clear and candid wrestling with both historical and theological questions, the latter is especially recommended.

5. That these stories are found only in Matthew and Luke is not in itself decisive. There are texts in Matthew alone and Luke alone that most mainline scholars see as going back to the time of Jesus. These include a number of parables. For example, only Luke reports the parables of the good Samaritan and the prodigal son, and only Matthew reports the parables of the workers in the vineyard and the unmerciful servant, yet most mainstream scholars see the core of these as going back to Jesus.

6. Matt. 1.1–17; Luke 3.23–34. Matthew traces Jesus's genealogy back to Abraham, Luke back to Adam. Moreover, from King David onward, they are very different.

7. Matt. 1.23; 2.6; 2.15; 2.18; 2.23. See my *Reading the Bible Again for the First Time* (San Francisco: HarperSanFrancisco, 2001), pp. 113–17; and Miller, *Born Divine*, pp. 155–74.

8. For this list, see Keith Hopkins, *Conquerors and Slaves, Sociological Studies in Roman History*, vol. 1 (Cambridge: Cambridge University Press, 1978), cited by John Dominic Crossan and Jonathan Reed, *In Search of Paul* (San Francisco: HarperSanFrancisco, 2004), pp. 235–36. Crossan and Reed's book is the most comprehensive and accessible account of Roman imperial theology as the cultural matrix for Paul, early Christianity, and Jesus.

9. The story is found in Suetonius, *The Twelve Caesars* (Augustus, 94.1–11), written in the early second century. Suetonius credits an earlier writer, Asclepia of Mendes. It is also found in Dio Cassius's *History of Rome* (45.1.2–2.4), written in the third century. For quotations of the texts, see Miller, *Born Divine*, pp. 140–45. The point, of course, is not whether these stories are factually true, but that Augustus as "Son of God" was the result of a divine conception.

10. For the full text, see Crossan and Reed, *In Search of Paul*, pp. 239–40. I first became aware of this inscription in Richard Horsley's *The Liberation of Christmas* (New York: Crossroad, 1989), p. 27. It is among those collected and reported by Gustaf Adolf Deissman a century ago in his *Light from the Ancient East*.

11. Crossan and Reed, *In Search of Paul*, p. 241. They continue: "There was decreed, for all time past, present, and future, but one overwhelming gospel, the good news of Augustus's advent, epiphany, and presence, the good news of a global Lord, divine Son, and cosmic Savior."

12. For the most thorough, elaborate, and elegant exposition of this approach, see John Dominic Crossan, *The Historical Jesus* (San Francisco: HarperSanFrancisco, 1991).

13. An example from a decade of working within the Jesus Seminar, a group of scholars who analyzed and then voted upon what parts of the gospels we regarded as memory. After a session in which I was frustrated by what seemed to me to be an overly mechanical application of criteria for discerning what was likely to be memory by one of the Fellows, I said to him, "You know, I think you

could program a computer to make decisions like you make them." He agreed with me and, I think, took it as a compliment. The process is more complex and, yes, subjective, than that.

CHAPTER FOUR

1. L. P. Hartley, *The Go-Between* (New York: Stein and Day, 1953), p. 3.
2. If we do not internalize our social world to a sufficient degree, we will be somewhere on the spectrum from quaintly eccentric to psychopathically narcissistic to criminally sociopathic.
3. For an excellent chapter-length treatment of the social world of Jesus, see William R. Herzog II, *Prophet and Teacher* (Louisville, KY: Westminster John Knox, 2005), pp. 43-69. See also Crossan, *The Historical Jesus* (San Francisco: HarperSanFrancisco, 1991); John Dominic Crossan and Jonathan Reed, *Excavating Jesus* (San Francisco: HarperSanFrancisco, 2001); Walter Wink, *Engaging the Powers* (Minneapolis: Fortress, 1992), pp. 13–104. Like that of many contemporary biblical scholars, my understanding of the dynamics of the ancient world has been shaped by Gerhard Lenski, *Power and Privilege: A Theory of Social Stratification* (New York: McGraw-Hill, 1966); see also his 1974 book coauthored with Jean Lenski, *Human Societies: An Introduction to Macrosociology*, 3rd ed. (New York: McGraw-Hill, 1974), especially pp. 177–230. Michael Mann, *The Sources of Social Power*, vol. 1 (Cambridge: Cambridge University Press, 1986), has also been influential.
4. Walter Brueggemann, *The Prophetic Imagination* (Philadelphia: Fortress, 1978), chap. 2.
5. For an excellent account of Herod and his reign, see Peter Richardson, *Herod: King of the Jews and Friend of the Romans* (Minneapolis: Fortress, 1999).
6. In the gospels, the temple authorities include the high priest, "chief priests," and "elders"; the last term refers to the heads of aristocratic families, not to elders known for their wisdom.
7. For a development of this notion, see Richard Horsley, *Jesus and the Spiral of Violence* (San Francisco: Harper & Row, 1987), pp. 20–58.
8. This is a central emphasis of E. P. Sanders in his work on Jesus, Paul, and Judaism at the time of Jesus. See especially his *Judaism: Practice and Belief, 63 BCE–66 CE* (Philadelphia: Trinity Press International, 1992).
9. Within Judaism, Torah in its most expansive sense includes not only the Jewish Bible, but postbiblical traditions included in the Mishnah and Talmud. This is a later development, of course.

CHAPTER FIVE

1. Another familiar expression of this is Ps. 139. The psalmist asks, "Where can I go from your spirit? Or where can I flee from your presence?" The answer is that

no matter where we go, God is there: "If I ascend to heaven, you are there; if I make my bed in Sheol, you are there. If I take the wings of the morning and settle at the farthest limits of the sea, even there your hand shall lead me, and your right hand shall hold me fast" (vv. 7–10). The author speaks of the three-story universe of the ancient imagination and affirms that there is nowhere outside of the presence of God.

2. His name was Otto Bratlie, then a professor at Concordia College in Moorhead, Minnesota. I think he may have been quoting or paraphrasing Karl Barth, though I am not sure.

3. See the insightful comments by Stanley Hauerwas and William Willimon in "Embarrassed by God's Presence," *Christian Century* (January 30, 1985): 98–100. They argue that both the modern church and modern theology are pervaded by the "practical atheism" of our time, a way of seeing and living that takes for granted that there is no reality beyond the visible.

4. William James, *The Varieties of Religious Experience* (New York: Macmillan, 1961); Abraham Heschel, *Man Is Not Alone: A Philosophy of Religion* (New York: Farrar, Straus & Giroux, 1951); Abraham Maslow, *Religious Values and Peak Experiences* (New York: Penguin, 1976); Rudolf Otto, *The Idea of the Holy* (New York: Oxford University Press, 1958; first published in German in 1917); Huston Smith, *Forgotten Truth: The Primordial Tradition* (New York: Harper & Row, 1977).

5. There are less dramatic and more common experiences of the sacred. A sense of divine presence can occur in the context of a worship service in the singing of hymns, the celebration of the liturgy, the enthusiasm of a Pentecostal service, or the silence of a Quaker service. Such experiences also sometimes occur in the dailiness of our lives. Though nourishing, they are often not as life-changing as the more dramatic experiences. But they are glimpses, intimations, of what is disclosed in the latter.

6. For other experiences of the sacred in the stories of the ancestors, see, e.g., Gen. 12.7–9; 15.1–17; 17.1–2; 18.1–33; 26.23–25; 32.22–31.

7. Though most of the Pentateuch concerns Moses, only a few chapters in the books of Kings speak of Elijah: 1 Kings 17–19; 21; 2 Kings 1–2.

8. The most accessible treatment of these figures is in an important book by Geza Vermes, *Jesus the Jew* (New York: Macmillan, 1973), pp. 65–78, 206–13. Also relevant are E. E. Urbach, *The Sages* (Jerusalem: Magnes, 1975), vol. 1, pp. 97–123; and, earlier, A. Büchler, *Types of Jewish Palestinian Piety* (New York: KTAV, 1968; first published in 1922), pp. 87–107, 196–252. In the thirty years since Vermes' book was published, some scholars have criticized his argument, primarily because the Jewish sources for these figures are several centuries later and thus of questionable historical value. But even if this criticism is given full weight, the stories still provide evidence for this type of religious figure in postbiblical Judaism. It is worthwhile pondering, if people of this type did not exist, why would stories about them with these characteristics have been created?

9. In her new novel *Christ the Lord Out of Egypt* (New York: Knopf, 2006), Anne Rice seeks to imagine what it was like for Jesus at age seven to live with an

awareness of God-consciousness. The appendix to her novel contains a sharp attack on what she sees as the excessive skepticism of much of mainstream Jesus scholarship. Rather ironically and inconsistently, she then bases her story on late apocryphal stories of Jesus's childhood that are not seen as historical by any scholar I know of, whether mainstream, conservative, or fundamentalist. Of course, as a novelist, she is completely entitled to do this. But her appendix misleadingly suggests that her work would have the support of conservative historical scholarship.

10. See also Isa. 64.1 for the image of a "tear" or "rent" in the heavens: "O that you would *tear open* the heavens and come down ..."

11. In earlier English translations, this is "the still small voice."

12. I owe the term to William James, even as I use it in a sense additional to his. I use it to refer to experiences of the "demonic," whereas James uses it to refer to mystical experiences associated with pyschological disorders such as delusional insanity and paranoia (*Varieties of Religious Experience*, p. 334). It is important to realize that mystical experience is an ambiguous phenomenon; it can lead to great evil. In her book *The Silent Cry: Mysticism and Resistance* (Minneapolis: Fortress, 2001), Dorothee Soelle refers to the mystical nationalism experienced by many Germans in the early years of the Third Reich. I see this as yet a third meaning of "diabolical" experiences. James suggests an empirical and pragmatic test for discerning the difference between authentic and diabolical mysticism: "By their fruits, you shall know them" (Matt. 7.16). Perhaps the difference between a vision and hallucination can also be discerned this way. If the experience leads to greater psychological functioning, it is a vision; if it leads to dysfunction, it is a hallucination.

13. Among the reasons for scholarly skepticism: (1) the story reports a private experience of Jesus—there were no witnesses; (2) the story uses "Son of God" language, which many scholars see as most likely post-Easter; and (3) with both the devil and Jesus quoting scripture, the story looks like a literary creation. The first objection seems the weakest. Though the story does report a private experience, Jesus's followers could have become aware of it because it became part of Jesus's teaching. If so, this suggests that he thought it had lessons for them too.

14. On *Gevurah*, see Urbach, *The Sages*, pp. 80–96; for his interpretation of this verse, see pp. 85–86.

15. On "Amen," see J. Jeremias, *New Testament Theology*. (New York: Scribner, 1971), pp. 35–36. According to his tables, it appears thirteen times in Mark, nine times in Q sayings, nine times in Matthew only, and three times in Luke as well as twenty-five times in John. Thus all the layers of the gospel tradition attest to it.

16. See the six antithetical statements found in the Sermon on the Mount, Matt. 5.21–22, 27–28, 31–32, 33–34, 38–39, 43–44. Some scholars accept the antithetical formulation of only the first, second, and fourth as authentic (e.g., Rudolf Bultmann, *The History of the Synoptic Tradition* [New York: Harper & Row, 1963], pp. 134–36). For a defense of the antithetical form as original to all six, see Jeremias, *New Testament Theology*, pp. 251–53.

17. Matthew has "Spirit of God," Luke has "finger of God"; however, the two expressions are synonymous.

18. Otto, *The Idea of the Holy*, especially 155–59. On p. 158, Otto writes: "The point is that the 'holy man' or the 'prophet' is from the outset, as regards the experience of the circle of his devotees, something more than a 'mere man.' He is the being of wonder and mystery, who somehow or other is felt to belong to the higher order of things, to the side of the numen itself. It is not that he himself teaches that he is such, but that he is *experienced* as such" (italics added). See also Otto's *The Kingdom of God and the Son of Man*, trans. F. V. Filson and B. L. Woolf (Grand Rapids, MI: Zondervan, 1951), especially pp. 162–69, 333–76.

19. The NRSV has "were afraid" rather than "were filled with awe." However, "awe" better expresses this meaning. As Otto puts it, in "these few masterly and pregnant words," Mark states "with supreme simplicity and force *the immediate impression of the numinous that issued from Jesus.*" *The Idea of the Holy*, p. 158; italics added.

20. Moses and Elijah are significant *not* because they represent "the law and the prophets," as is often stated in commentaries, for they were *not* symbolic of the law and prophets in the time of Jesus. Rather, they were the two great "holy men" of the Jewish Bible.

21. The accusation that Jesus was possessed by an evil spirit is also found in Q: Matt. 12.27–28; Luke 11.19–20.

22. The extended passage in Mark 3.19b–35 also illustrates a common literary technique used by Mark, called colloquially a "sandwich" technique, in which a story begins, is interrupted by another one, and then returns to the original story. This passage begins with his family, turns to the scribes from Jerusalem and Jesus's response to them (3.22–30), and then returns to his family (3.31–35). When Mark does this, he is indicating that the two stories are to be interpreted in light of each other. In this case, to see Jesus as insane or possessed is to fail to see the Spirit of God at work in him, and thus to dismiss him. This is what Mark means by "blaspheming" against the Holy Spirit (3.29).

23. Luke emphasizes the role of prayer in Jesus's life more than the other evangelists; in addition to 6.12, see 3.21; 5.16; 9.18; 9.28–29; 11.1. However, the picture is not due simply to Lukan redaction, as is clear from the references to Jesus's prayer life in the other gospels.

24. For a history of Jewish mysticism reaching back to the time of Jesus and earlier, see especially Gershom Scholem, *Major Trends in Jewish Mysticism* (New York: Schocken, 1946); *Jewish Gnosticism, Merkabah Mysticism, and Talmudic Tradition*, 2d ed. (Hoboken, NJ: KTAV, 1965). A connection between apocalypticism and visions of or journeys into another world is increasingly affirmed in studies of Jewish apocalyptic. See, e.g., John J. Collins, *The Apocalyptic Imagination* (New York: Crossroad, 1984), which speaks of two strands of tradition in Jewish apocalypses, one visionary and one involving otherworldly journeys.

25. The classic study of *abba* is J. Jeremias, *The Prayers of Jesus* (Naperville, IL: Allenson, 1967), though Jeremias overemphasized its distinctiveness, arguing that it

was *unique* to Jesus (an argument perhaps motivated by theological considerations). For a recent crystallization of the argument in light of subsequent scholarship, see James D. G. Dunn, *Jesus Remembered* (Grand Rapids, MI: Eerdmans, 2003), pp. 548–50.

26. See Vermes, *Jesus the Jew,* pp. 210–13.

27. Statistics from James D. G. Dunn, *The Christ and the Spirit,* vol. 1 (Grand Rapids, MI: Eerdmans, 1998), p. 8.

28. Because the dominance of "father" as term for God in Christian language has been extensively and rightfully criticized by feminist theology over the past several decades, I emphasize that it is not the *maleness* of father language that is significant, but its *familial* meaning as language of relationship and intimacy. It is also important to emphasize that "father" is a metaphor for God (as are king, shepherd, potter, mother, and so forth). God is not literally "father" and only metaphorically king, shepherd, potter, mother, and so forth. God is metaphorically all of these, but not literally any of these.

29. Reinhold Niebuhr, probably the most influential American-born theologian of the twentieth century, villified mysticism as beginning in mist, having "I" at the center, and ending with schism. Karl Barth, one of the two most important Protestant theologians of the century, spoke of mysticism as atheism.

30. Cited in Bernard McGinn, *The Foundations of Mysticism: Origins to the Fifth Century* (New York: Crossroad, 1991), p. 289. This book is the first volume of a very fine multivolume exposition of mysticism in the Christian tradition.

31. James, *Varieties of Religious Experience,* p. 328; p. 320, n. 28.

32. James, *Varieties of Religious Experience,* p. 300.

33. The subtitle of Dorothee Soelle's *The Silent Cry* makes the connection with elegant conciseness: *Mysticism and Resistance.* The book as a whole is about the relationship between mysticism and resistance to the way things are.

34. Even by quite conservative scholars, Luke's inaugural scene is commonly attributed to Luke. To a large extent, this is because the placement of the story is obviously the product of Luke's compositional work. These verses replace Mark's account of Jesus's "inaugural address" in Mark 1:15: "The kingdom of God is at hand." Moreover, the story reflects a central emphasis of Luke—Luke stresses the presence of the Spirit in Jesus more than the other gospels. In addition, the fact that the quotation from Isaiah is a composite of Isa. 61.1–2 and 58.6 makes it difficult to imagine that Jesus was reading from the scroll of Isaiah, as Luke reports. Thus the story is Luke's advance summary of who Jesus was and the themes of his activity. But, even though Luke most likely created this story, it aptly describes what we have seen to be true on other grounds. Thus, even if Luke was creating tradition (rather than reporting it), he saw well.

35. Jesus would not have known what the words "second person of the Trinity" meant. And if we had explained it to him, he perhaps would have been able to understand it—he was very bright. And then we can imagine him asking, "And that's me?" I think he would have been amused. And troubled. I think he would have said, "No, no—it's not about me."

CHAPTER SIX

1. See James Carroll, *Constantine's Sword: The Church and the Jews* (Boston: Houghton Mifflin, 2001) for a book-length treatment of this tragic history.

2. Of course, Matthew also affirms that the movement begun by Jesus is also for non-Jews. At the very end of the gospel, the risen Jesus says, "Go therefore and make disciples *of all nations*" (28.19). But this is a post-Easter command, and thus consistent with Matthew's report that in the pre-Easter setting, Jesus restricted his mission to Jews.

3. Roughly 30 percent of Mark's gospel deals directly or indirectly with miracles. In the first ten chapters of Mark, the percentage is about 47 percent. See John Meier, *A Marginal Jew,* vol. 2 (New York: Doubleday, 1994), p. 619.

4. Fever, Mark 1:29–31; leprosy, Mark 1:40–45; Luke 17:11–19 (ten lepers); paralysis, Mark 2:1–12; withered hand, Mark 3:1–6; bent back, Luke 13:10–17; hemorrhage, Mark 5:24b–34; deafness and dumbness, Mark 7:37; blindness, Mark 8:22–26; 10:46–52; dropsy (edema), Luke 14:1–6; severed ear, Luke 22:51; sick near death or paralysis, Luke 7:1–10 (= Matt. 8:5–13).

5. See also Mark 8:22–26, which reports that Jesus applied spit to the eyes of a blind man.

6. For the story of Hanina, see Vermes, *Jesus the Jew,* pp. 72–75.

7. Matt. 12.27; Luke 11.19; Mark 9.38–39; Mark 6.7–13; 9.18; Matt. 10.1–8; Luke 9.1–6; 10.17.

8. For studies of possession and exorcism, see I. M. Lewis, *Ecstatic Religion: An Anthropological Study of Spirit Possession and Shamanism* (Harmondsworth, England: Penguin, 1971).

9. See the provocative and illuminating discussion by M. Scott Peck in *People of the Lie* (New York: Simon and Schuster, 1983), pp. 182–211. Peck, a practicing psychiatrist, began his study of possession and exorcism believing that a clinical diagnosis within the framework of current psychological understanding would be possible. However, he and a team of professionals eventually became involved in two cases of "possession" (and exorcism) that he could not account for within a purely psychological framework.

10. See especially Lewis, *Ecstatic Religion*.

11. For a very illuminating description of the cosmology of such societies, see Mary Douglas, *Natural Symbols: Explorations in Cosmology* (New York: Pantheon, 1970), pp. viii–ix, 103, 107–24.

12. It is used over twenty times. See James D. G. Dunn, *Jesus Remembered* (Grand Rapids, MI: Eerdmans, 2003), p. 697; p. 177, nn. 22–23.

13. Arland J. Hultgren, *The Parables of Jesus* (Grand Rapids, MI: Eerdmans, 2000), pp. 2–5.

14. In sequence: Luke 15.11–32; 10.29–37; Matt. 20.1–15; 18.23–35; 25.14–30 (Luke 19.12–27); Mark 12.1–12.

15. More examples: "Which one of you?" (Luke 11.5; 14.28; 15.4; 17.7); "What woman?" (Luke 15.8); "What father among you?" (Matt. 7.9; Luke 11.1). See Hultgren, *Parables of Jesus,* p. 8, for these and more.

16. C. H. Dodd, *The Parables of the Kingdom* (New York: Charles Scribner's Sons, 1935, 1961), p. 5.

17. See the comment in Hultgren, *Parables of Jesus,* p. 9: "There is very little previous learning that Jesus's hearers need to bring to the occasion beyond what is gained through life experience. The subject of the parables is typically the familiar of everyday life: men and women working, losing, and finding; fathers and sons in strained and joyous relationships; kings, rich men, and slaves in stereotypical roles; domestic animals, seeds plants, vineyards, leaven, and the like."

18. For example, the parable of the good Samaritan as Luke 10.29–37 reports it concludes with, "Go and do likewise," that is, act compassionately, as the Samaritan did. So also the parable of the sheep and the goats in Matt. 25.31–46 involves an imperative: feed the hungry, clothe the naked, etc.

19. On this whole section, see my *Conflict, Holiness and Politics in the Teachings of Jesus,* rev. ed. (Harrisburg, PA: Trinity Press International, 1998), pp. 78–95, nn. 14–73, 306–14.

20. The meal practice of Jesus was my rite of initiation into the scholarly study of the historical Jesus. It was the primary focus of my doctoral dissertation at Oxford, completed in 1972 and published in significantly revised form in 1984 as *Conflict, Holiness and Politics in the Teachings of Jesus* (New York: Mellen), then reissued in a modestly revised form in 1998 (Harrisburg, PA: Trinity Press International). The topic of my 1972 thesis emerged from a conversation with my supervisor, George B. Caird, who asked me in 1969: "Let's assume that the Pharisees were good people and not hypocrites. What then was the conflict between Jesus and the Pharisees about?" As I pursued the question, I concluded that it was primarily about meal practice and what it signified.

21. This is emphasized especially by John Dominic Crossan in *The Historical Jesus* (San Francisco: HarperSanFrancisco, 1991), pp. 332–48. Some scholars are skeptical about Crossan's methodology and conclusions as a whole, but even they would agree that meals and healing are linked in the earliest layer of the gospel tradition.

22. S. Scott Bartchy, "The Historical Jesus and Honor Reversal at the Table," in *The Social Setting of Jesus and the Gospels,* ed. Wolfgang Stegemann, Bruce J. Malina, and Gerd Theissen (Minneapolis: Fortress, 2002), p. 175. See also Crossan, *The Historical Jesus,* pp. 341–42.

23. Bartchy, "The Historical Jesus and Honor Reversal at the Table," p. 176.

24. See Dunn, *Jesus Remembered,* pp. 599–605, esp. 602–3.

25. Though two of the criticisms are found only in Luke, the other two come from Mark and Q and thus have early independent attestation. Though the middle two do not mention tax collectors, they are set in the context of Jesus eating with tax collectors (Luke 19.1–10; 15.1).

26. The Pharisees virtually disappear from Mark's story of the Jerusalem period. They are mentioned only in the story of Jesus being asked if it is lawful to pay taxes to Caesar (12.13–17). They do not appear at all in the story of Jesus's arrest, trial, and execution.

27. NBC's *Today Show,* Good Friday, 1995.

CHAPTER SEVEN

1. I am using "information" in a broad sense to mean not simply "facts," but also method and larger conclusions flowing from the "facts."

2. For a fuller treatment of Israel's wisdom traditions, see my *Reading the Bible Again for the First Time* (San Francisco: HarperSanFrancisco, 2001), pp. 145–82.

3. *Reading the Bible Again,* pp. 151–61.

4. For this exposition, see H. Richard Niebuhr's insightful *The Responsible Self* (New York: Harper & Row, 1963). Niebuhr argues that our view of the "ultimate context" or "total environment" in which we live (that is, our view of "ultimate reality" or God) decisively affects our response to life. He lists and analyzes the four possibilities of seeing reality as indifferent, as hostile, as requiring appeasement, and as "friend." For the notion of "imaging" reality, see also Alan Jones, *Exploring Spiritual Direction* (New York: Seabury, 1982), pp. 83–98.

5. A phrase used by Carl Sagan in his television series and book *Cosmos* (New York: Random House, 1980).

6. In the United States, 90–95 percent of those polled say they believe in God. In Europe, the figure is much lower. Karen Armstrong reports that in England, the figure is about 35 percent (in a lecture given at the Chautauqua Institution).

7. As I recall the scene, Allen's character then asks her, "Want to see a movie tonight?" She replies, "I'm planning to kill myself." He responds, "How about tomorrow night?"

8. For example, Bruce Chilton, *Rabbi Jesus* (New York: Doubleday, 2000), pp. 63, 71–72. Moreover, if we were to see the parable as autobiographical, one could with equally good reason see the older, dutiful son as reflecting Jesus's experience—that he had a younger brother who behaved like the prodigal, returned, and was welcomed by his father, with Jesus remaining outside until he was changed by the father's question. But I don't think it's fruitful to press either possibility.

9. The passage is slightly different in the two gospels. The translation closely follows Matthew, with two changes. Masculine pronouns for God are changed into inclusive language; and the word "righteousness" is replaced with "justice." The reason for the latter change is that "righteousness" in the Bible most often means "justice," and not what "righteousness" means in the modern world, where it is often equated with scrupulous personal behavior.

10. Cf. Luke 6:35: "God is kind to the ungrateful and the wicked." Other relevant texts include Matt. 10:29–31; Luke 12:6–7.

11. Matthew uses the word "perfect" rather than "compassionate": "Be perfect, therefore, as your heavenly Father is perfect." About the difference, a few comments. Luke's version is commonly thought to be earlier than Matthew's. "Perfect" is a word with several meanings, in both Greek and English. It can mean never making a mistake, being completely free from sin, or being without flaw. The Greek word can also mean "brought to its end" or "completed," as in the English word "teleology." Matthew probably means "perfect" in this sense, as "fully devel-

oped" or "matured." See W. D. Davies and Dale Allison, *The Gospel According to St. Matthew,* vol. 1 (Edinburgh: Clark, 1988), pp. 560–64.

12. The King James Version, Revised Standard Version, and New Revised Standard Version all use "merciful." The New English Bible, Jerusalem Bible, and the Scholar's Version use "compassionate."

13. Here again the RSV and NRSV use the word "mercy" rather than "compassion." But given the association of "mercy" with a situation of wrongdoing, it does not apply here. Clearly "compassion" is meant.

14. Arland J. Hultgren, *The Parables of Jesus* (Grand Rapids, MI: Eerdmans, 2000), pp. 23–24. For an example of "ten thousand" as the largest number used in calculation, see Rev. 9.16, where a gigantic army is described as consisting of "twice times ten thousand times ten thousand."

15. I owe this possible way of hearing the parable to William Herzog II, *Parables as Subversive Speech* (Louisville: Westminster John Knox, 1994), pp. 79–97, and his *Prophet and Teacher,* pp. 146–51.

16. For this whole section on the semantic associations between "compassion" and "womb" in the Jewish Bible, see especially Phyllis Trible, *God and the Rhetoric of Sexuality* (Philadelphia: Fortress, 1978), chaps. 2–3.

17. E.g., Exod. 34.6; 2 Chron. 30.9: Neh. 9.17, 31; Ps. 103.8; Joel 2.13.

18. E.g., Pss. 25.6; 40.11; 51.1; 69.16; 77.9; 79.8; 103.4; 119.77; 145.9.

19. Translation from Trible, *God and the Rhetoric of Sexuality,* pp. 45, 50. For her exegesis, see pp. 40–50.

20. Passages from *Sibylline Oracles* 2, cited by John Dominic Crossan in Robert Miller, ed., *The Apocalyptic Jesus: A Debate* (Santa Rosa, CA: Polebridge, 2001), pp. 58–59.

21. See Davies and Allison, *The Gospel According to St. Matthew,* vol. 1, pp. 442–45.

CHAPTER EIGHT

1. See W. T. Stace, *Religion and the Modern Mind* (Philadelphia: Lippincott, 1952), p. 252.

2. William James, *The Varieties of Religious Experience* (New York: Macmillan, 1961), p. 393.

3. Until about three decades ago, scholars routinely used the term "Zealots" as the name of a Jewish group in the time of Jesus that advocated armed resistance to Rome. But, as is now commonly recognized, a careful reading of Josephus indicates that he does not use the term until his narration of the first year of the great Jewish revolt against Rome in 66 CE. He implies that the term first came into use then. So there probably was no group known as "Zealots" earlier in the century. But there were advocates of armed resistance going back to the time of Herod the Great and continuing through the first century.

4. For the reasons for seeing these stories as also reflecting historical memory, see John Meier, *A Marginal Jew,* vol. 2, pp. 686–94.

5. The story and its aftermath fill the whole of John's complex ninth chapter. In addition to the theme of blindness/darkness and sight/light, it also reflects a late first-century context in which Jews who had become follower of Jesus began to be ostracized by other Jews.

6. Norman Perrin, *Rediscovering the Teaching of Jesus* (New York: Harper & Row, 1967), p. 144. Perrin was one of the most important Jesus scholars of his generation. His claim that this is the *most* radical saying of Jesus perhaps overstates the case, but not by much.

7. The phrases are from Sam Keen, *The Passionate Life* (San Francisco: Harper & Row, 1983), chapters 6–7, an illuminating study of the stages of life shaped by Christian and cross-cultural religious perspectives.

8. For a systematic contrast between contemporary American and ancient Mediterranean understandings of the family, see Bruce Malina, *The New Testament World: Insights from Cultural Anthropology,* rev. ed. (Louisville: Westminster John Knox, 1993), pp. 117–48.

9. Bruce Malina and Richard Rohrbaugh, *Social-Science Commentary on the Synoptic Gospels* (Minneapolis: Fortress, 1992), p. 201.

10. Because the context in Matthew refers to teacher-student relationships, "father" in this verse has often been understood as an honorific term for a teacher rather than referring to the patriarchal head of family. The verse is preceded by "You are not to be called rabbi, for you have one teacher, and you are all students" and followed by "Nor are you to be called instructors, for you have one instructor, the Messiah." For the argument that "father" does refer to the head of a patriarchal family, see especially Elisabeth Schüssler Fiorenza, *In Memory of Her* (New York: Crossroad, 1985), pp. 149–50.

11. See especially Rodney Stark, *The Rise of Christianity* (San Francisco: HarperSanFrancisco, 1997), pp. 95–128. In a few of the later documents of the New Testament, this freedom is compromised, even negated, by the reintroduction of patriarchal authority. See especially 1 Timothy 2.8–14, a letter attributed to Paul but almost certainly written near the beginning of the second century by an early Christian for whom the real Paul (and Jesus) were too radical. Nevertheless, early Christianity for the first few centuries gave a role and freedom to women remarkably different from the conventions of Mediterranean society.

12. That the author of Proverbs meant a simple equation between righteousness and prosperity is not clear, but some have understood the sayings that way, both in the past and in the present. What is sometimes called "prosperity" Christianity does so.

13. Mark 1.16–20; 2.13–14; 6.8–9; Luke 9.57–58; Matt. 8.19–20.

14. The way of "holy poverty," known in many traditions including the Christian tradition (the preeminent postbiblical example is St. Francis, who embraced "lady poverty"), abolishes one of the fundamental distinctions culture imposes upon the world, the distinction between "mine" and "not mine." About what is mine I will be anxious, seeking to preserve it and perhaps add to it; I then easily become

centered in what is "mine." "Holy poverty" not only abolishes this distinction, but makes one radically dependent upon God.

15. Luke 8.1–3. Wealthy "sympathizers" would also include Joseph of Arimathea (Mark 15:43).

16. Malina, *The New Testament World*, p. 31; on honor, see especially pp. 28–62. Malina speaks of two kinds of honor: *ascribed honor*, based on birth, inherited wealth, or position; and *acquired honor*, flowing from the socially recognized claim to worth that a person acquires by excelling over others in social interaction (pp. 33–34).

17. Malina, *The New Testament World*, pp. 154, 157; on purity, see especially pp. 149–81. His treatment of purity exposits its cross-cultural meanings and then applies it to the world of Jesus.

18. For purity practices in Judaism at the time of Jesus, see E. P. Sanders, *Judaism: Practice and Belief, 63 BCE–66 CE* (Philadelphia: Trinity Press International, 1992), pp. 214–30; *Jewish Law from Jesus to the Mishnah* (Philadelphia: Trinity Press International, 1990), pp. 29–42, 131–236. I admire Sanders's work; impressively detailed and extraordinarily learned, it is of great value. Yet in my judgment and the judgment of a number of scholars, he minimizes the purity conflicts in the gospels as evidence of its importance in the mission and message of Jesus. See also Thomas Kazen, *Jesus and Purity Halakah: Was Jesus Indifferent to Purity?* (Stockholm: Almqvist and Wiksell, 2002).

19. In the book of Leviticus, prohibition against mixing seeds and cloth, 19.19; purification after intercourse and menstruation, 15.16–24. The great exception for most conservative Christians today is the prohibition of homosexual behavior in 18.22.

20. The author of Mark, writing some forty years after the time of Jesus, adds an editorial comment in 7.19: "Thus he declared all foods clean." That this is what Jesus meant is exceedingly unlikely. We know that the question whether followers of Jesus were to observe Jewish food laws was not resolved for a number of decades after Easter. It is thus impossible to imagine that Jesus had declared them to be no longer obligatory. But this recognition means only that Mark's editorial comment is later, not that Mark 7.14–15 is a post-Easter creation of Jesus's followers.

21. Matthew's version of what is probably (but not certainly) the same saying compares the Pharisees to "whitewashed tombs, which on the outside look beautiful, but inside they are full of the bones of the dead and of all kinds of filth" (23.27). For Matthew, the contrast is "outside" versus "inside," not that (as in Luke) the Pharisees are a source of defilement.

22. Tax collectors were among the unclean. The precise meaning of the term "sinners" is unclear, and its meaning depended upon the group using it. But it almost certainly refers to more people than the notoriously wicked, and minimally to those chronically nonobservant of purity rules. For a balanced treatment, see James D. G. Dunn, *Jesus Remembered*, pp. 526–32.

23. See Roberta Bondi's memory of how she understood repentance as a child in *Memories of God* (Nashville: Abingdon, 1993), pp. 153–54: If you had asked "me about what it took to get our sins forgiven, I would have told you: 'We have to repent of our sins.' If you had pushed me a little further to ask, 'And what does it mean to repent?' I would have said, 'To feel really, really bad about what a sinful person you are.'"

24. To amplify with a story that illustrates a nonexclusive way of interpreting John 14.6, about fifty years ago a Hindu professor preached on this text in a Christian seminary. After reading the text aloud, he announced that this text was absolutely true—Jesus is the only way. And, he continued, this way is known in all the world's enduring religions. His point is that Jesus was not the unique revelation of a way unknown anywhere else; rather, Jesus was that way become flesh, embodied, incarnate, in a life.

CHAPTER NINE

1. Other recent authors who emphasize the political as well as religious meaning of the Bible and early Christianity include Walter Wink, John Dominic Crossan, Walter Brueggemann, Jim Wallis, William Herzog, and Jack Nelson-Pallmeyer.

2. For a fuller account of Jewish responses, see John Dominic Crossan and Jonathan Reed, *Excavating Jesus,* rev. ed. (San Francisco: HarperSanFrancisco, 2001), pp. 177–223.

3. Josephus *Jewish War* 2.169–74; *Jewish Antiquities* 18.55–59. See Crossan and Reed, *Excavating Jesus,* pp. 184–85.

4. Josephus *Jewish War* 2.185–203; *Jewish Antiquities* 18.261–309; Philo *Embassy to Gaius* 203–348; see Crossan and Reed, *Excavating Jesus,* pp. 185–86.

5. Crossan and Reed, *Excavating Jesus,* pp. 186–87. They also correctly emphasize that these episodes mean that seeing active nonviolent resistance as a first-century option is not simply an anachronistic retrojection of the methods of Gandhi and Martin Luther King Jr.

6. For a book-length treatment of the week as reported by Mark, see John Dominic Crossan and Marcus Borg, *The Last Week* (San Francisco: HarperSanFrancisco, 2006).

7. With some variations, the story is also found in John 2.13–22. However, for thematic reasons, John places the episode at the beginning of Jesus's public activity, preceded only by the story of Jesus changing water into wine at the wedding in Cana.

8. This process happened in stages. The emperor Constantine legalized Christianity in 313 CE and sought to make it the unifying religion of the Roman Empire. By the end of the 300s, Christianity had become the official religion of the empire.

9. Properly speaking, separation of church and state is not the same thing as separation of religion and politics. The former means that government (the state) is not to support one religion over another, or even religion in general, or interfere with

the practice of religion. It is about freedom of religion from state interference or support. Often, however, Christians misunderstand this to mean separation of religion and politics, a very unbiblical notion.

10. See also Lev. 25.23: "The land is mine; with me you are but aliens and tenants."

11. See Chapter 4; for a fuller exposition, see my *Reading the Bible Again for the First Time* (San Francisco: HarperSanFrancisco, 2001), chap. 6.

12. Mark 6.15, 8.28; Luke 7.16.

13. Later in Mark 13, another saying refers to a coming sacrilege in the temple: "But when you see the desolating sacrilege set up where it ought not to be (let the reader understand), then those in Judea must flee to the mountains" (13.14). The "desolating sacrilege" echoes language used in Daniel to refer to a statue of Zeus erected in the temple by the Hellenistic ruler Antiochus Epiphanes in the second century BCE. It is uncertain whether Mark 13.14 goes back to Jesus; it could be a later creation that refers to Caligula's plan to erect a statue in the temple around 40 CE or to the Roman conquest and destruction of Jerusalem and the temple in 70 CE.

14. Luke 21.20–24 reports one more warning of Jerusalem's future, a passage that is seen as most likely reflecting after-the-fact knowledge of the events of 70 CE: "When you see Jerusalem surrounded by armies, then know that its desolation has come near. Then those in Judea must flee to the mountains, and those inside the city must leave it, and those out in the country must not enter it; for these are days of vengeance, as a fulfillment of all that is written. Woe to those who are pregnant and to those who are nursing infants in those days! For there will be great distress on the earth and wrath against this people; for they will fall by the edge of the sword and be taken away as captives among all nations; and Jerusalem will be trampled on by the Gentiles, until the times of the Gentiles are fulfilled."

15. I emphasize that the indictments were not against Judaism or the Jewish people not only for historical reasons, but also because these "judgment against Jerusalem" passages have often been a basis for Christian anti-Jewish attitudes over the centuries. See James Carroll, *Constantine's Sword*.

16. For a similar reading of this parable, see the extended exposition in Herzog, *Parables as Subversive Speech*, pp. 150–68.

17. Walter Wink, *Engaging the Powers* (Minneapolis: Fortress, 1992), pp. 175–93; *The Powers That Be* (New York: Doubleday, 1999), chap. 5; *Jesus and Non-Violence* (Minneapolis: Fortress, 2003), pp. 9–37. See also Crossan and Reed, *Excavating Jesus*, pp. 216–20.

18. Exod. 21.24; Lev. 24.20; Deut. 19.21.

19. For the linguistic argument, see Wink, *Jesus and Non-Violence*, pp. 9–14; *Engaging the Powers*, pp. 184–89.

20. John Reumann, *Jesus in the Church's Gospels* (Philadelphia: Fortress, 1968), p. 142.

21. The word is relatively recent, coined by the Lutheran theologian Abraham Calov in 1677. Within its meaning, he included death, judgment, heaven, and hell. See

Gerhard Sauter, "The Concept and Task of Eschatology: Theological and Philosophical Reflections," *Scottish Journal of Theology* 41 (1988): 499. According to *The Oxford English Dictionary*, the noun "eschatology" was first used in English in 1844 and the adjective "eschatological" in 1854.

22. The one apparent exception is 2 Pet. 3.10, which seems to speak of the destruction of the world of space and time, matter and energy: "Then the heavens [the sky] will pass away with a loud noise, and the elements will be dissolved with fire, and the earth and everything that is done on it will be burned up" (a variant reading has "will be disclosed"). Otherwise, the eschatological vision is of a transformed earth. Even the book of Revelation, the most intensely eschatological book in the Christian Bible, speaks of a *new* earth, not the end of the earth. See Rev. 21.1.

23. There is no agreed-upon designation for this kind of eschatology in the discipline. Thus what I call "imminent eschatology" is also sometimes called "apocalyptic eschatology," and I have sometimes used this phrase myself. But I am no longer satisfied with it, for the words "apocalypse" and "apocalyptic" mean simply a "revelation," an "unveiling," a "disclosure" of the final state of affairs; and one might have a revelation about the final state of affairs that is not imminent. Twenty years ago, I also used "eschatological Jesus" as shorthand for Jesus understood within the framework of imminent eschatology. I now think "imminent eschatology" is the most precise (and therefore least confusing) term.

24. Johannes Weiss, *Jesus' Proclamation of the Kingdom of God,* ed. and trans. R. H. Hiers and D. L. Holland (Philadelphia: Fortress Press, 1971; first edition published in German in 1892, second edition in 1900). Albert Schweitzer, *The Mystery of the Kingdom of God* (New York: Schocken, 1964; originally published in German in 1901); *The Quest of the Historical Jesus* (New York: Macmillan, 1968; originally published in German in 1906). Schweitzer's revised and expanded edition was published in German in 1913, and has only recently appeared in English as the "first complete edition," ed. by John Bowden (Minneapolis: Fortress, 2001).

25. The best known was the British scholar C. H. Dodd, who argued for "realized" eschatology, by which he meant that Jesus taught that the kingdom had *already* come. He first made the case in 1935 in *The Parables of the Kingdom*. See also his final book, *The Founder of Christianity* (New York: Macmillan, 1970).

26. Among the best-known contemporary scholars who argue for imminent eschatology are E. P. Sanders, *Jesus and Judaism* (Philadelphia: Fortress, 1985) and *The Historical Figure of Jesus* (New York: Penguin, 1993); John Meier, *A Marginal Jew*; Paula Fredriksen, *Jesus of Nazareth, King of the Jews* (New York: Knopf, 1999); Bart Ehrman, *Jesus: Apocalyptic Prophet of the New Millennium* (New York: Oxford University Press, 2001); and Dale Allison, *Jesus of Nazareth: Millenarian Prophet* (Minneapolis: Fortress, 1998).

27. 1 Thess. 4.13–18; 1 Cor. 15.51–52; Rom. 13.11–12.

28. The title of chap. 3 in Jonathan Kirsch's new book, *A History of the End of the World* (San Francisco: HarperSanFrancisco, 2006).

29. For example, Albert Schweitzer made a sharp distinction between the historical Jesus and the living (or spiritual) Christ. The former's mistaken eschatological convictions make him "a stranger to our time" and theologically irrelevant; only the Christ who still speaks to us is relevant for theology (*Quest*, p. 401). Indeed, the latter called him to Africa. His *Quest for the Historical Jesus* ends with what have been called the most famous words of twentieth-century theology: "He comes to us as One unknown, without a name, as of old, by the lakeside, He came to those men who knew Him not. He speaks to us the same word: 'Follow thou me' and sets us to the tasks which He has to fulfill for our time. He commands. And to those who obey Him, whether they be wise or simple, He will reveal Himself in the toils, the conflicts, the sufferings which they shall pass through in His fellowship, and as an ineffable mystery, they shall learn in their own experience Who He is" (*Quest*, p. 403). The words have been set to music as a Christian anthem by Jane Marshall, "He Comes to Us."

30. This was a major theme of my 1972 doctoral thesis at Oxford, published in significantly revised form in 1984 as *Conflict, Holiness and Politics in the Teachings of Jesus* (New York: Mellen), revised edition published in 1998 (Harrisburg, PA: Trinity Press International). I also treated this in an article in 1986, republished as chap. 4 in my *Jesus in Contemporary Scholarship* (Valley Forge, PA: Trinity Press International, 1994). See also chap. 5 in that book.

31. These include a strong majority within the Jesus Seminar. Well-published scholars holding this position include John Dominic Crossan, Stephen Patterson, and Walter Wink. In his own way, so does N. T. Wright, who accepts sayings about the imminent coming of the Son of Man as going back to Jesus, but understands them metaphorically as referring to the destruction of Jerusalem in the year 70. For a book-length debate between Dale Allison, one of the most persuasive advocates of imminent eschatology, and Crossan, Patterson, and me, see Robert J. Miller, ed., *The Apocalyptic Jesus: A Debate* (Santa Rosa, CA: Polebridge, 2001).

32. Translation of *Thomas* sayings from Stevan Davies, *The Gospel of Thomas* (Woodstock, VT: Skylight Paths, 2002).

33. For further development of this point, see my comments in Miller, ed., *The Apocalyptic Jesus*, pp. 43–48.

34. John Dominic Crossan argues that this cluster of material is foundational for glimpsing the historical Jesus, as it has multiple independent attestation in the earliest layers of the tradition. See *The Historical Jesus*, pp. 332–48.

CHAPTER TEN

1. Because I am writing this book during the same period of time that I wrote *The Last Week* (San Francisco: HarperSanFrancisco, 2006) with John Dominic Crossan, I occasionally use material from chapters 6 and 8 of that book in this chapter.

2. Discovered a few decades ago, the *Gospel of Judas* was made public early in 2006. Most likely written in the second half of the second century, the gospel expresses

a form of early Christianity commonly (but perhaps unfairly) known as Gnosticism. It views the created world (and thus the body) as something to be escaped. As Jesus orders Judas to "betray" him, he says: "You will exceed all of them. For you will sacrifice the man that clothes me."

3. Moreover, in John, the meal does not include what Christians often call "the words of institution" of the Lord's Supper or Eucharist. These are found only in the synoptic gospels and Paul. Rather, in John "the last supper" is the occasion for Jesus to wash his disciples' feet and to deliver his "farewell discourse" (John 13–17).

4. Mark 14.22–25; Matt. 26.26–29; Luke 22.17–20; and in Paul, 1 Cor. 11.23–26.

5. John 18.3 reports a "cohort" (imprecisely translated "detachment" in the NRSV) of imperial soldiers—six hundred men! Oddly, after Jesus says to them, "I am he," they fall to the ground (18.6). In awe? In worship? Then they get up and arrest him. It is impossible to visualize this as a historical scene, though it works as symbolism. Jesus has just uttered the most sacred name of God, "I am he," and so they prostrate themselves. Even the forces of empire recognize the sacred in Jesus—and then arrest and kill him anyway.

6. It is interesting to note that John does not report a trial or hearing before the council on the night or morning preceding Jesus's execution. John does mention that Jesus was brought before Annas and Caiaphas; the latter was the high priest, and the former his father-in-law (18.13, 24). But no council or meeting is convened. Instead, John reports a meeting of the council some time *before* Passover Week at which they decided to put Jesus to death (11.45–53).

7. Only John reports an extended dialogue between Pilate and Jesus, and it is full of delicious irony (18.28–19.16). Pilate is like an errand boy, shuttling back and forth between Jesus and the temple authorities. Pilate asks "What is truth?" The irony is that within John's theology, Jesus is "the truth" (14.6). The truth is standing right in front of Pilate, and he doesn't recognize it. In the climactic scene, Pilate has Jesus sit on the judge's seat (19.13, variant reading); as Pilate passes judgment on Jesus, Pilate himself is being judged.

8. Moreover, to imagine that darkness really covered the land for three hours leads to a very negative perception of the inhabitants of Jerusalem and the temple authorities. How could they be so obdurate as to miss the significance of what was happening? Why were they not terrified and led to rethink what was happening?

9. Luke 23.34, 43, 46; John 19.26–27, 28, 30.

10. Roberta Bondi, *Memories of God,* (Nashville: Abingdon, 1993), p. 153–54.

11. Mark Dever, "Nothing but the Blood," *Christianity Today* (May 2006): 29.

12. Dever, "Nothing but the Blood," p. 33.

13. For fuller but still concise expositions, see my *The Meaning of Jesus: Two Visions,* with N. T. Wright (San Francisco: HarperSanFrancisco, 1999), pp. 137–42; and *The Heart of Christianity* (San Francisco: HarperSanFrancisco, 2003), pp. 91–96.

14. Dallas Willard, *The Divine Conspiracy* (San Francisco: HarperSanFrancisco, 1997), p. 403, n. 8. The phrase "vampire Christians" was also included in his Web site when I visited it in August 2006.

15. Dietrich Bonhoeffer, *The Cost of Discipleship* (New York: Macmillan, 1963), p. 7 (first published in Germany in 1937). Bonhoeffer was executed by the Third Reich in April 1945, a month before the war ended. He was only thirty-nine.

16. For vigorous defenses of the historical factuality of the stories by conservative-evangelical scholars, see Lee Strobel, *The Case for Christ* (Grand Rapids, MI: Zondervan, 1988); *Jesus Under Fire*, ed. by Michael Wilkins and J. P. Moreland (Grand Rapids, MI: Zondervan, 1995); and Paul Copan, *Will the Real Jesus Please Stand Up?* (Grand Rapids, MI: Baker, 1998). For a more elaborate and sophisticated defense, see the massive volume by N. T. Wright, *The Resurrection of the Son of God* (Minneapolis: Fortress, 2003).

17. Mainstream scholars do not think that all of the thirteen letters attributed to Paul were written by him. A near consensus sees three of them (1 and 2 Timothy and Titus, commonly called the "pastoral letters") as written a generation or two after Paul. Scholars are divided about three more: Ephesians, Colossians, and 2 Thessalonians. There is virtual unanimity that seven definitely go back to Paul: Romans, 1 and 2 Corinthians, Galatians, 1 Thessalonians, Philippians, and Philemon. All or most of these seven were written in the 50s. 1 Thessalonians (commonly seen as the earliest) may have been written in the late 40s, and Philippians could have been written as late as the early 60s.

18. For Paul, the "apostles" are a larger group than the twelve, and include women. See Rom. 16.7, where a woman named Junia is said to be "prominent among the apostles."

19. There is some overlap between Paul's list and those in the gospel stories, but the correlation is not precise. Paul does not mention the women at the tomb. The gospels do not mention appearances to James the brother of Jesus or to five hundred people at one time (though some have wondered if this could be the Pentecost experience narrated in Acts 2).

20. According to the same letter, he received his gospel "through a revelation of Jesus Christ" (1.12). Second Cor. 12.2–4 may describe another such experience. See Alan Segal, *Paul the Convert: The Apostolate and Apostasy of Saul the Pharisee* (New Haven: Yale University Press, 1990), chap. 2.

21. For a fuller treatment of Paul as a Christ mystic, see my *Reading the Bible Again for the First Time* (San Francisco: HarperSanFrancisco, 2001), pp. 234–53. See also Gustaf Adolf Deissman, *Paul: A Study in Social and Religious History,* trans. by William E. Wilson (New York: Harper and Row, 1957), and Segal, Alan, *Paul the Convert.*

22. In Acts 9; 22; 26. The details differ somewhat in each account.

23. For Paul's concise description of his life before his conversion, see Phil. 3.4–6.

24. In a classic contemporary example, thinking that the truth of the Genesis stories of creation depends upon their factuality has led to disputes about "creation versus evolution," "intelligent design versus random evolution," and so forth. These disputes would not have occurred without the modern conviction that truth equals factuality. For many defenders of "the truth of Genesis," the truth of

these stories is dependent upon their factuality, with evolution as a competing factuality. A parabolic reading of these stories would eliminate this conflict and place the issue where it really belongs: to whom does the earth belong? Is the earth the creation of God and the gift of God, wondrous and calling forth awe, plenteous and calling forth gratitude and adoration, and intended for the whole of creation? Or is it ours, to divide up and do with as we please?

25. Mark 16.9–20, printed in most Bibles at the end of Mark and usually identified as a later "longer" ending. Some scholars argue that Mark's gospel likely did not end with v. 8, perhaps because Mark did not have a chance to finish it or perhaps because the ending got separated from the rest of the manuscript. But most scholars affirm that 16.8 is the original ending.

26. Matthew 28.9–10, 16–20; Luke 24.13–35, 36–49; John 20.11–18, 19–23, 24–29; 21.1–23. All of them are treated in the final chapter of Borg and Crossan, *The Last Week.*

27. John Dominic Crossan, *Jesus: A Revolutionary Biography* (San Francisco: HarperSanFrancisco, 1994), p. 197. Crossan sums this up in two three-word sentences: "Emmaus never happened. Emmaus always happens." I agree, but I have dropped the first part in order to avoid the distraction of arguing about whether it happened or not.

28. For the historical argument that God's triumph over the powers was the central meaning of Good Friday and Easter for the first millennium of Christianity, see Gustaf Aulen, *Christus Victor* (New York: Macmillan, 1969; originally published in 1931).

29. For a fuller treatment of the path of personal transformation, see my *The Heart of Christianity,* chap. 6, pp. 103–25.

EPILOGUE

1. E. H. Carr, *What Is History?* (New York: Vintage, 1961).

2. Some evangelical authors who are not part of the Christian right are cited in note 6 below. I also note that most African American evangelicals and Pentecostals are not part of the Christian right. Though many may be theologically conservative, most are not politically conservative.

3. Is abortion a serious moral issue? Yes. And we should do all that we can to reduce the number of abortions. To be pro-life should not be about outlawing abortion, but about making it rare. We can learn from other countries where abortion is legal and yet their abortion rate is far lower than ours.

4. I note some exceptions. In 2003, the Evangelical Environmental Network sponsored a national campaign called "What Would Jesus Drive?" to raise consciousness about fuel-efficient cars. In 2006 a group of eighty-six evangelical leaders issued the "Evangelical Climate Initiative" that warned about global warming and called for legislation to address the crisis. However, other evangelical leaders pressured the National Association of Evangelicals not to endorse the document. See Randall Balmer, *Thy Kingdom Come, An Evangelical's Lament* (New York:

Basic Books, 2006), pp. 160–63. His chapter 5 (pp. 143–65) treats the divisions among evangelicals about the environment.

5. For a readable and fascinating account of how the political right manipulates the Christian right to support economic and tax policies that are against its best interest, see Thomas Frank, *What's the Matter with Kansas?* (New York: Henry Holt, 2005). For the growing gap between the wealthy and the rest of us, see Kevin Phillips, *Wealth and Democracy: A Political History of the American Rich* (New York: Random House, 2002).

6. In particular, see Randall Balmer, *Thy Kingdom Come;* Jim Wallis, *God's Politics* (San Francisco: HarperSanFrancisco, 2005); Jimmy Carter, *Our Endangered Values: America's Moral Crisis* (New York: Simon and Schuster, 2005). See also Mark Noll, *The Scandal of the Evangelical Mind* (Grand Rapids: Eerdmans, 1995), for his critique of anti-intellectualism within evangelicalism, and Ronald J. Sider, *The Scandal of the Evangelical Conscience* (Grand Rapids: Baker, 2004). More generally, see the books of Brian McLaren, especially *A Generous Orthodoxy* (Grand Rapids: Zondervan, 2005).

7. See especially the important new book by Diana Butler Bass, *Christianity for the Rest of Us* (San Francisco: HarperSanFrancisco, 2006), based on her "on the ground" intensive study of a large number of thriving mainline congregations. Her earlier book on this subject is also important, *The Practicing Congregation: Imagining a New Old Church* (Herndon, VA: Alban Institute, 2004). See also *The Emerging Christian Way,* ed. by Michael Schwartzentruber (Kelowna, BC, Canada: Copperhouse, 2006).

8. Luke Timothy Johnson, *The Real Jesus: The Misguided Quest for the Historical Jesus and the Truth of the Traditional Gospels* (San Francisco: HarperSanFrancisco, 1995).

9. Kenneth Burke, *The Philosophy of Literary Form,* 3d ed. (Berkeley: University of California Press, 1973; originally published in 1941), pp. 110–11. For the full quotation, see my *The Heart of Christianity* (San Francisco: HarperSanFrancisco, 2003), pp. 19–20. I thank my graduate student Josh Beach for introducing me to Burke.

10. Jaroslav Pelikan, *Jesus Through the Centuries* (New Haven: Yale University Press, 1985).

Author Index

Allen, Woody, 169
Allison, Dale, 325nn.11, 21, 330n.26
Anselm, Archbishop of Canterbury, 268
Asclepia of Mendes, 316n.9
Aulen, Gustaf, 334n.28

Balmer, Randall, 334n.4, 335n.6
Bartchy, S. Scott, 323nn.22, 23
Barth, Karl, 305–6, 321n.29
Bass, Diana Butler, 335n.7
Bondi, Roberta, 267, 328n.23, 332n.10
Bonhoeffer, Dietrich, 270, 333n.15
Borg, Marcus, 328n.6, 334n.26
Bornkamm, Günther, 315n.12
Bowden, John, 330n.24
Brown, Raymond, 315n.4
Brueggemann, Walter, 317n.4, 328n.1
Büchler, A., 318n.8
Bultmann, Rudolf, 319n.16
Burke, Kenneth, 310, 335n.9

Caird, George B., 323n.20
Calov, Abraham, 329n.21
Capon, Robert, 9–10, 313n.4
Carr, E. H., 334n.1
Carroll, James, 322n.1, 329n.n15
Carter, Jimmy, 335n.6
Chilton, Bruce, 324n.8
Collins, John J., 320n.24
Copan, Paul, 333n.16
Crossan, John Dominic, 316nn.8, 10,
    11, 12, 317n.3, 323n.21, 325n.20,
    328nn.1, 2, 3, 329n.17, 331nn.34,
    334nn.26, 27

Davies, Stevan, 314n.4, 331n.32
Davies, W. D., 325nn.11, 21
Deissman, Gustaf Adolf, 316n.10, 333n.21
Dever, Mark, 332nn.11, 12

Dio Cassius, 316n.9
Dodd, C. H., 153, 323n.16, 330n.25
Douglas, Mary, 159, 322n.11
Dungan, D. L., 314n.5
Dunn, James D. G., 321nn.25, 27,
    322n.12, 323n.24, 327n.22, 331n.31

Ehrman, Bart, 330n.26

Farmer, W. R., 314n.5
Filson, F. V., 320n.18
Fiorenza, Elisabeth Schüssler, 326n.10
Fox, Richard, 313n.2
Frank, Thomas, 335n.5
Fredriksen, Paula, 330n.26
Frost, Robert, 191

Galileo, 15, 21, 314n.12

Harris, Sam, 313n.7
Hartley, L. P., 317n.1
Hauerwas, Stanley, 318n.3
Herzog, William R., II, 317n.3, 325n.15,
    328n.1, 329n.16
Heschel, Abraham, 113, 318n.4
Hiers, R. H., 330n.24
Holland, D. L., 330n.24
Hopkins, Keith, 316n.8
Horsley, Richard, 316n.10, 317n.7
Hultgren, Arland J., 322n.13, 325n.14

James, William, 112, 113, 115, 132, 192,
    318n.4, 319n.12, 321nn.31, 32, 325n.2
Jefferson, Thomas, 13, 313n.8
Jenkins, Jerry, 313n.1, 313n.6
Jeremias, J., 319nn.15, 16, 320n.25
Johnson, Luke Timothy, 304, 335n.8
Josephus, 30, 31, 90, 117, 228, 275,
    314n.3, 325n.3, 328nn.3, 4

Kazen, Thomas, 327n.18
Keen, Sam, 326n.7
Kierkegaard, Søren, 60
Kirsch, Jonathan, 330n.28

LaHaye, Tim, 313n.1, 313n.6
Lao Tzu, 166, 167, 191
Lenski, Gerhard, 317n.3
Lenski, Jean, 317n.3
Levertov, Denise, 60, 315n.3
Lewis, C. S., 18–19, 313n.10
Lewis, I. M., 322nn.8, 10
Lindsey, Hal, 11

McGinn, Bernard, 321n.30
McLaren, Brian, 335n.6
Malina, Bruce J., 323n.22, 326nn.8, 9,
    327nn.16, 17
Mann, Michael, 317n.3
Marshall, Jane, 331n.29
Maslow, Abraham, 113, 318n.4
Meier, John, 27, 42, 314n.1, 322n.3,
    325n.4, 330n.26
Miller, Robert J., 316nn.4, 7, 9, 325n.20,
    331nn.31, 33
Moreland, J. P., 333n.16

Nelson-Pallmeyer, Jack, 328n.1
Niebuhr, H. Richard, 324n.4
Niebuhr, Reinhold, 321n.29
Nolan, Albert, 49, 315n.14
Noll, Mark, 335n.6

Otto, Rudolf, 113, 318n.4, 320nn.18, 19

Patterson, Stephen, 314n.4, 331n.31
Peck, M. Scott, 322n.9
Pelikan, Jaroslav, 335n.10
Percy, Walker, 3
Perrin, Norman, 326n.6
Phillips, Kevin, 335n.5
Plath, Sylvia, 132
Powell, Mark Allan, 315n.9
Prothero, Stephen, 313n.2

Raine, Andy, 315n.10
Reed, Jonathan, 316nn.8, 10, 11, 317n.3,
    328nn.2, 3, 5, 6, 329n.17

Reumann, John, 329n.20
Rice, Anne, 318n.9
Richardson, Peter, 317n.5
Rohrbaugh, Richard, 326n.9
Rossing, Barbara, 313n.5

Sagan, Carl, 324n.5
Sanders, E. P., 317n.8, 327n.18, 330n.26
Sauter, Gerhard, 330n.21
Scholem, Gershom, 320n.24
Schwartzentruber, Michael, 335n.7
Schweitzer, Albert, 330n.24, 331n.29
Segal, Alan, 333n.21
Sheldon, Charles, 305
Sider, Ronald J., 335n.6
Simon, Richard, 24
Skinner, John T., 315n.10
Smith, Huston, 113, 309, 318n.4
Smith, Wilfred Cantwell, 313n.11
Sobel, Dava, 314n.12
Soelle, Dorothee, 319n.12, 321n.33
Spinoza, Baruch, 24
Stace, W. T., 325n.1
Stark, Rodney, 326n.11
Stegemann, Wolfgang, 323n.22
Strobel, Lee, 333n.16
Suetonius, 316n.9

Theissen, Gerd, 323n.22
Thoreau, Henry David, 191
Throckmorton, Burton H., Jr., 314

Urbach, E. E., 318n.8, 319n.14

Vermes, Geza, 318n.8, 321n.26, 322n.6

Wallis, Jim, 299, 328n.1, 335n.6
Weiss, Johannes, 330n.24
Willard, Dallas, 270, 332n.14
Willimon, William, 318n.3
Willkins, Michael, 333n.16
Wilson, William E., 333n.21
Wink, Walter, 247, 250, 317n.3, 328n.1,
    329nn.17, 19, 331n.31
Woolf, B. L., 320n.18
Wright, N. T., 331n.31, 332n.13, 333n.16

Scripture Index

OLD TESTAMENT
Genesis 3.24, **200**
Genesis 12.7–9; 15.1–17;
   17.1–2; 18.1–33;
   26.23–25; 32.22–31,
   318n.6
Genesis 28.17, **115**
Genesis 43.30, **183**
Genesis 45.5–8, **272**

Exodus 10.21–23, **265–66**
Exodus 20.2–3, **99**
Exodus 21.24, **329n.18**
Exodus 34.29–35, **116, 126**

Leviticus 15.16–24,
   327n.19
Leviticus 19.2, **159, 214**
Leviticus 19.19, **327**
Leviticus 24.20, **329n.18**
Leviticus 25.8–12, **202**
Leviticus 25.23, **100,
   329n.10**

Deuteronomy 6.4–9, **96**
Deuteronomy 6.13, **124**
Deuteronomy 6.16, **124**
Deuteronomy 8.3, **123**
Deuteronomy 19.21,
   329n.18
Deuteronomy 32.15, **218**
Deuteronomy 34.10–12, **116**

1 Samuel 8.4–22, **101**
1 Samuel 8.11–18, **102**
1 Samuel 9.1–10.16, **101**
1 Samuel 9.16, **101**
1 Samuel 10.1, **102**

1 Kings 3.26, **183**
1 Kings 17–19; 21, **318n.7**
1 Kings 19.5–8, **122**
1 Kings 19.12, **121**

2 Kings 1–2, **318n.7**
2 Kings 2.11, **116**

Job 42.5, **115, 133**

Psalms 18.2, **218**
Psalms 22, **266**
Psalms 24.1, **239**
Psalms 31.2, **218**
Psalms 46.10, **114**
Psalms 62.2, **219**
Psalms 110.1, **264**
Psalms 120–134, **106**
Psalms 122.1–2, 6, **106**
Psalms 126.1–2, **106**
Psalms 132.13–14, **106**

Proverbs 10.4, **208**
Proverbs 13.21, **208**
Proverbs 15.6, **208**
Proverbs 19.15b, **208**
Proverbs 22.4, **208**

Isaiah 2.2–4, **107**
Isaiah 5.1, **104**
Isaiah 5.1–7, **237**
Isaiah 5.7, **104**
Isaiah 6.1–3, **116**
Isaiah 7.11, **104**
Isaiah 9.2, **63**
Isaiah 20, **231**
Isaiah 35.5–6, **147, 162**
Isaiah 51.1, **219**

Isaiah 53.5, **8**
Isaiah 56.7, **234**
Isaiah 58.6; 61.1–2,
   321n.34
Isaiah 60.1–3, **63–64**
Isaiah 61.1, **116, 121, 147**
Isaiah 61.1–2; 58.6,
   135, 201

Jeremiah 7.4, **235**
Jeremiah 7.5–7, **235**
Jeremiah 7.11, **235**
Jeremiah 13, 27–28, **231**
Jeremiah 15.9, **266**
Jeremiah 31.20, **183**

Ezekiel 1.1, **116**
Ezekiel 4, **231**
Ezekiel 10, **242**
Ezekiel 11.5, **116**

Daniel 7.13–14, **264**

Joel 2.2, **266**

Amos 2.7, **103**
Amos 4.1, **103**
Amos 5.11, **103**
Amos 5.21–24, **104**
Amos 6.4–6, **103**
Amos 8.9, **266**

Micah 1.5, **104**
Micah 2.2, **104**
Micah 3.1–2, **104**
Micah 4.4, **252**

Zephaniah 1.15, **266**

Zechariah 9.9, **37–38**
Zechariah 9.9–10, **232**

Malachi 3.1, **119**

NEW TESTAMENT
Matthew 1.23, **285**
Matthew 2.10, **63**
Matthew 2.15, **66**
Matthew 3.7–9, **118**
Matthew 3.10,12, **119**
Matthew 3.13–17, **40**
Matthew 3.17, **121**
Matthew 4.1–11, **122**
Matthew 4.24–25, **150**
Matthew 5–7, **141**
Matthew 5.1–7.27, **157**
Matthew 5.3, **189**
Matthew 5.6, **189**
Matthew 5.8, **216**
Matthew 5.13, **156**
Matthew 5.15, **156**
Matthew 5.21–22, 27–28,
    31–32, 33–34, 38–39,
    43–44, **319n.16**
Matthew 5.38–41,
    43–45, **247**
Matthew 5.45, **175**
Matthew 5.48, **175**
Matthew 6.2, 16–18, **213**
Matthew 6.5–6, **213**
Matthew 6.9b–13, **35**
Matthew 6.11–12, **188**
Matthew 6.19–21, **210**
Matthew 6.22, **156**
Matthew 6.22–23, **195**
Matthew 6.24, **155,
    210, 218**
Matthew 6.25–33, **175**
Matthew 6.26, 28, **196**
Matthew 6.28, **155**
Matthew 6.33, **109,
    190, 260**
Matthew 7.2, **300**
Matthew 7.3, 5, **195**
Matthew 7.3, **53**

Matthew 7.7, **257**
Matthew 7.9–11, **174**
Matthew 7.13–14, **193**
Matthew 7:16, **319n.12**
Matthew 7.16–18, **156**
Matthew 7.24–27, **72, 194**
Matthew 8.2, **53**
Matthew 8.5–13, **147**
Matthew 8.11, **187**
Matthew 8.12; 13.42, **180**
Matthew 8.19–20,
    326n.13
Matthew 8.22, **156, 197**
Matthew 10.5–6, **146**
Matthew 10.8–11, **259**
Matthew 10.29–31,
    324n.10
Matthew 10.34–35, **207**
Matthew 10.37, **206**
Matthew 10.38, **221**
Matthew 11.3, **120**
Matthew 11.4–5, **147, 162**
Matthew 11.11, **120**
Matthew 11.18–19, **217**
Matthew 11.19, **160**
Matthew 12:27–28,
    320n.21
Matthew 12.28, **110, 126,
    148, 256**
Matthew 12.41–42,
    162, 180
Matthew 13.16–17, **162**
Matthew 13.33, **152, 257**
Matthew 13.44, **152, 256**
Matthew 13.45, **256**
Matthew 13.45–46, **152**
Matthew 14.13–21, **74**
Matthew 14.22–33, **39**
Matthew 14.27, **59**
Matthew 14.28–31, **59**
Matthew 14.33, **40**
Matthew 15.14, **156, 195**
Matthew 15.24, **146**
Matthew 16.2–3, **196, 300**
Matthew 16.13–16, **41**
Matthew 16.16, **42**
Matthew 17.1–8, **127**

Matthew 18.4; 23.12, **212**
Matthew 18.23–34, **177**
Matthew 19.23, **211**
Matthew 20.1–15, **181**
Matthew 20.2–16, **71**
Matthew 21.1–7, **37**
Matthew 21.5, **37**
Matthew 21.7, **38**
Matthew 21.28, **152**
Matthew 21.31, **257**
Matthew 23.4, **245**
Matthew 23.6, **212**
Matthew 23.9, **156, 207**
Matthew 23.13, **257**
Matthew 23.23, **245**
Matthew 23.24, **53, 156**
Matthew 23.25, **216**
Matthew 23.27, **217,
    327n.21**
Matthew 23.29–31, **204**
Matthew 23.37, **108**
Matthew 23.37–38, **242**
Matthew 24–25, **179**
Matthew 25.1–13, **179**
Matthew 25.14–30,
    179, 246
Matthew 25.26–27, **246**
Matthew 25.28–30, **247**
Matthew 25.31–46, **178,
    323n.18**
Matthew 26.11, **45**
Matthew 26.26–29,
    332n.4
Matthew 26.64, **263**
Matthew 27.25, **143**
Matthew 27.62–66;
    28.4, **282**
Matthew 28.2–3, **282**
Matthew 28.8, **282**
Matthew 28.9–10, 16–20,
    334n.26
Matthew 28.11–15, **282**
Matthew 28.16, **284**
Matthew 28.16–20, **284**
Matthew 28.17, **284**
Matthew 28.18–20, **284**
Matthew 28.19, **322n.2**

Mark 1.4, **118**
Mark 1.7–8, **119**
Mark 1.9–11, **40**
Mark 1.10, **109, 120**
Mark 1.11, **120**
Mark 1.12–13, **122**
Mark 1.14–15, **137**
Mark 1.15, **140, 219, 251, 256, 321n.34**
Mark 1.16–20; 2.13–14; 6.8–9, **326n.13**
Mark 1.19–20, **206**
Mark 1.21–28, **149**
Mark 1.22, **125**
Mark 1:29–31; 1:40–45, **322n.4**
Mark 1.32–33, **150**
Mark 1.34, **149**
Mark 1.35, **128**
Mark 1.39, **149**
Mark 1.40–42, **147**
Mark 1.45, **150**
Mark 2, 3, 7, **141**
Mark 2, **121**
Mark 2:1–12, **322n.4**
Mark 2.9, **203**
Mark 2.15–16, **217**
Mark 2.16, **160**
Mark 2.27, **155**
Mark 3, **127**
Mark 3.1–6, **322n.4**
Mark 3.5, **147**
Mark 3.9–10, **150**
Mark 3.19b–35, **320n.22**
Mark 3.21, **127**
Mark 3.22–30, **320n.22**
Mark 3.31–35, **320n.22**
Mark 3.32, **206**
Mark 3.33–35, **206**
Mark 4.12, **195**
Mark 4.26–29, **257**
Mark 4.30–32, **257**
Mark 5.1–20, **56, 149**
Mark 5.9, **202**
Mark 6.4, **131, 240**
Mark 6.7–13, **259**
Mark 6.15; 8.28, **329n.12**

Mark 6.15, **131**
Mark 6.30–44, **74**
Mark 6.46, **128**
Mark 6.47–52, **39**
Mark 6.51–52, **39**
Mark 7, **216**
Mark 7.1–2, 5, **216**
Mark 7.14–15, **327n.20**
Mark 7.15, **215**
Mark 7.19, **73, 327n.20**
Mark 7.21, **216**
Mark 7.24–30, **149**
Mark 7.32–35, **147**
Mark 8.18, **195**
Mark 8:22–26; 10:46–52, **322n.4**
Mark 8:22–26, **322n.4**
Mark 8.22–10.52, **54**
Mark 8.22–26, **56, 196**
Mark 8.27–28, **131**
Mark 8.27–30, **41**
Mark 8.29, **42, 141**
Mark 8.30, **47**
Mark 8.31; 9.31; 10.33–34, **55, 141**
Mark 8.34, **220, 290**
Mark 8.34; 9.35; 10.35–45, **55**
Mark 8.35–36, **221**
Mark 8.38; 14.62, **254**
Mark 9.1, **256**
Mark 9.2–4, **127**
Mark 9.14–29, **149**
Mark 10.15, **257**
Mark 10.17–31, **210**
Mark 10.23, **211, 257**
Mark 10.32, **127**
Mark 10.42–43, **244**
Mark 10.46–52, **56, 196**
Mark 10.51–52, **56**
Mark 11.1–7, **37**
Mark 11.1–10, **230**
Mark 11.2–3, **231**
Mark 11.15–17, **233**
Mark 11.18, **236**
Mark 11.27–33, **236**
Mark 11.29–30, **125**

Mark 12.1–12, **237**
Mark 12.6, **262**
Mark 12.13–17, **238, 323n.26**
Mark 12.30, **109, 218**
Mark 12.34, **257**
Mark 12.38–39, **212**
Mark 12.38–40, **244**
Mark 13, **256, 329n.13**
Mark 13.1–4, **242**
Mark 13.24–27, **254, 264**
Mark 13.30, **256**
Mark 14.2, **262**
Mark 14.10–11, **262**
Mark 14.22–25, **332n.4**
Mark 14.32–50, **263**
Mark 14.36, **129**
Mark 14.62, **148, 263**
Mark 15.1–5, **264**
Mark 15.6–14, **264**
Mark 15.25, **265**
Mark 15.27, **265**
Mark 15.34, **266**
Mark 15.38, **266**
Mark 15.39, **266**
Mark 15.40–41, **267**
Mark 15.43, **327n.15**
Mark 16.1–8, **282**
Mark 16.8, **334n.25**
Mark 16.9–20, **334n.25**

Luke 1.32,35, **66**
Luke 1.52–55, **64**
Luke 1.68–71, **64**
Luke 1.78–79, **63**
Luke 2.9, **63**
Luke 2.10–14, **68**
Luke 2.29–32, **65**
Luke 2.32, **63**
Luke 3.1, **77**
Luke 3.7–8, **118**
Luke 3.9,17, **119**
Luke 3.21–22, **40**
Luke 4.1–13, **122**
Luke 4.14, **148**
Luke 4.18–19, **135, 201**
Luke 4.24, **131**

Luke 6.12, **128**
Luke 6.18, **149**
Luke 6.20, **155**
Luke 6.20–23, **189**
Luke 6.20–26, **208**
Luke 6.20–49, **157**
Luke 6.23; 3.21; 5.16;
   9.18; 9.28–29, **320n.23**
Luke 6.24–26, **189**
Luke 6.35, **324**
Luke 6.36, **109, 175, 178**
Luke 6.37, **300**
Luke 6.39, **53, 156, 195**
Luke 6.41–42, **195**
Luke 6.43–44, **156**
Luke 6.44, **53**
Luke 6.47–49, **72, 194**
Luke 7.1–10, **147, 322n.4**
Luke 7.16, **329n.12**
Luke 7.19, **120**
Luke 7.22, **147, 162**
Luke 7.28, **120**
Luke 7.33–34, **217**
Luke 7.34, **160**
Luke 8.1–3, **327n.15**
Luke 8.3, **145**
Luke 9.10–17, **74**
Luke 9.18–20, **41**
Luke 9.20, **42**
Luke 9.23, **290**
Luke 9.28–36, **127**
Luke 9.51–19.27, **142**
Luke 9.57–58, **326n.n13**
Luke 9.60, 156, **197**
Luke 9.61–62, **206**
Luke 10.4–9, **259**
Luke 10.23–24, **162**
Luke 10.25–37, **246**
Luke 10.29–37, **176,
   323n.18**
Luke 11.2b–4, **35**
Luke 11.9, **257**
Luke 11.11–13, **174**
Luke 11.19–20, **320n.21**
Luke 11.20, **110, 126,
   148, 256**
Luke 11.31–32, **162, 180**

Luke 11.33, **156**
Luke 11.34, **156, 195**
Luke 11.38, **216**
Luke 11.39, **216**
Luke 11.42, **245**
Luke 11.43, **212**
Luke 11.44, **217**
Luke 11.46, **245**
Luke 11.47–48, **204**
Luke 11.52, **257**
Luke 12.6–7, **324n.10**
Luke 12.8–9, **254**
Luke 12.15, **208**
Luke 12.16–21, **209**
Luke 12.22–31, **175**
Luke 12.24,27, **196**
Luke 12.31, **109, 190, 260**
Luke 12.33–34, **210**
Luke 12.51–53, **207**
Luke 12.54–56, **196, 300**
Luke 13.10–17, **202,
   322n.4**
Luke 13.20–21, **152, 257**
Luke 13.23–24, **193**
Luke 13.28–29, **187**
Luke 13.31–33, **242**
Luke 13.33, **131, 240**
Luke 13.34, **108**
Luke 13.34–35, **242**
Luke 14:1–6, **322n.4**
Luke 14.7–11, **212**
Luke 14.26, **206**
Luke 14.27, **221**
Luke 14.28–33, **221**
Luke 14.34, **156**
Luke 15.1–2, **217**
Luke 15.1–32, **246**
Luke 15.2, **160, 170**
Luke 15.11–32, **169, 201**
Luke 15.24, 32, **198**
Luke 16.1–10, **72**
Luke 16.13, **210, 218**
Luke 16.19–31, **209**
Luke 17:11–19, **322n.4**
Luke 17.20, **256**
Luke 18.14, **212**
Luke 18.24, **211**

Luke 19.1–10; 15.1,
   232n.25
Luke 19.1–10, **145**
Luke 19.7, **160**
Luke 19.11–27, **246**
Luke 19.22–23, **246**
Luke 19.24–27, **247**
Luke 19.41–44, **243**
Luke 19.42, **108**
Luke 21.20–24, **329n.14**
Luke 22.3, **262**
Luke 22.17–20, **332n.4**
Luke 22.51, **322n.4**
Luke 22.70, **263**
Luke 23.1–2, **143**
Luke 23.6–12, **143**
Luke 23.34, 43, 46, **332n.9**
Luke 23.40–43, **265**
Luke 24.6–7, **283**
Luke 24.9, **282**
Luke 24.13–35, 36–49,
   334n.26
Luke 24.13–35, **285**
Luke 24.26–27, **272**
Luke 24.37–43, **289**
Luke 24.50–53, **288**

John 1.5, 9; 9.5, **64**
John 1.9, **197**
John 2, **120**
John 2.1–11, **57**
John 2.13–22, **328n.7**
John 3.1–10, **199, 220**
John 3.16, **184, 223, 306**
John 5.8, **203**
John 6.1–15, 25–59, **74**
John 6.35, 51, **74**
John 9.5, **197**
John 9.25, **133**
John 11.1–44, **198**
John 11.23–25, **198**
John 11.25, **198**
John 11.44, **199**
John 11.45–53, **332n.6**
John 13–17, **332n.3**
John 13.2, 27, **262**
John 13.34, **185**

John 14.6, **222, 332n.7**
John 17.3, **144**
John 18.3, **332n.5**
John 18.13, 24, **332n.6**
John 18.28–19.16, **332n.7**
John 18.31, **271**
John 19.13, **332n.7**
John 19.26–27, 28, 30, **332n.9**
John 20.11–18, 19–23, 24–29; 21.1–23, **334n.26**
John 20.19–23, **286**
John 20.24–29, **286**
John 20.28, **45**

Acts 1.3, **288**
Acts 1.8, **148**
Acts 9; 22; 26, **333n.22**
Acts 9.2, **191**
Acts 9.3–6, **113**
Acts 9.18, **133**
Acts 17.28, **111**
Acts 22; 26, **113**

Romans 1.3–4, **66**
Romans 5.8, **184**

Romans 6, **220**
Romans 6.1–11, **291**
Romans 8.15, **129**
Romans 13.11–12, **330n.27**
Romans 16.7, **333n.18**

1 Corinthians 2.8, **279, 290**
1 Corinthians 9.1, **277**
1 Corinthians 11.23–26, **332n.4**
1 Corinthians 13.13, **184**
1 Corinthians 15.5–8, **277**
1 Corinthians 15.35–50, **289**
1 Corinthians 15.51–52, **330n.27**

2 Corinthians 5.16, JB, **44**
2 Corinthians 5.17, **291**
2 Corinthians 12.2–4, **333n.20**
2 Corinthians 12.24, **291**

Galatians 1.15–16, **277**
Galatians 2.19–20, **220, 291**

Galatians 4.6, **129**
Galatians 5.1, **203**

Philippians 2.5–11, **278**
Philippians 3.4–6, **333n.23**

Colossians 2.15, **290**

1 Thessalonians 4.13–18, **330n.27**

1 Timothy 2:8–14, **326n.11**

1 Peter 1.18–20, **272**

2 Peter 3.10, **330n.22**

1 John 4.7, **184**
1 John 4.11, **184**
1 John 4.16, **184**

Revelation 19.11–21, **12**
Revelation 21.1, **330n.22**

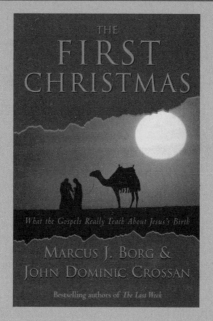